GENES, ENVIRONMENT AND HEALTH:

Anthropological Perspectives

GENES, ENVIRONMENT AND HEALTH:
Anthropological Perspectives

Editors:
Krishan Sharma
R.K. Pathak
Shalina Mehta
Indu Talwar

SERIALS PUBLICATIONS
NEW DELHI (INDIA)

First Published - 2007

ISBN: 81-8387-079-1

Published by

SERIALS PUBLICATIONS
4830/24, Prahlad Street, Ansari Road
Darya Ganj, New Delhi-110002 (India)
Phone: 23245225. Fax: 91-11-23272135
E-mail: serials@satyam.net.in

CONTENTS

LIST OF CONTRIBUTORS

Abhik Gosh, Department of Anthropology, Panjab University, Chandigarh-160014

A.K. Gupta, Department of Human Development and Sociology, PAU, Ludhiana.

A.K. Kapoor, Department of Anthropology, University of Delhi, Delhi-110007.

A. Pathak, Department of Neurosurgery, PGIMER, Chandigarh-160012.

Archna Handa, Department of Human Dev. And Sociology, PAU, Ludhiana.

Balbir Kumar, Department of Human Dev. And Sociology, PAU, Ludhiana.

Dolly Monisha, Department of Human Biology, Punjabi University, Patiala-147002

Ganesh Chandra Mallick, Department of Anthropology, University of North Bengal, West Bengal-734430.

Hemanta Bag, Department of Anthropology, University of Delhi, Delhi-110007.

K.C. Tarachand, Post-Graduate Department of Studies in Anthropology, Karnatak University, Dharwad-580003.

Kusum Lata Dogra, Department of Anthropology, Panjab University, Chandigarh.

Krishan Sharma, Department of Anthropology, Panjab University, Chandigarh.

K. Rajasekhar Reddy, Department of Anthropology, University of Mysore, Manasa Gangothri, Mysore-570006.

Indu Talwar, Department of Anthropology, Panjab University, Chandigarh-160014

Nongmeikapam Inoaba Singh, Department of Anthropology, Panjab University, Chandigarh-160014.

Parul Sharma, Department of Anthropology, Panjab University, Chandigarh.

Payal, Department of Anthropology, Panjab University, Chandigarh-160014.

Preeti Bajwa, Department of Anthropology, Panjab University, Chandigarh-160014

R.S. Balgir, Division of Human Genetics, Regional Medical Research Centre, Indian Council of Medical Research, Chandrasekharpur, Nandan Kanan Road, Bhubaneshwar-7521023.

Shalina Mehta, Department of Anthropology, Panjab University, Chandigarh.

S.K. Pal, Department of Anthropology, Panjab University, Chandigarh-160014.

S. Prabhakar, Department of Neurology, PGIMER, Chandigarh-160012.

Shilpy Gupta, Department of Anthropology, University of Delhi, Delhi-110007.

S.P. Singh, Department of Human Biology, Punjabi University, Patiala-147002.

Subir Biswas, Department of Anthropology, University of North Bengal, West Bengal-734430.

Tripta, Department of Anthropology, Panjab University, Chandigarh-160014.

Twinkle Pal, Department of Anthropology, University of Delhi, Delhi-110007.

Updesh, Department of Anthropology, Panjab University, Chandigarh-160014.

V. Jagdeesh, Department of Anthropology, Karnataka University, Dharwad-580003

PREFACE

Anthropology is the science of man dealing with man's extreme curiosity about his origin, migration, cultural and biological diversity and his relationships to other members of the animal kingdom. It was around the year 1800, when anthropology appeared as an autonomous discipline of knowledge cutting across humanistic and natural science boundaries. Since the acceptance of Darwin's theory of natural selection as a major evolutionary force, anthropology has focused on health and disease among human populations because of their linkage with natural selection. Human genetics is the cardinal/seminal discipline which throws light on the causes of human biological diversity. Anthropologists have always maintained that in addition to genetic causes, health and disease have social, local and cultural constructs. Anthropologists have played key role in identifying causes of failure of ambitious public health intervention projects. These projects were alien to normative practices of the communities. They often encroached upon people's worldviews and were insensitive to the felt needs of the communities. They ignored diversity of indigenous systems of health management. Inability of most nation states to meet the Alma Atta's declaration that vowed to 'provide health for all by 2000' has compelled the community of health researchers, planners and funding agencies to recognize the fact of medical pluralism and the need to expand the scope of researches on human health. With this recognition also comes the onus of conducting researches with caution, care and utmost sensitivity. From Tuberculosis to HIV/AIDS, the domain of health has shifted from individual health to fundamentals of social fabric of society. On the other front, advances made in the field of ' bio-medicine' in ever unfolding mysteries of DNA-that bring us closer to man's ability to recreate life brings forth issues pertaining to ethics in bio-medicine research. These are new frontiers for consideration in empirical researches.

Epidemiological studies have shown that the diseases do not equally affect all human populations. It is also well acknowledged that there are some hot spots for various diseases. Infectious diseases had a large impact on the evolution and differentiation of human populations. Those who have some natural resistance to disease are more likely to survive and pass their genes on to their offspring. The discipline of 'ecological' or 'bio-cultural' anthropology has acquired a niche for itself. Its focus on the ecology of disease in the human group has been largely responsible for explanations of 'evolutionary approach to human adaptation'. The impact of environmental stresses for instance high altitude or migration on human health has opened fresh vistas for anthropologists to explore.

The present book is the outcome of the activities pursued with the above mentioned perspectives in view. In the first chapter, Krishan Sharma reviews the trends in anthropology over the last 100 years from the perspective of the theme chosen for the book. The science of genetics emerged as a separate discipline in the year 1900 and this had a profound impact on the discipline of anthropology especially from the perspective of health and disease. Genomic studies at molecular level have revolutionized the fields of anthropology and medicine. Some major paradigm shifts have been noted in the discipline of anthropology during the 20th century and the novel approaches are being followed in the 21st Century. Environmental changes are having tremendous impact on human species' biology and thus providing tremendous scope for planned anthropological studies. Some of these areas have been highlighted in this chapter. Some current information has been provided on certain traditional genetic markers employed in anthropological genetic studies for the benefit of young readers. The other topics of this book, covering different aspects of health, disease and culture from anthropological perspectives, would fall under sub-fields of Medical Anthropology, Anthropological Genetics, Human Ecology and Cultural Anthropology. In the following paragraphs, the contributory papers of various authors are briefly reviewed.

Hemanta Bag and A.K. Kapoor discuss the ways of management of health in a 'primitive tribe', the Kondhs of Kalahandi District of Orissa. The Kondh consult Gur/Pujari/Jani for treatment of various diseases. They believe that, some of the diseases are caused by wrath of deities, evil spirits, and ghosts of the dead body. They use indigenous medicines for treatment, also visit the PHCs (Primary Health Centres) but are not satisfied with the services of the PHC.

K.C. Tarachand reports health care practices of Hakkipikki, a semi-nomadic tribe of Karnataka. In his opinion, they are specialists in indigenous medicine to cure certain diseases which are common to one and all.

Twinkle Pal examines the people of Karjan village in the Kullu District of Himachal Pradesh for their cognition of health and diseases. She has found that they have their own concepts regarding health and illness, various beliefs and practices concerning different ailments. According to their understanding, healthy man is that who can work without any difficulty and illness is perceived as a condition when a person is not able to work and confined to the bed.

Shilpy Gupta and A.K. Kapoor discuss human rights, development and tribe in an interactive manner. In their opinion, there are as numerous and diverse development programmes as are the Scheduled tribes themselves in India.

Parul Sharma and Krishan Sharma in their article report oral health status of Gaddi children from Kangra District of Himachal Pradesh. They find higher prevalence of dental caries in males than in females. The study shows significant correlation of DMF scores with age, family income, dietary habits, eating sugar or gur after meals and timing of cleaning teeth. The results favour the hypothesis that different etiological factors interact to cause dental caries.

V Jagdeesh has worked on health and hygiene of Lamani tribe of Appenahalli settlement in Bellary District of Karnataka. Lamani tribe is unique in its customs, traditions, dress, patterns and belief system and are highly scattered but distributed more in northern Karnataka region.

Dolly Monisha and S.P. Singh examine the prevalence of abdominal obesity in post-menopausal women, aged 50-60 years, from lower socio-economic strata of Chandigarh. They emphasize that anthropometric parameters of abdominal adiposity, such as waist circumference and waist-hip ratio (WHR) should be evaluated during clinical check-ups of healthy post-menopausal women. With the onset of menopause, they become more susceptible towards cardiovascular disease risk. As redistribution of fat takes place towards abdominal region, it becomes necessary to investigate them. Socio-economic status and event of menopause seem to play key role in the abdominal obesity among post-menopausal women of lower SES.

Krishan Sharma and R. Aggarwal report growth patterns of urban and rural adolescent Punjabi girls with reference to age at menarche. They found that the post-menarche urban and rural adolescent girls had significantly larger body dimensions and adiposity indices than pre-menarche girls. Rural girls had larger dimensions and advanced sexual maturity than rural girls. Their results indicated occurrence of plasticity for these continuously distributed traits.

Talwar, Payal, Updesh and Preeti Bajwa report physical growth and nutritional status of Scheduled Caste children of Naraingarh Tehsil in Ambala District of Haryana with the help of selected anthropometric measurements. The incidence of stunting was substantially higher than wasting. The results indicated that girls were nutritionally poorer than boys.

Kusum Lata Dogra examines adolescent Brahmin girls from Bhimtal, Utaranchal. She found that the Brahmin girls of Bhimtal had greater mean weight when compared to all India sample of ICMR, but were much lighter than NCHS sample.

Ajeet Jaiswal reports changes in lung functions and airway reactivity resulting from exposure to textile dust and the role of other indirect factors in relation to these changes of textile workers of District Varanasi of Uttar Pradesh. In his opinion, the exposure to textile dust is responsible for acute and consistent decrease in lung function as well as a slight increase in airway reactivity.

K. Rajasekhara Reddy's paper presents certain palmar dermatoglyphics characteristics of Madigas from Districts of Cuddapah(MDCDP) and Chittoor(MDCTR) in Andhra Pradesh. He found that the mean mainline index values were highly variable in both MDCDP and MDCTR groups. Right hand showed higher transversality than the left in all the Madiga series. Mean atd angle was relatively higher in female than in male series in both MDCDP and MDCTR groups.

R.S. Balgir examines the innovative developments in human health care and diseases in India. According to him, several health-related issues of humans are crying for attention today. Genetic disorders are encountered in almost every community, locality, clinic or hospital in India. The practice of genetic medicine seeks to provide the answer.

Krishan Sharma examines genetic and environmental factors in menstrual characteristics and premenstrual syndrome in twins ranging in age from 14 to 24 years from Punjabi population of Chandigarh. He found that the prevalence of Premenstrual Syndrome (PMS) was higher in DZ twins than in MZ twin pairs. Genetic analysis revealed insignificant genetic component of variation for PMS scores, duration of menstrual flow and length of menstrual cycle. Results showed significant genetic component of variation for age at menarche.

Krishan Sharma's next paper analyses genetic susceptibility to periodontal diseases on the basis of the twin study. He found that the prevalence rates of caries and calculus were marginally higher in DZ twins than in MZ twins, while conversely prevalence of gingivitis was higher in MZ twins than in DZ twins. According to him, the genetic component of variation for the intensity of dental caries was not substantially high.

Krishan Sharma and Tripta examine prevalence of dental caries in relation to ABO blood groups and ABH secretion in adolescent children. They found no significant differences in dental caries with reference to sex and caste groups. O blood group individuals had lowest prevalence and blood group A individuals had higher prevalence. ABH secretors had lower prevalence of dental caries than non-secretors.

S.K. Pal, K. Sharma, A. Pathak and S. Prabhakar, in their paper on association of ABO blood groups and secretor status with epilepsy, demonstrate statistically significant differences between symptomatic versus controls and idiopathic versus symptomatic, but insignificant differences between idiopathic versus controls, for the frequency of ABH secretors/non-secretors. The results support the hypothesis that ABH secretion status might be associated with the susceptibility to epilepsy.

Abhik Ghosh examines National Health Policy of India and how Indians manage to work around various kinds of medico-legal and ethical systems. Such systems often show characteristics of local cultures within India and these cannot be separated from the local community from which these spring. In his opinion, only small portion of medical malpractice cases come to court and most cases are lost due to loopholes in the laws.

Archna Handa, A.K. Gupta and Balbir Kumar, on the basis of the interviews of the inmates of Senior Citizen Homes, report their socio-personal and psychological problems. The respondents mainly suffer eye and heart ailments, besides joint pains and blood pressure. They mainly suffer from psychological problems of isolation, loneliness and consequent emotional vacuum in their personal lives.

Shalina Mehta and Nongmeikapam Inoaba Singh, in their paper on dialogues on morality and ethics in perceptions on masculinity and sexuality, examine methodology and interpret narratives to address complex questions of sexuality and ethics. According to them, evolving sensitivities to differing discourse on cross-cultural conversations on sexuality is the urgent need of the hour to evolve effective intervention strategies to meet the challenge of HIV/AIDS.

Subir Biswas and Ganesh Chandra Mallick report findings of their investigations on sex biased health practices among Rajbansis-a numerically predominant Scheduled Caste Community of West Bengal. Rajbansis, like many other communities of India, have their own health care system which reflects sex biases. This type of sex biased health care system and disease treatment pattern may be one of the major causes behind low sex ratio in this community.

We are grateful to the Vice-Chancellor, Punjab University Chandigarh for financial support and permission to arrange a National Seminar. This publication is a sequel of that exercise. We are also grateful to our colleagues, research scholars, especially Parul Sharma and Aakriti Sharma and students for their cooperation and help.

Editors

1

ANTHROPOLOGY IN HEALTH AND DISEASE: TRENDS CHATTER OF THE PAST HUNDRED YEARS WITH A VISION FOR THE FUTURE IN VIEW OF NEW CHALLENGES FACING THE HUMAN SPECIES

Krishan Sharma

The study of health and disease in biological anthropology has a long and significant tradition, partly because of its implications in natural selection, and also since a number of founder contributors were trained as physicians and not as natural scientists, including Pierre Paul Broca, the founder of French anthropology and Ales Hrdlicka, the founder editor of American Journal of Physical Anthropology. Angel (1981) document beginning of palaeopatholological studies in the first half of the 19th century. Palaeopathological and bioarchaelogical investigations have played an important role in the reconstruction of population history. These permit a comparison of similar populations to assess the impact of demographic, social, economic, and political conditions on a specific population. These studies are done on the skeletal and dental health indicators across populations. Such studies continue to enjoy an important niche in the discipline of biological anthropology even in the present context. Before discussing the topic further, it would be worthwhile to know the status of anthropology at the dawn of the 20th century.

Anthropology became an autonomous discipline in the 19th century. It started as a very generalist science of man and established an alliance with prehistory and ethnology to study man from the holistic perspective. With ascendancy of natural sciences, Darwinian Theory had an enormous impact on the anthropologists in the later half of the 19th century. The emphasis in the continental Europe shifted from cultural and social aspects to anatomy, physiology and psychological aspects to study natural history of man. However, the alliance among anthropology,. prehistory and ethnology was maintained in different countries for different amounts of time. It still exists in the Anglo-Saxon countries and the countries influenced by them, e.g., U.K., U.S.A., France, India, etc. On the contrary, in the majority of European countries the term of anthropology excludes socio-cultural anthropology and is defined as a natural science dealing with the human biological variations in time and space. At the dawn of 20th century, anthropology was a full- blown discipline with well defined scope. Its aim was to study man's place in animal kingdom by the comparative study of morphology (Duckworth, 1904). Anuchin (1902), founder of Russian Anthropological Journal in 1900, defined anthropology as branch of natural sciences studying a collective man in all varieties of his types in time and space.

The technique of anthropometry, elaborated by Quetelet (1870), has been always an important part of anthropological tradition. This has been used to study morphology of humans, living, dead and skeletal remains. Anthropometry technique may be claimed as an anthropological technique that is being used by other disciplines. By 1920s and 30s, millions of measurements had been made, which provided basic data for the rising schools of statistics. These measurements were used to classify people into primary, secondary and tertiary races as the synthetic discipline of Anthropology at that time was passing through "what is known as the typological phase", a conceptual scheme dominant among biological sciences of that era. Moreover, there was rise of racism between the two world wars.

The dawn of the 20th century also witnessed the birth of science of genetics with triple rediscovery of Mendel's work in 1900. Landsteiner discovered the first blood group system, i.e., ABO blood groups, in the same year. Sir Archibald E Garrod laid the foundation of the discipline of biochemical genetics in the year 1909 by showing that four human metabolic disorders were inherited according to the Mendelian principles. The genetics of ABO blood groups was correctly understood by 1920s by Bernstein. Hirschfeld and Bernstein applied these in racial studies. The discovery of new blood enzymes provided additional dimension to document geographical variations in human populations/races. Human genetics took off rapidly with application of the newly rediscovered Mendelian laws to various human traits. However, many behavioral and social traits were uncritically included into the Mendelian mould. Charles Davenport was the protagonist of the eugenic movement in the USA, which was initiated by Francis Galton in England. Mixing true genetic knowledge with pseudoscience, the existence and dangers of defective genes in traits such as pauperism, insanity, epilepsy, alcoholism, criminality and feeble mindedness were publicized. Consequently, compulsory sterilization laws were passed in many states of U.S.A. and Germany followed suit. Euthanasia programme followed that of sterilization in Germany under Nazis. In sterilization and euthanasia programmes, physicians, anthropologists, psychologists and human geneticists were involved in selecting those to be sterilized or to be killed. Under this programme, 5-6 million Jews and about 500,000 Gypsies were killed in Germany. Joseph Mengele had Ph.D. degree in Physical Anthropology besides M.D. degree. He worked as postdoctoral fellow in medical genetics and race biology with Vershuer. Medical genetic programmes still face hostile public reaction and looked with suspicion in Germany. However, most notable German anthropologists succeeded in keeping themselves away from the scourge of Nazi racism, e.g. von Eickstedt, von Luschan, Saller, Schwidelsky, etc.

Epidermal ridge patterns on palms and soles are other congenital markers that have been traditionally used in anthropological studies. These ridges are differentiated during the third and fourth fetal month. Once formed, these patterns do not change throughout the life of an individual. Their applications in medicine was highlighted by Cummins (1939), who studied characteristic dermatoglyphic changes in Down Syndrome patients and concluded that factors responsible for the occurrence of mongolism were operative prior to the fourth month of fetal life. Since then, a voluminous literature has been published on the use of dermatoglyphics in medical disorders (see Schaumann and Alter, 1976). The comparison of finger and palmar dermatoglyphics within and between MZ and DZ twins and between twins and singletons has provided important clues about life in the womb and the effect of environmental factors during prenatal growth period (Sharma and Bakshi, 2005). A host of environmental factors during embryogenesis affect dermatoglyphic characteristics as well as individual's susceptibility to diseases.

To have an idea of type of research done in biological anthropology during 1920s and 30s, we checked through the proceedings of the First International Congress of Anthropological Sciences that was held in London in July 1934. Only, two sessions were related to biological anthropology:1) Anatomy and Physical Anthropology; 2) Anthropometry and Standardization of Techniques. Of 58 papers in session 1, 11 were on growth and development, 6 on fossils, 16 on blood groups and genetics, 9 on comparative anatomy & man's place among primates and the remaining on other aspects of anatomy and physiology. There were 39 papers on anthropometry and standardization of techniques. There was a full session on "Demography and Population Problems", where 13 papers were presented on various aspects of demography and 2 papers on migration and disease. This exercise reveals that till 1930s, the emphasis in biological anthropology was on anatomical/morphological and blood group variations in human populations. The science of dermatoglyphics was yet to take its roots in anthropology.

However, the situation had begun to change and ripples were noticed on the surface of anthropology due to various innovative approaches that developed during the first half of the 20th century. There was phenomenal rise of ecology as an approach to understand the complexity of population-environmental interaction, which was followed by the rise of health ecology that included basic and applied studies in medical ecology, medical anthropology, health and nutrition. These revolutionary nascent approaches led to the realization among anthropologists of futility of typological approach to categorize humans into primary, secondary and tertiary races. A major paradigm shift was witnessed in our discipline towards researches on human adaptation to environment. The focus shifted to understand the process and mechanism of human evolution and human variation. The knowledge of human population genetics, evolutionary processes and ecological approach provided theoretical basis for interpreting genetic polymorphisms as adaptations. "Adaptation to the environment", as a paradigm for anthropological research had, by that time, begun to incorporate ecological theory as an expanded view of the human environment (Newman, 1953; Baker, 1962; Livingstone, 1962). This striking new phase of Anthropology was called "New Anthropology" by Sherwood Washburn (1951). A classic book emphasizing these paradigms was published by Harrison et al. (1964). The text included five major divisions written by the stalwarts of their times: Human evolution (Harrison and Weiner), human genetics (Harrison), biological variations in modern populations (Barnicot), human growth and constitution (Tanner) and human ecology (Weiner).

The above developments and after effects of the second world war led to the emergence of a new discipline called, "ergonomics/human engineering". It was felt that that the equipment should be so designed that it should not only be operational within the comfortable limits of human capacity but also should be optimal for use and enhance human capacity. For this purpose fundamental principles were derived from functional anatomy, body mechanics, physiology, anthropometry and psychology. Ergonomics continues to be an area where anthropological knowledge is used as an input for the development of biotechnology. Similar applications led to the rise of another new discipline of sports anthropology.

It had been realized by 1940s that much of the genetic diversity necessary for evolutionary change arose through mutations, both chromosomal and genic. Thus, efforts to measure mutation rates of various organisms kept occupied biologists especially after the acceptance of synthetic theory of evolution. Studies of mutation rates in man have focused primarily upon the extent to which newly mutated genes contribute genetic burden carried by human populations (see Trimble and Smith, 1977). A Nobel laureate, Herman J Muller, in 1950s drew attention to mutation load in man and tried to assess it quantitatively (Muller, 1950). At that time, several investigations were launched to estimate frequencies of hereditary diseases in human populations. The discovery of chromosomal diseases came as a new impetus in the study of mutational load. The studies were undertaken to understand the impact of harmful genes in precise biological, medical and social terms. The analysis of published data on burden of genetic pathology reveals that frequency of genic, chromosomal, congenital anomalies and other multifactorial disorders is about 60-75 per 1000 births (Committee on Mutagenesity of Chemicals in Food, 1981). The incidence of severe type of hereditary diseases is 1-2%. Annual number of births of homozygous or compound heterozygotes for major haemoglobinopathies is about 217, 800 (WHO, 1983). It would mean that about 300 million people are heterozygous for haemoglobinopathies alone. The total contribution of hereditary diseases to the causes of child mortality has been growing over the last 70-100 years in human populations. The burden of hereditary pathology is not only limited to lethal effects, but impacts public health as well. The pathologic manifestation of genic hereditary diseases occurs in 25% of parents at birth, 70% at 3 years of age, and 90% by the end of puberty (Costa et al., 1985). The genetic pathology is also known to affect the lifespan and life function and studies are being done to estimate these effects (Costa et al., 1985). These studies indicate extra expenditure on health care due to our genetic load, due to environmental change including degradation, and pollution. Such studies would continue to receive greater anthropological attention for health and nutritional appraisal of populations. It has been recently estimated that the key regions of our DNA that control when genes are switched on and off, have been altered by around 140,000 naturally occurring mutations over the last 6 million years. This has left humans with sloppy gene control mechanism which makes us susceptible to diseases, or directly causes genetic disease.

Geographic variations of the blood groups and other genetic markers continued to dominate the anthropological genetic studies since 1940s. The maintenance of genetic polymorphisms, and geographical variations in the frequency of such genes were correlated with environment, and disease susceptibility. The works of Haldane (1949), Allison (1954), Livingstone (1958), Motulsky (1964) on the role of infectious diseases in human evolution, genetic resistance to disease, and protective role of human red cell traits in an environment where malaria was endemic, have become classics in human population genetics and the study of human genetic adaptation.

The role of malaria as an evolutionary force is now an accepted fact. Malaria has been a major cause of child mortality in many parts of the world. The malarial parasite *Plasmodium falciparum* causes more than 1 million deaths every year in Africa alone. This malarial species is estimated to cause about half a billion episodes of disease each year (Snow et al., 2005). Hundreds of millions are affected by other species of Plasmodium: *P.vivax*, *P.malariae*, and *P.ovale*. Such a situation prevails at a time when human species is at advantage of possessing affective controls against malaria through drugs and other measures. It can be safely assumed that mortality was much higher earlier. At that time, it would not be surprising to project malaria alone as the strongest evolutionary force in the recent history of human genome. Human red cell traits like sickle cell haemoglobin (HbS), thalassemia, glucose-6-phospho-deydrogenase (G6PD) deficiency and other haemoglobinopathies like HbC and HbE etc., affect millions of families today and are documented under genetic load. Malaria is assumed as the evolutionary force behind these erythrocyte defects. These are diseases in homozygous state, but heterozygotes have a tremendously reduced risk of severe malaria. Research in this field has not abated since the classic work of Allison and Livingstone of 1950s. The focus has now shifted to genomic studies. The most striking example of the different single nucleotide polymorphisms (SNPs) which confer protection against malaria are Glu 6 Val (HbS), Glu 6 Lys (HbC) and Glu 26 Lys (HbE) (see Flint et al., 1998; Tishkoff and Williams, 2002; Kwiatkowski, 2005).

Similarly, various blood group genetic markers have also been associated with differential susceptibility to diseases. There are thousands of research papers written since 1940s on association of ABO blood groups with differential susceptibility to diseases. ABO locus has been mapped on chromosome 9q34.2 and Hh locus on 19q13.3. Though it is difficult to argue with the general pattern that emerges from the large body of statistical data, yet some of the findings on the microbe receptors and the association with important proteins seem convincing in suggesting that blood group antigens do play some important biological role in differential susceptibility to diseases. A counter argument has been forwarded. Lack of A, B, and H antigens on RBC's in individuals with the Bombay phenotype (O_h) do not seem to affect erythrocyte function, integrity or survival (Poschmann et al., 1974). There are no reports suggesting increase propensity to infection or disease in these individuals. It can be argued here that perhaps presence of A, B, and H antigens are biologically important rather than their absence in causing differential susceptibility to disease. In nutshell, the association of blood group antigens is not surprising, because cell surface molecules containing blood group epitopes play important roles in modulation of protein function, infection and cancer. Bacteria also have the ability to circumvent the host's immune system by acquiring host's blood group substances on their surface and thereby, preventing a host response. The differential susceptibility of different ABO blood group persons to a pathogen may be related to the differential ability of bacteria to adsorb blood group epitopes. The association of A blood group with stomach ulcers and cancer may thus be explained on the basis of above hypothesis, because these diseases may also be caused interalia by bacteria. Two pathologists, Prof. Barry Marshall and Dr Robin Warren have been awarded the Nobel Prize in Medicine for the year 2005, on their discovery that a bacterium causes stomach ulcers and gastric cancer. (See papers of Pal et al. and Sharma and Tripta in the proceedings of this volume on association of blood groups with diseases).

ABH secretion is another genetic marker that has been traditionally used in anthropological studies. This marker is also of great clinical importance for its association with disease susceptibility. ABO(H) histo-blood group antigens are oligosaccharide antigens constructed by sequential action of specific glycosyltransferases. These antigens are expressed not only in erythrocyte membranes but also in tissues such as salivary gland and digestive mucosa. Since H antigen is a precursor of A and B antigens, the α(1,2)-fucosyltransferase is one of the essential enzymes for the tissue expression of ABH antigens, which are composed of four types of chains: types 1,2,3 and 4. The type 2 chains are expressed mainly in erythrocyte membranes as insoluble glycolipids, while saliva and digestive mucosa mainly have the type 1 antigens as soluble glycoproteins. Biochemical genetic studies have shown that at least two distinct α (1, 2)-fucosyltransferases are present in human tissues. One is the H gene (FUT 1)-encodes α (1, 2)- fucosyltransferase (H enzyme) that regulates expression of the ABH antigens in erythrocyte membranes, and the other is the Secretor gene (FUT 2)-encodes α (1, 2)-fucosyltransferase (Se enzyme) that regulates expression of ABH antigens in secretory glands and secretory fluids (see Oriol et al., 1981; Kelly et al., 1995). Lack of the FUT 2-encoded enzyme activity would lead to failure of H antigens in secretory fluids. FUT 1, FUT 2, and a pseudo gene of FUT 2 are located within 100-kb region in chromosome 19 q (Kelly et al., 1995). Point mutations and pseudo genes in this region are responsible for the non-secretor phenotype in human populations. Consequently non-secretor phenotype in different populations may be because of different Se-enzyme-deficient alleles like se 1, se 2, se 3, se 4, etc. There is need to undertake these studies on Indian populations, where none exists.

Another clinically important blood group system that has been tremendously used in anthropological genetic studies is Rh (Rhesus) blood group system. It also has huge clinical importance. Its historic discovery was made by Levine and Stetson (1939). Early researchers soon realized its complexity and controversy rose about its genetics and molecular biology. Weiner (1944) viewed Rh as a single protein containing multiple antigenic epitopes (Rh_0, rh', hr', rh'', hr''). Race (1944) opined that there existed three closely linked genes, each coding for an independent protein specific for a different Rh antigen (C/c, D/d or E/e). It is now firmly established that Rh antigens are carried by two non glycosylated palmitoylated proteins encoded by two closely linked genes, RHD and RHCE, mapped to p. 34-36 of chromosome 1 in the order of 5'-RHCE-RHD-3' (Carritt and Kemp, 1997). RHD gene codes for RhD proteins and RHCE has four allelic forms (ce, cE, Ce, CE). Rh antigen expression at the RBC surface requires the presence of the Rh- associated glycoprotein (Rh AG) encoded by a gene located on chromosome 6 (see Avent and Reid, 2000 and Huang et al., 2000). The Rh proteins have been reported to facilitate transportation of ammonia and carbon dioxide (Marini et. al., 2000; Soupene et al., 2001).

Similarly, Duffy blood group antigens have been associated with susceptibility to malaria. These are carried on the Duffy glycoprotein. The Duffy glycoprotein acts as a receptor for the malarial parasite, *Plasmodium vivax* (Miller et al., 1976; Peiper, 1997). The Duffy null phenotype {F_y (a-b)}, which acts as a refractory to invasion of *P.vivax* merozites, evolved under selective pressure in Africa to circumvent infection (Hamblin and Di Rienzo, 2000). Its frequency varies from 75% to even 100% at different places in African blacks. It can be concluded that some proteins in the RBC membrane that carry blood group antigens appear to be receptors for specific ligands and for bacteria, suggesting that they play direct role in the pathogenesis of the disease. Duffy blood group has been mapped on chromosome 1q 22-23.

The science of genomics has revealed that there are about 10 million polymorphisms in human genome. These provide tremendous variability among unrelated individuals. This legacy of our evolution looks wonderful, but comes at a price. Genes, besides having benign effects, also influence health. Geneticists have helped unfolding genetic abnormalities leading to disease. The genetic analysis reveals that genetic variation explains about 40% of the variation in the susceptibility to common diseases and about 70% for complex multifactorial disorders like schizophrenia, apart from lethal/ sub- lethal mendelian genes. The gene variants influencing common diseases only predispose us, but do not cause these. It is here where life style and other factors play their role.

Genetic epidemiology is another new discipline, the foundation of which was laid during the classic works of 1950s by Livingstone, Motulsky, Neel, and Schull etc. Genetic epidemiology has been defined as a science that deals with etiology, distribution and control of disease in group of relatives with inherited causes of disease in populations (Morton, 1982). The word inherited in this definition is used in a broad sense to include both biological and cultural inheritance. Partitioning the genetics and environmental components in the etiology of disease constitutes one of the major goals of genetic epidemiology. Twin and family studies are conducted to estimate the proportion of liability in a given population due to genetic differences between individuals and familial effects. The genetic structure of the population may also be studied to segregate genetic factors which decrease or increase the risk of the disease or disorder. The word disease is also used in the broadest sense of health and disease. The complex diseases are generally associated with complex multifactorial traits. Many of these are quantitative in nature. A major effort in the gene mapping process is the detection of loci that influence quantitative traits and these are referred to as quantitative trait loci (QTL). QTL analysis plays a critical role in the genetic detection of complex human diseases. Feingold (2001) has provided an excellent review of QTL-mapping methods. These days genetic epidemiology is an important area of research of medicine and biological anthropology.

Human ecology is an area which bridges the gap between culture and nature. The topics like the ecology and demography of the past and present human societies and their impact on the health of those populations and the world's ecosystems have always been very attractive to the funding and governmental agencies. Many major research projects have been carried in this area (Baker et al. 1986; Friedlaender, 1987; Little, 1989).

Anthropology of food is another up coming area of research in the field of Ecological Anthropology. The fascination for food is rooted in hundreds of thousands years of food insecurity facing humans. To an ordinary man, food tends amount to heaven. This is as true today as it was in the past. Thanks giving ritual to the God after every meal is hallowed in Indian tradition. The diversity of climate, costumes, products and people have led to the evolution of what are called flavors, cuisines, hot and cold concepts. Preparation involves choice of ingredients, their proper seasoning employing various skills handed over generations and using various cooking methods: boiling, stewing, braising, frying, steaming, crisping, baking, and simmering, and so on... This is a very fertile area for anthropological research that can generate lot of funding because of its application in health and disease. Discovery of India in the realm of food reverberates with millennial echoes-'*annam vai Brahman*' (food is the supreme cosmic reality). Food taboos are observed in all cultures. The new age lifestyle has revived an interest in traditional health related roots of native cuisines. Food festivals are organized to expose people to pan-Indian flavours. The concepts of hot and cold in relation to food consumption are embedded in Indian tradition. It is believed that for a healthy state of an individual, hot-cold balance must be maintained. It is in this belief foods are said to have hot-cold dichotomy. All food items are believed to have either hot or cold effect. However, there is no uniformity among ethnic groups to classify a food into hot or cold category. A food item may associate with hot effect in one culture and cold effect in another. Then, there are food legends. This is another virgin area of research from biological anthropology perspective.

Ecological variation in food availability has been an important stressor through human evolutionary history (Leonard and Robertson, 1992). It continues to shape the biology of traditional human populations even today (De Garine and Harrison, 1988). Interpopulational variation in the prevalence of ability to digest lactose during adulthood, and diabetes mellitus are well known examples of nutritional adaptation and suggest how distinct dietary and metabolic adaptations can emerge rapidly over evolutionary time (Simmons, 1970; McCracken, 1971; Kobberling and Tattersall, 1982). Mongoloid and Negroid population have highest frequency of lactose intolerance. Adult lactose persistence is said to be controlled by an autosomal dominant gene (Scrimshaw and Murray, 1988). The locus for adult lactose intolerance has been mapped on chromosome 2 (Enattah et al., 2002). Human ecology seeks to analyze the role of human populations in changing their environment and the effects of environment on human populations. A natural outgrowth of this development has been the rise of health ecology as a grouping of basic and applied studies in medical ecology, epidemiology, medical anthropology, health and nutrition (Little, 1982, p. 421). Ecological anthropologists have studied patterns of energy production and use in a community or a population as a function of the type and extent of local energy acquisition exchange relationships with other groups and other activities, including biological and economic, that are important in maintaining group function (Nydon and Thomas, 1989).

Anthropologists are now deeply involved in the study of disease within human ecosystems. Figure 1 is a schematic chart of the flow of events

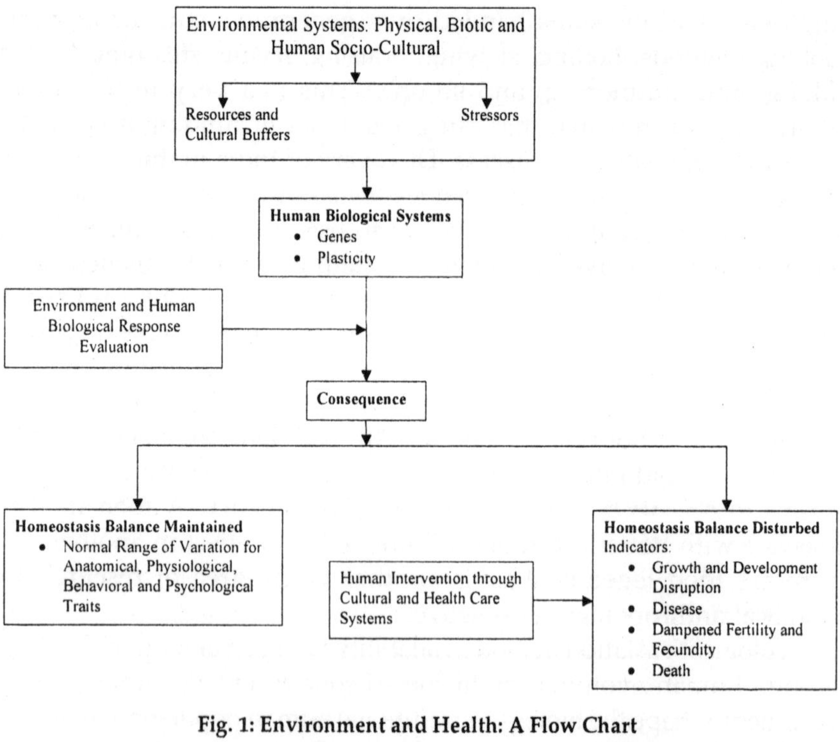

Fig. 1: Environment and Health: A Flow Chart

related to anthropology, environmental systems and health. Greene (1974, 1977) conducted intensive research on endemic goiter in the Andean region of Ecuador and examined a large number of measures of morphology, growth, neurological maturation, diet, and taste sensitivity to PTC (phenyl thiocarbamide) within the context of a model employing interactions among three components of ecosystems; biological, socio-cultural, and environmental. PTC tasting is a classic phenotype that has been used in numerous surveys of human populations. PTC tasting has been proposed to be associated with dietary preferences (Tepper, 2003) that in turn lead to differential susceptibility to thyroid related disorders such as goiter (Greene, 1974) and also epilepsy- a disease having multifactorial etiology (Sharma, 2005). The gene responsible for PTC tasting ability has been now localized on chromosome 7, and there is also evidence that another locus on chromosome 16 influences PTC tasting ability (Drayna et al., 2003).

The analysis of the ecology of Kuru is another illustration of the application of a holistic approach model, by integrating cultural and biological components of anthropology to focus upon the disease as the outcome. This example is usually cited in anthropological literature as an overt recognition of the role of anthropological research in providing health care by studying diseases of the world's most remote societies. A Nobel Prize was awarded jointly to DC Gajadusek and BS Blumberg in 1978 for their work on neurological viruses and transmission of Hepatitis, respectively (Johnston and Low, 1984). Patterns of nutritional and metabolic variation among human populations provide additional insights into the influence of environmental and cultural factors on the evolution of nutrition in human species.

The racial and ethnic disparities in prevalence rates of certain diseases in the United States have been attributed to variations in the genetic, physiologic and factors associated with racial discrimination which create higher stress (see Cooper, 2004). For example, hypertension among African Americans (20-74 years old) is 34%, which is considerably higher than European Americans (22%) (NCHS, 1996). The problem is attributed to as a consequence of a genetic adaptation for efficient sodium storage under tropical conditions (Denton, 1982). Anderson et al. (1991) attribute it to increased sympathetic nervous activity, as a result of higher sodium retention. Dressler (1991) argued that hypertension among African American is largely a product of social stress. Similarly non-insulin dependent (adult onset) diabetes mellitus (NIDDM) is a disease thought to be the product of an interaction between genes and environment. Life style factors play an important role in the etiology of NIDDM. Neel (1962) proposed thrifty genotype hypothesis that would allow quick release of insulin to enhance glucose storage during times of plenty. Barker (1994) proposed a nongenetic thrifty phenotype model to explain the etiology of NIDDM. This model assumes that prenatal and postnatal malnutrition results in decreased β-cell mass of the pancreas and increased resistance to insulin in the muscle tissue. These conditions in presence of adult over nutrition lead to the development of diabetes (Hales and Barker, 1992).

The early onset of adult type Diabetes mellitus in many human populations, e.g., India, has been attributed to changes in dietary habits, sedentary lifestyle and certain base pair substitutions (genic mutations).

Human growth status is studied as an indicator of health of an individual as well as that of a population. The study of human growth has always been an integral part of biological anthropology. As anatomy and anthropometry have been part of anthropology since 19th century, an interest in human growth and development is natural for anthropologists. Growth has a substantial genetic component, but we are yet to identify most of the specific genes that affect body size and shape. The children are known to resemble their parents in body size and shape. Their resemblance is generally attributed to the cumulative effect of additive polygenes, besides cultural component (Sharma et al., 1984). Physical growth variations are also seen as developmental plasticity and as a strategy for human adaptation to environmental factors/stressors as coded in human genome. The auxological epidemiology in Europe and the United States of America (U.S.A) has been reviewed by Tanner (1981). Auxological epidemiology regards stunting due to adverse environmental conditions as an indicator of environmental pressures (Johnston, 1981; Schell, 1991). Environmental stressors may cause reduced growth and small body size. Culture can also act as a stress factor (Schell, 1997). Lasker (1969) developed a paradigm for the study of human adaptation based in part on several investigations in which human growth appeared as an adaptive response to environmental stressors like heat or cold (Eveleth, 1966), hypoxia (Frisancho et al., 1975). The effects of air pollution from combustion products like automobile exhaust (Williams et al., 1977), and other pollutants like radiation, noise etc. (Sutow et al., 1965; Schell, 1991) on human growth have been studied.

A question that may be raised here is that whether the average body size would be the same in all human populations, if they are exposed to the same environment. Though the answer cannot be a plain yes, yet we know that African American, European and European American living in affluent countries like USA, Canada, Western Europe, and Australia show similar patterns of growth in height during childhood and adolescence. Most of the studies of well off children in developing countries (India and South America) have found that growth in childhood does not differ greatly from the growth of children in affluent countries. The role of specific nutrients in growth performance has been extensively studied in experimental animals, but the picture is much less clear in human populations. Not many such studies have been done on Indian populations.

The impact of migration on human biology is of considerable importance to anthropology (see Mascie-Taylor and Lasker, 1988). Humans have been migrating from one place to another since antiquity and wherever they have lived, they have been reproductively successful. They have been plagued by diseases and ill health which kept their numbers in check until recently. As their number grows, they expand first nearby and later into more distant environments. They bring their native diseases to the new territories of their migration. For example, migrants from Europe introduced such diseases into the New World which were common in Europe like small pox, measles, typhoid and plague during the 16th and 17th century AD. These diseases were unknown to original inhabitants of the America. They had no biological resistance to the diseases and thus affected everyone, young, adult, old at that time. Food production stopped and the every day life collapsed due to large number of deaths that occurred due to these diseases. For example, Maya population in Guatemala declined by almost 94% from 1526 to 1625 AD (Lovell and Lutz, 1996).

Rural to urban migration is one of the most prevalent types of human movement. The effects of such migrations on demography, human growth and health have been intensively studied. The city habitat is a unique ecological niche that is evolutionally novel for human species, since man was never exposed to such a habitat during the course of his evolution. These movements are now occurring very rapidly, though such migrations had taken place during all periods of recorded history (OECD, 1999). McNeil (1979) introduced a new approach to history and migration studies, as he viewed much of history and most of migrations as driven by disease. The concentration of a large and dense population in an urban area established the conditions for the fast communication and spread of infectious diseases. From hunter gatherers to settled village life had set up the conditions for the infection of anthrax, brucellosis and tuberculosis in human populations. Urban life increased the chances of spread of much more devastating epidemic diseases like cholera, smallpox and plague (Cockburn, 1967; Armelagos and Dewey, 1970). The migrants tend to adapt to the new environment. Livingstone (1958) has traced how migration and extensive agricultural activity led to human modification of environment resulting in conditions conductive for mosquitoes to grow in large numbers in West Africa. Soon thereafter malaria became endemic in that region and resulted in high mortality of children. Natural selection led the establishment of the polymorphic sickle cell trait as a human adaptation to the disease.

A major phenomenon of modernization and urbanization is the epidemiological transition. After initial higher mortality due to infectious diseases in urban areas, mortality rates decreased in western countries due to biological adaptation of human host and pathogen toward each other as well as improved sanitation, water treatment, and public health measures. However, relatively high rates of deaths from endemic diseases were still part of urban ecology. But slowly, mortality due to infectious diseases decreased and replaced by degenerative diseases. Omran (1971) classified this shift from infectious to non-infectious disease as epidemiological transition, whereby pandemics of infections are gradually displaced by degenerative and man made diseases as the chief cause of mortality. These include cancer, allergy, stroke, coronary heart disease, increased incidence of spontaneous abortions and genetic diseases. The entire industrialized Western world has completed this epidemiological transition. A significant anthropological contribution is recognized in the comparative epidemiology. India is witnessing high urban population growth. Its urban population has grown by six times since independence. As a result, nearly 35 crore (about 27%) Indians are now living in urban areas. Studies of epidemiological transition are very much relevant in Indian settings.

Intensive industrialization has also brought environmental destruction and change. The industrial revolution fueled economic growth, which created tremendous job opportunities in the industrial towns. The pull of more money, more amenities and an expectation of higher living standards in urban areas resulted in massive urban in-migration from rural areas. City concentrates not only people, but also goods and services, which lowers transport cost. It fuels more growth. Consequently, you have large and dense populations in the urban areas. These characteristics generate many types of problems. These, interalia, include provisions for water supply, waste managements, unemployment, poverty, social conflicts, pollution and biological problems of disease and ill-health. These aspects have invited attention of scholars studying ecology of cities. Population explosion would further fuel demands of more food, services and energy. Man made pollution is increasing in alarming proportions. Anthropometric combustion of fossil fuels is adding to the pollution and resulting in environment change. The pollution levels become highest in the winter. The satellite data reveal spatial and temporal levels of air pollution due to emissions from fossil fuel combustion, biomass burning and fumes from exhausts of automobiles, etc. The recent satellite data reveal increased pollution level over China. Prof. Larry Di Girolambo from the University of Illinois, U.S.A., has reported a thick brown cover of soot and dust draping over the state of Bihar and surrounding areas at 1-3 Km altitude. It was about 7 times worst than global winter averages. The haze is suspected to have sources in old fashioned kitchen burning wood, cow dung, and use of smoky Chula, diesel and vehicular emissions. International Kyoto Protocol has been signed to regulate greenhouse-gas emissions, but some large countries are yet to ratify it, and many others are yet to initiate any concrete step.

Anthropogenic combustion of fossil fuels causes increase in mean concentration of carbon dioxide in the atmosphere. Carbon dioxide has the property of absorbing long-wave energy that in turn warms the earth's atmosphere. Additional input of carbon will produce further warming and may contribute to greater intensity of heat. Global average temperatures are projected to increase between 1.4° and 5.8°C by the end of this century (Intergovernmental Panel on Climate Change, 2001). The extreme droughts are projected to increase with warmer ambient temperatures. The extreme drought and heat wave episodes have the potential to significantly alter long-term continental carbon balances. These changes will affect the abilities of plants to resist pathogen attacks (Boyer, 1995). The year 2005 witnessed a large number of disasters. Beginning with the last year's tsunami, disasters broke all geographical barriers in 2005-earth quake in Kashmir, Iran and Indonesia, hurricanes in USA and Brazil, floods in Mumbai, Chennai, Hyderabad and Bangalore, and unprecedented torrential rains in China. The economic loss was more than 200 billion US$. Scientific analysis reveals that storms have become more intense in the last several decades.

Intensive industrialization has led to indiscriminate exploitation of natural resources causing tremendous environmental pollution and destruction. Many new toxic substances like polychlorinated biphenyles (PCBs) and doxins that were created proved injurious to human health. Excessive uses of chemicals and insecticides in agriculture have increased their contents in food articles. The inhaling of asbestos is known to cause mesothelioma (a painful form of lung cancer). Its use and manufacture have been banned by about 40 countries since the time when the first case linking asbestos with cancer was reported in 1924. Its demand has shrunk in developed countries, but in India, it is about 200 crore industry with 14 large- and 673 small-scale units. Asbestos, DDT, PCBs and many others are the ugly faced demonic materials of the past that were earlier considered to be advantageous now need to be discarded.

Untreated sewage from towns and cities is being canalized into rivers/ streams or affecting ground water without being treated. The rivers are being polluted. Jamuna River is the most polluted in Delhi. Bhopal gas tragedy killed 15274 and 573,000 people were affected as per records. Another recent chemical slick has been reported in the news papers (Indian Express, 3rd December, 2005, reported by Pallavi Aiyar) from Harbin city in China's northeast Heilongjiang province which is inhabited by 4 million people. On November 13, 2005, about 100 tones of the carcinogenic chemicals, benzene and nitrobenzene were discharged into the Songhua River following a blast in Jilin province. The spill was kept secret for about a week and during this period the slick made headway towards Harbin city. People continued to use river water for drinking and washing. The water supply to the city was then cut off for five days. In the mean while, the slick had further headed towards the Russian border city of Khabarovsk. Beijing ordered a probe and made a rare public apology to Moscow. Increasing population and migration to urban areas have also resulted in encroachment of catchment's areas such as ponds and tanks. Thousands of tanks and water bodies have been lost over the years in Delhi and Tamil Nadu. In some cases, tanks have been destroyed due to effluent discharge from tanneries and factories. These tanks are important sources for storage of rainwater and recharging of ground water. Numerous such examples of damage to environment and ecology can be cited that would have anthropological implications.

The theory of population genetics tells us that advantageous alleles may turn disadvantageous with change in the environmental factors. Environmental factors have played very crucial role in evolution and in the prevalence of diseases. Human populations are experiencing rapid changes in environmental factors. Man made pollution is increasing. The World Health Organization has estimated that the warming and precipitation trends due to anthropogenic climate changes since the mid-1970s have already claimed more than 150,000 lives and approximately five million 'disability-adjusted life years' (DALYs) per year through increasing incidence of diseases such as diarrhea, malaria and malnutrition that occur mainly in developing countries(see Ezzati et al, 2004). Increase in the incidence of many other prevalent human diseases and mortality like cardiovascular and respiratory diseases has also been linked to climate fluctuations. The future global warming and changes in the climate would result in increased morbidity and mortality in many areas of the world, like regions around Pacific and Indian Oceans that are currently subjected to large rainfall variability (Patz et al, 2005). Human species is already living in era of disasters like tsunami, landslides, drought, hurricane, flooding, avian flu, and mad cow disease, AIDS etc, which is affecting millions of people.

These findings are of immense concern to the authorities engaged in providing health care at different levels. There is need to investigate health statistics of various Indian states with reference to pollution level which would provide data about various disease hotspots. For example, the incidence of respiratory diseases including lung cancer is high in Himachal Pradesh (Sharma et al, 2005). There are newspaper reports of increased incidence of cancer at some places in Bathinda district of Punjab. Highest incidence of Ischemic heart disease and hyper levels of triglycerides are observed in northwest Indians. Drug peddling is rampant in six Himachal Pradesh districts- Chamba, Kullu, Mandi, Sirmour, Kinnaur and Shimla. 2200 hectares of area and 1800 hectares of forest land are under cannabis and poppy cultivation in the state of Himachal. Such information would help to locate causative factors.

The question of global collapse is invariably raised by some people, but it was generally dismissed as bogey. Now, even sensible people are talking of its possibility. The threat factors are climate change, resource depletion, and population imbalances. In the past, many societies like Maya of Mexico and Polynesians of Eastern Island have collapsed because of the very same reasons. These were isolated civilizations. But due to globalization, now if one part of the world is affected, the trouble can be quickly exported. If modern civilization collapses, it will do so everywhere. All of us now stand or fall together. Due to rapid and large scale movement of people related to tourism, business, employment, etc., the spread of diseases from a small localized area to take pandemic proportion is very fast. The whole world has been reduced to a global village status due to such large scale movements of people almost daily. New diseases are spreading very fast. The story of the fast spread of severe acute respiratory syndrome (SARS) can be told as an illustration. On February 22, 2003, a physician from the Guangdong province of China, stayed overnight in a hostel in Hong Kong. During his brief stay, he transmitted a corona virus (CoV) to other guests, who then spread the disease throughout the world with great speed. However, the response of the world community, coordinated by WHO, was also equally swift. In less than 4 months, the outbreak was controlled. Avian influenza is another example. The deadly H5N1 strain of bird flu has resulted in the deaths of more than 91 people and 100 million chickens in Asia since 2003. Most human cases have been traced to direct contact with sick birds, but the virus could mutate and become easily transmissible between humans. Once that happens, the disease would soon spin out of control and could kill up to three million people in Asia as per estimates of the Asian Development Bank (ADB). The reports of human-to-human avian flu cases are also percolating. Avian flu has swept across a wide swathe of South East Asia, parts of Central Asia, North Africa and Europe. It has recently been detected in India. First report came from the tribal pocket of northern Maharashtra's Nandurbar district. Further reports came from adjoining places. The affected birds were culled.

1970s and 1980s witnessed spurt in studies on anthropological demography. Anthropological demography is the study of the biosocial characteristics of human population and their development through time. Anthropology adds the comparative, evolutionary and holistic approaches to traditional demography. By such additions, anthropological demographers study cross-cultural variations in social behavior, biology and population dynamics. Demographic indicators like fertility, mortality and morbidity serve as health indicators of a population. All these indicators have bio-cultural regulators. During hominid evolution, life span and life expectancy at all ages among humankind have changed and increased through interaction of evolutionary and cultural forces. It is commonly commented that in the 21st century, only unfortunate ones will not be able to celebrate their 70th birth year. Biological anthropologists and Anthropological demographers have shown keen interest in the ageing and senescence processes. In Indian context, 2.5 million children die every year and this account for one in five deaths in the world. It has been further reported in the "Status of Children in India Inc" by HAQ Centre for Child

Rights that one in every three malnourished children in the world lives in India. India also has the largest number, about six hundred thousand, of sexually abused children in the world. Children continue to die due to malnutrition, caused by a combination of factors like inadequate or inappropriate food intake, gastrointestinal parasites and childhood diseases and improper child care during illness.

Anthropological perspective of the acquired immunodeficiency syndrome (AIDS) caused by human immunodeficiency virus (HIV) is another current topic of inquiry (see Bogin, 2001). The demographic perspective of HIV/AIDS around the world shows that the distribution of the disease is not uniform. The World Health Organization (WHO) estimated that 40 million of people of all ages were living with HIV/AIDS in the year 2005, and sub-Saharan Africa represented 70% of all cases. India accounts for about 5.1 million HIV positive people, next only to South Africa. Recent UNAIDS report however, says that India has overtaken South Africa. India had 5.7 million cases against 5.5 million in South Africa by the end of 2005. AIDS epidemic has claimed more than 3 million lives and close to 5 million people have acquired the HIV in 2005 (UNAIDS/WHO, 2005). Many social and cultural factors have contributed to the differential spread of HIV/AIDS in different nationalities of people, e.g., migration, conflict, danger and stigma, and the list of such factors can be expanded. A very curious incidence has been noticed recently. An unaffected wife has filed a complaint with the police that her HIV/AIDS affected husband has been threatening her to have unprotected sex with him. She has been running from pillar to post to save her. In another incidence, an affected person threatened his adversaries that he would infect them with HIV/AIDS by biting or other ways if they do not comply. The veracity of these threats may be doubtful, but it created fear psychosis in affected people. There is need to ponder over these issues.

The disease is also a biological entity. There are many other sexually transmitted diseases (STDs), like genital herpes, syphilis, gonorrhea and chlamydia. STDs often cause infertility if left untreated in traditional cultures, which would have further social and biological consequences. These STDs existed in the populations since long, while AIDS was first diagnosed in 1981 in a small population of homosexual men. Today AIDS is a pandemic disease. A number of biological and cultural factors have led to rapid expansion and devastating effect of HIV/AIDS in tropical Africa and Asia. These regions are also plagued by diseases like malaria, tuberculosis and other infectious diseases superimposed by factors like poverty and poor nutritional status, etc. The interactions among social, cultural, behavioral and biological factors illustrate the biocultural nature of human health and disease.

Innovations in medical technology have been liberally used by biological anthropologists to pursue research in nascent fields of inquiry and thereby widening the scope of anthropological research. X-ray, ultra sound, computed tomography (CT) and magnetic resonance imaging (MRI) scanning are routinely used in clinical investigations. All these techniques have many potential applications in anthropological research. An ultrasound imaging system using pulse-echo technique and nominal frequency (3.5 MHz) longitudinal waves can be used to assess sex and estimate age of human skeletal remains from intact teeth. Ultra sound is also being used in prenatal growth studies. Ruff and Leo (1986) have reviewed the applications of CT scanning in anthropological research. MRI is being used in evolutionary and neuroanthropological studies (Allen et al., 2005). Recently, functional MRI technique has been used by Helen Fisher and others from Rutgers University, New York to study anthropology of love. The anthropology of love is as crucial as its chemistry to decipher how it has evolved in time and memory and how it is interlinked with myths. Electroencephalography (EEG) is a useful method to assess cognitive functioning across populations living in varied ecological settings and thus may be very useful in assessing determinants of human cognitive evolution. Infact, most of the clinically used techniques have applications in anthropological research. There is a need to strengthen research liaison between anthropological institutes and medical research institutes for the benefit of science.

The methodological break through of 1980s in the field of molecular genetics had significant effect on the anthropological genetics in the reconstruction of the human history, in the studies of human variation and migration routes and mapping of genes associated with complex traits and diseases. The effect was so hard that in 1993, a group of anthropological geneticists felt that there was a need to have a separate association to cater to the growing needs and interests of anthropological geneticists and consequently American Association of Anthropological geneticists was formed in 1994 with the journal of Human Biology being its official journal. The impact of genomic studies on anthropological geneticists was so strong during 1990s that the use of gene products, blood groups and blood proteins has almost been abandoned in favor of more informative DNA markers. Anthropological genetics is at one of the exciting points in its history of about 100 years. So much of information was never available earlier to facilitate the search for genes that influence normal human variation and adaptability. Identification of the genes responsible for human Mendelian diseases can now be routinely and readily accomplished. One would only require DNA samples, associated phenotypes, internet connection to the public genome database, a thermal cycler and a DNA-sequencing machine.

The completion of human genome project in the year 2003 was a landmark event in human genetics. Publication of the draft DNA sequence of chimpanzee genome is another notable event of the year 2005. The data show that human and chimpanzee genomes differ by only

1.23% in terms of nucleotide substitutions. Their comparative genomics provide information about mutations at different gene loci in Homo lineages which make them more susceptible to diseases like diabetes mellitus, coronary heart disease, etc. The understanding of the genetic basis of physical and behavioral traits that distinguish humans from other primates poses the greatest challenge in the present context for the discipline of biological anthropology. Pan and Homo lineages separated from their ancestral stock about 5-7 million years ago. There is need to implicate genes involved during this separation. 98% of the human DNA has non-coding sequences. Comparative genomics, population genetics, gene expression analysis and medical genetics have begun to make complementary inroads into the complex genetic architecture of human evolution (see Carroll, 2003).

These achievements provide an unparalleled opportunity to advance our understanding of the role of genetic factors in human health and disease. These developments would facilitate development, evaluation and application of genome-based diagnostic methods for prediction of susceptibility to disease, the prediction of drug response, the early detection of illness and the accurate molecular classification of disease. It is assumed that pharmaceutical houses would target all 30,000 human-protein-coding genes to develop drugs. Genomic based tools are being developed that would help in improving the health of all. Genetic medical intervention is now a reality.

Gene influences not only health and disease, but also normal human traits and behaviors. The research in behavior genetics would help in understanding the pathways that underlie attributes like cognition, diurnal rhythms and behavioral characteristics like anger, depression, criminal attitude, etc. The data generated through Human Genome Project have provided rich source of information having relevance to anthropology. It is now possible to identify and localize the specific genes that influence normal human variation and human adaptability on a large scale. This would help in the understanding of human microevolution.

Most genomic variations are shared between all populations, but certain alleles are more frequent in some populations than in others. However small these differences may be, they are useful in defining broad geographically based groupings. Analysis of hundreds of polymorphic loci sampled across the globally distributed populations have revealed the existence of genetic clustering that roughly matches with groups that have historically occupied large continental and sub-continental regions (Rosenberg, 2002). There are many similarities between the distribution of genetic variation and distribution of physical traits within and between human populations (American Association of Physical Anthropologists, 1996; Keita and Kittles, 1997). It has been usually argued in many circles that these patterns of variation provided a biological justification for the use of traditional racial categories (Risch et al., 2002). Others contradict saying that same data undercut traditional notions of racial groupings (King and Motulsky, 2002; Tischkoff and Kidd, 2004).

The question that can be raised here is whether we are completing a full circle by undertaking and using genomic studies to categorize humans into geographically based groupings. Have we really been able to discard the concept of race in anthropology? Infact, problems surrounding the word "race" forced researchers to promote the alternative word "ethnicity" (Huxley and Haddon, 1936; Hutchinson and Smith, 1996). However, the word ethnicity also suffers from several shortcomings and the two terms are often used interchangeably (Oppenheimer, 2001). To be straight, there is no U-turn, because tracing human history remains one of major aims of anthropology. Anthropology uses population substructure as a unit of inquiry. Ethnicity is such an important aspect of many societies that is difficult to ignore this in genetic research. How do the gene travel or circulate among human groups is determined by the culture. These concepts can not be ignored in genetic research. Human groups also vary widely in economic, social and psychological exposed a very different environment as a consequence of their membership of a particular group. These genetic and environmental differences among human populations have been used to study health disparities among groups and to explain various hot spots for various diseases. Anthropology and biomedical literature is replete with hundreds of examples suggesting higher susceptibility of various ethnic groups to certain diseases. It has been hypothesized that common variants present in the ancestral population before the dispersal of modern humans from Africa play an important role in human diseases (Goldstein and Chikhi, 2002).How to come out of this dilemma of using or not using ethnic or ancestral categories? A number of journals have issued guidelines stating that researchers should carefully define the terms they use for populations. Efforts to go beyond the use of racial/ethnic categories in genetic research would require a very broad range of additional variables (Chakravarti and Little, 2003).

It may be important to record here that genomic data is also being exploited for political considerations as genetic data was done in the past for stirring racial feelings. The example from Croatia can be cited. Its science minister has reportedly been asking the school teachers to promote teaching in the classrooms that recent genomic data reveals that the Croats are only distantly related to other Slavic populations such as the Serbs, but closely related to Finns. Croatian scientists are reportedly very angry at the spurious claim made and do not accept the claim of any racial differences between Croats and Slavs (see Abbot, 2005). The question of ethnicity is too deep in human psyche to obliterate easily.

The genetic literature is replete with examples showing that technology innovations can be misused. The example of amniocentesis, a prenatal diagnostic test for detection of fetal abnormalities, may be cited here as an illustration. The test first began in India in 1974 to detect fetal anomalies in families having higher risk. But it was misused for prenatal sex determination, and first clinic was established in Amritsar (Punjab) in 1979. Later there was mushrooming of private clinics all over the country. To check the misuse, the Pre-Natal Diagnostic Techniques (Regulation and Prevention of Misuse) Act, 1994 was enacted by the Union Government that banned sex determination tests all over the country. The implementation of the act waited till 1997. The misuse of the test resulted in selective killing of female fetuses. Census of India (2001) data from the Northwest India, i.e., especially from the states of Punjab and Haryana, show declining sex ratios. Punjab has the lowest sex ratio of 798 in the 0-6 age group. It is estimated that about one in 25 unborn girls are aborted every year. There are many other cultural issues related with sex selection at birth. There is rampant sex selection in China due to stringent one-child norm and there are about 40 million bachelors, and number is destined to increase if no remedial steps are taken.

The technological innovations have made gene manipulation in humans a reality due to the developments of techniques allowing the transfer of genes into mammalian cells. Patients are being treated by gene therapy to correct genetic defects. The application of these revolutionary technological innovations and the genomic and other data so generated have raised many ethical, social and legal consequences. There are reports that humans are being subjected to medical experimentation without maintaining adequate safeguards and/or without keeping the highest ethical standards. Perhaps it was true earlier also, but awareness was less then. The aggrieved parties have now started seeking legal remedies. A recent case of gene therapy can be cited as an illustration. The gene therapy trial used a modified virus to deliver a gene that was intended to produce a liver enzyme that was deficient in a teenager, Gelsinger. Gelsinger died from an immune reaction to the adenovirus vector in the year 1999. In an out of court settlement, employers of the three researchers who conducted the trial were to pay fines of one million U.S. dollars and the clinical researchers were to face restrictions on their work. This case has been widely publicized so as to tighten rules on the conduct of clinical trials. The justice department alleged that the researchers and their institutions made false statements regarding the safety of the trials to the National Institute of Health, U.S.A.(see Cheek, 2005).

Consequently new laws are being codified and made stringent. Human Tissue Act comes into force in April 2006 in the U.K. The law introduces new safeguards which will make keeping any tissue samples problematic-even a pinprick of blood. Every research investigation will need specific informed written consent. Specimens will need to be destroyed once the work is done. Objections are being raised against such stringent laws which may make medical research difficult and thus undermining the ability of researchers to find the causes of disease. However, one may question the validity of an informed written consent in poor underdeveloped countries, where many people are poor and illiterate.

Some other applications of genomics have also been criticized for being highly controversial and the propriety of such explorations like development of genomic databases is being questioned by some members of the public. Genomic databases are being established by many countries. For example, some countries have made it mandatory to keep genomic profile of their defence personnel, e.g., USA, UK. India is also planning to follow suit. Similarly, it may be argued that genetic profiling of individuals would help in the assessment of disease risk and health planning. But such data sets can be misused and exploited by those involved in different professions. These would create a lot of social unrest and raise many ethical, social and legal issues. For example, the possibility of misuse of genetic knowledge for occupational discrimination: (1) should a person's higher genetic risk to develop a late onset disease information be leaked to the prospective employers or others? (2) should persons with certain genetic defect be allowed in some professions, e.g., persons with genetic colour vision defect to be employed in aviation industry? Health insurance is another thorny issue. Detective agencies may lap at genomic databases to answer various types of queries from various clients, e.g., matrimonial services, placement agencies, etc. There is needed to ponder over these issues and frame laws, because freedom of scientific inquiry is not unbounded, howsoever such a freedom be cardinal for human progress. It is important for the society to define the appropriate and inappropriate use of genomics. There is need to discuss these issues over wider platforms before enacting laws. New laws should meet these new needs with adequate safeguards. Bio-ethicists, sociologists, anthropologists, human geneticists, lawyers and theologians should minutely ponder over genetic, legal, social and ethical issues in order to make recommendations regarding public policy to be followed by the state.

DNA tests have tremendous applications in judicial proceedings and can revolutionize the court proceedings. Many genetic tests for health and behavioral traits have the potential to predict diseases and conditions that have no prospect of treatment or cure. These tests are providing new challenges for judges- whether to admit or compel genetic tests to confirm or predict genetic diseases and conditions in judicial contexts like culpability, causation, sentencing, liability and damages. Hoffmann and Rothenberg (2005) have recently conducted a survey of different trial court judges in Marryland (USA) to illicit their views. The respondents were asked whether they would admit a positive genetic test for schizophrenia to establish that the defendant did not have the necessary criminal intent/ guilty mind (*mens rea*) to commit the crime. Respondents were also asked whether they would compel a test for a condition that predisposes an individual to bout of rage during their hearing proceedings. A large majority of judges said they would not compel a genetic test for assessing their genetic predisposition in a criminal sentencing. But in civil cases in the context of causation for tort liability and determination of damages a majority of judges said that they would compel a genetic test to establish that the defendant's negligence was not the cause of plaintiff's injury, but the cause was his developmental disabilities. The judges reasoned that since the plaintiff's health was an issue, the defendant had a right to use this. As the genetic tests provide virtually conclusive evidence of identity, thousands of such cases on the horizon would pose new challenges for the judiciary and public.

Before discussing the contributions of cultural anthropology in health and disease, it may be prudent here to distinguish biomedical approach from cultural approach in studies on health and disease. Biomedical approach is characterized by elements like anatomy, physiology, the processes that cause pathology including socio-cultural. Some biomedical problems may be phrased in terms of evolutionary theory, most are not. These problems become of interest to biological anthropology when they are linked to populations following holistic and comparative approaches. The "biomedical model" of disease is in fact a name given to the philosophical thought and assumption underlying western allopathic medicine under which, the disease is a physical entity that occurs in identifiable location due to pathogenic causes. It addresses the disease, its diagnosis and treatment. The modern medicine ignores other indigenous systems of health management and calls them as alternative/ complimentary medicine and/or ethnomedicine. These are ayurveda, homeopathy, acupressure/ acupuncture, hypnotherapy, naturotherapy and reiki, etc. The so called alternative medicine believes that the cause of disease is always psychic or emotional or else due to certain imbalances in the body and/or mind. These approaches including homoeopathy are considered as "no more than a placebo effect" by modern medicine (Shang et al., 2005). But this argument would not please those who have been cured by complimentary medicine. The protagonists of homoeopathy would swear by the validity of this art, and are of opinion that its science is mysterious. Some new concepts, phenomena and sciences are needed to elucidate the science of homoeopathy. Similar line of argument may be favored by protagonists of other approaches. Ayurveda and Yoga have already made inroads into the western cultures. Today, China has captured 26% of the global market in traditional medicinal plants, while India has managed to garner 9%. According to figures from the department of Ayurveda, Yoga, Unani, Sidha, and Homoeopathy (AYUSH), 70% of Indians use Indian systems of medicine. Indian Vedic Homa therapy propagates that healthy environment has healing properties.

Illich (1975) drew attention to the major ills of medical establishment, which sent shock waves across the medical world. Illich used the medical term *'Iatrogenic'* to refer to illness produced by doctors and hospitals. His strongest criticism was at the cultural level. Human experience of hundred thousands of years have developed various cultural and spiritual ways to cope with certain realities of life like, ageing, illness, pain and death. Now, by over-medications, are we taking away from the society these cultural coping mechanisms? The protagonists of indigenous systems of medicine have highlighted the failures and/or serious side effects of using allopathic medicine. Antihistamines containing phenylpropanolamine may cause stroke (Actifed has been banned by the government). Cetrizine may depress motor coordination and cause gastro-intestinal discomfort and kidney impairment. Recently, Vivox, a pain killing drug, has been reportedly withdrawn from the market after a lawsuit claimed it caused heart attacks. Viagra, the drug popularly used to treat male impotency, has been indicated for causing sudden blindness. Thalidomide, prescribed to treat nausea in pregnant women in 1950s, led to the birth of thousands of children suffering from phocomelia, characterized by limb deformities. This drug was consequently banned world over. Clioquinol, an anti-diarrhea drug, is said to cause paralysis among thousands of people globally. Despite these limitations, it cannot be denied that allopathic medicine has, in many ways, revolutionized the science of diagnosis and treatment of diseases and cured billions of people over time. It has improved life span of people and led to another demographic transition that is being observed in the developed countries. Population growth has become zero or negative and aged people are increasing. These put extra burden on the state to provide health care and to maintain economic growth.

Cultural anthropology provides various theoretical orientations to the study of the dimensions of health and disease from cultural perspective. It has been emphasized that these concepts exist only within the constructs of a particular culture and therefore cannot be studied without understanding these conceptual properties. Anthropologists have emphasized that disease causation models are embedded in the culture of many societies and their ignorance has resulted in the failures of many ambitious public health intervention projects. The specialists in this branch of knowledge are called medical anthropologists. They have termed the mechanistic and reductionism approach of biomedicine as "the machine metaphor". Medical anthropology studies health care as a part of cultural analysis of health behavior, beliefs and values and the rules of analysis are the same that are employed in general ethnography as health care systems are viewed as cultural systems (Kleinman, 1978). Weidman (1979) defines health culture as all phenomena related to the maintenance of well-being and problems of sickness with which people cope in traditional ways within their own social networks. Thus health care domain under above perspective includes cognitive and social systems, beliefs and practices which provide a framework of rules and meanings for appropriate health behavior in a particular cultural setting. There are many models which do not focus solely on the cultural definition of health, but emphasize the sick role and social aspects of illness behavior and medical care (Foster, 1978). Variations in health behavior are explained on the basis of differences in factors like education levels, socio-economic class, sex, religion, etc. Culture is included in these models from a perspective of differences in illness behavior of various ethnic groups (Wolff and Langley, 1968).

Medical anthropologists explore field applications of various new health care improvement programmes/services to study the kinds of resistance shown by various communities against these programmes. They also study the resistance of medical personnel and, bureaucracy to change their models and explanations of health care delivery. Communities may reject new health services if there is conflict between the programme imposed and their folk beliefs regarding health and body functioning. Because of an adversarial position between traditions, folk and professional systems, this model is referred to as the "adversary model" (Foster and Anderson, 1978). Medical anthropological research can help to find ways to make these health care delivery programmes acceptable to the communities by making them compatible with their culture, beliefs and expectations. Medical anthropological research has demonstrated that the community ideas of health may be very strong and interwoven with their cultural and religious beliefs. Medical anthropology in itself has now become a burgeonic field. Many universities in North America and Europe now offer courses related to anthropology of health. There has been a lot of proliferation of research interests in the last 25 years in this field which now encompasses a range of concerns, varying from a historically predominant cross-sectional study of local health beliefs and practices to the cultural construction of biomedicine (see Johnson and Sargent, 1990).

A moot point may be raised here as a follow-up of the conflicting issues and explanations forwarded under the cultural and biomedical approaches of anthropology, that is, whether biological and cultural anthropologists are at logger heads and drifting apart from each other due to incompatibility of views shared by them. There are people who would argue that biological anthropology has become highly scientific and technology oriented due to revolutionary innovations in these fields in the last 25 years. As a result there of, many cultural anthropologists have started indicating that they have nothing to contribute to tradition of scientific and evolutionary thought in anthropology (see Cartmill, 1994). But anthropologists have always emphasized that anthropology is the science which helps to dismantle the intellectual barriers that separate humanities from natural sciences (Ingold, 1992). Bio-cultural approach to study humans following holistic and comparative approaches has always been central to the anthropology and the tradition would go on despite all talks of cultural anthropology without anthropologists and biological anthropologists without anthropology. These hiccups can not create hindrances in the fast growth path which anthropology is traversing, at least in the North America if not yet in India. The anthropology circles should highlight evolutionary, environmental destruction and change and other related theoretical directions that underlie the work in anthropology while celebrating the year 2009 as the 200th anniversary of Charles Darwin's birth and 150th anniversary of the publication on the origins of species.

Darwin (1859) noted a curious problem which was proving fatal to the theory of evolution. He found that social insects like bees have large populations of neuters or sexless females. These bees have distinctive behavioral and anatomical characteristics and yet they can not propagate their type being sterile. They live as a "servile class". The theory of population genetics tells that kin selection migration increase frequency of related genes in any given population. The concept of population as a unit of evolution is universally accepted. Fitness of an individual and that of group is another evolutionary important attribute. It has been often noted that even distant biological relatives may enhance the fitness of another individual(s). There are numerous such examples in animal kingdom. Vampire bats are bats that feed on blood (hematophagy) and are native to the Americas. Bats regularly regurgitate blood and donate it to other members of their group who failed to feed that night (see Altringham, 1996). Zoological literature is replete with examples of animals which give alarm signals to warn their fellow counterparts of the presence of predators, in turn increasing their own chances of falling prey. We note such a behavior in human groups too. This behavior of a select few enables many to pass on their genes to the succeeding generation though themselves they might not have been able to do that successfully in the absence of support. Such a social group may be an extended family/ community or may be extended on a mega scale to include civilization (see Sharma, 2006). In the modern genetic parlance, this concept may be extrapolated to hypothesize the presence of a "spiritual gene" or aggregation of such genes that motivates people to defend have-nots and the weak and thereby enhancing their fitness and many times at their own peril. Recently, Hamer (2005) has claimed that he has found a gene (VMAT2) that controls the flow to the brain of chemicals which play a key role in emotions and consciousness among individuals who are able to consistently reach a transcendent spiritual mental state. This gene has been called the 'God gene'. The nomenclature of the gene may be a misnomer. Though his work has been severely criticized by his colleagues, yet we come across examples of individuals with sacrificial tendencies. The factor of social engineering through legislation and many other such related issues, that may have far reaching evolutionary effects, need to be studied scientifically. Neuro-and philosophical-anthropologists need to ponder over these issues that have aroused great curiosity.

REFERENCES

Abbot A. (2005), Race Claims Spark Fury over Croatia's School Curriculum. *Nature* 437:463.

Allen J.S., Bruss J. and Damasio H. (2005), MRI analysis of the calcarine and lunate sulci in modern humans. *Am. J. Phys. Anthropol. Suppl.*40: 64.

Allison A.C. (1954), Protection Afforded by the Sickle-cell Trait Against sub Tertian Malarial Infection. *Br. Med. J.* 1:290-294.

Altringham J.D. (1996), *Bats: Biology and Behavior*. Oxford: Oxford University Press.

American Association of Physical Anthropologists (1996), AAPA Statement on Biological Aspects of Race. *Am J. Phys. Anthropol:* 101: 569-570.

Anderson N.B., McNeilly M. and Myers H. (1991), Autonomic Reactivity and Hypertension in Blacks: A Review and Proposed Model. *Ethnicity Dis.* 1: 154-185.

Angel J.L. (1981), History and Development of Palaeoanthropology. *Am. J. Phys. Anthropol.* 56: 509-515.

Anuchin D.N. (1902), On Tasks and Methods of Anthropology. *Russian Anthropological Journal* 3:62.

Armelagos G.J. and Dewey J.R. (1970), Evolutionary Response to Human Infectious Diseases. *Bioscience* 20: 271-275.

Avent N.D. and Reid M.E. (2000), The Rh Blood Group System: A Review. *Blood* 95: 375-387.

Baker P.T. (1962), The Application of Ecological theory to Anthropology. *Am. Anthropol.* 64: 15-22.

Baker P.T., Hanna J.T. and Baker T.S. (eds). (1986), *The Changing Samoans: Behavior and Health in Transition*. Oxford: Oxford University Press.

Barker D.J.P. (1994), *Mothers, Babies and Disease in Later Life*. London: BMJ Publishing Group.

Bogin B. (2001), *The Growth of Humanity*. New York: Wiley-Liss.

Boyer J.S. (1995), Biochemical and Biophysical Aspects of Water Deficits and the Predisposition to Disease. *Annu. Rev. Phytopathol.* 33: 251-274z.

Carritt B., Kemp T.J. and Poulter M. (1997), Evolution of the Human RH (Rhesus) Blood Group Genes: A 50 year old Prediction (Partially) Fulfilled. *Hum. Mol. Genet.* 6: 843-850.

Carroll S.B. (2003), Genetics and the Making of *Homo Sapiens*. *Nature* 422: 849-857.

Cartmill M. (1994), Reinventing Anthropology: American Association of Physical Anthropologists. Annual Luncheon Address. *Yrbk. Physical Anthropol.* 37: 1-9.

Chakravarti A. and Little P. (2003), Nature, Nurture and Human Disease. *Nature* 421: 412-424.

Check E. (2005), Sanctions Agreed over Teenager's Gene-therapy Death. *Nature* 433: 674.

Cockburn T.A. (ed). (1967), Infectious Diseases: *Their Evolution and Eradication.* Springfield, Ill: Charles C. Thomas.

Committee on Mutagenicity of Chemicals in Foods (1981), *Report on Health and Social Subjects* 24. London: HMSO.

Cooper R.S. (2004), Genetic Factors in Ethnic Disparities in Health. In: Anderson N.B., Bulatao R.A., Cohen B. (eds): *Critical Perspectives on Racial and Ethnic Differences in Health in Later Life.* Washington DC: National Academy Press, pp. 267-309.

Costa T., Seriver C.R. and Childs B. (1985), The Effect of Mendelian Disease on Human Health: A Measurement. *Am. J. Med. Genet.* 21: 231-242.

Cummins H. (1939), Dermatoglyphic Stigmata in Mongoloid Imbeciles. *Anat. Rec.* 73: 407-415.

Darwin C. (1859), *The Origin of Species*, London: John Murray.

De Garine I. and Harrison G.A. (eds). (1988), *Coping with Uncertainty in Food Supply.* Oxford: Oxford University Press.

Denton D. (1982), *The Hunger for Salt: An Anthropological, Physiological and Medical Analysis.* New York: Springer-Verlag.

Drayana D., Coon H., Kim U.K., et al. (2003), Genetic Analysis of a Complex Trait in the Utah Genetic Reference Project: A Major locus for PTC taste Ability on Chromosome 7q and a Secondary Locus on Chromosome 16 p. *Hum. Genet* 112: 567-572.

Dressler W.W. (1991), Social Class, Skin Colour and Arterial Blood Presence in Two Societies. *Ethnicity Dis.* 1: 60-70.

Dubus R. (1965), *Man Adapting.* New Haven: Yale University Press.

Duckworth W.L.H. (1904), *Morphology and Anthropology.* Cambridge: Cambridge University Press.

Enattah N.S., Sahi T., Savilahti E., et al. (2002), Identification of a Variant Associated with Adult type Hypolactasia. *Nat. Genet.* 30: 233- 237.

Eveleth P. (1966), The Effect of Climate upon Growth. *Ann N.Y. Acad. Sci.* 134:750.

Ezzath M., Lopez A.D., Rodgers A. and Murray C.J.L. (eds). (2004), *Global and Regional Burden of Disease due to Selected Major Risk Factors.* Geneva: WHO.

Feingold E. (2001), Methods for Linkage Analysis of Quantitative Trait Loci in Humans. *Theor. Popul. Biol.* 60: 167-180.

Flint J., Harding R.M., Boyace A.J. and Clegg J.B. (1998), The Population Genetics of the Haemoglobino-pathies. *Baillierres Clin. Haematol.* 11: 1-51.

Foster G.M. (1978), Medical Anthropology. In Logan MH and Hunt EE (eds): *Health and Human Condition.* North Sciutate, MA: Duxberry Press, pp. 2-11.

Foster G.M. and Anderson B.G. (1978), *Medical Anthropology.* New York: John Wiley.

Friedlaender J.S. (ed). (1987), *The Solomon Islands Projects: A Long-Term Study of Health, Heredity and Modernization.* Oxford: Clarendon Press.

Frisancho A.R., Farrow S., Lockette W., et al. (1999), Role of Genetic and Environmental Factors in the in Creased Blood Pressure of Bolivian Blacks. *Am. J. Hum Biol.* 11: 489-498.

Frisancho A.R., Velasquez T. and Sanches J. (1975), Possible Adaptive Significance of Small Body size in the Attainment of Aerobic Capacity Among High Altitude Quechua Natives. In Watts E., Johnston F.E. and Lasker G.W. (eds). *Biosocial Interactions in Population Adaptation.* The Hague: Mouton.

Goldstein D.B. and Chikhi L. (2002), Human Migrations and Population Structure: What we know and why it Matters. *Ann. Rev. Genomics Hum. Genet.* 3:129-152.

Greene L.S. (1974), Physical Growth and Development, Neurological Maturation and Behavioral Functioning in two Ecuadorian Andean Communities in which Goiter is endemic II. PTC Taste Sensitivity and Neurological Maturation. *Am. J. Phys. Anthropol.* 41: 139-151.

Greene L.S. (1977), Hyper Endemic Goiter, Cretinism and Social Organization in Highland Ecuadour. In Greene LS (ed): *Malnutrition, Behavior and Social Organization.* New York: Academic Press. pp. 55-94.

Hadley T.J. and Peiper S.C. (1997), From Malaria to Chemokinc Receptor: The Emerging Physiologic Role of the Duffy Blood Group Antigen. *Blood* 89: 3077-3091.

Hadley T.J., Klotz F.W., Pasvol G., Haynes J.D., McGinniss M.H., Okubo Y., Miller L.H. (1987), Falciparum Malaria Parasites Invade Erythrocytes that Lack Glycophorin A and B (M_kM_k): Strain Differences Indicate Receptor Heterogeneity and Two Pathways for Invasion. *J. Clin. Invest.* 80: 1190-1193.

Haldane J.B.S. (1949), Disease and Evolution. *Ricerca Sci. Suppl.* 19:3-10.

Hales C.N. and Barker D.J.P. (1992), Type 2 (non-insulin dependent) Diabetes Mellitus: the thrifty Genotype Hypothesis. *Diabetologia* 35: 595-601.

Hamblin M.T., Di Rienzo A. (2000), Detection of the Signature of Natural Selection in Humans: Evidence from the Duffy Blood Group Locus. *Am. J. Hum. Genet.* 66: 1669-1679.

Hamer D.H. (2005), *The God Gene: How Faith is Hardwired into our Genes.* New York: Knopf Publishing Group.

Harrison G.A. and Jefferies D.J. (1977), Human Biology in Urban Environments: A Review of Research Strategies. In Baker P. (ed): *Problems in the Biosphere: Some Research Strategies and Designs, MAB Technical Notes 3.* Paris: UNESCO, pp. 65-85.

Harrison G.A., Weiner J.S., Tanner J.M., and Barnicot N.A. (1964), *Human Biology: An Introduction to Human Evolution, Variation, Growth and Ecology.* Oxford: Oxford University Press.

Hoffmann D.E. and Rothenberg K.H. (2005), When should Judges Admit or Compel Genetic Tests? *Science* 310: 241-242.

Huang C.H., Liu P.Z. and Cheng J.G. (2000), Molecular Biology and Genetics of the Rh Blood Group System. *Seminar Hematol.* 37: 150-165.

Hutchinson J. and Smith A.D. (eds). (1996), *Ethnicity.* New York: Oxford University Press.

Huxley J. and Haddon A.C. (1936), *We Europeans: A Survey of Racial Problems*. New York: Harper.

Illich I. (1975), *Medical Nemesis: The Expropriation of Health*. London: Marian Boyars. 184 p.

Ingold T. (1992), Editorial. *Man (ns)* 27:693-696.

Intergovernmental Panel on Climate Change (2001), *The Scientific Basis: Contribution of Working Group 1 to the Third Assessment Report* 1-944. Cambridge: Cambridge University Press.

Johnson T.M. and Sargent C.F. (eds). (1990), *Medical Anthropology: Handbook of Theory and Method*. New York: Greenwood Press.

Johnston F.E. (1981), Physical Growth and Development and Nutritional Status. *Federation Proc.* 40:25-83.

Johnston F.E. and Low S.M. (1984), Biomedical Anthropology: An Emerging Synthesis in Anthropology. *Yrbk. Phys. Anthropol.* 27: 215-226.

Keita S.O.Y. and Kittles R.A. (1997), The Persistence of Racial Thinking and the Myth of Racial Divergence. *Am. Anthropol.* 99: 534-544.

Kelly R.J., Rouquier S., Giorgi D., Lennon G.G. and Low J.B. (1995), Sequence and Expression of a Candidate for the Human Secretor Blood Group? (1,2) Fucosyltransferase Gene (FUT 2). Homozygosity for an Enzyme-inactivating Nonsense Mutation Commonly Correlates with the Non-secretor Phenotype. *J. Biol. Chem.* 270: 4640-4649.

King M.C. and Motulsky A.G. (2002), Mapping Human History. *Science* 298:2342-2343.

Kleinman A. (1978), Concepts and a Model for the Comparison of Medical Systems as Cultural Systems. *Soc. Sci. Med.* 12B:85-94.

Kobberling J. and Tattersall J. (eds). (1982), *The Genetics of Diabetes Mellitus*. New York: Academic Press.

Kwiatkowski D.P. (2005), How Malaria has Affected the Human Genome and what Human Genetics can Teach us about Malaria. *Am. J. Hum. Genet.* 77: 171-192.

Leonard W.R. and Robertson M.L. (1992), Nutrition Requirements and Human Evolution: A Bioenergetic Model. *Am. J. Hum. Biol.* 14 : 179-195.

Levine P. and Stetson R.E. (1939), An Unusual Case of intra Group Agglutination. *JAMA* 113: 126-127.

Little M.A. (1982), The Development of Ideas on Human Ecology and Adaptation. In Spencer F(ed): *A History of American Physical Anthropology* 1930-1980, pp. 405-433. New York: Academic Press.

Lasker G.W. (1969), Human Biological Adaptability. *Science* 166: 1480-1486.

Little M.A. (1989), Human Biology of African Pastoralists. *Yrbk. Phys. Anthropol.* 32: 215-247.

Livingstone F.B. (1958), Anthropological Implications of Sickle Cell Gene Distribution in West Africa. *Am. Anthropol.* 60: 533-562.

Livingstone F.B. (1962), Population Genetics and Population Ecology. *Am. Anthropol.* 64: 45-52.

Livingstone F.B. (1964), Aspects of the Population Dynamics of the Abnormal Haemoglobin and Glucose-6- Phosphate Dehydrogenase Deficiency Genes. *Am. J. Hum. Genet.* 16: 435-450.

Lovell W.G. and Lutz C.H. (1996), "A Dark Obverse": Maya Survival in Guatemala, 1520-1994. *The Geographical Rev.* 86: 398-407.

Marini A.M., Matassi G., Raynal V., et al. (2000), The Human Rhesus Associated Rh AG Protein and a Kidney Homologue Promote Ammonium Transport in Yeast. *Nature Genet.* 26: 341-344.

Mascie-Taylor C.G.N. and Lasker G.W. (eds). (1988), *Biological Aspects of Human Migration*. Cambridge: Cambridge University Press.

McCracken R.D. (1971), Lactase Deficiency: An Example of Dietary Evolution. *Curr. Anthropol.* 12: 479-517.

McNeil W.H. (1979), Historical Patterns of Migration. *Curr. Anthropol.* 20: 95-102.

Miller L.H., Mason S.J., Clyde D.V., McGinniss M.H. (1976), The Resistance Factor to Plasmodium Vivax in Blacks: the Duffy-blood-group Genotype, F_yF_y. *N. Eng. J. Med.* 295: 302-304.

Morton N.E. (1982), *Outline of Genetic Epidemiology*. Basel: S. Karger.

Motulsky A.G. (1964), Hereditary Red Cell Traits and Malaria. *Am. J. Trop. Med. Hyg.* 13: 147-158.

Muller H.J., (1950), Our Load of Mutations. *Am. J. Hum. Genet.* 2: 111-176.

National Centre for Health Statistics (NCHS) (1996), *Health, United States, 1995*. Hyattsville, Md: Public Health Service.

Neel J.V. (1962), Diabetes Mellitus: A "Thrifty" Genotype Rendered Detrimental by "Progress"? *Am. J. Hum. Genet.* 14: 353-362.

Newman M.T. (1953), The Application of Ecological Rules to the Racial Anthropology of the Aboriginal New World. *Am. Anthropol.* 55: 311-327.

Nydon J. and Thomas R.B. (1989), Methodological Procedures for Analyzing Expenditure. In Pelto G.H., Pelto P.J. and Messer E. (eds): *Research Methods in Nutritional Anthropology*. Tokyo: United Nations University.

OECD (1999), The City in the Global Village. The OECD (Organization for Economic Corporation and Development). *Observer* 217/218: 33-35.

Omran A.R. (1971), The Epidemiologic Transition. *Milbank Mem Quart* 49:509-538.

Oppenheimer G.M. (2001), Paradigm Lost: Race, Ethnicity and the Search for New Population Taxonomy. *Am. J. Public Health* 91: 1049-1055.

Oriol R., Damlovs J. and Hawkins B.R. (1981), A New Genetic Model Proposing that the Se Gene is a Structural Gene Closely Linked to the H Gene. *Am. J. Hum Genet* 33: 421-131.

Patz J.A., Campbell-Lendrum D., Holloway T. and Foley J.A. (2005), Impact of Regional Climate Change on Human Health. *Nature* 438:310-317.

Poschmann A., Fischer K., Seidl S., et al. (1974), ABH Receptors and Red Cell Survival in a "Bombay" Blood. Immunofluorescence Studies by Phytohaemagglutinins and Helix Agglutinins. *Vox Sang* 27: 338-346.

Quetelet A. (1870), *Anthropometrie,ou Mesure des Differences Facultes de Phorens*. Brussels.

Race R.R. (1944), An Incomplete Antibody in Human Serum. *Nature* 153: 771-772.

Reisch N., Burchard E., Ziv E. and Tang H. (2002), Categorization of Humans in Biomedical Research: Genes, Race and Disease. *Genome Biol.* 3(htpp://genomebiology.com).

Rosenberg N.A., Pritchard J.K., Weber J.L., Cann H.M., Kidd K.K., Zhivotovsky L.A. and Feldman M.W. (2002), Genetic Structure of Human Populations. *Science* 298: 2381-2385.

Ruff C.B. and Leo F.P. (1986), Use of Computed Tomography in Skeletal Structure Research. *Yrbk. Phys. Anthropol* 29:181-196.

Schaumann B. and Alter M. (1976), *Dermatoglyphics in Medical Disorders.* New York: Springer Verlag.

Scrimshaw N.S. and Murray E.B. (1988), The Acceptability of Milk and Milk Products in Populations with a High Prevalence of Lactose Intolerance. *Am. J. Clin. Nutr.* 48 (Suppl 1): 1083-1159.

Schell L.M. (1991), Effects of Pollutants on Human Prenatal and Postnatal Growth: Noise, Lead, Polychlorinated Compounds and Toxic Wastes. *Yrbk. Phys. Anthropol* 34: 157-188.

Schell L.M. (1997), Culture as a Stressor: A Revised Model of Bio-cultural Interaction. *Am. J. Phys. Anthropol.* 102:67-77.

Shang A., Huwiler-Muntener K., Nartey L., et al. (2005), Are the Clinical Effects of Homoeopathy Placebo Effects? Comparative Study of Placebo-controlled Trials of Homoeopathy and Allopathy. *Lancet* 366: 726-732.

Sharma M. (2006), How Spiritual Gene Could Have Arisen? *The Economic Times, Friday, May, 12.*

Sharma K. (2005), Genetic Epidemiology of Epilepsy. *Neurology India* 52:486-491.

Sharma K. and Bakshi S. (2005), Genetic Analysis of Bilateral Dermatoglyphic Asymmetry in Twins and their Parents. *Anthropologischer Anzeiger* 63: 165-188.

Sharma K., Banerjee B.G. and Sinha A.K. (2005), Health Status of a Hill Community: An Assessment through Utilization of Health Care Services at Block Level in the State of Himachal Pradesh. *South Asian Anthropologists* 5: 1-17.

Sharma K., Byard P.J., Russell J.M. and Rao D.C. (1984), A Family Study of Anthropometric Traits in a Punjabi Community:1. Introduction. *Am. J. Phys. Anthropol.* 63: 389-395.

Simmons F.J. (1970), Primary Adult Lactose Intolerance and the Milking Habit: A Problem of Biologic and Cultural Interrelations II. The Culture Historical Hypothesis. *Am. J. Dig. Dis.* 15: 695-710.

Snow R.W., Guerra C.A., Noor A.M., Myint H.Y., Hay S.I. (2005), The Global Distribution of Clinical Episodes of *Plasmodium Falaciparum* Malaria. *Nature* 434: 214-217.

Soupene E., Ramirez R.M., Kustu S. (2001), Evidence that Fungal MEP Proteins Mediate Diffusion of the Uncharged Species NH_3 Across the Cytoplasmic Membrane. *Mol. Cell Biol.* 21: 5733-5741.

Sutow W.W., Conrad R.A. and Griffth K.M. (1965), Growth Status of Children Exposed to Fallout Radiation on Marshall Islands. *Pediatrics* 36:721.

Tanner J.M. (1981), *A History of the Study of Human Growth*. Cambridge University Press.

Tepper B.J., Keller K.L., Ullrich N.V. (2003), Genetic Taste Markers and Preferences for Bitter and Pungent Foods. In: Hofmann T., Pickenhagen W., Ho CT(eds.) : Taste Research-Chemical and Physiological Aspects. *Am. Chem. Soc. Sym. Ser.* 867, 60-74.

Tishkoff S.A. and Kidd K.K. (2004), Implications of Biogeography of Human Populations for "Race" and Medicine. *Nat. Genet*. 36: S21- S27.

Trimble B.K. and Smith M.E. (1977), The Incidence of Genetic Disease and Impact on Man of an Altered Mutation Rate. *Can. J. Genet Cytol.* 19: 375-385.

UNAIDS/WHO (2005), AIDS Epidemic Update (Dec. 2005). http://www.unaids.org/en/resources/epidemiology.asp.

Washburn S.I. (1951), The New Physical Anthropology. *Trans N.Y. Acad. Sci. Ser.* 2, 13: 298-304.

Weidman H. (1979), Falling out: A Diagnostic and Treatment Problem Viewed from a Transcultural Perspective. *Soc. Sci. Med.* 13B: 95-102.

Weiner A.S. (1944), The Rh Series of Allelic Genes. *Science* 100:595.

Williams L., Spence M.A. and Tideman S.C. (1977), Implications of the Observed Effect of Air Pollution on Birth Weight. *Soc. Biol.* 24:1.

Wolff B.B. and Langley S. (1968), Cultural Factors and Pain Response: A Review. *Am Anthropol* 70: 494-501.

WHO (1983), *World Health Statistics*. Geneva: WHO.

Part-I

TRIBAL HEALTH

2

HEALTH MANAGEMENT AMONG THE KONDH: A PRIMITIVE TRIBE OF DISTRICT KALAHANDI, ORISSA

Hemanta Bag and A.K. Kapoor

INTRODUCTION

Health has been defined by WHO (World Health Organisation) as "a state of complete physical, social and mental well being and not merely the absence of disease or infirmity (1971)". The definition of health as a state of well being indicates that health is not an activity; rather it is the outcome of all activities, which make up the lives of individuals, households, community, societies and cities. The result of health activities can be measured by the information feedback to management.

The management of health takes place at three levels: Grass root level- it provides the first point of contact between individual and the delivery system where people obtain primary health facilities having primary centre, sub centers and dispensaries. Intermediate level-when the facilities referred to as agencies at the grass root level are inadequate; individuals are referred to agencies at intermediate level for better curative services and testing facilities. e.g. Hospitals. At the apex level, health institutions provide specialized care and super special services and medical research.

Despite all these, every society recognizes notion of social health and social illness. But every culture, irrespective of its simplicity and complexity, has its own beliefs and practices concerning diseases and illness. They evolve their own system of medicine in order to treat diseases in its own way. In the diagnosis of disease, primary consideration is to find out its cause. Every culture has indigenous ideas of diseases causation. Disease usually is related to victims or patient's surrounding and the relationship between the patient and the surrounding is interpreted culturally.

Few of the studies have been carried out in tribal population focusing on health dimensions like causes of diseases and curing practices (Marriott, 1955; Ali, 1980; Chaudhuri, 1986; Basu, 1994; Swain, 1994; Mishra and Kapoor 2001; Bag and Kapoor, 2004) and reported that, the tribal have their own medical system i.e. a mixture of religion, magic, science and tradition. They have their own theory of disease and illness i.e. caused by manifestation of evil spirit, wrath of certain spirits, breach of some taboo or hostile spirit of the dead. They have their own curative practices i.e. magico-religious practices.

In the present paper an attempt has been made to study the management of health through ethnomedical practices and modern medical practices among the Kondhs- A Primitive tribe of Kalahandi District, Orissa.

AREA AND PEOPLE

Kalahandi district occupies the South-Western portion of Orissa and is situated between 19 degree 3′ N and 21 degree 5' N latitude and 82 degree 30′ E and 83 Degree 74′ E longitude. It is bounded in the North by the District of Balangir and Nawapara, on the South by the District of Rayagada, on the West by the District of Nawarangpur and Raipur (Madhya Pradesh) and on the East by the District of Rayagada and Boudh. It extends over an area of 8,364.89 Sq.K.Ms. Total population of Kalahandi District is 1334372. Out of which, (49.995 per cent) 667126 are males and (50.005 per cent) 667246 are females. Density of Population in Kalahandi District is 168/Km^2. Total numbers of literate persons are 518951 (46.20 per cent). Out of which, (62.88 per cent) 352751 are males and (29.36 per cent) 166200 are females.

MATERIAL AND METHODS

The intensive and extensive fieldwork was carried out in seven Villages i.e. Paria, Turpi, Khalan, Kalam, Sundimunda, Shargiguda and Chheliamal of Kalahandi District, Orissa from February 2004 to June 2004. The primary data was collected from 306 households using various anthropological tool and techniques. Secondary data was also collected from census report and other government and non-government publications.

Socio-economic Aspect

The total Kondh population under study is 2064. Out of which, 1065 (51.60 per cent) are males and 999 (48.40 per cent) are females. There are 364 (17.64 per cent) literate, out of which (9.45 per cent) 195 are males and (8.15 per cent) 169 are females. It has been observed that, 40.50 per cent are engaged in agriculture, 26.20 per cent daily wage labour, 30.70 per cent forest economy, 2.60 per cent other works. It has been found that 84.97 per cent nuclear families, 14.05 per cent are joint families, 0.98 per cent are polygynous families. The average household size is 6.75. The clan or *Kuda* is a larger kinship group. On the basis of function, the Kondh clan can be divided into four sub clans namely, Mondal, Majhi, Jani and Pujari. Jani look after the worship of deities, Pujari assist the Jani in religious matter. Mondal looks after the overall well being and Polito-jural administration of the village and Majhi assists the Mondal.

RESULTS AND DISCUSSION

The sample size of the present study comprised of 306 households of seven villages i.e. Paria, Turpi, Khalan, Kalam, Sundimunda, Shargiguda and Chheliamal of Kalahandi District, Orissa. Out of which 242 (79.08%) are males and 64 (20.92%) are females as heads of the families as well as the main informants. The total number of Kondh population under study is 2064, out of which 1065 (51.60%) are males and 999 (48.40%) are females.

Out of 2064 peoples, in the last six month i.e. July 2003 -January 2004, 383 (18.57%) peoples were suffered from various diseases and illness. Out of 383, 204 (53.26%) are males and 179 (46.74) are females.

Table 1
No. of Cases of Illness in Last Six Months

Sl. No.	*Have you suffering from any illness or diseases in last six months?*	*Male (n) (%)*	*Female (n) (%)*	*Total (n) (%)*
1.	Yes	204 (19.15)	179 (17.92)	383 (18.57)
2.	No	801(80.85)	820 (82.08)	1621 (8143)
3.	total	1065 (100.00)	999 (100.00)	2064 (100.00)

From Table 1, it has been observed that in the last six months 383 (18.57) per cent of people suffered from various diseases and illness. But 204 (19.15) per cent of males are suffering from various diseases and illness and 179 (17.92) per cent of females are suffering from various diseases and illness

REASONS FOR DISEASE AND ILLNESS

To find out the reasons of diseases and illness we have taken 242 (79.08%) males and 64 (20.92%) females as heads of the families as well as main informants. They have their own explanations of disease and illness, on the basis of which they develop their peculiar ways of curing diseases and illness.

From Table 2, it has been observed that, 29.41 per cent of Kondhs believe that disease and illness are caused by wrath of certain evil spirits. Where as 24.51 per cent believe that the disease and illness are caused by due to wrath of gods. But 46.08 per cent believe that disease and illness are cause by due to physical disorders.

From table 3, it has been observed that, from July 2003 to January 2004 the Kondh are suffering from Malaria (31.33%), Cough (21.15%),

Scabies (3.92%), Headache (8.09%), Scorpion bite (2.08%), Stomach pain (3.13%), Small Pox (5.22%), Dental Pain (3.92%), Sore Eyes (3.66%) etc.

Table 2
Reasons for Falling Ill

Sl. No.	Why do you think a person becomes ill?	Male (n) (%)	Female (n) (%)	Total (n) (%)
1.	Due to wrath of evil spirit.	69 (28.52)	21 (32.81)	90 (29.41)
2.	Due to wrath of God.	60 (24.79)	15 (23.44)	75 (24.51)
3.	Due to physical disorders	113 (46.69)	28 (43.75)	141 (46.08)
	Total	242 (100.00)	64 (100.00)	306 (100.00)

Table 3
Name of Diseases and No. of Cases in the Last Six Months

Sl. No.	Name of disease	Male (n) (%)	Females (n) (%)	Total (n) (%)
1.	Malaria/fever	67 (32.84)	53 (29.61)	120 (31.33)
2.	Cough	45 (22.06)	36 (20.11)	81 (21.15)
3.	Scorpion bite	5 (2.45)	3 (1.67)	8 (2.08)
4.	Dental Pain	8 (3.92)	7 (3.91)	15 (3.92)
5.	Dysentery	13 (6.37)	22 (12.28)	35 (9.14)
6.	Sore eyes	8 (3.93)	6 (3.34)	14 (3.66)
7.	Head ache	17 (8.33)	14 (7.82)	31 (8.09)
8.	Stomach pain	4 (1.96)	14 (7.82)	18 (3.13)
9.	Scabies	5 (2.45)	2 (1.12)	7 (3.39)
10.	Weakness	7 (3.43)	3 (1.67)	10 (2.61)
11.	Stones	1 (0.49)	1 (0.58)	2 (0.52)
12.	Small Pox	11 (5.39)	9 (5.03)	20 (5.22)
13.	Accident	4 (1.96)	1 (0.58)	5 (1.31)
14.	Typhoid	9 (4.42)	8 (4.46)	17 (4.43)
	Total	204 (100.00)	179 (100.00)	383 (100.00)

To find out the first approach for treatment we have taken 242 (79.08 per cent) males and 64 (20.92 per cent) females as heads of the families as well as main informants.

From table 4, it has been observed that the 36.81 per cent first approached to tribal practitioner for their illness or diseases whereas 18.14 per cent first approach to the PHC for their treatment and 19.32 first approached to the private doctor for their treatment. But 25.07 per cent first approach to the herbalist for their treatments.

From table 5, it has been observed that 34.32 per cent of Kondh go for treatment of illness or diseases within 1-3 days, 29.08 per cent go for treatment within 4-6 days, 15.04 per cent go for treatment with in 7-9 days, 9.80 per cent go for treatment within 10-12 days, 7.18 per cent go for treatment with in 13-15 days and 4.58 per cent go for treatment above 15 days.

Table 4
First Approach for Treatment

Sl. No.	Whom you approach first when fall ill	Male (n) (%)	Female (n) (%)	Total (n) (%)
1.	Tribal practitioner	77 (37.74)	64 (35.75)	141 (36.81)
2.	PHC	37 (18.14)	35 (19.55)	72(18.80)
3.	Herbalist	51 (25.00)	45 (25.15)	96 (25.07)
4.	Private Doctor	39 (19.12)	35 (19.55)	74 (19.32)
	Total	204 (100.00)	179 (100.00)	383 (100.00)

Table 5
Time Frame for Treatment

Sl. No.	After how many days you go for treatment of illness when you fall ill?	Male (n) (%)	Female (n) (%)	Total (n) (%)
1.	1-3 days	86 (35.54)	19 (28.69)	105 (34.32)
2.	4-6 days	75 (30.99)	14 (21.88)	89 (29.08)
3.	7-9 days	34 (14.05)	12 (18.75)	46 (15.04)
4.	10-12 days	21 (8.68)	9 (14.06)	30 (9.80)
5.	13-15 days	17 (7.02)	5 (7.81)	22 (7.18)
6.	Above 15 days	9 (3.72)	5 (7.81)	14 (4.58)
	Total	242 (100.00)	64 (100.00)	306 (100.00)

Table 6
Decision Making for Consulting Medical Practitioner

Sl. No.	Whom you consult before taking any treatment?	Male (n) (%)	Female (n) (%)	Total (n) (%)
1.	Head of Household	181 (74.79)	38 (59.38)	219 (71.59)
2.	Elderly males	32 (13.22)	13 (20.31)	45 (14.72)
3.	Clan chief	18 (7.44)	8 (12.50)	26 (8.50)
4.	Collective decision	11(4.55)	5 (7.81)	16 (5.29)
	Total	242 (100.00)	64 (100.00)	306 (100.00)

Table 6 shows the responsibility of decision-making in family for consulting medical practitioners among the Kondh. It has been observed that in large majority of cases among the Kondh (71.59) per cent, the decision is taken by the head of the household. A collective decision for consulting medical practitioners is taken only in 5.29 per cent of cases in consulting medical practitioner. But only 8.50 per cent of cases the decision is taken by clan chief to consult medical practitioner where as 14.72 per cent of cases decision is taken by elderly males to consult medical practitioners.

PATTERN OF TREATMENT

It has been found that the Kondhs practices both Ethnomedical System (Traditional medical system) and Modern Medical System for curing illness and diseases.

Home Remedies

In case of home remedy female plays an important role. Some of the home remedies are described as follows: In the case of *Phada* means boil which contain pus; they apply Karanj's leaf and custard oil on it. If there is ear pain caused by piercing of ear, they apply saliva over it. If a patient does not get cured within 1-2 days; he/she may be taken either to the *(Baid)* Herbalist/*Gunia or Guru* (Witch doctor)/*Pujari* (Priest)/medical Doctor. *Gunia* and *Guru* both are witch doctors. But *Gunia* is individual affairs and *Guru* has some assistance they are known as *"Chella"*. *Pujari* is the worshipper of village deity.

TRADITIONAL MEDICAL PRACTICES

(i) Magico-religious Practices

It has been observed that 20.71 per cent of Kondhs first approach to the tribal practitioner locally called *Guru/Gunia/Pujari* for their treatment. The *Gunia* or *Guru* represents a particular Deity. When the Deity appears through him, his body starts shivering rapidly and his contacts with this world breaks for a short span of time. During such moments he tells the causes of ailments and suggests remedies. He performs the following rites in succession.

1. First throws some raw rice over the patient after reciting some spells, then he gives "Spiritual ash"*(Chhar)* purified by reciting mantras (hymns).
2. If he is not cured then a thread is tied around his arms.
3. If this does not produce any result then chicken or pigeon are sacrificed.
4. If still it does not help, goat or lamb sacrifice is performed.
5. If a patient does not get cured, then he/she taken to the PHC.

For the epidemics diseases like cholera and small pox they also perform ritual at the community level. On the appointed day, all the villagers are assembled in the *'Dhurni'* worship place. Each family offers *Mudhi and ghee and fire.* On behalf of the villagers one chicken and pigeon is sacrificed.

From Table 7, it has been observed that 141 people approach to the tribal practitioner i.e. 36.81 per cent. In case of Scabies, Stones and Accident, very few Kondhs approach to the tribal practitioner for their treatment.

(ii) Herbal Medicine

The Kondhs used various herbal medicine and healing lotions, which they are prepare themselves with the help of various herbs and plants, found in the forest. Some of the herbs and plants, which are used for medicinal value and remedies of disease or illness described as follow;

Table 7
Name of Disease and Types of Treatment: Tribal Practitioner (Spiritual)

Sl. No.	Name of the disease	Male (n) (%)	Female (n) (%)	Total (n) (%)
1.	Malaria/ fever	28 (36.36)	20 (31.25)	48 (34.04)
2.	Cough	18 (23.37)	15 (23.43)	33 (23.40)
3.	Scorpion bite	2 (2.60)	1 (1.56)	3 (2.13)
4.	Dental Pain	3 (3.90)	2 (3.13)	5 (3.55)
5.	Dysentery	3 (3.90)	7 (10.94)	10 (7.09)
6.	Sore eyes	2 (2.60)	2 (3.13)	4 (2.84)
7.	Head ache	5 (6.49)	7 (10.94)	12 (8.51)
8.	Stomach pain	2 (2.60)	5 (7.81)	7 (4.96)
9.	Scabies	1 (1.30)	1 (1.56)	2 (1.41)
10.	Weakness	3 (3.90)	1 (1.56)	4 (2.84)
11.	Stones	1 (1.30)	-	1 (0.71)
12.	Chicken Pox	5 (6.49)	1 (1.56)	6 (4.26)
13.	Accident	1 (1.30)	-	1 (0.71)
14.	Typhoid	3 (3.90)	2 (3.13)	5 (3.55)
	Total	77 (100.00)	64 (100.00)	141 (100.00)

1. *Fever/malaria:* The root of palsa (Saccharum species) are powdered and kept in an earthen pot with water 3-4 hours. About 100 ml of this water is given to the patient thrice a day. Leaf of the pumpkin boiled in water and bathed with this water.
2. *Cough:* 2 to 4 grams of roots of Badi Anola, tulsi 'Basil' in equal amount are crushed in mahu rasa (Basis latifolia) and mixture given to the patient twice a day. Some cases people keep a piece of root of Badi Anola in the mouth for curing cough.
3. *Scorpion bite:* The roots of Kaincha 'Crab eye' plant are rubbed on a stone with water and the paste applied to the bite. Sometimes the leem (neem), (Azadirachta indica) nirmuli and satavari leaves are also used to induce vomiting.
4. *Dysentery:* The roots of tatua (Datura stromium) are crushed and kept overnight in a pot of water. About 100ml of this water is given twice a day.
5. *Headache:* The roots of Kadaba (Zizyphus jujube) creeper are crushed with water and applied on the forehead. The leaves of Gutuchita creeper are tied on head.

From Table 8 it has been observed that 96 patients approach to the tribal practitioner i.e. 25.07 per cent. In case of malaria (45.10 per cent), cough (29.41%), scorpion bite (1.96%) are approached to the herbalist for their treatment.

ALLOPATHIC TREATMENT

There are 7 hospitals in Kalahandi District, Orissa, Out of which one is district hospital situated in Bhawanipatna. There are 8 primary health centres with labour room, 39 primary health centre, 140 primary health canter (in door beds), 343 hospitals (in door beds), 7 x-ray facilities, 9 ambulance facilities, 3 ECG facilities, one blood bank facilities, 213 sub centers, 151 sub centres with ANM residents.

There is no primary health centre, sub centers or dispensary in the Paria, Turpi, Chheliamal, Kholandi, Shurgiguda, Shundimunda and Kalam. In Paria village, there is only one private practitioner. The primary health centre situated at Karlapada.

Table 8
Name of Diseases and Types of Treatment: Herbalist

Sl. No.	*Name of the diseases*	*Male (n) (%)*	*Female (n) (%)*	*Total (n) (%)*
1.	Malaria/ fever	23 (45.10)	14 (31.11)	37 (38.54)
2.	Cough	15 (29.41)	13 (28.89)	28 (29.17)
3.	Scorpion bite	1 (1.96)	1 (2.22)	2 (2.07)
4.	Dental Pain	1 (1.96)	1 (2.22)	2 (2.07)
5.	Dysentery	2 (3.92)	5 (11.11)	7 (7.29)
6.	Sore eyes	-	-	-
7.	Head ache	1 (1.96)	2 (4.44)	3 (3.13)
8.	Stomach pain	2 (3.92)	2 (4.44)	4 (4.17)
9.	Scabies	-	-	-
10.	Weakness	2 (3.92)	1 (2.22)	3 (3.13)
11.	Stones	-	-	-
12.	Chicken Pox	1 (1.96)	2 (4.44)	3 (3.13)
13.	Accident	-	-	-
14.	Typhoid	3 (5.89)	4 (8.89)	7 (7.29)
	Total	51 (100.00)	45 (100.00)	96 (100.00)

Table 9
Distances From the PHC and No. of Patients Visited to the PHC

Sr. No.	*Name of the village*	*Distance from the PHC (in k.ms)*	*Total no. of Patients*	*No. of patients visited to the PHC (n) (%)*
1.	Paria	9	67	16 (22.22)
2.	Turpi	9	46	14 (19.44)
3.	Chheliamal	8	64	19 (26.39)
4.	Shundimunda	10	43	12 (16.67)
5.	Kholandi	14	55	6 (8.33)
6.	Shargiguda	15	48	2 (2.78)
7.	Kalam	17	60	3 (4.17)
	Total		383	72 (100.00)

From Table 9, it has been observed that out of 383 patients, 72 patients approached to the PHC for their treatment. The PHC is nearer to the villages Paria, Turpi, Chheliamal and Sundimunda in comparison to other village. From Paria (22.22%), Turpi (19.44%), Chheliamal (26.39%) and Shundimunda (16.67%) are visited to the PHC.

From Table 10, it has been observed that, out of 383 patients, 72 patients visited to the PHC for different diseases and illness. For malaria 15 patients (20.83%), cough 8 patients (11.11%), dysentery 9 patients (12.50%) are visited to the PHC for their treatment.

From Table 11, it has been observed that, out of 383 patients, 74 patients visited to the PHC for different diseases and illness. For malaria 20 patients (27.03%), cough 12 patients (16.22%), dysentery 9 patients (12.16%) are visited to the PHC for their treatment.

Table 10

Name of Disease and Types of Treatment: (PHC) Allopathic (Doctor)

Sr. No.	*Name of the disease*	*Male (n) (%)*	*Female (n) (%)*	*Total (n) (%)*
1.	Malaria/ fever	7 (18.91)	8 (22.85)	15 (20.83)
2.	Cough	5 (13.51)	3 (8.57)	8 (11.11)
3.	Scorpion bite	1 (2.70)	-	1 (1.39)
4.	Dental Pain	3 (8.11)	1 (2.86)	4 (5.56)
5.	Dysentery	3 (8.11)	6 (17.14)	9 (12.50)
6.	Sore eyes	3 (8.11)	1 (2.86)	4 (5.56)
7.	Head ache	5 (13.51)	3 (8.57)	8 (11.11)
8.	Stomach pain	-	4 (11.43)	4 (5.56)
9.	Scabies	2 (5.41)	1 (2.86)	3 (4.17)
10.	Weakness	1 (2.70)	1 (2.86)	2 (2.78)
11.	Stones	-	1 (2.86)	1 (1.39)
12.	Chicken Pox	3 (8.11)	3 (8.57)	6 (8.32)
13.	Accident	2 (5.41)	1 (2.86)	3 (4.17)
14.	Typhoid	2 (5.41)	2 (5.71)	4 (5.56)
	Total	37 (100.00)	35 (100.00)	72 (100.00)

Table 11

Name of Disease and Types of Treatment: Private Doctor

Sl. No.	*Name of the disease*	*Male (n) (%)*	*Female (n) (%)*	*Total (n) (%)*
1.	Malaria/ fever	9 (23.09)	11 (31.43)	20 (27.03)
2.	Cough	7 (17.96)	5 (14.29)	12 (16.22)
3.	Scorpion bite	1 (2.56)	1 (2.86)	2 (2.70)
4.	Dental Pain	1 (2.56)	3 (8.57)	4 (5.40)
5.	Dysentery	5 (12.82)	4 (11.43)	9 (12.16)
6.	Sore eyes	3 (7.69)	3 (8.57)	6 (8.10)
7.	Head ache	6 (15.38)	2 (5.71)	8 (10.81)
8.	Stomach pain	-	3 (8.57)	3 (4.05)
9.	Scabies	2 (5.13)	-	2 (2.70)
10.	Weakness	1 (2.56)	-	1 (1.36)
11.	Stones	-	-	-
12.	Chicken Pox	2 (5.13)	3 (8.57)	5 (6.76)
13.	Accident	1 (2.56)	-	1 (1.36)
14.	typhoid	1 (2.56)	-	1 (1.36)
	Total	39 (100.00)	35 (100.00)	74 (100.00)

CASE STUDY-I

Suresh Majhi, aged 35 years, a resident of Paria village. He has a long hair. His main occupation is agriculture but he is also practiced healing as a part time work. Bhauro Maa possess him. He narrated his experience; he said that once he gets possessed, all around him look very small. He is never conscious in possessed state. He does not remember anything about his actions during trance. He can only cure by using divination method. He does not have much knowledge about herbs or other treatment methods. His father was possessed by Maa. But his grandfather was not. He claims that he provides treatment to his patients on the basis of what the Maa tells him. He can cure for all illness caused by supernatural agent. If the patient is suffering from disease, his treatment does not cure the patient and is such a case doctor has to be consulted. Sometimes people go for both doctor's medicine and his treatment.

CASE STUDY-II

Gobind Majhi, aged 45 years, a resident of turpi village. He narrates me that, kondhs used herbal medicines which they prepare themselves with the help of various plants found in the forest for lighter ailments. However, if sickness continues for a longer period, in spite of taking the traditional treatment from spiritual doctors, they consult an allopathic physician for the treatment of sickness. He said, in the past we always used to consult Gunia or Pujari for treatment of sickness. However, in a few cases allopathic and herbal treatments also continue side by side. He gave an example of his brother who suffered from tuberculosis for two years and did not take any treatment for it. After much pressure from the family members, he went to the Gunia or Guru. The Guru gave him some medicines and he remained under his treatment for three months. But when the disease entered its critical stage he went to the T.B. Hospital, which is situated at the Kamathana, it was 35 K.Ms. far away from his village.

CASE STUDY-III

Keshab majhi aged 49 years, a resident of Turpi village. He narrates me that, why the people have lost faith on the guru or the treatment by herbal medicine. He told me that his sister lost her son because of the Guru. His version was that, we always believed that guru (tribal practitioner) would treat our child that is why all of us first go to him. Guru also assures us that patient would get well. On this assurance our faith in him continues and we left everything to him. The dependence and reliance on him lead to the death of our child. So, after this incident nobody prefers to consult the Guru rather travel the long distances to Primary Health Centre.

CASE STUDY-IV

Basanti Jani, aged 27 years is suffering from Pet Dukha (Stomach pain). According to her husband, she was taken to gunia one day before puni (full moon day) or a day before ouasa (Chaudas) then Gunia gives her the treament. The gunia takes some paddy grains in his hand and chants some mantra and then goes in trance. His body starts shivering and then he tells the cause of ailment. He tells the name of the deity which is angry with the sick person and tells the person to made offering to deity. Only then sick person will be cured. The gunia is given ghee, coconut, and sugar. The Gunia does not take any because if he takes money his power will be finished.

CASE STUDY-V

Sharvan majhi, a resident of Kalam village told that when a child dies while taking milk or during breast-feeding it is, believed to be caused by a ghost known as Mirchuk Masan. The dead body of child is kept in a place, digs and then covered with mud. For avoiding such death the Gunia ties a black thread around neck and forearm of the children. It will protect the child from evil eye. According to Sharavan, a child named Bhaj died 2 years back he was six months old.

CASE STUDY-VI

Gundi Majhi, a resident of Themera village is suffering from night blindness. Initially he consulted a Gunia for treatment. But there was no improvement in his condition then He went to Karlapada for treatment where he was told to go to Bhawanipatna to get treatment in the big hospital. He said that in all cases this process he has already spent money. He said when Gunia fails to cure the disease then they consult private doctor or go to PHC and even if the doctor's at PHC fail to bring any improvement in the condition of the sick person then they go to Kesinga for treatment.

The concepts that tribal don't accept the modern medical care system is not true in case of Kondh. The accusation has become something like a myth and as a matter of fact, If the facilities are available they are ready to accept it. The above analysis shows that Kondhs accept the modern medical care system. They have faith in all the medical treatments (Spiritual, Herbal and allopathic). Thus we see how Kondh are managing themselves through various health practices for better health care, which are available to them.

ACKNOWLEDGEMENTS

It will be a mistake on our part if we fail to mention our sincere thanks to the Kondhs of Kalahandi District, Orissa for their help, immense co-operation and necessary assistance. We are grateful to Mr. Lima, Block Development Officer, Dr. Rath, Medical Officer and many more for their timely help, co-operation and assistance. Last but not least, the study has been supported by ICSSR in the form of Doctoral Fellowship to Hemanta Bag.

REFERENCES

Ali A. (1980), Health and Genetic Problem of Kutia Kondhs of Burlubaru Village, Phulbani District, Orissa. The Newsletter. Govt. of India, Ministry of Home Affairs, Tribal Development Division, New Delhi, 1 (2) 103-114.

Bag H. and Kapoor A.K. (2004), Religious Beliefs and Practices Among Kondhs: A Primitive Tribe of District Kalahandi, Orissa. In M.K. Raha (eds): *Man and Life.*, Kolkota: ISRAA Publication.

Basu S.K. (1994), Health Problems and Health Care of the Tribal Population of India. In N. Mahanti (eds): *Tribal Economy and Wasteland Development*. New Delhi: Inter-India Publications. pp. 137-146.

Census of India (2001), Orissa, District Census Handbook, Kalahandi District, Kalahandi.

Chaudhuri B. (1986), Medical Anthropology in India with Special Reference to Tribal Population. In B. Chaudhuri (eds): *Tribal Health: Socio-Cultural Dimensions.* New Delhi: Inter India Publication.

Misra P. and Kapoor A.K. (2001), Emerging Roles of Medical Anthropology for Health Providers who are Engaged in Tribal Development: A Study Among Saharia of Rajasthan. In M.K. Bhasin and S.L. Malik (eds): *The Science of Man in the Service of Man:* Delhi: Department of Anthropology, University of Delhi, pp. 177-190.

Marriot M. (1955), Western Medicine in a Village of Northern India. In B.D. Paul (eds): *Health, Culture and Community.* New York: Russel Sage.

Swain S. (1994), Health, Disease and Health Seeking Behaviour of Tribal People of India. In S. Basu (eds): *Tribal Health in India.* New Delhi: Manak Publication.

3

HEALTH CARE PRACTICES OF HAKKIPIKKI: A TRIBE IN TRANSITION

K.C. Tarachand

India is known for diverse cultures and races. It has given shelter to a number of tribes which are racially, linguistically, culturally and economically different. Many foreign dignitaries who visited India were amazed by the different life styles and living conditions of these tribes. Among such tribes the Hakkipikki, a scheduled tribe of Karnataka is one and it is totally unique with regard to its health care and its related aspects.

The aim of this paper is to throw sufficient light on Hakkipikki's health practices over a period of time. Hakkipikki, a semi-nomadic tribe in the recent past has transformed itself to a absolutely well settled one. Several factors are responsible for this change. The government of Karnataka has recognised them as Scheduled Tribe and has given several concessions. As a result owing to these benefits, Hakkipikki has changed considerably.

Hakkipikki, one of the very old tribes of India, is termed differently in different parts of Karnataka state such as Melshikari, Vagri, Farsi and Sikkaliger. This is a scheduled tribe in Karnataka state. Since time immemorial, these people were moving from place to place, from one jungle to the other having trapping of birds as their prime occupation. Over the years due to the shortage of forest lands, they have shifted their allegiance from trapping birds to various new activities which include selling of rare commodities, giving indigenous medicine, and to some extent the cultivation of land. A limited literature is available on them and these materials are not sufficient in understanding them fully. (Maan, 1980) is the only source to know something about them. This is partly because of the fact that this population constantly moved from place to place for so many reasons so that no governmental agencies could take note of these people, about their habitat, way of life and what they do. Here an attempt has been made to know and understand who are these people, from where they came to Karnataka, what they do, how could they become the experts of indigenous medicine which is very unique in character to prevent and cure innumerable diseases, and to what extent people have developed faith in their medicinal system and curing methods.

Hakkipikki traces their origin since birth of humanity. It is also believed that their ancestors immigrated into Karnataka from the present states of Gujarat and Rajasthan. They came to Karnataka via Andhra Pradesh and they still remember the name of a town 'Jetpalli' near Hyderabad where their ancestors lived for a considerable period of time (Maan, 1980). Hakkipikki claimed their descent from 'Vikhli', though recognizing Dadaji as the supreme god to whom they consider as the originator of the entire humanity and existing Gods and Goddesses. According to 1991 census, the population of Hakkipikki in Karnataka is 6281. These people are distributed in different parts of Karnataka state such as H.D. Kote, Pakshiraj Pura near Mysore, Kolar, Chintamani and in Channagiri and Hastapanahalli in Shimoga district. The Hakkipikki speak a dialect namely 'Vagriboli' which is a mixture of Gujarathi, Marwari and Rajasthani among themselves. Apart from this, they also know and speak Tamil, Telugu, Malayalam, Kannada and Hindustani. This was possible because of their constant moving from place to place having continuous association with the local population. Hakkipikki are divided themselves into four clans, i.e., Gujarathia, Panwar, Kaliwalo and Mewar. But this classification is based on the religious basis and the hierarchy was properly maintained in the olden days.

Maan (1980) opines that Gujarathia among Hakkipikki are taken as the first and direct descendents of Vikhli. Hence Gujarathia occupies the top position followed by Panwar, Kaliwalo and Mewara in that order. Apart from these four divisions, they are also divided into two sub groups based on the sacrificial rituals; the group which sacrifice goat for worship and the group sacrificing buffaloes. Earlier these groups were totally endogamous but now inter marriages are also taking place. Forest is the main natural resource of the Hakkipikki. Trapping of birds and animals forms a part of Hakkipikki life and selling them is their traditional occupation. They also sell herbs, roots and leaves of medicinal plants collected in the forest. Apart from this now they are also cultivating land which they got from the government under various welfare schemes. At present majority of the Hakkipikkis of Shimoga district are depending upon agriculture. Very few Hakkipikkis still go out to trap birds and also to sell the indigenous medicine which is prepared by themselves.

Hakkipikkis of Shimoga district of Karnataka state are well settled in their own village named Hastapanahalli. The village has 362 households. The population of this village is 2080. Males 1070 and Females 1010. The population of Hakkipikki includes all the four major clans. Very few amongst them are still engaged themselves in their traditional occupation of trapping birds but majority of them have become business men and still others are working as landless agricultural labourers. The Hakkipikkis of this area are enjoying all privileges which are meant for Scheduled Castes/Scheduled Tribes. Since they are Scheduled Tribe they have got several concessions from the government which include free housing, free electricity, borewells to their lands and also availed all types of loans. At present, Hakkipikkis are fast changing and as a result they are educating their children and they have a government primary school exclusively for their children. They have good drinking water facility and free health checkup camps are arranged by the district administration. They have got even political representation. At present, there are two members who are working as village panchayat members.

Hakkipikki by the virtue of their close association with the Nature and constant moving from one jungle to other in the past have become well versed in locating, identifying the rare medical plants and using them in preparing medicine. They have become the perfect specialist of indigenous medicine and out of this they have treated and cured and number of diseases in their own typical way. Hakkipikkis even today go very often to the neighbouring villages for curing patients who are suffering from several diseases. They convince the people about their quality of medicine and its importance and also its no side effects in such a manner that people will readily agree to take their medicine for curing their disease. They are equally intelligent in convincing people about good health and long life. Since Hakkipikkis are well settled in their villages it is not too difficult to convince people about the authenticity of medicine and its effectiveness in curing diseases to the people of nearby villages. As a result the people not only trust them but also prefer to buy medicine from the Hakkipikkis which according to them is not only pure but also 100% effective in curing ailments.

Diseases are as old as man himself. Since from the days of antiquity, our primitive people have developed several mechanisms to deal with various diseases, health disorders by adopting their own mechanisms of taking medicine which was available in nature to cure/overcome them. But in the beginning, this was purely based on trial and error method. Over the years man developed some sort of faith in this medicine, which was absolutely as pure as the nature itself (Maan, 1980). But as and when man developed, he also engaged himself in identifying various medicinal valuable plants and some of the roots, leaves and herbs and processing them indigenously and started giving it to people to overcome their health disorders. Even today Hakkipikkis claim that they are the pioneers in ayurvedic medicine. Hakkipikkis treat and cure a number of diseases. Hakkipikkis do not give free medicine to others but they don't take money from their own people for the same purpose. At present the selling of herbal/indigenous medicine is more an economic activity rather than a social service. Hakkipikki gives medicine for a number of diseases and have successfully cured the following disorders.

1. *Head Poison:* Hakkipikki cures this by giving juice of red prawn of the pond mixed in the lemon juice and rubbed on the head and forehead of the sufferer. After this a cup of butter milk is given to drink and later water from seven new mud vessels are being poured on the head continuously. By doing so it is believed that this Head Poison will be cured.
2. *Dog Bite:* To cure this sufferer will be made to drink water from the house of the owner of the dog and lime is applied on the place of bite.
3. *Head Ache:* This is a peculiar way of curing. Both the arms are tied and made to smelt broken onion for five minutes. By doing so it will cured.
4. *Cold or Flu:* Garland prepared out of garlic will be tied around the neck of the sufferer. If the garland becomes dry then it is believed that it is cured.
5. *Dysentery:* The germing plant of banana is converted into paste and mixed with milk, is given to drink to the sufferer to cure this problem.
6. *Skin Disease:* The milk of adventitious seeds will be applied to the affected part for two to three times daily for one week. By doing so the skin disease will be controlled.
7. *Tooth Ache:* The past of claw has to be kept at the affected teeth for half an hour without a single split or by applying the milk of papaya fruit to the affected teeth. Hakkipikki opines that patients with this problem comes to them very often in big number.
8. *Secretion of white Semen:* This is one of the very common health disorders found among women folk. To treat this problem Hakkipikki uses the germ of white Dasawala or Daswala flowers, Kasturi water and milk are mixed up and kept till next morning. The affected women will be made to drink this mixture in a empty stomach. By doing so it is believed that body becomes cool and also cures the diseases like cough, joint pain, sluggishness and acidity.
9. *For Smooth Delivery:* Hakkipikki advises to drink the water mixture of coriander and ginger or coffee without milk three four times a day to the pregnant woman. So that the delivery takes place smoothly without causing much problem.
10. *Baldness:* Pattamande nut and a mixture of coconut oil is applied for the regeneration of hair. Locally this oil is known as *'Khatichan'*. It is prepared out of Bears fat.
11. *Arthritis:* This is one of the common problems found among the aged people. It affects them very much. The pain will be severe and as a result they can not walk and move properly. The Hakkipikki cures this problem by applying the mixture of peacock oil, iguana oil, and crocodile's oil being mixed with lemon juice and applied on knee joint, elbow joint for smooth functioning.

12. *Paralysis:* To cure this Hakkipikki suggests the applying of wild pigeon's blood on the affected part and the eating of the flesh by the person. For this Hakkipikki are in great demand because they trap the wild pigeon easily and they charge exorbitantly.
13. *Ear leakage:* For this four five drops of breast milk will be mixed with little salt and drops them in ear. This will be cured by doing so for three four days.
14. *Piles:* Hakkipikki identifies three types of piles such as (1) Itching pile (2) Germ Pile and (3) Blood Pile. For this they use upper layer of the animal resembling pangolin is to be powered and applied in the affected portion.
15. *Fits:* This is one of the common diseases found amongst most of the people. This is caused by the weakness of nervous system. To prevent this they use neem juice (rubbing the neem leaves in the hand) with gorajina given to the affected person to drink and at the same time two three drops of this will be put in the nostrils.

Apart from the above mentioned diseases, the Hakkipikkis also prepare and give medicine to the diseases which are exclusively meant for women. As a result the Hakkipikkis in this area have become very famous for their medicine. The most striking point about Hakkipikki is that the local people do not recognize Hakkipikki as the Trappers and Sellers of rare birds and animals but as experts of ayurvedic medicine. These are the unique health care practices of Hakkipikkis which we don't find so accurately amongst other tribes. Hakkipikkis are highly cautious and take all necessary care in preparing medicine to administer to the patients. So far no patient in any part of Shimoga district who took medicine from Hakkipikkis have raised any objections about their medicine. This is Hakkipikki's venture in attracting the local people towards their medical practices.

REFERENCES

Mann R.S. (1980), *Hakkipikki : Trapper and Seller.* Calcutta: Anthropological Survey of India.

Misra P.K. and Malhotra K.C., eds., (1982), *Nomads in India.* Calcutta.

Naik V. Unpublished Ph.D. thesis entitled, *A Socio-Economic Study of Hakkipikki – A Scheduled Tribe of Karnataka with Special Reference to Shimoga District* Karnatak University, Dharwad.

Vidyarthi L.P. and Rai B.K. (1972), *Tribal Culture in India.* New Delhi: Concept Publisher.

4

COGNITION OF HEALTH AND DISEASE AMONG THE PEOPLE OF VILLAGE KARJAN, DISTRICT KULLU, HIMACHAL PRADESH

Twinkle Pal

INTRODUCTION

Health and illness are two polar categories, the actual society can be placed somewhere on the continuum. Health is defined as '...a state of complete physical, mental and social well-being and not merely the absence of disease or infirmity' according to World Health Organization (1946). But the above definition seems to be more of a utopian notion as different cultures define health differently. For the Thulungs of Nepal, health is an aspect of good order of one's work. Illness on the other hand is an aspect of afflictions, which relates to disorder in one's relationship to ancestors (Spring, 1978:39). According to Talcott Parsons (1951), during illness the patient is exempted from performing his normal social duties, is helpless in the sick state, is in need of help and is expected to recover fast. Thus illness is a deviation from the normal. No one wants to remain in a state of illness. But illness is certainly not disease. Disease is purely a pathological concept where the illness qualities to be a disease is established by the specialist.

In every society the way in which health or illness is defined is a reflection of cultural categories. To the Jaunsari's the term health means 'right conditions of the body' (Rezvi, 1986: 2). In Ayurvedic system, it is the harmonious relationship of five elements, dhatu, which is supposed to be the cause of good health. Illness is also culturally defined. This cultural universal is based on the notion of relativism which means that what may be illness in one context may not be defined as illness in another context. In rural Greece measles, chicken pox and whooping cough are not considered disease and are rarely reported in government records as diseases as they are considered compulsory in the process of growing up. In Panchgani, Madhya Pradesh, goiter is not considered as a disease as it does not impair in everyday work. In upper Mississippi, chills with fever are regarded as essential for good health. These are the views held by people, however they are not supported by medical science.

In traditional societies, the cause of illness and impairment is sought in the domain of magic and religion. Thus the medicine man identifies the cause in the world of spirits, which are to be coerced, coaxed and pleased. Compared to this, in a complex society, which essentially adheres to biomedical system, health and disease are understood in terms of 'germ theory'. Microorganisms cause most disease; professional doctors prescribe the diagnosis and treatment.

The medical anthropologists submit that the concept of health and diseases, as well as those of curative and therapeutic practices, are deeply rooted in social system. Rivers (1924) and Clements (1932) think that the cultural beliefs and ideas portray the medicine in the traditional fabric of the society. Native cultural aspects of the concepts surrounding the health and illness and treatment in such a society need not be inferior or wrong since each belief pattern has its own basis. We understand relevance on contextually. Let me have a look at a village of Himachal Pradesh, Karjan, with the perspective mentioned above.

AIM OF THE STUDY

During Dec. '2002 I happen to visit Karjan, a village in district Kullu, Himachal Pradesh. The trip to Karjan was made to write an account of different medical systems prevalent in the village, in the partial fulfillment of the degree of the Master of Science, in the Department of Anthropology, University of Delhi.

METHOD

With the aim to study the different medical systems prevalent in the village, Karjan, a month long intensive fieldwork was carried out in December' 2002. During the fieldwork data was carried out using the techniques of participant observation and interviews. I had prepared an interview guide before starting my research in order to channelise and streamline my questioning in the field. Apart from this case-study and life history were the other techniques employed.

FIELD AREA AND PEOPLE

The village Karjan, where fieldwork was carried out, is situated on the left bank of the famed river Beas in Himachal Pradesh. A metalled road locally called 'Bam tat' i.e. 'left bank' dissects the village lengthwise, running from north to south. The settlement pattern is more or less irregular. The caste factor apparently does not affect the settlement pattern of the village too much. However, Rajput houses are generally located nearer the metalled road and Harijan houses further up the terrain.

Karjan is a multicaste village. The demarcation of people into various caste groups is unambiguous and absolute. People identified eight castes in the village. Every caste follows its traditional occupation. However, agriculture is caste-free. Practice of agriculture depends on the ownership of cultivable land. The village follows traditional commensal restriction. Karjan is patriarchal and patrilineal. Family is the unit of production and consumption. Joint family type is quite popular in the village. As far as the marriage and its form are concerned, monogamy is the predominant form.

RESULTS AND DISCUSSION

After carrying out a month long fieldwork it became very apparent that people of Karjan have developed various social institutions, etiological theories and therapeutic techniques to enable them to cope with social and other dislocation occasioned by illness-induced disabilities. Although Karjan is situated in the vicinity of Manali and is open to exogenous changes through improved means of communication, the instrumental aspect of growing modernity has not replaced the traditional structure. This is reflected in their unquestioned belief in the supernatural and other socio-cultural adaptive strategies that have modulated their medical systems. Among the villagers of Karjan carrying out normal day's routine is sign of being healthy. The daily routine entails getting up early in the morning, collecting firewood from the hills, going to the fields, cooking food etc. If the person's face glows and has its natural colour and if one has a good appetite one is considered healthy. Any sign of bad health would be reflected if one is unable to carry out these tasks. One who is unable to lift a head log of wood, who cannot attend the cattle or stays in the bed for long and feels lazy, falls under the category of being unhealthy.

With regard to the key of healthy living and cause of illness, people do not differ much. According to them what contributes to health is fresh vegetables, fresh air, a lot of milk and avoiding fried food. The villagers classify the food items into category of either 'hot' or 'cold'. For instance, milk, chilies, meat are considered 'hot', while curd, cucumber and fruits are considered as 'cold'. Thus incorrect dietary habits, say, taking 'hot' food in summers, are believed to cause illness. Thus to correct the imbalance caused through improper dietary habits various restrictions and preferences are followed. For the treatment of 'hot' ailments like fever, 'hot' food like meat, chillies are not given to the affected individuals. People of Karjan emphasize that doing physical work is good for healthy living. They do not exercise separately but the physical work they do during the day is a form of exercise in itself. They stress that one should not abandon traditional practices like going out to the forest to collect fuel or taking care of the cattle.

An ethnomedical profile of the community reveals that the villagers do not regard skin diseases, common cold and cough, stomachache and headache, etc, as severe ailments as they do not curtail the normal activities of a person. The villagers generally resort to domestic remedies in case of common cold and cough, and also during the initial days of fever. But they think that herbal medicine is the best remedy for skin afflictions and insect bite. Theories of disease causation lay both in personalistic and naturalistic realm. A personalistic system, following Foster and Anderson, is one in which illness is perceived as being the result of active, purposeful intervention of a 'sensate' agent who may be a supernatural being (a deity or god), a non-human being (such as ghost, ancestor or evil-spirit) or a human being (a witch or a sorcerer). The sick person is literally a victim, the object of aggression or punishment directed specifically against him. The people of Karjan generally attribute causes of paralysis, lasting fever, miscarriage and sudden death to the wrath of sensate agent. Thus according to the villagers sudden and persistent illness is caused by the wrath of sensate agent. For such illness assistance of village priest or goor (spirit-medium) is sought.

On the other hand, ailments attributed to natural causes such as dietary imbalance, bad weather, physical disturbance, etc, embrace headache, stomachache, cold, cough and fever. In this category, illness is naturalistic and explained in 'impersonal', systemic terms. For such ailments assistance of either domestic remedies or modern medicine is sought. However while collecting several case studies during the fieldwork I encountered cases where the illness aggravated and they returned to the village and reverted to the herbalist and magico- religious administration of the specialist.

For most unexplainable experiences, a supernatural connotation is ascribed to them, they are used to explain events that are beyond normal understanding and control of which is beyond their technical competence. This is reflected in an incident narrated by a lady called Chamlo Devi. She told that one day all of a sudden she had severe stomachache. After consuming mixture of rock salt and herb, wild harr, the pain subsided. But after a few hours it was back. She went to the sub-center next day and brought back few medicines. Since the pain refused to go she was asked to consult the doctor in Manali. The doctor doubted that she have developed a stone. The X-ray reports, however, were normal. Meantime her stomachache refused to go and it would get aggravated all of a sudden at odd hours. Finally one day they visited Parasher Rishi temple. The goor of that temple told the concerned family had planned to build a small temple in their new house. They have moved into their new house but the temple has still not been constructed. The goor told that Parasher Rishi, the local deity, wants his place in the house. The family soon got a small temple constructed in the front courtyard of their house. She said that within a few days after pleasing the local deity the pain began to subside and today she is healthy.

The people of the village thus recognize a supernatural causation of illness. Here illness is seen as a manifestation of wrath of evil spirits. Human sufferings, at individual or community level are subscribed to the effect of supernatural entities. They have a very strong belief that smaller gods and goddesses cause illness thus rejecting the germ theory of disease causation. All the diseases for which no apparent reason can be discerned are attributed to the supernatural realm and for such categories of illness help of magico-religious practitioner is sought. People believe that one can out of enmity and jealousy cause harm to others by praying to god and goddess to cause harm. Villagers believe that certain offerings as prescribed by magico-religious beliefs and practitioners of the village then later placate these deities.

In the traditional medical system in the village, the goor occupies a central place. He acts as an emissary of higher divine power, adroit in his capability to communicate with the transcendental. The priest of the temple combines the role of herbalist too. The villagers ignorant of the scientific explanation of various phenomena have developed a largely magical world outlook. The goor or the magical healer of the village does not have any specialized paraphernalia for curing disease, but are gifted with a special power. When 'possessed' by the spirit, wherein he becomes the medium between man and supernatural, a goor tells whether causation lies in the supernatural or natural realm and if the cause lies in the supernatural realm, then the goor tells the different ways to placate superhuman spirit in the state of trance itself. During my stay in the village I happen to witness the entire ceremony of goor getting possessed by the spirit. Once in trance, a lady, Poorna Devi, comes and tells the goor about her niece, Sonali, who is having high fever. They tried all sorts of medicines including allopathy but there was no improvement. In trance, Bhola Ram, the goor tells that somebody has cast an evil eye on her. He gives her flowers and rice grain charged with magical spell for Sonali and tells her to bathe Sonali with holy water at Vashisht, a holy place near Karjan. When I went to talk to Poorna after two days, I saw Sonali playing in the front courtyard of the house. Poorna told me that Sonali was bathed with the holy water at Vashisht that very evening and her condition began to improve by night. When I asked her that did they stop giving Sonali allopathic medicine? Poorna answered that they were giving her allopathic medicine but maintained that it was local deity Docha-Mocha's blessing that actually helped Sonali to recover.

I came across several such cases in the village where people had either availed the allopathic medicine or had initially been admitted to the local hospital in Manali, but later, when they their condition did not improve, they came back to avail the ethno medical practices in the village. People in the village do not give up allopathic medicine but along with it they would be consulting the goor or the village priest. This gives them the added confidence that even their goddess Docha-Mocha is helping them to restore back to normal health. Thus it imparts psychological satisfaction to the people.

CONCLUSION

After conducting a fifteen days' fieldwork and observing the village life closely and interviewing both young and old, I arrived at the following understanding regarding the medical systems in the village. The choice of the medical system made by the sick largely depends on his or her age. It is seen that the grandparental generation in the village, in case of minor and many serious ailments first resort to domestic remedies. If they do not get cured they shift to the herbalist and they may also seek divine intervention, start visiting the goor, performing various rituals and/or sacrifices to appease and pacify the supernatural power. If the allopathic system does not prove really helpful then they discontinue it, though the system of supernatural healing may continue. However the young in the village, even for minor ailments like common cold and cough, immediately opt for allopathic medicines. If the disease persists, they are not feed up with the medicines and do not generally give up the allopathic medical system, though they may combine it with other kind of treatments, say herbal medicine or supernatural healing. Thus it is seen that the medical pluralism is present in the village.

ACKNOWLEDGMENT

I am obliged to the Department of Anthropology, University of Delhi, for organising the trip to Karjan, Himachal Pradesh. I extend my heartiest thanks to the people of Karjan for sharing their native medical knowledge. I also thank them for making my stay comfortable and pleasant in the village. I am also grateful to my Supervisor, Prof. (Dr.) Vinay Kumar Srivastava without whose suggestions and support I would not have been able to complete this work.

REFERENCES

Barua N. (1955), *Medical Pluralism and the Effects of Supernatural Healing: A Field Study of the Bhils in Udaipur District.* M.Sc. dissertation, Department of Anthropology, University of Delhi, Delhi.

Bhasin V. and Srivastava V.K. (1991), Medical Anthropology: A Review. *Journla of Human Ecology,* 2(1): 1-19.

Evans-Pritchard (1937), *Witchcraft, Oracles and Magic among The Azande.* London: Oxford University Press.

Foster G.M. and Anderson B. (1978), *Medical Anthropology,* New York, Brisbane and Toronto: John Wiley and Sons.

Goode W.J. and Hatt P.K. (1983), *Methods in Social Research.* Mc.Graw-Hill International Book Company.

Hasan K.A. (1979), *Medical Sociology of Rural India.* Ajmer: Sachin Publication.

Joshi P.C. (1984), *Illness, Health and Culture: Dynamics of Therapy in Central Himalayan Tribe.* Ph.D. dissertation, Department of Anthropology, University of Delhi, Delhi.

Notes and Queries in Anthropology (1951), London: Royal Anthropological Institute, Routledge.

5

HUMAN RIGHTS, DEVELOPMENT AND TRIBE: A STUDY AMONG THE LAHOULIS OF HIMACHAL PRADESH

Shilipi Gupta and A.K. Kapoor

INTRODUCTION

A hallmark of a civilized country is the regard it has, to protecting the human dignity and freedom of all sections of its people without discrimination. This is a part of the drive for human development in any country. Human development can have no meaning unless there is a serious attempt to ensure human rights to all. The fact that the rhetoric of Human rights is often used as a weapon in geo-political struggles cannot be a ground for ignoring human rights.

Regard for human dignity cannot just be in theory but has also to be reflected in practice. To ensure this, a country has to evolve the necessary development machinery both through its constitution and institutions suited to the genius of its people. More the diversity, in the genius of people, more will be the variety in the types of development programs. As if self evident, all these words-human rights , its violation , development programs etc are always, only visualized keeping in mind the under-privileged , or the minorities or for that matter, the tribal groups , in Indian context. It can be sardonically said that, except for extremely small privileged minority of elite, there are no human rights, or development for any.

After Africa, India is the second country to host a large number of diverse communities. Each community has its own cultural and economic differentiation besides specific ethnic identities (Pathy, 2003). Since more than five decades, numerous academicians, administrators and policy - makers have been recommending, evaluating and altering the development policies for Scheduled Tribes. Yet nothing new happened nor was the exercise abandoned. Kapoor (1990 and 1996) has outlined various strategies and suggestions for the applied aspect of research for tribals.

One must then ask few questions as to:

- Why even after more than a half century of the emergence of the issue of development, there persists such wide spread poverty and destitution.
- More to the point, what can be immediately done to eliminate or redress the problem?
- Whether the development or the policy prescriptions that have been tried out thus far might not have missed out some basic truths?
- Even if the development programs are absolutely relevant for the specific community, but is the information about the program getting percolated to the grass root level?
- If people are aware about the programs running in their community and or area, then are they taking the cognizance of its impact?

Development is a value loaded concept. Keeping all the dimensions in mind, it can be defined as ' change in desired direction within stipulated time '. That means, aims, motives and policies once sketched should be left after completion only. However, as often happens in our "soft state", the gap between policy and performance is enormous. If people are impoverished because of development, its spirit and ethos are subjected to criticism. (Gupta and Kapoor, 2003).

The whole idea of development revolves around the awareness of an individual or an group, about their surroundings or about their rights. For majority of Scheduled Tribes these programs virtually do not exist. They are either apathetic to these programs, or feel that they have been cheated. So in this context, the *'rights based'* approach to development may be seen to have some crucial relevance. This approach calls for regarding the Right to Development (RTD) as a basic human right. This Right to Development was formally recognized as an international human right, when the United Nations adopted the Declaration on the Right to Development in 1986. However, in 1993, there was full consensus among all nations, to regard RTD as a basic human right, when this was adopted at the Second UN World Conference on human rights in Vienna. The first article of the Declaration of 1986 states: "The right to development is an inalienable human right by virtue of which every human person and all people are entitled to participate in, contribute to and enjoy economic, social , cultural and political development, in which all human rights and fundamental freedoms can be fully realized." (Nayak, 2003).

Again, here at this juncture it is inevitable to mention the important role played by the awareness factor. Development is a Right, which means it's the people's discretion to develop or not, this fact is not much popular among Scheduled Tribes; as it is seen that those who have been forcefully pushed towards development are facing the consequences. (Gupta, 2004).

"At the level of critical policy decisions and implementations of welfare and development programmes it can be said that there is only ad hoc involvement of the anthropologists. Even while implementing development programmes in the tribal areas and while proposing to alleviate the pressings problems, counsel of the anthropologists is only accepted as an interpreter of primitive men" (Kapoor and Singh, 1991).

"In practically all the welfare oriented policies, most of the changes have been brought about through legislation. The application of various laws to these scheduled areas without any machinery will look into their possible consequences on the tribals and how non–tribals have reacted to such legislation which has remained untouched by the social scientists. Thus, there is a need to study the role of law a tool of directed social change with reference to the tribals and in wider national context, if it is to fulfill its function as a paramount instrument of social order". (Kapoor, 1999).

The present situation, has make a caricature of the development programs and indicates the callousness shown towards these weaker section, in the rubric of "directed change".

In the present paper, an attempt has been made to study Human Rights, Development and Tribe in an interactive manner.

MATERIALS AND METHODS

Keeping all these aspects of Development, forced development, right to development, human rights (in general), a study was conducted in the tribal area of Lahoul and Spiti district of Himachal Pradesh for one year in parts, from June 2003 to June 2004. While in the field, the data from 300 households has been collected from 24 villages of five different valleys of Lahoul Block. Various anthropological tools and techniques like Interview Schedules, Focus Interviews, Non-participant as well as Participant observation; Focus Group Discussions has been used. The tribal group of Lahoul block of the district is known as "Lahoulis". The Scheduled Tribe Order (Amendment) Act, 1976 as promulgated under Presidential order, declares 'Lahaula' (Spelling as used by the author) as Scheduled Tribe throughout the state of Himachal Pradesh. (Parmar, 1996).

Study Area: Lahoul and Spiti district is one of the frontiers districts of India and is geographically the largest district in the state of Himachal Pradesh. It accounts for 24.8 per cent area of the state. The total area of the district is 13,835 km sq and the population is 33,224. Out of which 22,674 tribals are in Lahoul and 10,550 are in Spiti. The average density of population is 2 persons per square kilometer. (Census, 2001).

Lahoulis: The word 'Lahouli' is a blanket term. It's a broad generic term , including Brahmins, Ranas, Thakurs (Rajputs), Kanets or Bhots and Scheduled Castes like Lohars (iron smiths), Dagis or Shippis (carpenters),

Hessis (land–less labourers or musicians) are broadly classified as Lahoulis (Gupta and Kapoor, 2005). In there features, a combination of Mongolian and Aryan traits was observed. Their slightly high cheek bones and almond like eyes are the indicators of a Mongolian origin where as their straight noses are an index of Aryan blood. In Lahoul, there are followers of Hinduism and Buddhism. Those who follow Buddhism are called Bhots and those who practice Hinduism are called Swanglas. Marriage between Bhots and Swanglas is acceptable to the society. Buddhists have nine 'clans' or '*rus*' and Hindus have five clans. However, a *rus* is a strictly exogamous unit. No marriage can be performed if boy and girl belong to the same *rus*. It comes under the prohibited category of relationships. Even joking relationship is a taboo between the persons of the same *rus*.

Villages of this scheduled tribe are predominantly located on the sun facing side of the river.

RESULTS AND DISCUSSION

In Lahoul where agriculture is the main occupation and amount of land holdings influence the status of the family in their society. It is found on the basis of the data collected from 300 households of Lahoulis, that the average land holdings of a household is 14.13 *beigha*. Only 1.33 per cent has land above 30 *beigha*. In Lahoul, joint family system is preferred. 51.67 per cent of families are joint. However, a number of separation cases year after year indicate a tendency is developing among the people of Lahoul to live separately in nuclear families, as 48.33 per cent are nuclear families.

It is found 91 per cent of people practice monogamy. It can be said that much practiced institution of polygamy is now on decline, as only 9 per cent cases of polygamy could be found. Out of 9 per cent, 8 per cent are the cases of polyandry (plurality of husband) and 1 per cent of polygyny (plurality of wife).

42.67 per cent respondents follow Hinduism and 57.33 per cent follow Buddhism. It has been observed in Lahoul that cross cousin marriages are prevalent only among the Bhots and not among Hindus. Average age of marriage for this schedule tribe is 23.79 years. Average age of marriage for Lahouli male is 24.93 years and for females is 22.66 years. Literacy rate among Lahouli population is 71.46 per cent. Literacy rate for females is 61.91 per cent and for males is 80.52 per cent.

Human Rights and Development in Lahoul: India is a signatory of the International Bill of Human Rights, which was drafted on December 10, 1948, when the General Assembly adopted the Universal Declaration of Human Rights. The rights given in the Declaration are categorized into two broad headings-first refers to civil and political rights and second refers to economic, social and cultural rights. Various types of rights are outlined in both these two categories. These are:

(i) Right to life
(ii) Freedom to torture
(iii) Freedom from slavery
(iv) Freedom from arbitrary arrest and detention
(v) Freedom of movement
(vi) Equality before courts
(vii) Equal protection of law
(viii) Freedom of thought
(ix) Freedom of religion
(x) Freedom of expression
(xi) Freedom to seek, receive and impart information
(xii) Right of peaceful assembly
(xiii) Right to marry
(xiv) Right of minorities to enjoy their own culture, religion and language
(xv) Right to work
(xvi) Right to social security
(xvii) Right to an adequate standard of living
(xviii) Right of everyone to education
(xix) Right to take part in cultural life

Inspite of, such an extensive detailing of all these rights, which, one, is entitled to, merely by the fact, of the right, of being human, man's struggle is still perpetual and pace of development is still laggard.

In the tribal belt of Lahoul and Spiti district, it was very difficult to make the respondent comprehend the meaning of the word 'Human Rights'. Table 1 presents the perception of Lahoulis about Human Rights. It has been observed that, 46.33 per cent could not explain at all the meaning of the word 'Human Rights', even after discussions , thus coming into the category of 'unaware'.

Table 1
Perception of Human Rights

Level of Awareness	*Respondents*	*Per cent*
Unaware	139	46.33
Partially Aware	137	45.67
Fully Aware	24	8.00
Total	300	100.00

45.67 per cent are those who could explain the meaning by giving examples, thus being partially aware. Only 8 per cent respondents were fully aware, who gave the definition with examples. Thus it can be defined collectively as "Rights given to a person, being a human by the constitution are called human rights."

Table 2 depicts that 54 per cent of the informants are unaware as they don't know why rights are framed and 46 per cent are aware as they gave various reasons which all meant similar that–all would have equal opportunity, nobody would be weak in the society, all would be equal.

Table 2
Rights Framed

Reasons for Framing Rights	*Respondents*	*Per cent*
Unaware	162	54.00
Aware	138	46.00
Total	300	100.00

On the range of seven, the numbers of human rights told by the informants were arranged

As shown in Table 3 , where 'None' stands for those who are absolutely unaware as they couldn't tell even one human right out of eighteen and 'Above ten' category stands for fully aware i.e. who could tell more than ten human rights out of eighteen .

Table 3
Human Rights Awareness Among Lahoulis

Rights Awareness	*Respondents*	*Per cent*
None	142	47.33
One-two	31	10.33
Three-four	71	23.67
Five-six	31	10.33
Seven-eight	9	3.00
Nine-ten	10	3.33
Above ten	6	2.00
Total	300	100.00

47.33 per cent (which is the maximum also) respondents lie in first category, who could tell none of the human rights. Only 2 per cent of the respondents could tell more than 10 human rights. These are the lawyers, civil servants, or police officials. From Table 3 , it can also be derived that if 47.33 per cent respondents couldn't tell even a single human rights, than 52.67 per cent were those which include as less as single human right or as much as above 10.

A further analysis of these 158 respondents in Table 4 shows that, 80.38 per cent of respondents ticked on Right to Education and 79.75 per cent knew about right to work. The reason for such type of response could be assign to the fact that since its a tribal belt most of the people here are aware of their tribal status and thus the benefits. Children are given free education, plus other facilities. Moreover, educational programmes run in the district are a major source of motivation for people to get inclined towards education .Since Lahoul has an agricultural economy, so everybody in the area works .This could be the probable reason for their awareness of right to work.

The top five answers are 'Right to Education', 'Right to Work', 'Freedom of Religion', 'Right to Life' and 'Freedom of Movement'.

Table 4
Awareness About Human Rights

Human Rights	*N = 158*	*Per cent*
Right to Education	127	80.38
Right to Work	126	79.75
Freedom of Religion	99	62.66
Right to Marry	79	50.00
Right to Life	66	41.77
Freedom of Movement	46	29.11
Equality before Courts	37	23.42
Freedom of Thought	35	22.15
Equal protection of Law	30	18.99
Right of Minorities	16	10.13
Freedom to seek Information	16	10.13
Freedom from Torture	15	09.49
Right to Social Security	09	05.70
Right to Adequate Standard of Living	05	03.16
Freedom from Slavery	05	03.16
Right to take part in Cultural Life	04	02.53
Freedom from Arrest	04	02.53
Right to Peaceful Assembly	04	02.53
Freedom to Seek Information	03	01.90

Looking at this pattern of answers it can be said that for Lahoulis the basic meaning of human rights is very rustic and uncomplicated and is also away from the constitutional labyrinth of covenants, charters etc. All they understand and demand is very basic. Lahoulis define Human Rights as "Right to Education, Work, Life, Movement and Religion".

Table 5
Attitude Towards Violation of Rights

Take the Injustice Done	*Respondents*	*Per cent*
Take an Action	117	39
Leave it after Few Discussion	78	26
Never Bother	105	35
Total	300	100

Table 5 takes a note of attitude of Lahoulis towards Human rights and its violation, 35 per cent reply came from those who said they would not be bothered by the violation of their rights. Most of the informants in this category were either the elderly people or were the females. 39 per cent said they would take an action against the unjust done to them 26 per cent said they would leave the issue after discussing it.

Human Rights Violation in Lahoul: Lahoul is a small tribal society, isolated from the rest of the world for more than half of the year. The geographical terrain of the area is a major barrier to the information. The simplicity of life and occupation here projects a picture that there can be no violation of human rights in the area. Infact, there is no reported constitutional violation of human rights in the area. It is also the reason, that there is not even a single case registered in the State Human Rights Commission, at Shimla.

Like every tribal society, Lahoulis also have a set of customary laws, like no property rights for females, marriage by elopement, polygamous marriage etc. Customary laws are observed with a lens eye, with respect to violation of human rights. There is no constitutional violation of human rights, but surely it is quite perceptible in the customary laws from the etic's perspective. The violation is subtly engraved in the ways, in which customary laws are functional in the society.

Development in Lahoul: Development in Lahoul began, way back in 1960s, when the two different geographical units-Lahoul and Spiti were put together to form a new district of Himachal Pradesh. Prior to the formation of the new district, this region was a part of Kangra district of Punjab. After getting a different status of a district, the area started getting developed. Single line administration was introduced in the area. Government started pumping a lot of money in the area through one or another program, which is continuing till date.

Following programms are run by Government in the area:

1. Swaranjayanti Gram Swarozgar Yogna (SGSY)
2. Jawahar Gram Samridhi Yojna (JGSY)
3. Indra Awas Yojna (IAY)
4. Employment Assurance Scheme (EAS)
5. National Social Assistance Program (NSAP)
6. Credit Cum Subsidy Rural Housing Scheme
7. Food for Work Program
8. Sampoorna Grameen Rozgar Yojna (SGRY)
9. Natural Calamity Scheme (NCS)
10. Pradhan Mantri Gram Sadak Yojan (PMGSY)
11. Desert Development Program (DDP)

Table 6 shows the awareness of Lahoulis about the Development Programmes running in their block. 50.33 per cent are aware of the various programmes being run by the government and 49.67 per cent are totally unaware. This ignorance may be because of two reasons – either the programmes are not well propagated or people are disinterested. The reason being 'unawareness'. People are so much engrossed in their lives and routine that they neither find time nor are interested in knowing about these development programs. Resultant, they don't know if they can develop. Their unawareness forces them to lead the under-developed way of life.

Table 6
Awareness of Development Programmes

Development Programs	*Respondents*	*Per cent*
Aware	151	50.33
Unaware	149	49.67
Total	300	100.00

Lahoulis are unaware even about the scholarship given to the students in the school. Table 7 presents the data showing their awareness about the Scholarship Programmes.

Table 7
Awareness of Scholarship Programmes

Scholarship Programmes	*Respondents*	*Per cent*
Aware	116	38.67
Unaware	184	61.33
Total	300	100.00

38.67 per cent of the respondents are aware of the scholarship schemes for the students 61.33 per cent are absolutely uninformed of any such programme.

Table 8 presents the data showing the Awareness about the Right to Development (RTD) among Lahoulis. The right to development is an inalienable human right by virtue of which every human person and all peoples are entitled to participate in, contribute to, and enjoy economic, social, cultural and political development, in which all human rights and fundamental freedoms can be fully realized.

Table 8
Awareness of Right to Development

Right to Development	*Respondents*	*Per cent*
Yes	12	4.00
No	288	96.00
Total	300	100.00

96 per cent of the respondents are absolutely unaware of their right to development and only 4 per cent knew that its their right to accept or reject the development programme.

Reason may be any, but the result is same. Inspite of huge calculations and massive investments in these programmes, desired results could never be achieved. There is a link between Human Rights awareness and development. If people are aware about their rights, if they are vigilant about all that, they are entitled to get and if they are sensitive to judge what all they are not getting, then the development of the sector is sure enough. They would know that its their Right to Develop.

The picture in Lahoul has changed quite a few shades from the past three decades; but the pace of development is very slow. Reason behind this is the non- participation of Lahoulis because of their ignorance. Secondly, the ruggedness of the area is also a detrimental factor. The conditions are worse in the interior villages as compared to district head quarters. Lahoulis in those villages are more unaware about any development activity going on in the head quarter village; as the interior villages are difficult to access because of absence of roads. (For example the distance by road from the village Agaher, Tindi Panchayat till District Head Quarters at Keylong is 80 km.).

SUGGESTIONS

There is a need for researchers to re-think critically the nature of anthropological research in the global era, and the kind of contribution that anthropology can make to issues of development and modernity. (Arce & Long, 2000). Following are the suggestions given:

1. Human Rights are concerned with the tribals constitutional laws and amendments relating to policy issues, their exploitation and to safe guard their interest. All these modalities of functioning and draft declaration require careful appraisal and analysis, where in, the role of anthropologists should not be undermined. (Gupta, 2002).
2. To find out the reasons behind the unawareness of people towards human rights, anthropological inquiry should examine the relationship between orders of power-enshrined in both nation-state and trans-national institutions and their constitution in everyday settings.
3. Their study should explore rights at the level of social practice: how are rights applied-and what are they applied for-in everyday legal processes. (Wilson & Mitchell, 2003).
4. Infrastructure development becomes crucial in the less developed countries.
5. Education is the only way, which can annihilate their miseries. The education system is the corner-stone of any democracy, human rights and governance.

6. It can be said that tribals must be raised to that particular level where they decide for their own development.

ACKNOWLEDGEMENT

Thanks are due to Director-General BPR&D, Ministry of Home Affairs, Government of India, New Delhi, for awarding the fellowship grant to SG under which the field work was conducted, which is gratefully acknowledged.

We express our heart felt gratitude to the people of Lahoul for their cooperation and assistance.

REFERENCES

Arce A. and Long N. (2000), Reconfiguring Modernity and Development from An Anthropological Perspective. In Alberto Arce & Norman Long (eds): *Anthropology, Development and Modernities.* London: Routledge, pp. 1-31.

Census of India (2001), Himachal Pradesh Series 3 – Provisional Population Totals, Paper 1 and 2.

Gupta S. and Kapoor A.K. (2003), Development or Globalization for Scheduled Tribes-An Anthropological Perspective. In A.K. Kalla and D.K. Bhattacharya (eds.): *Understanding People of India: Anthropological Insight,* Proceedings of P.C. Biswas Centenary National Seminar, Department of Anthropology, University of Delhi, Delhi, pp. 385-91.

Gupta S. and Kapoor A.K. (2005), Ethnicity and Social Variability Among Lahouli. In M.K. Raha (ed.): *Tribal Cultures of India.* Calcutta. (In Press).

Gupta S. (2002), Human Rights and Primitive Tribe–An Anthropological Perspective. In S.K. Chaudhuri and S.S. Chaudhuri (eds.): *Primitive Tribes in Contemporary India.* (In Press).

Gupta S. (2004), Police, Population and Human Rights: An Interface Study in Cross-Cultural Perspective. Report Submitted to *Bureau of Police Research and Development,* Ministry of Home Affairs, Government of India, Delhi. (Unpublished)

Kapoor A.K. (1990), Genetics and Tribals: An Anthropological Perspective. *South Asian Anthropologist,* 11(2): 55-62.

——(1996), Tribe, Anthropologist and Future. In R.S. Mann (ed.): *Tribes of India: Ongoing Challenges.* New Delhi: M.D., pp. 67-80.

——(1999), Law and Scheduled Tribes: A Socio-Legal Perspective. In V.K. Pant and B.S. Bisht (eds.): *Backward Communities: Identity, Development and Transformation.* Delhi: Gyan , pp. 175-182.

Kapoor A.K. and Singh R. (1991), Human Biology in India: A Plea for Future Strategies. In I.J.S. Bansal et al, (eds): *New Horizons in Human Biology.* New Delhi: Today and Tomorrow's , pp. 223-229.

Nayak P.B. (2003), Development and Human Rights. *Economic and Political Weekly,* XXXVIII (37); 13-19 Sept.: 3894-96.

Parmar H.S. (1996), Lahaula. In Sachchidananda and R.R. Prasad (eds.): *Encyclopedic Profile of Indian Tribes.* Vol. III. New Delhi: Discovery, pp. 545-547.

Pathy S. (2003), Destitution, Deprivation and Tribal Development. *Economic and Political Weekly*, XXXVIII (27), 5-11 July: 2832-36.

Wilson R.A. and Mitchell J.P. (2003), *Human Rights in Global Perspective-Anthropological Studies of Right, Claims and Entitlements.* London: Routledge.

6

CARIES PREVALENCE, ORAL HYGIENE AND SOCIO-ECONOMIC STATUS IN ADOLESCENT GADDIS OF HIMACHAL PRADESH

Parul Sharma and Krishan Sharma

INTRODUCTION

Dental caries or decaying of teeth, the most common disease of humans, is characterized by decalcification and disintegration of the hard dental tissues like enamel, dentine and cementum. It affects persons of all races, countries, and economic strata and may occur at any stage or in either sex. Although bacteria on teeth are the direct cause of dental caries, a large number of microbiological, environmental and host's biological factors interact to determine whether or not an individual will be affected by this disease and if affected, how and to what extent. For this reason, dental caries is considered to be a multifactorial disease (WHO, 1984). Caries is believed to be the same disease throughout the world, yet the impact of various etiological factors can be quite different in different individuals and in different parts of the world (WHO, 1992). Dental caries begin with acid demineralization of the outer enamel surface and if not arrested or treated, the dissolution of enamel surface continues into the dentine and pulp with increasing cavitations and loss of tooth substance. Toothache is common accompanying sign of decay. The end result is the total loss of the crown of the tooth, often associated with abscess and other types of secondary infection (WHO, 1997).

The Indian subcontinent is characterized by tremendous amount of cultural, geographic, environmental and ethnic variability and therefore, presumably within and between population differences occur in the prevalence of oral health and of dental diseases. Prevalence of caries has been studied with reference to age, sex, geographical area, population, intelligence quotient, bio-social factors and type of dentition: primary, mixed and secondary. The dental epidemiological studies on different

Indian populations give contradictory results. A very high prevalence of periodontal diseases was reported during 1940s and 1950s, as about 70% children were reported to suffer from gingivitis (see Mistry, 1983). Prevalence of dental caries in children and adolescents, ranging in age from 6-17 years, varied between 50-60% (see Talim, 1983). Later studies during 1960s and 1970s too reported prevalence of dental caries in the similar range of 50 to 70% (Gill and Prasad, 1968; Tiwari and Chawala, 1979; Singh and Singh, 1981). Mistry (1983) observed that earlier dental literature from 1941 to 1981 lacked uniform recording index, standardization and non-calibration of the investigations, etc.

The differences in prevalence and severity of periodontal diseases in various Indian populations have been correlated with differences in geographical, ethnic, sex, and socio-economic factors. On the contrary, Mistry (1983) is of the opinion that these differences in prevalence of disease are primarily due to consequences of oral hygiene and only secondarily (to lesser degree) a consequence of demographic factors. In 1960, the Government of India constituted a school health committee (Govt.of India, 1961) which recommended medical examination of children at the level of entry into school and thereafter every 4-5 years. But this recommendation has never been implemented or practiced in schools.

The majority of Indian studies are on subjects ranging in age from 10-60 years, and such a wide age variation is not appropriate for any meaningful epidemiological investigation. The literature review reveals that no study on oral health status among Gaddi population has been undertaken to study prevalence of dental caries with reference to socio-economic traits, oral hygiene, dietary habits, sex differences and age factors. On the basis of existing literature and popular beliefs, the following hypotheses were framed to be tested in this study: (1) Prevalence of dental carries is higher in females than in males; (2) Prevalence of dental carries is higher in children who belong to low-income group; (3) Prevalence of dental carries is higher in children who consume sugar or jaggery after meals; (4) Prevalence of dental carries is lower in children who brush or clean their teeth daily.

MATERIALS AND METHODS

Gaddis are the inhabitants of Bharmour sub-division of Chamba District and also settled in the belt of Kangra district lying in the shadow of Dhauladhar. Gaddi is a generic name and the tribe is stratified into two horizontal divisions of upper and lower castes. The Gaddis belong to Hindu fold. They possess certain specific social traits. The abundance of Sanskrit words in their dialect confirms that their ancestors were Sanskrit-speaking people. Under the generic name of Gaddis, they constitute a number of castes of unequal status. They are divided into four main classes, the Brahmins, the Rajputs, the Khatris and the Menials or low castes comprising

Kolis, Riharas, Badhis, Sipis and Halis. Out of these various groups, the study is limited to Gaddi Rajput children. Gaddis with their distinctive cultures and customs form an inseparable part of the cultural mosaic of Himachal Pardesh.

The study was carried on 94 school-going Gaddi Rajput children ranging in age between 14-18 years, of both sexes. Data was collected along the foothills of Dhauladhar in Kangra District from schools in Dharamshala. Children from adjacent villages mainly Kandi, Dadnu, Trapda, Ther, Mohli, Juhl, Khadota etc. came to study here. General information such as age, sex, family, educational status, income and occupational status of the subjects and their parents was collected. Apart from recording and observing teeth for the prevalence of dental caries; their dietary habits and oral hygiene habits were recorded. Clinical examination was performed making use of direct and indirect sunlight in the school building. Each subject was examined sitting in a regular chair. The teeth were examined systematically for dental caries with a probe and a dental mirror and the findings were recorded on a specially prepared Proforma. The instruments were rinsed off in fresh water, dried with cotton towel and disinfected with a surface disinfecting solution before using these for making observations in other children's mouth and in between the examination. The intensity or extent of dental caries in terms of the number of teeth affected per person is measured through DMF index. The DMF is the average number of permanent teeth per person which are decayed, missing because of caries or filled. Children were asked certain set of structured questions relating to their diet, oral hygiene and oral habits. The data thus collected was subjected to statistical analysis.

RESULTS

Table 1 shows frequency distribution of demographic, socio-economic traits, oral hygiene, dietary habits and caries prevalence with reference to sex. Majority of subjects (52.5%) belonged to families having income less than Rs. 3000/- per month. The literacy rate in the mothers is very low compared with the fathers as the majority of the mothers (76.6%) were illiterate. The majority of the subjects (88.3%) have mixed diet. Two-third of them rinses their mouth after meals. Frequency of sugar and jaggery eaters after meals was low (15.1% males and 12.2% females). 6.4% of males and 2.4% of females do smoking. 26.4% of males chew tobacco, 9.5% of males and 9.7% of females do thumb sucking and the sex differences for these traits are significant. It has been found that 41.5% of males and 53.7% females breathe through mouth. About 50% of the subjects clean their teeth daily. Brushing is the most common mode of (42.6%) cleaning teeth and about 58% of the subjects either use *datun* alongwith brush or only use *datun*. Depending upon the local flora, chewing sticks (*datun*) used to clean their teeth are of different materials. Commonly used chewing sticks include *Prunus(Aaru), Lantana indica(Phulnu), Eruca sativa(Tirmira)*. Majority (96.8%) of the subjects clean their teeth before breakfast. Occlusal and buccal (34%) are the most commonly brushed surfaces. Short to and fro (56.4%) and long to and fro (22.3%) are the techniques of brushing the teeth. Presence of dental caries is higher (50.9%) in males as compared to females (31.7%). Significant sex differences are observed for dental caries and smoking habits.

Table 1
Frequency Distribution of Demographic, Socio-economic Traits, Oral Hygiene, Dietary Habits and Caries Prevalence

Trait	*Male*		*Female*		χ^2	*Total*	
	N	*%*	*N*	*%*		*N*	*%*
Age Group							
14	8	15.1	5	12.2	1.6	13	13.8
15	12	22.6	6	14.6		18	19.2
16	9	17	9	22		18	19.2
17	14	26.4	11	26.8		25	26.6
18	10	18.9	10	24.4		20	21.3
Family Income							
1500-3000	26	49.1	23	56.1	2	49	52.1
3001-4500	19	35.9	13	31.7		32	34
4501-6000	6	11.3	2	4.9		8	8.5
6001-7500 and above	2	3.7	3	7.3		5	5.4
Education Father							
Illiterate	20	37.7	14	34.2	1.3	34	36.2
Primary	18	34	11	26.8		29	30.9
Middle and above	15	28.3	16	39		31	32.9
Education Mother							
Illiterate	44	83	28	68.3	3	72	76.6
Primary	7	13.2	9	22		16	17
Middle and above	2	3.8	4	9.8		6	6.4
Diet							
Vegetarian	4	7.6	7	17.1	2	11	11.7
Mixed	49	92.5	34	82.9		83	88.3
Do You Rinse Your Mouth After Meal							
No	15	28.3	11	26.8	0.1	26	27.7
Yes regularly	15	28.3	13	31.7		28	29.8
Yes occasionally	23	43.4	17	41.5		40	42.6
Do You Take Sugar Gur or Any Other Sweet Thing After Meals							
No	45	84.9	36	87.8	1.4	81	86.2
Yes sugar	5	9.4	2	4.9		7	7.4
Yes gur	2	3.8	1	2.4		3	3.2
Yes any other	1	1.9	2	4.9		3	3.2
Do You Have Any of These Habits							
No	29	54.7	36	87.8	16.3*	65	69.2
Yes smoking	5	9.4	1	2.4		6	6.4
Yes tobacco chewing	14	26.4	0	0		14	14.9
Yes thumb sucking	5	9.5	4	9.7		7	7.5
Do You Breathe Through Mouth							
No	31	58.5	19	46.3	1.4	50	53.2
Yes	22	41.5	22	53.7		44	46.8

Contd....

Trait	Male N	Male %	Female N	Female %	χ^2	Total N	Total %
Incidence of Brushing or Tooth Cleaning							
Daily	25	47.2	20	48.8	0.1	45	47.9
Rarely	6	11.3	5	12.2		11	11.7
Occasionally	22	41.5	16	39		38	40.4
Material Used							
Brush	26	49.1	14	34.2	2.1	40	42.6
Datun stick	9	17	9	22		18	19.2
Both brush and *datun* stick	18	34	18	43.9		36	38.3
Medium Used							
Tooth paste	42	79.3	30	73.2	3.1	72	76.6
Tooth powder	2	3.8	2	4.9		4	4.3
Banna stick	2	3.6	1	2.4		3	3.2
Aroo or *pajja* stick	4	7.6	4	9.8		8	8.5
Phulnu stick	3	5.7	2	4.9		5	5.3
Tirmira stick	0	0	2	4.9		2	2.1
Timing of Brushing or Datun							
Before breakfast	51	96.2	40	97.6	0.1	91	96.8
Before breakfast and after dinner	2	3.8	1	2.4		3	3.2
Method of Brushing							
Buccal surface	15	28.3	18	43.9	4.1	33	35.1
Occlusal and buccal surface	22	41.5	10	24.4		32	34
Occlusal buccal and lingual surface	7	13.2	4	9.8		11	11.7
No data	9	17	9	22		18	19.2
Technique of Brushing							
Circular	1	1.9	1	2.4	0.4	2	2.1
Short to and fro	31	58.5	22	53.7		53	56.4
Long to and fro	12	22.6	9	22		21	22.3
No data	9	17	9	22		18	19.2
Presence of Dental Caries							
Absent	26	49.1	28	68.3	3.5**	54	57.5
Present	27	50.9	13	31.7		40	42.6
DMF Score							
0	26	49.1	28	68.3	6.1***	54	57.5
1	12	22.6	5	12.2		17	18.1
2	3	5.7	4	9.8		7	7.5
3	7	13.2	2	4.9		9	9.6
4	4	7.6	2	4.9		6	6.4
5	1	1.9	0	0		1	1.2

*p<0.05 **0.05<p<0.10 ***0.10<p<0.50.

Results of one-way analysis of variance of DMF scores and prevalence of dental caries with reference to various socio-economic traits, oral hygiene and dietary habits are given in the Table 2. The results were found significant for sex, paternal education and habit of taking sugar or jaggery after meals.

Rank correlation coefficients between DMF scores with socio-economic traits, oral hygiene and dietary habits are given in Table 3. Significant correlation ($p<0.05$) was found for age group, family income, dietary habit, consumption of sugar or jaggery and timing of brushing or cleaning teeth.

Table 2
Result of One-way Analysis of Variance of DMF Score and Prevalence of Dental Caries with Reference to Various Socio-economic Traits, Oral Habits and Oral Hygiene

Trait	*Dental Caries*			*DMF Score*			*ANOVA*
	Absent	*%*	*Present*	*%*	*Mean*	*S.D.*	*F-test*
Sex							
Male	26	49.1	27	50.9	1.51	0.5	
Female	28	68.3	13	31.7	1.32	0.47	
Age Group							2.979*
14	5	38.5	8	61.5	1.15	1.28	
15	11	61.1	7	38.9	0.72	1.13	
16	12	66.7	6	33.3	0.39	0.61	
17	17	68	8	32	0.72	1.28	
18	9	45	11	55	1.7	1.78	
Family Income							0.2339
1500-3000	33	67.3	16	32.7	0.82	1.42	
3001-4500	15	46.9	17	53.1	1.03	1.18	
4501-6000	3	37.5	5	62.5	1.13	1.36	
6001-7500and above	3	60	2	40	1	1.73	
Education Father							4.2395*
Illiterate	14	41.2	20	58.8	1.44	1.58	
Primary	19	65.5	10	34.5	0.66	1.14	
Middle and above	21	67.7	10	32.3	0.61	1.05	
Education Mother							1.1539
Illiterate	40	55.6	32	44.4	0.94	1.33	
Primary	9	56.3	7	43.8	1.13	1.54	
Middle and above	5	83.3	1	16.7	0.17	0.41	
Diet							
Vegetarian	9	81.8	2	18.2	0.36	0.92	
Mixed	45	54.2	38	45.8	1	1.37	
Do You Rinse Your Mouth After Meal							0.9586
No	15	57.7	11	42.3	0.96	1.46	
Yes regularly	13	46.4	15	53.6	1.18	1.36	
Yes occasionally	26	65	14	35	0.73	1.24	
Do You Take Sugar Gur or Any Other Thing After Meals							5.719*
No	49	60	32	39.5	0.75	1.15	
Yes sugar	1	14.3	6	85.7	2.71	1.6	
Yes gur	2	66.7	1	33.3	1.67	2.89	
Yes any other	2	66.7	1	33.3	0.67	1.15	
Do You Have Any of These Habits							2.1383
No	40	61.5	25	38.5	0.77	1.18	
Yes smoking	5	83.3	1	16.7	0.67	1.63	
Yes tobacco chewing	5	35.7	9	64.3	1.71	1.77	
Yes thumb sucking	4	44.4	5	55.6	0.75	1.04	
Do You Breathe Through Mouth							
No	31	62	49	38	0.84	1.3	
Yes	23	52.3	21	47.7	1.02	1.39	
Incidence of Brushing or Tooth Cleaning							1.3719
Daily	30	66.7	15	33.3	0.69	1.24	
Rarely	5	45.5	6	54.5	1.09	1.38	
3-4Times a week	19	50	19	50	1.16	1.42	
Material Used							0.3144
Brush	20	50	20	50	1.02	1.4	
Datun stick	12	66.7	6	33.3	0.72	1.23	
Both brush and *datun* stick	22	61.1	14	38.9	0.92	1.34	0.3793

Contd....

Trait	*Dental Caries*				*DMF Score*		*ANOVA*
	Absent	*%*	*Present*	*%*	*Mean*	*S.D.*	*F-test*
Medium Used							
Tooth paste	40	55.6	32	44.4	0.96	1.35	
Tooth powder	2	50	2	50	1.25	1.89	
Banna stick	2	66.7	1	33.3	1.33	2.31	
Aroo or *pajja* stick	5	62.5	3	37.5	0.63	0.92	
Phulnu stick	3	60	2	40	0.8	1.3	
Tirmira stick	2	100	0	0	0	0	
Timing of Brushing or Datun							
Before breakfast	52	57.1	39	42.9	0.92	1.34	
Before breakfast and after dinner	2	66.7	1	33.3	1	1.73	
Method of Brushing							0.5755
Buccal surface	18	54.5	15	45.5	0.97	1.31	
Occlusal, buccal	18	56.3	14	43.8	0.84	1.25	
Occlusal, buccal,lingual	6	54.5	5	45.5	1.36	1.86	
No data	12	66.7	6	33.3	0.72	1.23	
Technique of Brushing							1.3409
Circular	2	100	0	0	0	0	
Short to and fro	33	62.3	20	37.7	0.85	1.29	
Long to and fro	7	33.3	14	66.7	1.38	1.53	
No data	12	66.7	6	33.3	0.72	1.23	
Dental Caries							
Absent	54	57.4	40	42.6	0	0	
Present	40	42.6	54	57.4	2.17	1.22	

*P < 0.005.

Table 3
Rank Correlation between Mean DMF Scores and Varioussocio-economic Traits, Oral Hygiene and Dietary Habits

Trait	*Correlation*
Sex	0.086
Age Group	0.374*
Family income	0.364*
Education father	0.01
Education mother	0.252
Diet	0.46*
Do you rinse your mouth after meal	0.039
Do you take sugar *gur* or any other Thing after meals	0.37*
Do you have any of these habits	0.326
Do you breathe through mouth	0.337
Incidence of brushing	0.29
Material used	0.091
Medium used	0.161
Timing of brushing	0.423*
Method of brushing	0.01
Technique of brushing	0.154

*P < 0.05.

DISCUSSION

We find an average of 1.51 DMF score in males and 1.32 in females. The magnitude of index can be regarded as low. WHO (1991) recommends less than 2 DMF score in twelve year olds as desirable goal in European children. Gaddis have lower than 2 DMF score despite the fact that no oral health facilities are available to these people.

Table 4
Comparison of Prevalence of Dental Caries in Northern India

Place/Population	*Age Range*	*Prevalence of Dental Caries*	*Mean DMF*	*Reference*
Chandigarh	6-16	81.60	3.93	Tewari and Chawla (1977)
Amritsar (Punjab)	13-14	62.96	1.53	Chopra et. al. (1983)
Ludhiana (Punjab)	14-19	88.72	5.18	Gauba et. al. (1986)
Lucknow (U.P.)	13-14	18.71	-	Gangwar et. al. (1990)
SC Males of Dharampur (H.P.)	14-15	33.33	0.60	Duggal (2001)
SC Females of Dharampur (H.P.)	14-15	35.00	0.70	Kaur (2001)
Male Gaddis of Kangra (H.P.)	14-19	50.10	1.51	Present study
Female Gaddis of Kangra (H.P.)	14-19	31.00	1.32	Present study
Combined	14-19	42.55	1.42	Present study

The comparison of prevalence of dental caries and mean DMF score has been made in Table 4 which shows that Gaddis on average have lower prevalence of dental caries. However, the prevalence rates are similar to Scheduled Caste (SC) children of Himachal Pradesh reported by Duggal (2001) and Kaur (2001). But, the prevalence rates in their studies included children in the age range of 14-15 years, whereas our sample has children ranging in age from 14-19 years. The prevalence and mean DMF in Gaddis is much lower than that reported by Gauba et al. (1986) who report very high prevalence of dental caries and mean DMF score in rural areas of Ludhiana District of Punjab.

Prevalence of dental caries has been reported to be higher in females than in males by Shourie (1941), Dutta (1965) and Govilla (1983). Our results on Gaddi children do not favour the hypothesis that females are more susceptible to dental caries than males as significantly higher prevalence ($p<0.05$) was found in males (50.94%) than females (31.7%). Our results are compatible with those of Chopra 1983), Vaish (1983), Gangawar et al. (1990) and Sharma and Mittal (2003) in reporting higher prevalence of dental caries in males. These sex differences cannot be explained on the basis of gender differences in oral hygiene habits like rinsing mouth after meals, taking sugar or jaggery after meals, tooth brushing, material used medium used, method of brushing, technique of brushing and timing of brushing because no gender differences were observed for these variables. However, incidence of tobacco chewing and smoking has been found to be significantly higher in males than in females. No sex differences were found for family income and education of parents.

Prevalence of dental caries has been usually associated with socio-economic differences. We tested the hypothesis that prevalence of dental caries is higher in children who belong to low income group. Our results do not support this hypothesis as we found lowest prevalence of dental caries in children whose family income was lowest. However, rank correlation coefficient between family income and DMF score was statistically significant. There are also contradictory reports in literature regarding this aspect. Dutta (1965) found higher prevalence among lower classes, while Chandra (1979) found higher prevalence in higher classes.

The results of the present study validate the hypothesis that prevalence of dental caries is higher in children who consume sugar after meals. However, the number of such subjects was very low (13.8%) and hence any conclusion on prevalence of caries with reference to above category is tentative.

The results of present study are compatible with the hypothesis that prevalence of dental caries is lower in children who clean their teeth daily. Prevalence of dental caries has also been investigated with reference to the type of diet, i.e., vegetarian and non-vegetarian (mixed). Our results showed higher prevalence of dental caries in non-vegetarians than vegetarians. However, it may be added here that the number of vegetarians was very low compared to non-vegetarians and this was true for both males and females. Gangawar et al. (1990) found no significant differences in caries between vegetarians and non-vegetarians.

In our study we have taken large number of correlated factors, e.g., oral hygiene, oral habits and socio-economic status, etc. These factors are known to affect prevalence and extent of dental caries. We studied the role of these factors in both prevalence and extent of dental caries; indicator for the later was DMF score. Results of ANOVA of DMF score and rank correlation between DMF score and various correlated factors show that only three of the sixteen (18.75%) factors namely, sex, family income and rinsing the mouth after meals are significantly correlated with dental caries. Hereby, we affirm the role of our Indian tradition of rinsing our mouth after meals tends to lower the prevalence of dental caries.

SUMMARY

A sample of 94 Gaddi children (53 Males and 41 females) from Kangra District of Himachal Pradesh was studied to assess their oral health status. The children ranged in age from 14 to 18 years. Their dietary habits, oral hygiene habits, socio-economic status were also recorded. The results showed that the dental caries was present in 42.6% of the children. Prevalence of dental caries was higher in males (50.9%) than in females (31.7%) and the differences were statistically significant. The mean DMF scores were 1.51 in males and 1.32 in females. One-way analysis of variance of DMF Scores revealed significant age differences. Mean DMF Scores were significantly higher in subjects whose fathers were illiterate and who took sugar or *gur* after their meals. Dietary habits revealed that vegetarians had less caries prevalence (18.2%) than those who also had non-vegetarians diet (45.8%). 27.7%of the subjects did not rinse their mouth after meals and 86.2% did not eat sugar/jaggery after meals. 46.8% of subjects, who breathed through mouth and they had higher caries prevalence (47.7%) than their counterparts who did not breathe through mouth. 47.9% of the subjects cleaned their teeth daily and prevalence of dental caries in them was less (33.3%) than those who cleaned their teeth rarely (54.5%) or occasionally (50.0%). The majority of the subjects (96.8%) cleaned their teeth before breakfast. This study showed significant correlation between DMF scores and age groups, family income, dietary habit, consumption of sugar or *gur* after meals and timing of cleaning teeth. The results favoured the hypothesis that different etiological factors interact to cause dental caries.

REFERENCES

Chandra S. and Chawla T.N. (1979), Incidence of Dental Caries in Lucknow School Going Children. *J. Ind. Dent. Assoc.* 51: 109-110.

Chopra S., Vacher B.R. and Taneja J.R. (1983), Dental Caries Experience During the Period of Mixed Dentition. *J. Ind. Dent. Assoc.* 55: 99-104.

Dutta A. (1965), A Study on the Prevalence of Periodontal Disease and Dental Caries Amongst School Going Children in Calcutta. *J. Ind. Dent. Assoc.* 37: 367.

Duggal S. (2001), *A Study of Permanent Teeth Emergence and Oral Health Status among the Scheduled Caste Males of Dharampur, District Solan (H.P.) M.Sc. Project Report,* Panjab University, Chandigarh.

Gaikwad R.S. and Indurkar M.S. (1993), Prevalence of Dental Caries in School Going Children of Aurangabad in the Year 1992. *J. Ind. Dent. Assoc.* 64: 325.

Gangwar S.K., Idris M.Z., Bhusan V., Nirupam S., Saimbi C.S. and Jain V.C. (1990), Bio-social Correlates of Dental Caries in Rural Area of Lucknow. *J. Ind. Dent. Assoc.* 61: 93-97.

Gauba K., Tewari A. and Chawla H.S. (1986), Frequency Distribution of Children According to Dental Caries Status in Rural Areas of Northern India (Punjab), *J. Ind. Dent. Assoc.* 55: 395-399.

Gill P.S. and Prasad B.G. (1968), Dental Health Survey of Primary School Children in a Rural Area of Lucknow. *J. Ind. Dent. Assoc.* 40: 2-7.

Govilla A.K., Parihar K.S. and Sapra S. (1983), Prevalence of Dental Caries, Gingivitis and Dental Fluorosis in School Children of the Rural Area under PHC-DABRA. *Ind. J. Comm. Med.* 8(3): 75.

Govt. of India (1961), *Report of School Health Committee.* New Delhi: Central Health Education Bureau.

Kaur K. (2001), *A Study of Permanent Teeth Emergence and Oral Health Status among the Scheduled Caste Females of Dharampur, District Solan (H.P.)* MSc. Project Report, Panjab University, Chandigarh.

Mistry K.M. (1983), The Changing Pattern of Oral Disease in India then Need for a Preventive Approach. *J. Ind. Dent. Assoc.* 55: 387-393.

Sen R. (1997), Oral Diseases. *Youth Health.* 46: 6.

Sharma K. and Mittal S. (2003), Oral Health in a Rural Agricultural Community: The Link between Oral Hygiene and Dental Pathology among the Gujjars of Northwest India. In Sahay V.S. and Singh P.K. (eds.): *Dimensions of Researches in Indian Anthropology*, Vol. I. New Delhi: Serials Publications. pp. 407-438.

Shourie K.L. (1941), Dental Caries in Indian Children. *Ind. J. Med. Res.* 29: 709.

Singh D.K. and Singh R.P. (1981), Prevalence of Dental Caries in School Going Children of Patna. *J. Ind. Dent. Assoc.* 53: 267.

Talim S.T. (1983), The Problem of Dental Caries and Periodontal Disease in India. *J. Ind. Dent. Assoc.* 55: 395-399.

Tewari A., Chawla H.S. and Malik C.P. (1979), Prevalence of Periodontal Disease in Northern Region of India: Chandigarh. *J. Ind. Dent. Assoc.* 51: 263.

Tewari A. (1991), Risk Markers for Oral Diseases. In Johnson N.W. (ed.): *Dental Caries*. Cambridge: Cambridge University Press.

Vaish R.P. (1983), Prevalence of Caries among Tribal School Children in Phulbani District, Orissa. *J. Ind. Dent. Assoc.* 55: 455-45.

Vaish R.P. (1982), Prevalence of Caries amongst School Going Tribal Children in Ganjam District, Orissa. *J. Ind. Dent. Assoc.* 54: 375-377.

WHO (1984), Prevention Methods and Programmes for Oral Diseases: Report of WHO Expert Committee. *Tech. Rep. Ser.* 713.

WHO (1992), Advances in the Prevention of Oral Diseases. *Tech. Rep. Ser.* 822-828.

WHO (1997), *Oral Health Service-Basic Methods*. Geneva: WHO.

7

HEALTH AND HYGIENE OF LAMANI TRIBE: A CASE STUDY OF APPENAHALLI SETTLEMENT IN BELLARY DISTRICT OF KARNATAKA STATE

V. Jagadeesh

INTRODUCTION

Human population would have vanished long long ago, had it not been developed the modern modes and methods of controlling diseases. Health and human development form integral components of overall socio-economic development of any nation. Every society has its own way of its cultural systems to perceive and realise the concepts of health, hygiene, diseases, treatment and care differently and this results in variations in understanding the causes of an illness and its treatment across the communities. In all traditional societies the system of medicine was based on magic, religion or plants. These were used for curing a sickness either separately or in combination with other systems of medicine.

This article deals with beliefs and practices, related to Lamanis with regard to their food patterns, ideas regarding hygiene, community sanitation and their concepts about illness and associated beliefs, their notions about supernatural and spirits as well as treatment in seeking behaviour.

MATERIALS AND METHODS

For collection of data I have used both primary and secondary methods of data collection. Primary data collection involved such methods as personnel interviews, questionnaire through participant observation. Secondary method of data collection involved references of books, journals, reports, encyclopedia, and dictionaries etc. I also attended some relevant Lamani conferences in the state to collect more details about the health and hygiene conditions of other Lamani settlements. This experience of mine during field work was indeed fruitful and rewarding as I was able to collect a plethora of literature pertaining to this article. Apart from this, I could get a first hand knowledge and understanding of the problems, perspectives of a Lamani tribe. This field work was carried out during summer vacation of my college days, that is, from March 25 to April 25, 2004.

Lamanis who call themselves migrants from Rajasthan are unique settlements in Karnataka State. They live scattered over the state, but they are distinctly identified by several names like Lamani, Lambada, Banjara and Sukali (in Andhra Pradesh). According to the encyclopedia of religion and ethics "their origin is probably Dravidian, but they now all trace their descent from the Brahmin or Rajput tribes of North India".

Appenahalli thanda is a settlement of Kudligi taluka, Bellary District in the Karnataka State. This is about 38 Kilometers from Kudligi taluka and 40 Kilomiters away from Bellary district. The main food crops in the settlement are *ragi, jawar* and rice. *Ragi* is consumed in the form of *Mudda* along with Khodi and some times with daal kurry. Mudda is prepared from the flour of ragi, after boiling in hot water and made round balls out of it. Khodi is a mixture of green chillis, brinjal, salt and tomato. Jawar is consumed in the form of Baati along with Khodi and daal. Baati is thick flattend bread, prepared from the flour of ragi, jawar or baajri.

They know the food preparation with vegetables but due to poverty, they never go to the market to purchase of vegetables. Many varieties of vegetables consumed by them are not grown in the settlement. Usually for breakfast mudda is consumed before 9 A.M. For lunch Baati is preferred at around 2 pm. For dinner, rice with daal, Khodi is consumed around 7.30 to 8 pm. Once or twice in a month they use protein pulses like gram, toori, wheat and vegetables. Food consumed during festivals and other social occasions like marriage, Sagai (Betrothol ceremony), rituals related to births, pregnancies and deaths are however, quite different from the food consumed on a daily basis. The consumption of alcohol is not a taboo in the settlement especially at the time of marriage and death ceremonies during which both men and women drink. Country liquor is made generally out of gol (raw jaggery) and mixed with chaal (Bark of sindhi tree). During recent years consumption of country liquor on certain ceremonial occasions has become very popular among youths of this community. But some people who have visited Lard Venketesh at Tirupati, Andrapradesh avoided consumption of alcohol. Those who are economically well-off go to nearby city and drink beer and whisky. They usually agree that consumption of alcohol is always accompanied with Boti lagamon (Mutan curry) and Kukadir lagaman (Chiken curry). The Food consumed in the settlement is broadly divided in to vegetarian and non vegetarian. The farmer includes green chillis, brinjal, tomato and the latter includes non vegetarian includes, mutton, chicken and eggs. Occasionally group of yougsters go to the forest for hunting pigs. If they succeed in hunting, they share and consume pork with locally made alcohol. Some families, that avoid taking non vegetarian food, consume alcohol only.

Based on the above explanation we can draw a conclusion that they are quite unaware of adverse effect then food system causes on human health. Men and women of all age group, pregnant women, children, youngster, oldmen, sickone are all found consuming the same food. Due to lack of awareness, they fall sick and may become anemic. On the contrary they trace it to their ancestors for most of the disease and offer sacrifice hen or a goat for remedy. Children in the settlement generally eat more Ammli (white tamarind) and gole (Jaggery) due to which indigestion takes place naturally and fall ill. It is believed battened that massaging the body on a regular basis leads to energy and growth up to the age of one year.

In the settlement, almost all agree that mother's milk is the best food but generally they give solid food to a baby after one year. It consists of ganji (paste) of ragi, salt and jawar rooti, occasionally rice and daal. During sickness, one or two days they take care of providing hot water for drinking, taking him to a private doctor, in bullock cart or by government bus. Supposing he or she fails to recover with in two days, generally they say that ascribe it to some spirit and it never allows him to become a normal man. Pregnent women are taken special care with regard to their food pattern. It is believed that the food containing protein is given, for the well being of fetus growth in the mothers womb. Morning they give hot water for bathing, break fast like milk, wheat flour bread, for lunch cooked rice, toor daal or maoong daal with ghee. Twice a day fruits, like banana, custard apple etc. are consumed. In fact a special mixture of dry coconut, ghee, jaggery and honey is also consumed and curd and milk of a buffalo is regularly taken with food. They also give mutton, chicken and egg occasionally. Consumption of fish is avoided during pregnancy, as they believe that consumption of fish leads to many diseases. Especially people with better economy, are of the opinion that human body must maintain a balance between the environment and its changes so they use balanced food. It is also believed that the type of food they take must be change in male and female according to their physical change. It is included starting from the fetus to the old.

With respect to the body and hygiene, one must keep the body clean in order to maintain healthy phyque. This belief is shared by all. But it changes from one to another. Among Lamanis of Appenahalli tribe, since they live in huts with joint families, regular bathing is not found among male and female members of the family. Generally, men go to the wells occasionally, and females take bath weekly in the corner of a hut behind certain standing stone like structure. Those who are economically well-off, bath during the morning hours between seven to nine. All Lamanis believe that hot water for bathing removes tiredness and makes the body smooth. In the summer, majority of male and female prefer to bath in cold water. Frequency of washing one's face and hands is rarely found, and the use of soaps is rare among them but economically well-off people use soap daily. However, if it is believed that use of soap cools the body and cleans the skin. Fingernails are trimmed at regular intervals. Women folk say that for them to keep their nails clean is very much important because they work in the fields, kitchen and cleaning cattle sheds and simultaneously they should take care of small babies and children. They say that change of clothes on regular bases is considered important but men and women change their clothes on alternate days in summer. During winters the frequency of changing cloth is lesser. It is believed that clothes do not get dirty as the temperature is low. Clothes are washed only by women. They first dip in a soap powder and then on a huge stone which is fixed in front of their huts. Cloths are then beaten in order to clean. An extra soap is used to clean dirtier portion of shirts and dhotis and subsequently hung for drying. Cheplu (Foot wear) are rarely used. Usually when they go to the market they wear chappals. Usually in the settlement they never use them. When they go to the forests and fields they use cheplu in order to protect their feet from the thorns. Children, however, move, play and even go to schools bare footed. Only on ceremonial occasions one can find some children wearing slippers. Drinking water is being supplied by borewells maintained by panchayats and it is distributed through pipelines with taps fixed at specific point. Drinking water is stored in earthen pots, which keeps it cool and also they use steel and plastic vessels for storing water. Except few families in the settlement pots containing drinking water are always covered with steel plate or with a clean cloth. They have the fear of getting the water contaminated with the lizard and domestic insects which are highly poisonous and harmful to the body. Majority of huts are relatively unclean because both men and women work in the fields.

The matter of Environmental sanitation, people extend the concept of cleanliness beyond the boundaries of their dwellings and feel that dirt in their surroundings are the root cause of illness. No drainage facility is found the settlement. All most all huts have pits in a corner of house yard for collection of waste domestic water as well as for urination. The water filled in pits is also thrown on common space like pathways and near by roads. In the rainy season these pits create unsanitary conditions. Solid waste materials are also thrown in these pits which are mainly responsible for multiplication and substance of harmful germs and insects like mosquitoes and houseflies. Those who have cattles, keep them behind dwellings attached to their residing walls. In same cases the shed is on the side of a house. Huts without space at the backside as well as at the sides keep the cattle in the corner of the huts. Cattle dung is collected in pits.

Some families use dung to make fuel and is also mixed with clay for plastering walls and floors of huts. Dung is not considered as dirty and they never thought that diseases may emanate from them and affect human beings. On the other hand they believe that closed cattle shed brings healthier and western atmosphere. Some families are of the opinion that cattle sheds are unclean places from where germs and bacterias emerge which harm the human beings. Majority of the families in the settlement does not keep goats, sheeps or hen. All these together make the public space dirty and prone diseases. In the rainy season, rains play havoc in such areas causing water logging and overflowing of filth and mud. The washing places of their surrounding huts also become more hazardous. The belief prevails that rain brings prosperity and illness (headack cold, fever). But the village environment and sanitation are affected with moist and unhealthy form during the rainy season.

Diseases, response to them and beliefs associated to it. According to them healthy person is one who is able to do all his routine work without being excessively exhausted and without disturbing sleep and appetite. Lamanis in the settlement eat and work well. It is a good sign but youth are of opinion that shining face and ability to communicate properly is the good character of a healthy personality. Generally, if a person is considered sick it is an indication of abnormal health, is not in a position to sleep well and with sunken eyes and weak body. Excessively crying baby is considered to be ill and suffering from stomach problems. While a healthy child plays well eats and has a normal motion. In Appenahalli settlement, people usually categorise Tav (fever) in different way. Falling sick of fever on alternative days is related to the belief of unhappiness of deceased ancestors in the house. Falling sick of fever fortnightly is related to changing condition in the weather. If the fever is due to cold and cough they relate it to the excessive work in the fields. Some people in the settlement are of the opinion that fever can cause different aches like, headache, stomach ache, pain in the waist, and aching bones and joint pain. In the settlement we can divide diseases into two categories namely common and uncommon. Under common diseases we can see minor illness, prolonged or major illness, and illness such as cold, flue, headache, skin diseases etc. and under uncommon diseases typhoid, jaundice, cholera, dengue, leprosy, paralysis and polio. Some common diseases are not serious diseases in which patients are expected to be cured with in a weak or even earlier to it, by taking a short course of medicine. Often there is no need to consult doctor or Bhagat (priest). In fact, in curing common diseases most of them follow traditional home medicine. For uncommon diseases patients recover only after long periods and the treatment for them is also very expensive while in many cases complete recovery is uncertain. Lamanis believe that for avoiding common diseases they offer sweets to Valer Bhavani (Air deity), for she is angry with this settlement for the delay in offering sweets. While offering they never use non-vegetarian food. In addition to this for measles and small pox they treat differently. At draught season usually measles and the goddess of pox visits the settlement due to this, there will be abnormal or disturbed environment takes place. If any person in the house is suffering from measles, a special ritual is performed to please the goddess of measles. It is believed that the goddess has appeared. On such occasions cooking of any non-vegetarian food is prohibited. It is believed that if non-vegitarian food is cooked the measles would increase and the person suffering may die. A person with measles will be kept in separate room. He will be covered with leaves of neem. The specific puja with neem leaves and sweet is performed to please the goddess.

Cases of snake bite and scorpion bites are common in the settlement. If a person is bitten by snake or scorpion, one of the family members goes immediately to the house of Magician (who is called by the name) Lucchanaik who is expert in curing such bites by chanting of mantras. One, who informs regarding snake bite to him, is slapped very strongly by him and goes to a man who is suffering. He will ask him to sit infront, and takes incense sticks, the smoke or fragnance as to be inhaled by the suffery. Simultaneously Magician gives dry chillies for chewing. That is followed by continuous chanting of mantras for about one hour. This will be continued half an hour or one an hour. Then he asks patient regularly about the condition. Such beliefs are more in the settlement. They proudly claim that he has cured more than a hundreds of such cases. Even people will go in search of him rather than a doctor. Later he will be paid of Rs. 1000 or a goat or with a pair of new dress as a regard to his service. People say that it is a gift given willingly without any force. The magician never demands money or any gift for his service. He believes that if he demands money or any gift in return for the service provided his mantra will become ineffective as soon as he demands it. This vidya (knowledge) of snake bite/scorpion bite treatment by chanting mantra is hereditary passed on from father to son for centuries.

Generally people suffering from common diseases and when home remedies do not respond they take help of professionals. The local healers generally practicing it as hereditary occupation. When a person is ill all together for eg. The members in the family, neighbouring people and friends take decision regarding treatment. If a case is serious they take suggestion from educated in the village and consult the head of the settlement called "Nayak". Patients to a are generally taken to a doctor and bhagats (local priest) about whom people have heard or known from those who have got treatment already. On the basis of the capacity of a household they purchase medicine. If family is good in terms of economy, the full course of medicines is purchases and if family is poor they take one or two doses first and if found to be effective, the rest of the doses are purchased. Poor families often borrow loans from friends, relatives as well as money lenders.

DISCUSSION

Explanation given on the above aspects is an attempt to make holistic apprcach towards the idea of understanding the knowledge, attitudes, perceptions and practices relating to the overall health and hygiene system of Lamani tribe of Kudgi taluk in Bellary district of Karnataka state. With regard to food pattern in the settlement is unsystematic, not planned properly in terms of health. Food and drink that provides sustance and reflexive to a human body are clearly perceived in terms of specific types with set norms of consumption by age and sex as well during illness and times. In relation with body and hygiene, economically well-off people are very much aware of purity and pollution. Environmental or community sanitation is generally neglected in the settlement. A well developed drainage system is not found in the settlement especially during the monsoon. The settlement become extremely worst with regard to mode of isolating human and animal excrete and other solid waste disposal.

The health and hygiene system in a democracy like ours has to be successful, the health and hygiene of rural masses has to be improved by providing awareness at first stage and also a good modern medical facilities followed by well developed community sanitation. Educating rural mass through mass media, regular medical camps, etc also play an important role in improving health and hygiene conditions of rural India.

SUMMARY

Human population would have vanished long long ago, had it not been developed the modern modes and methods of controlling diseases. Lamanis who call themselves migrants from Rajasthan are unique settlements in Karnataka State. They live scattered over the state, but they are distinctly identified by several names like Lamani, Lambada, Banjara and Sukali (in Andhra Pradesh).This article deals with beliefs and practices, related to Lamanies with regard to their food patterns, ideas regarding hygiene, community sanitation and their concepts about illness and associated beliefs, their notions about supernatural and spirits as well as treatment in seeking behaviour. Explanation given on the above aspects is an attempt to make holistic approach towards the idea of understanding the knowledge, attitudes, perceptions and practices relating to the overall health and hygiene system of Lamani tribe of Kudgi taluk in Bellary district of Karnataka state.

REFERENCES

Caudill W. (1969), Applied Anthropology in Medicine. A.L. Kroeber (ed.) *Anthropology Today*, Berkely: University of California Press.

Gurumurthy K.G. (1970), *Vyavaharika Manavashastra (Applied Anthropology)*. Dharwad, Karnatak University Press.

Halber B.G. (1986), *Lamani Economy and Society in Change*. Delhi: K.M. Mittal Publications.

Jagadeesh V. (2005), *The Study of Lamani Tribe: An Anthropological Perspective*. Bangalore.

Mead, Margaret (1962), Nutrition, Maternal and Child Care. In Foster G.M. (ed): *Traditional Cultures and Technological Change*. New York: Warper.

Part-II
MORPHOLOGICAL VARIATIONS

8

PREVALENCE OF ABDOMINAL OBESITY WITH THE ONSET OF MENOPAUSE AMONG POST-MENOPAUSAL WOMEN OF LOWER SOCIO-ECONOMIC STRATA OF CHANDIGARH

Dolly Monisha and S.P. Singh

INTRODUCTION

Waist size is associated with metabolic markers of disease risk in post-menopausal women and is easily measurable circumference. VanPelt *et al.*, (2001) recommended that health care professional should monitor changes in waist circumference in post-menopausal women with respect to body weight and metabolic screening, as minimal increase in abdominal adiposity may contribute to unfavorable changes in metabolic complications. It has been clinically approved that body fat redistributes to the abdominal region during and after the menopause, which may be attributed to the effects of estrogen deficiency on adipocyte metabolism and fat patterning (Rebuffe-Scrive et al, 1987). Increased central adiposity in women is a greater predictor of heart disease, diabetes and death than generalized obesity (Manson et al, 1995).

A large body of epidemiological evidence has shown that abdominal obesity is a more potent risk factor for many cardiovascular diseases (CVDs) than generalized obesity (Kvist *et al.*, 1988; Bouchard *et al.*, 1990; Wei *et al.*, 1997; Taylor et al., 1998; *et al.*, Siedell *et al.*, 1988; Dipietro *et al.*, 1999). In a recent study of the prevalence of abdominal obesity in the United States, 24 million adult men and 40 million adult women suffered from abdominal obesity (Okosun *et al.*, 1999). The tendency of both abdominal obesity and type 2 diabetes coexist (Björntorp, 1992; Groop et al., 2001; Okosun et al., 2001) suggesting that the high prevalence of type 2 diabetes in the United States may be caused by the high prevalence of abdominal obesity, particularly among non-Hispanic blacks and Hispanics (Okosun *et al.*, 1999).

Several studies found that waist circumference (WC) is more closely associated with VAT and central adiposity than is either waist-to-hip ratio or body mass index (BMI; in kg/m²) (Ashwell *et al.*, 1996; Han *et al.*, 1998; Turcato *et al.*, 2000). A recent report by Seidell *et al.* (2001) suggests that people with a small WC and large hip circumference have a lower risk of cardiovascular disease. Lean et al. (1996) studied 1918 adults from a general population in north Glasgow and found that WC could be used in health promotion programs to identify adults who need weight management to avoid obesity-related diseases. Booth *et al.* (2000) found that even self-reported WC estimates are useful for monitoring overweight and obesity in epidemiologic surveys.

Epidemiologic studies have clearly shown that central adiposity is highly correlated with the presence of hypertension, coronary heart disease, type-II diabetes, and increased mortality risk (Grinker *et al.*, 2000; Bouchard, 1988; Osukun *et al.*, 2000). Abdominal obesity is associated with increased visceral adipose tissue (VAT) mass (Clasey *et al.*, 1999; Pouliot *et al.*, 1994), and VAT is independently associated with glucose and insulin concentrations in both men and women (Fujioka *et al.*, 1997; Garaulet *et al.*, 2000).

Both body mass index and waist circumference, waist-to-hip ratio are the anthropometric indicators most frequently used to assess general obesity and central obesity. Epidemiological studies have demonstrated that both BMI and waist circumference, WHR are powerful predictors of type II diabetes (Coldtiz *et al.*, 1995 and Haffner, 1990). The World Health Organisation currently defined overweight in Asian population as a BMI of 23-29.9 kg/m² and obese as a BMI of $\geq$ 30 kg/m² (Choo, 2002).

The present study was conducted to investigate:

(a) Prevalence of abdominal obesity with onset of menopause; (b) Is waist circumference a better anthropometric indicator of disease risk?

MATERIALS AND METHODS

The present cross-sectional study was conducted on the population of 300 post-menopausal women residing in various colonies of Chandigarh, representing lower socio-economic class during April 2002 to January 2004. Various anthropometric measurements using standard techniques (Lohman et al., 1988) were undertaken including body weight measured using weighing scale, abdominal obesity from the waist circumference and waist-to-hip ratio. Waist-to-Hip ratio is also good indicator of various disease risk associated with it. Accordingly, values of WHR ranging from 0.80 to 0.90 cm in women have been defined as critical (Willett et al, 1999). Lean et al. (1995) developed the cut-off values of Waist circumference associated with disease risk and adopted by the WHO (1997), in women, which are as follows:

Body Mass Index has been calculated as:

BMI = Body Weight (kg)/Height^2 (meter)

Waist-to-Hip ratio has been calculated as:

WHR = Waist Circumference (cm.)/Hip Circumference (cm.)

Waist circumference has been calculated as:

Low risk	≤ 79 cm
Increased risk	= 80-87 cm
Substantially increased risk	≥ 89 cm.

RESULTS

The present sample has been distributed into six yearly groups after the onset of menopause to study the influence of menopause on fat distribution. The anthropological characteristics of the present population are presented in the Table 1 and Table 2.

Table 1
Mean, Standard deviation and Standard Error of Mean

Years after onset of menopause	*Weight (kg)* X	S.E.M.	S.D.	*Height (cm)* X	S.E.M.	S.D.	*BMI* X	S.E.M.	S.D.
2-3 yrs	50.6	1.71	5.92	153.7	0.50	4.29	21.33	0.60	2.09
4-5 yrs	49.7	1.12	5.73	153.9	0.81	2.82	21.35	0.35	1.76
6-7 yrs	53.3	0.92	7.06	152.3	0.81	4.14	22.49	0.33	2.54
8-9 yrs	53.9	1.03	8.16	152.3	0.18	4.14	22.78	0.38	2.99
10-11 yrs	54.9	0.93	7.65	153.6	0.48	3.81	22.87	0.33	2.72
12-13 yrs	53.6	0.88	7.52	154.7	0.51	4.19	22.65	0.32	2.75

Table 2
Mean, Standard deviation and Standard Error of Mean

Years after onset of menopause	*Waist (cm)* X	S.E.M.	S.D.	*Hip (cm)* X	S.E.M.	S.D.	*WHR* X	S.E.M.	S.D.
2-3 yrs	76.1	1.70	5.88	95.8	1.15	3.97	0.79	0.012	0.04
4-5 yrs	76.1	1.22	6.20	95.2	0.99	5.06	0.80	0.007	0.03
6-7 yrs	78.7	1.08	8.33	95.1	0.87	6.65	0.83	0.006	0.04
8-9 yrs	80.1	0.97	7.69	95.8	0.82	6.53	0.84	0.005	0.04
10-11 yrs	81.2	0.99	8.13	96.8	0.79	6.5	0.84	0.005	0.04
12-13 yrs	79.0	0.96	8.24	94.6	0.82	6.99	0.83	0.005	0.05

Following WHO classification of BMI (for Asian population) the percentage distribution of the present sample are given in the Table 3. Women representing lower socio-economic strata have indicated prevalence of being in grade-I overweight category with their percentage increasing from 16.8% during initial years to maximum of 55.5% of the studied sample during 8-9 years after the onset of menopause followed by decline. However the studied sample of post-menopausal women of lower socio-economic strata are in normal or healthy category of BMI, the cases of malnutrition according to BMI are comparatively very marginal, maximum of 11.5% during 4-5 years and minimum of 3.4% during 6-7 years in grade–III category of thinness were reported in the studied sample of lower socio-economic strata.

Table 3
Percentage Distribution and Incidence of Obesity and Malnutrition According to BMI Criteria after the Onset of Menopause

BMI	*GRADE*		*2-3 yrs*	*4-5 yrs*	*6-7 yrs*	*8-9 yrs*	*10-11 yrs*	*12-13 yrs*
<16	Grade III	N	0	0	0	1	1	0
	Thinness	%	0.0	0.0	0.0	1.5	1.5	0.0
16-16.99	Grade II	N	0	0	2	1	1	1
	Thinness	%	0.0	0.0	3.4	1.5	1.5	1.4
17-18.49	Grade I	N	1	3	2	6	4	4
	Thinness	%	8.3	11.5	3.4	9.2	6.0	5.6
18.5-22.99	Normal	N	9	18	29	21	29	41
		%	75.0	69.2	50.0	32.3	43.3	56.9
23-29.99	Grade I	N	2	5	25	36	36	26
	Overweight	%	16.7	19.2	43.1	55.4	55.4	36.1
30-39.99	Grade II	N	0	0	0	0	0	0
	Overweight	%	0.0	0.0	0.0	0.0	0.0	0.0
≥ 40	Grade III	N	0	0	0	0	0	0
	Overweight	%	0.0	0.0	0.0	0.0	0.0	0.0

With the onset of menopause 91% of the studied sample was found to be at low risk category of waist circumference during initial years, thereafter their %age has been decreasing till 41.8% (10-11years) followed by steep increase. Only 8.3% of the studied sample was found to be in the substantially increased risk category during initial years with slight decline followed by increase of 25.4% (Table 4).

Table 4
Disease Risk Associated with Waist Circumference after the Onset of Menopause in Lower SES
Waist Circumference (cm)

Risk	*2-3 yrs*		*4-5 yrs*		*6-7 yrs*		*8-9 yrs*		*10-11 yrs*		*12-13 yrs*	
	N	%	N	%	N	%	N	%	N	%	N	%
Low ≥ 79 cm	11	91.7	18	69.2	29	50.0	26	40.0	28	41.8	45	62.5
Increased 80-87 cm	0	0.0	7	26.9	17	29.3	25	38.5	22	32.8	14	19.4
Subs Increased ≥ 88 cm	1	8.3	1	3.8	12	20.7	14	21.5	17	25.4	13	18.1

Post-menopausal women of lower socio-economic strata have shown tendency towards high-risk category (e" 0.85 cm) of waist-to-hip ratio with their percentage observing a trend of increase from 8.3% to 46.3% in the studied sample (Table 5). However, their %age has observed decrease in the very low (d" 0.80 cm).

Table 5
Recommended Standards of Disease risk for the Women Belonging to Lower SES after the Onset of Menopause

Disease risk	*Years after onset of menopause*											
	2-3 yrs		*4-5 yrs*		*6-7 yrs*		*8-9 yrs*		*10-11 yrs*		*12-13 yrs*	
	N	%	N	%	N	%	N	%	N	%	N	%
Very low	10	83.3	17	65.4	20	34.5	19	29.2	15	22.4	22	30.6
Low	1	8.3	7	26.9	19	32.8	16	24.6	21	31.3	21	29.2
High	1	8.3	2	7.7	19	32.8	30	46.2	31	46.3	29	40.3

Figure 1: Percentage Distribution of Post-menopausal Women According to Body Mass Index

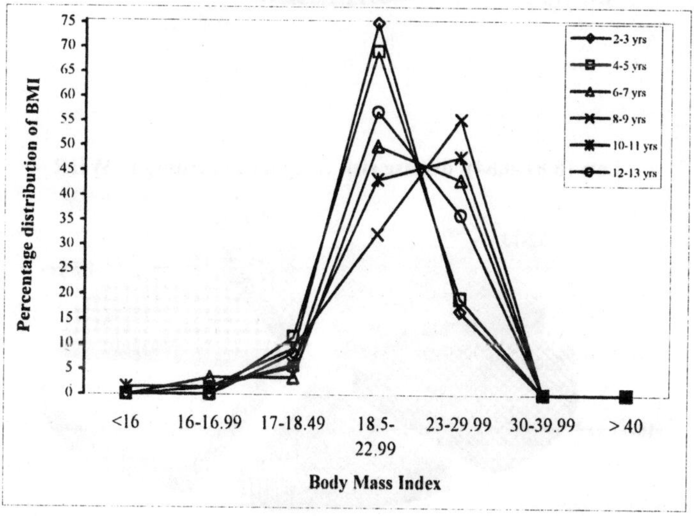

Figure 2: Prevalence of Risk Factors Associated with Waist Circumference after the Onset of Menopause

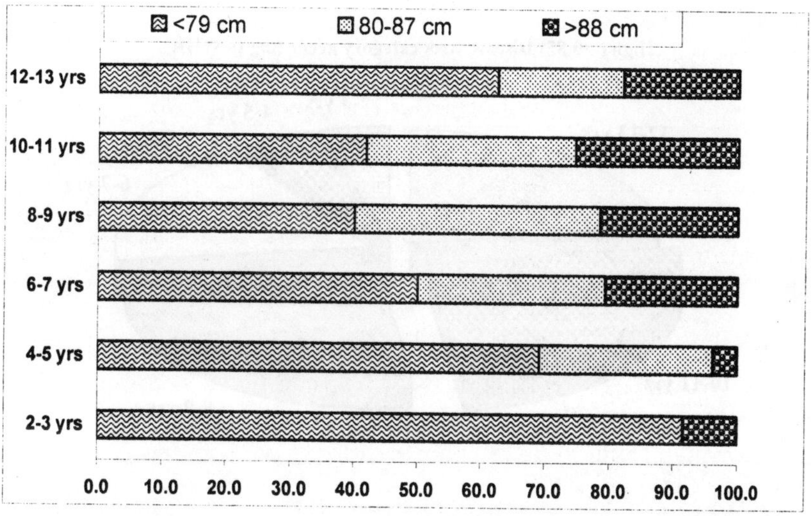

Figure 3: Percentage Distribution of WHR

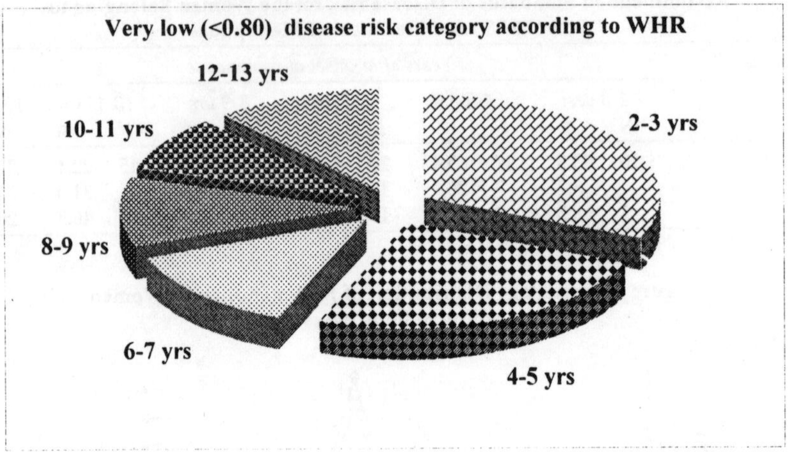

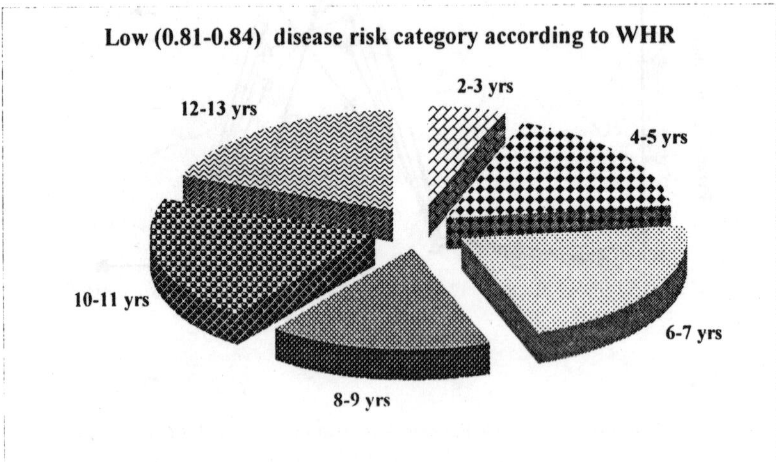

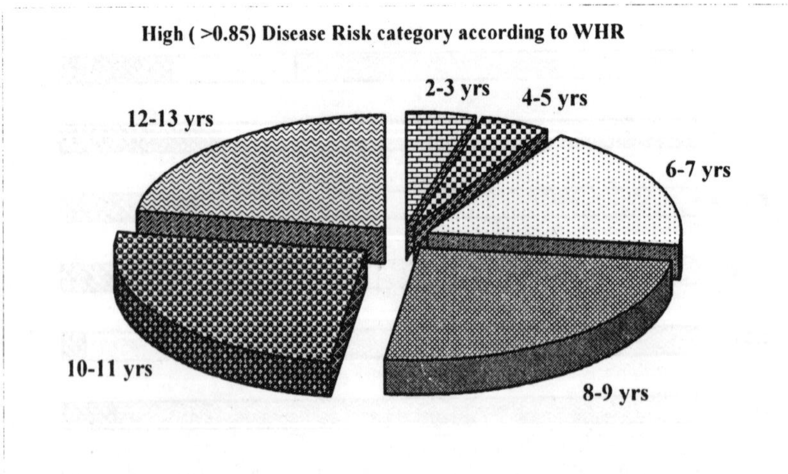

DISCUSSION

The present study indicated the prevalence of abdominal obesity with the onset of menopause as indicated by the waist circumference and WHR. A trend of increase was observed in both waist circumference and WHR over the 10-year period after the onset of menopause in a unfavorable direction as minimal increase in the abdominal obesity favors the CVD risk factors and disease associated with it. BMI has also observed a trend of increase, however compared to the other two indicators of abdominal obesity the BMI has indicated healthy population.

Mishra *et al.* (2001) studied urban slum population of Delhi where WHR was found to be higher in females indicating abdominal adiposity. De Vegt *et al.* (2001), in the Hoorn Study it was observed that waist-to-hip ratio (WHR) and not body mass index (BMI) is an important independent predictor of incident of diabetes in 50–75-y-olds. Rosenthal et al. (2004) studied the Chinese women aged 40-70 year, observed that with increasing central obesity the risk of diabetes also increased, primarily among women with low WHR.

Han *et al.* (1997), has identified that the people with larger waist circumference are at increased risk of cardiovascular diseases. Sobal *et al.* (1989) showed that low-income women from minority groups have the greatest likelihood of being overweight.

Sonnenschein *et al.* (1993) observed that the WHR of middle-aged women are influenced by menopausal status. Bjorntorp, (1993) stated that the increasing WHR with menopause has been to be linked to the possible role of estrogen in the regulation of visceral fat mass in women.

CONCLUSION

The present study conducted on the post-menopausal women of Chandigarh has shown prevalence of abdominal obesity with onset of menopause. Anthropometric parameters for abdominal adiposity such as waist circumference and WHR should be considered while going for clinical check-ups in healthy post-menopausal women. With the onset of menopause they become more susceptible towards cardiovascular disease risk, as redistribution of fat takes place towards abdominal region, it become necessary to investigate them. Socio-economic status and event of menopause seem to play key role in the abdominal obesity among post-menopausal women of lower SES.

REFERENCES

Ashwell M., Cole T.J. and Dixon A.K. (1996), Ratio of Waist Circumference to Hip is a Strong Predictor of Intra-abdominal Fat. *BMJ* 313: 559–60.

Björntorp P. (1992), Abdominal Obesity and the Metabolic Syndrome. *Ann Med* 24: 465-468.

Booth M.L., Hunter C., Gore C.J., Bauman A. and Owen N. (2000), The Relationship between body mass index and waist circumference: implications for estimates of the population prevalence of overweight *Int. J. Obes. Relat Metab Disord* 24:1058–61.

Bouchard C., Bray G.A. and Hubbard V.S. (1990), Basic and Clinical Aspects of Regional Fat Distribution *Am. J. Clin Nutr* 52: 946-950.

Bouchard C. and Johnson F.E. (1988), *Fat Distribution During Growth and Later Healthy Outcomes.* New York: Alan R. Liss, pp.193–201.

Choo V. (2002), WHO Reassesses Appropriate Body-mass Index for Asian Populations. The *Lancet* 20; 360 (9328): 235.

Clasey J.L., Bouchard C., and Teates C.D. (1999), The use of Anthropometric and Dual Energy X-ray Absorptiometry (DXA) Measures to Estimate Abdominal Visceral Fat in Men and Women. *Obes. Res.* 7:256–64.

De Vegt F., Dekker J.M. and Jager A. (2001), Relation of Impaired Fasting and Postload Glucose with Incident Type 2 Diabetes in a Dutch Population: The Hoorn Study. *JAMA* 285: 2109–2113.

Dipietro L., Katz L.D. and Nadel E.R. (1999), Excess Abdominal Adiposity Remains Correlated with Altered Lipid Concentrations in Health Older Women *Int. J. Obes Relat Metab Disord* 23: 432-436.

Fujioka S., Matsuzawa Y., Tokunaga K. and Tarui S. (1987), Contribution of Intra-Abdominal fat Accumulation to the Impairment of Glucose and Lipid Metabolism in Human Obesity. *Metabolism* 36: 54–9.

Garaulet M., Llamas F.P., Fuente T., Zamora S. and Tebar F.J. (2000), Anthropometric, Computed Tomography and Fat Cell Data in an Obese Population: Relationship with Insulin, Leptin, Tumor Necrosis Factor-alpha, Sex Hormone Binding Globulin and Sex Hormones *Eur. J. Endocrinol* 143: 657–66.

Grinker J.A., Tucker K.L., Vokonas P.S. and Rush D. (2000), Changes in Patterns of Fatness in Adult Men in Relation to Serum Indices of Cardiovascular Risk: The Normative Aging Study. *Int. J. Obes Relat Metab Disord* 24: 1369–78.

Groop L. and Orho-Melander M. (2001), The Dysmetabolic Syndrome *J. Intern Med.* 250: 105-120.

Han T.S., McNeill G., Seidell J.C. and Lean M.E. (1997), Predicting Intra-abdominal Fatness from Anthropometric Measures: The Influence of Stature *Int. J. Obes Relat Metab Disord* 21: 587-593.

Han T.S. and Lean M.E.J. (1998), Self-reported Waist Circumference Compared with the 'waist watcher' Tape Measure to Identify Individuals at Increased Health Risk Through Intra-abdominal Fat Accumulation *Br. J. Nutr* 80: 81–8.

Kvist H., Chowhury B., Grangard U., Tylen U. and Sjöström L. (1988), Total and Visceral Adipose Tissue Volumes Derived from Measurements with Computed Tomography in Adult Men and Women: Predictive Equations *Am. J. Clin Nutr* 48: 1351-1361.

Lean M.E.J, Han T.S. and Deurenberg P. (1996), Predicting Body Composition by Densitometry from Simple Anthropometric Measurements *Am. J. Clin Nutr.* 63: 4-14.

Manson J.E., Willet W.C., Stampfer M.J., et al., (1995), Body Weight and Mortality among Women. *New Engl. J. Med.* 333: 677-685.

Millar W.J. and Wigle D.T. (1986), Socio-economic Disparities in Risk Factors for Cardiovascular Diseases. *Can. Med. Assoc. J.* 134: 127-32.

Mishra A., Pandey R., M. Rama Devi, Sharma R., Vikaram N.K. and Khanna N. (2001), High Prevalence of Diabetes, Obesity and Dyslipidaemia in Urban Slum Population in Northern India *Int. J. Obesity* 25: 1722-1729.

Okosun I.S., Chandra K.M., Choi S., Christman J., Dever, G.E. and Prewitt T.E. (2001), Hypertension and Type 2 Diabetes Comorbidity in Adults in the United States: Risk of Overall and Regional Adiposity *Obes. Res.* 9: 1-9.

Okosun I.S., Prewitt T.E. and Cooper R.S. (1999), Abdominal Obesity in the United States: Prevalence and Attributable Risk of Hypertension *J. Hum. Hypertens.* 13: 425-430.

Osukun I.S., Tedders S.H., Choi S. and Dever G.E.A. (2000), Abdominal Adiposity Values Associated with Established Body Mass Indexes in White, Black and Hispanic-Americans. A Study from the Third National Health and Nutrition Examination Survey. *Int. J. Obes. Relat Metab Disord* 24: 1279–85.

Pouliot M.C., Despres J.P. and Lemieux S. (1994), Waist Circumference and Abdominal Sagittal Diameter: Best Simple Anthropometric Indexes of Abdominal Visceral Adipose Tissue Accumulation and Related Cardiovascular Risk in Men and Women *Am. J. Cardiol* 73: 460–468.

Rebufe-Scrive M., Lonnorth P., Wesslau C., Smith U. and Bjorntorp P. (1987), Regional Adipose Tissue Metabolism in Men and Postmenopausal Women. *Int. J. Obesity* 11: 347-355.

Rosenthal A.D., Jin F., Shu X.O., Yang G., Elasy T.A., Chow W.H., Ji B.T., Xu H.X., Li Q, Gao Y.T. and Zheng W. (2004), Body fat Distribution and Risk of Diabetes Among Chinese Women *Int. J. Obesity* 28 (4): 594-599.

Seidell J.C., Perusse L., Despres J.P. and Bouchard C. (2001), Waist and Hip Circumferences have Independent and Opposite Effects on Cardiovascular Disease Risk Factors: The Quebec Family Study *Am. J. Clin. Nutr.* 74: 315–321.

Siedell J.C., Oosterlee A., Deurenberg P., Hautvast J.G.M.J. and Ruys J.H.J. (1988), Abnormal Fat Depots Measured with Computed Tomograph: Effect of Obesity, Sex and Age *Eur. J. Clin Nutr.* 42: 805-807.

Sobal J. and Stunkard A.J. (1989), Socioeconomic Status and Obesity: A Review of Literature. *Phychol. Bull.* 105: 260-275.

Sonnenschein E.G., Kim M.Y., Pasternack B.S. and Toniolo P.G. (1993), Sources of Variability in Waist and Hip Measurements in Middle-aged Women *Am. J. Epidemiol.* 138: 301-309.

Taylor R.W., Keil D., Gold E.J., Williams S.M. and Goulding A. (1998), Body Mass Index, Waist Girth, and Waist-to-hip Ratio as Indexes of Total and Regional Adiposity in Women: Evaluation Using Receiver Operating Characteristic Curves *Am. J. Clin. Nutr.* 67: 44-49.

Turcato E., Bosello O., Francesco V.Di, Harris T.B., Zoico E., Bissoli L. and Fracassi E. (2000), Waist Circumference and Abdominal Sagittal Diameter as Surrogates of Body fat Distribution in the Elderly: Their Relation with Cardiovascular Risk Factors. *Int. J. Obesity* 24; 1005-1010.

Van Pelt R.E., Evans E.M., Schechtman K.B., et al. (2001), Waist Circumference Vs. Body Mass Index for Prediction of Disease Risk in Postmenopansal Women. *Int. J. Obesity* 25: 1183-1188.

Wei M., Gaskill S.P., Haffner S.M. and Stern M.P. (1997), Waist Circumference as the Best Predictor of Noninsulin Dependent Diabetes Mellitus (NIDDM) Compared to Body Mass Index, Waist/hip Ratio over other Anthropometric Measurements in Mexican Americans—a 7-year Prospective Study. *Obes. Res.* 5: 16-23.

Willett M.D., William P.H., Dietz H. and Colditz G.A. (1999), Guidelines for Healthy Weight. *New Engl. J. Med.* 341: 427-434.

9

PATTERNS OF BODY AND ABDOMINAL ADIPOSITY GROWTH IN RELATION TO MENARCHE STATUS IN URBAN AND RURAL PUNJABI ADOLESCENT FEMALES

Krishan Sharma and R. Aggarwal

INTRODUCTION

People develop phenotypic adaptations to the local environments. These include irreversible changes in growth during childhood and adolescence as well as the development of disease immunities that occur even in adulthood (Weissman et al., 1978). Rural to urban migration is one of the most prevalent types of human movement affecting all nations and cultures. The earliest studies of the biology of urban migrants deal with physical growth. The urbanization and industrialization in the early 19th century was associated with decline in health status as measured by height and weight of people (see Tanner, 1981). The review of studies from 1880 to 1920 shows that rural children in the Europe and the U.S.A. were taller than their urban peers (Meredith, 1979; Malina et al., 1981; Steegmann, 1985). The rural height advantage persisted till 1930s after which the urban children are consistently taller and heavier than rural children (Eveleth and Tanner, 1976; Meredith, 1979; Susanne 1984).

The urban children are known to mature earlier for tooth eruption and menarche age (Panek and Piaseck, 1971). Similar trends are observed in relatively less developed countries (ICMR, 1972). The urban resident migrants are generally better educated, of higher socio-economic status, younger, and less traditional in cultural values than rural sedentes (Butterworth and Chance, 1981). These social characteristics correlate positively with physical size and health. There is another aspect of rural-to-urban migration. A large number of migrants to cities in India who come in search of job are either illiterate or less educated. They are employed as labourers or industrial workers in factories or for some other petty jobs. Such people make their homes in slum areas in and around cities. They are relatively at disadvantage than city residents in experiencing benefits of urban environment. These areas are unhygienic and highly congested with very high population density. The physical growth of children in such areas is not significantly better than those living in the impoverished rural areas (Davies et al., 1974; Graham et al., 1979). The urban slum children have been reported to be shorter and lighter than nearby rural children (Malina et al., 1981).

Bogin and MacVean(1981) studied growth and development of three groups of children living in Guatemala city. They observed that urban children from low socio-economic group, living in impoverished areas of the city but not in urban slums, were significantly taller and heavier than rural children of the same age. Similarly urban children of city-born parents were significantly taller than urban children of rural-born migrant parents. However, children with one city-born and one rural-born parent were the tallest. The families of rural-born parents were of significantly lower socio-economic status than families of the other two kinds of parents.

In sum, rural sedentes can be differentiated both socially and biologically from urban-living migrants. The common feeling that rural children are generally at a disadvantage is not universally true, as variability within each group is so great that it is not possible to characterize biologically the typical rural or the average urban migrant. This means that any rural group can be made to look like urban migrants in terms of growth and health. Menarche is the most commonly reported indicator of maturation during adolescence. The fat patterning is associated with morbidity and is independent of the total amount of fat (Hartz et al., 1984). In view of above background, the present study was undertaken to contrast measures of body size and adiposity between urban and rural girls in relation to menarche status.

MATERIALS AND METHODS

A cross-sectional growth data were collected on a sample of urban and rural adolescent girls in the age range of 12 to 15 years from the Khanna town and adjoining rural areas. Place of residence was the inclusive criterion to decide urban or rural status. Khanna town lies between 30°-42′-11″North Latitude and 76°-13′-32″ East Longitude. It has a Municipal Corporation and has been classified as a class I town (Census of India, 2001). Any urban area with a population of 100,000 or more is treated as city and class I town. According to the Revenue Records of Panjab Government, Khanna town was established by Kahana Rajput and derived its name from him. It is a subdivision and tehsil headquarter of the Ludhiana district in the state of Punjab.

The subjects were apparently healthy school going girls. The parents' education levels in urban and rural girls were comparable, but rural sample enjoyed relatively higher monthly income. Agriculture was the major occupation of the subjects' fathers in the rural sample. The mothers were predominantly housewives (95%). In the urban sample, majority of the

Figure 1: Map of Ludhiana District Showing Location of the field Work area

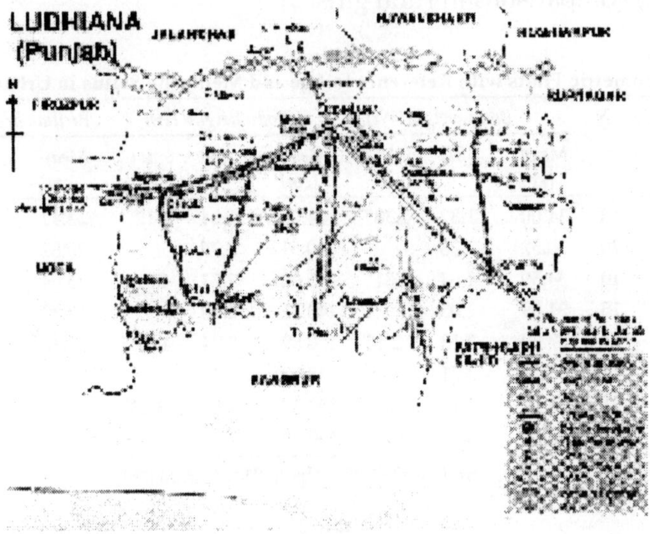

fathers were working either as skilled or unskilled workers and about 18% were professionals. The mothers were mostly housewives (85%).

The routine diet of the subjects included chapattis, vegetables, milk and milk products, pulses, rice and occasionally eggs. The rural subjects had three meals a day, while the urban subjects had a glass of milk in the morning, besides two major meals. Each subject was measured for six anthropometric measurements following methods of Weiner and Lourie (1969). Waist circumference was measured midway between umbilicus and xiphoid levels. Abdomen circumference was measured at umbilicus. The information on menarche status was collected by status-quo method. Body adiposity was studied with the help of three body indices:

(i) Hip adiposity index (HAI)= Hip girth (cm)/(wt(kg)/Ht(m))½

(ii) Abdomen adiposity index (AAI)= Abdomen girth (cm)/(wt(kg)/Ht(m))½

(iii) Waist-Hip-Ratio (WHR)= (Waist girth (cm))×100/Hip girth(cm)

The data were statistically analyzed using tests of mean, standard deviation (SD), coefficient of variation (CV) and t-test to draw inferences.

RESULTS

Table 1 and Table 2 show that post-menarche girls have larger body dimensions than pre-menarche girls. The differences are statistically significant in 11 of 12 (91.7%) comparisons among urban and 10 of 12 (83.3%) comparisons among rural girls.

Table 3 and Table 4 show that both urban and rural post-menarche girls have higher adiposity indices than pre-menarche girls. The differences are statically significant in 7 of 12 (58.33%) comparisons in urban and 5 of 12 (41.67%) comparisons in rural girls.

Table 1
Anthropometric Traits with Reference to Age and Menarche Status in Urban Girls

Age (yrs)	*Menarche status*	*N*	*Body weight(Wt)*			*Body height(Ht)*			*Bi-iliac breadth (BIB)*		
			Mean (kg)	*SD*	*t*	*Mean (cm)*	*SD*	*t*	*Mean (cm)*	*SD*	*t*
12	O	10	34.00	1.82	4.38***	144.00	1.84	4.12***	22.42	0.77	4.40***
	NO	20	30.57	2.38		140.51	2.75		20.82	1.21	
13	O	10	34.50	1.64	3.81***	145.08	1.71	4.81***	23.04	0.73	2.13*
	NO	15	31.69	2.05		140.71	2.80		22.30	1.01	
14	O	11	37.60	2.13	2.45*	150.89	0.94	4.07***	23.46	0.32	4.382***
	NO	14	35.23	2.71		148.93	1.46		22.52	0.72	
15	O	21	38.25	3.16	1.63	153.37	1.88	3.13**	23.76	0.60	5.81***
	NO	9	36.00	3.60		150.60	2.35		22.50	0.52	

O = Occurred, NO = Not-Occurred, *P<0.05, **p<0.01, ***p<0.0001.

Table 2
Anthropometric Traits with Reference to Age and Menarche Status in Rural Females

Age (yrs)	*Menarche status*	*N*	*Body weight(Wt)*			*Body height(Ht)*			*Bi-iliac breadth (BIB)*		
			Mean (kg)	*SD*	*t*	*Mean (cm)*	*SD*	*t*	*Mean (cm)*	*SD*	*t*
12	O	8	37.85	1.34	8.09***	146.64	2.33	5.37***	22.72	0.53	6.82***
	NO	17	33.12	1.54		141.40	2.37		20.65	0.99	
13	O	12	38.66	1.55	3.87***	149.41	2.45	2.21*	23.81	0.93	3.07**
	NO	13	35.27	2.57		147.00	2.79		22.50	1.18	
14	O	15	40.00	1.03	9.30***	152.61	1.77	4.21***	23.72	0.37	8.48***
	NO	10	35.55	1.33		149.50	1.91		22.27	0.47	
15	O	23	41.13	5.71	1.25	156.23	3.25	1.37	24.51	0.51	7.55***
	NO	7	38.00	5.83		154.25	3.37		22.65	0.59	

*p<0.05, **p<0.01, ***p<0.0001.

Table 3
Adiposity Indices with Reference to Age and Menarche Status in Urban Girls

Age (yrs)	*Menarche status*	*N*	*Hip adiposity index (HAI)*			*Abdomen adiposity index (AAI)*			*Waist-hip-ratio index (WHR)*		
			Mean (kg)	*SD*	*t*	*Mean (cm)*	*SD*	*t*	*Mean (cm)*	*SD*	*t*
12	O	10	14.83	0.62	2.55*	14.25	0.65	3.49**	90.35	2.36	1.31
	NO	20	14.22	0.61		13.40	0.59		89.26	1.67	
13	O	10	15.06	0.58	1.06	13.33	0.59	3.09**	90.56	2.44	0.72
	NO	15	14.80	0.65		12.78	0.23		89.92	1.85	
14	O	11	15.93	0.72	3.27**	13.76	0.70	1.63	89.25	4.21	2.10*
	NO	14	14.96	0.75		13.31	0.68		86.31	2.20	
15	O	21	16.07	0.36	4.43***	13.87	0.25	1.03	86.87	3.18	4.89***
	NO	9	15.44	0.35		13.77	0.26		82.67	1.52	

*p<0.05, **p<0.01, ***p<0.0001.

Table 4
Adiposity Indices with Reference to Age and Menarche Status in Rural Girls

Age (yrs)	*Menarche status*	*N*	*Hip adiposity index (HAI)*			*Abdomen adiposity index (AAI)*			*Waist-hip-ratio index (WHR)*		
			Mean (kg)	*SD*	*test value*	*Mean (cm)*	*SD*	*test value*	*Mean (cm)*	*SD*	*test value*
12	O	8	14.97	0.35	3.83***	13.30	0.37	2.81**	89.55	1.62	0.24
	NO	17	14.22	0.63		12.71	0.68		89.38	1.88	
13	O	12	14.72	0.68	1.57	13.59	0.52	0.54	91.21	2.63	0.93
	NO	13	14.27	0.76		13.49	0.41		90.23	2.62	
14	O	15	14.88	0.58	2.66*	13.94	0.71	2.19*	89.22	4.35	0.63
	NO	10	14.21	0.66		13.44	0.38		88.38	2.00	
15	O	23	15.90	0.61	0.78	13.98	0.43	0.89	87.80	1.98	3.34**
	NO	7	15.68	0.66		13.81	0.44		84.85	2.07	

*p<0.05, **p<0.01, ***p<0.0001.

The median age at menarche in urban girls (13.36±1.12 years) is higher than rural girls (12.93±1.09 years). Rural-urban means of various traits were compared by t-tests. These results, depicted in Table 5, show that differences between urban and rural means are statistically significant in 12 of 16 (75%) comparisons for body weight and stature, while in only 9 of 32 (28%) comparisons for pelvic breadth and adiposity indices; thus showing that urban-rural divide is less conspicuous for pelvic width and adiposity indices than body weight and stature. Negative signs of t-tests show that rural females have higher dimensions than their urban counterparts in all age groups.

Table 5
Comparison of Means with t-test between Urban and Rural Means

Age (yrs)	*Menarche status*	*Wt* *t*	*Ht* *t*	*BIB* *t*	*HAI* *t*	*AAI* *t*	*WHR* *t*
12	O	-5.17*	-2.69*	-1.06	-0.58	3.91*	0.85
	NO	-3.79*	-1.05	1.26	0.01	3.28*	-0.20
13	O	-6.11*	-4.73*	-2.13*	1.26	-1.10	-0.60
	NO	-4.10*	-5.93*	-1.26	1.99	-5.58*	-0.41
14	O	-3.45*	-3.20*	-1.94	3.98*	-0.64	0.02
	NO	0.38	-0.79	1.03	2.23*	-0.62	-2.40*
15	O	-2.09*	-3.61*	-4.46*	0.74	0.96	-1.15
	NO	-0.80	-2.44*	-0.53	-0.87	-0.25	-2.34*

*p<0.05.

DISCUSSION

Our data do not support the hypothesis that urban migrants have higher height and body weight than the rural sedentes (ICMR, 1972; Mascie-Taylor, 1984). Anthropometric variables are more related to socio-economic, nutritional, cultural, and genetic factors than mere residential status. The rural children living in the peripheral areas of the cities have liberal access to the boons of urban life like public health services, medical treatment, education services, etc. Consequently, they have higher anthropometric dimensions and nutritional status than peri-urban or urban children when socio-economic differences are controlled (Sharma et al., 2003; Sharma and Sharma, 2005). The results of this study are in consistent with the above generalization.

The variation in timings of pubertal events among individuals within a population is well documented. Menarche occurred after peak-height-velocity in all girls in the Harpenden Growth Study (Tanner et al., 1976). Consequently, post-menarche girls would tend to have higher skeletal dimensions than pre-menarche girls of the same age group. The results of this study are consistent with the above observation.

The anthropometric studies of fat distribution have identified three different body types: gynoid, intermediate, and android. Gynoid type is characterized by lower body fat predominance, and androids are characterized by upper body fat predominance. These anthropometric types constitute a risk factor for morbidity which is independent of total body fat mass (Rimm et al., 1988). The women with a typical gynoid body would have a WHR of 70%. The results of this study show decrease in WHR with increase in age among adolescent urban and rural girls. But in all age groups, mean WHR index was higher than 70% in both pre-and post-menarche girls. Post-menarche girls had higher WHR and AAI than pre-menarche girls. The differences between them were statistically significant in 50% age groups. The results indicate that post-menarche girls have higher abdominal fat than pre menarche girls.

Frisch and Revelle (1971) hypothesized a direct relationship between the attainment of a specific body weight during adolescent spurt and menarche. They proposed that critical body weight of 47 to 48 kg was necessary for menarche to occur. The critical weight hypothesis was later altered (Frisch et al., 1973; Frisch, 1976) to incorporate body composition estimates. The revised hypothesis suggested that critical body component of relative fatness of 22%-24% was necessary for occurrence of menarche. The results of the present study do not support the hypothesis of critical body weight. Mean body weight of post-menarche adolescent girls varied from an average of 37.85 kg at age 12 and 41.13 kg at age 15 years.

Ellison (1981) and Worthman (1993) hypothesized that a median age of menarche was associated with the median age of females when they have biilliac breadth of 24cm. But, pelvic width of 24 cm is not critical for menarche to occur (Ellison, 1981). Our data show that mean pelvic width of post-menarche girls at age 12 is lower than 24 cm, but in later age groups the pelvic breadth is about 24 cm.

To study the effects of attaining menarche on skeletal and adiposity traits, coefficients of variation (CV) were studied with regard to discovering whether there are ontological patterns of change in variation over time. The results of the analysis are given in Table 6. There is consistent increase in CV over time from age 12 to 15 years for body weight in both rural and urban adolescent girls, but for minor variations in certain age groups. The increase in coefficients of variation is 54.39% in post-menarche urban girls, and 28.37% in pre-menarche urban girls from age 12 to 15 years. This increase is 292.1% and 230.1% in post- and pre-menarche rural girls over time in the same age span. Though the trend is similar in rural and urban girls, yet there are significant differences in the magnitude.

Table 6
Coefficient of Variation (CV) for Anthropometric Traits/indices with Reference to Age and Menarche Status

Age (yrs)	*Menarche status*	*CV for Anthropometric Traits and Indices* *Wt*	*Ht*	*BIB*	*HAI*	*AAI*	*WHR*
(A) Urban girls							
12	O	5.35	1.28	3.43	4.20	4.53	2.61
	NO	7.79	1.96	5.81	4.26	4.41	1.87
13	O	4.75	1.18	3.17	3.86	4.42	2.69
	NO	6.47	1.99	4.53	4.37	1.78	2.06
14	O	5.66	0.62	1.36	4.55	5.08	4.72
	NO	7.69	0.98	3.20	5.03	5.10	2.55
15	O	8.26	1.23	2.52	2.23	1.82	3.66
	NO	10.00	1.56	2.31	2.27	1.89	1.84
(B) Rural girls							
12	O	3.54	1.59	2.33	2.34	2.80	1.81
	NO	4.65	1.68	4.79	4.41	5.34	2.10
13	O	4.01	1.64	3.91	4.64	3.85	2.88
	NO	7.29	1.90	5.24	5.32	3.02	2.90
14	O	2.58	1.16	1.56	3.90	5.12	4.88
	NO	3.74	1.28	2.11	4.67	2.86	2.26
15	O	13.88	2.08	2.08	3.83	3.10	2.26
	NO	15.34	2.19	2.60	4.21	3.18	2.44

In contrast to body weight, opposite trend is observed in CVs for bony and adiposity traits. Coefficient of variation for pelvic breadth decreases by 26.53% in post-menarche and 60.24% pre-menarche urban girls and by 10.73% and 45.72% respectively in rural girls from age 12 to 15 years. Similarly, CV for abdomen adiposity index decreases by 59.82% in post-menarche and 52.61% in pre-menarche urban girls. These results indicate that growth responses are complex and synergistic in nature. The urban and rural environment factors seem to play some role for body weight in particular. Table 6 also shows that coefficients of variations are generally lower in post-menarche girls than pre-menarche girls for different bony and adiposity traits. The lowering of CV in post-menarche girls compared to pre-menarche girls indicate that stabilizing selection forces might be separating against lower and higher values of these continuously distributed polygenic traits. These results also indicate the existence of plasticity in these quantitative traits with regard to nutritional, cultural, and other environmental factors, which are known to affect the phenotypic expressions of these traits.

SUMMARY

The study was conducted on a cross-sectional sample of 215 adolescent Punjabi girls (110 urban and 105 rural) ranging in age from 12 to 15 years from Khanna town and adjoining villages. Post-menarche urban and rural adolescent girls had larger body dimensions and adiposity indices than their pre-menarche counterparts. The differences were statistically significant in 18 of 24 (75%) comparisons among rural girls. Median age at menarche was higher in urban girls (13.36±1.12 years) than rural girls (12.93±1.01 years). The differences between urban-rural means were statistically significant in 12 of 16 (75%) comparisons for body weight and stature, while in only 9 of 32 (56.25%) comparisons for pelvic breadth and adiposity indices. In general, rural females had larger body and fat dimensions than their urban counterparts. Coefficient of variation (CV) increased over time from 12 to 15 years for body weight in both urban and rural girls. On the contrary, CV decreased for stature, pelvic breadth and adiposity indices. These results indicated the existence of general plasticity in these polygenic continuously distributed traits and operation of selection forces.

REFERENCES

Bogin B. and MacVean R.B. (1981), Bio-social Effects of Migration on the Development of Families and Children in Guatemalan Children. *American Journal of Public Health* 71:1373-1377.

Butterworth D. and Chance J.K. (1981), *Latin American Urbanization.* Cambridge: Cambridge University Press.

Census of India (2001), *Series 4.Punjab Provisional Population Totals.* Punjab: Director of Census Operation.

Davies C.T.M., Mbelwa D. and Dore C. (1974), Physical Growth and Development of Urban and Rural East African Children, Aged 7-16. *Annals of Human Biology* 1:257-268.

Ellison P.T. (1981), Threshold Hypothesis, Developmental Age and Menstrual Function. *American Journal of Physical Anthropology* 54: 337-340.

Eveleth P.B. and Tanner J.M. (1976), *World-Wide Variations in Human Growth.* Cambridge: Cambridge University Press.

Frisch R.E. (1976), Fatness of Girls from Menarche to Age 18 years, with a Nomogram. *Human Biology* 48:353-359.

Frisch R.E. and Revelle R. (1971), Height and weight at Menarche and a Hypothesis of Menarche. *Arch Dis Child* 46: 695-701.

Frisch R.E., Revelle R. and Cook S. (1973), Components of weight at Menarche and he Initiation of Adolescent Growth Spurt in Girls: Estimated Total Water, Lean Body weight and fat. *Human Biology* 45: 469-483.

Graham G.G., MacLean W.C. Jr., Kallman C.H., Rabold J. and Mellits E.D. (1979), Growth Standards for Poor Urban Children in Nutrition Studies. *American Journal of Clinical Nutrition* 32:703-710.

Hartz A.J., Rupley D.C. and Rimm A.A. (1984), The Association of Girth Measurements with Disease in 32,856 Women. *American Journal of Epidemiology* 119: 71-80.

ICMR (1972), *Growth and Physical Development of Indian Infants and Children.* Technical Report Series no. 18. New Delhi: Indian Council of Medical Research.

Malina R.M., Himes J.H., Stepick C.D., Lopez F.G. and Buschang P.H. (1981), Growth of Urban and Rural Children in the Valley of Oaxaca, Mexico. *American Journal of Physical Anthropology* 55: 269-280.

Mascie-Taylor C.G.N. (1984), The Interaction between Geographical and Social Mobility. In Boyce A.J. (ed.): *Migration and Mobility.* London: Taylor and Francis, pp. 161-178.

Meredith H.V. (1979), Comparative Findings on Body size of Children and Youth Living at Urban Centers and in Rural areas. *Growth* 43:95-104.

Panek S. and Piaseck M. (1971), Nowa Huta: Integration of the Population in the Light of Anthropometric Data. *Materialyi Prace Anthropology* 80:1-249.

Rimm A.A., Hartz A.J. and Fischer M.E. (1988), A Weight Shape Index for Assessing Risk of Disease in 44,820 Women. *Journal of Clinical Epidemiology* 41:459-465.

Sharma K., Banerjee B.G. and Aggarwal R. (2003), Sexual Maturation, Anthropometric, and Physiological Variations Among Urban and Rural Punjabi Girls. In Kalla A.K. and Bhattacharya D.K. (eds.): *Understanding People of India: Anthropological Insight.* Delhi: Department of Anthropology, Delhi University, pp. 58-67.

Sharma K. and Sharma P. (2005), Adolescent Growth Trends in Urban and Rural Punjabi Girls from Gurdaspur. *South Asian Anthropologist* 5: 209-216.

Steegmann A.T., Jr. (1985), 18th Century British Military Stature: Growth Cessation, Selective Recruiting, Secular Trends, Nutrition at Birth, Cold, and Occupation. *Human Biology* 57:77-85.

Susanne C. (1984), Biological Differences between Migrants and Non-migrants. In A.J. Boyce (ed): *Migration and Mobility.* London: Taylor and Francis, pp: 179-195.

Tanner J.M. (1981), *A History of the Study of Human Growth.* Cambridge: Cambridge University Press.

Tanner J.M., Whitehouse R.H., Marubini E. and Resele L.F. (1976), The Adolescent Growth Spurt of Boys and Girls of the Harpenden Growth Study. *Annals of Human Biology* 3:109-126.

Weiner J.S. and Lourie A. (eds.) (1969), *Human Biology: A Guide to Field Methods*. Oxford: Blackwell.

Weissman I.L., Hood L.E. and Wood W.B. (1978), *Essential Concepts in Immunobiology*. Melno Park: Benjamin/Cummings.

Worthman C.M. (1993), Biocultural interactions in Human Development. In Pereira M.E. and Fairbanks L.A. (eds.): *Juvenile Primates: Life History, Development and Behavior*. New York: Oxford University Press, pp. 339-357.

10

PHYSICAL GROWTH AND NUTRITIONAL STATUS OF SCHEDULED CASTE CHILDREN OF NARAINGARH TEHSIL, AMBALA DISTRICT, HARYANA

Indu Talwar, Payal, Updesh and Preeti Bajwa

INTRODUCTION

Health is a crucial attribute of human resource and a healthy human population is the most desired national asset. The health and nutritional status of a population is reflected in the growth of its children. Malnutrition is the major health problem in the developing countries like India. Prospective studies in India have shown the dramatic increased risk of death among severely malnourished children (Rohde, 1996). Most of these deaths are due to the synergistic action of undernutrition and infections. The synergism of hunger and disease leaves its marks on those who survive past childhood resulting in growth retardation in either height, weight or both, reduced mental capacity and reduced work capacity. Vast majority of such children are from underprivileged sections of our society. Many studies have shown that preventing all grades of malnutrition is a powerful strategy for improving child survival (Sharma, 1992; Gaur and Singh, 1994; Pelletier, 1994; Schroeder and Brown, 1994; Gaur et. al., 1995; Schroeder and Martorell, 1997; Fawazi et. al., 1997; Yoon et. al., 1997; Monyeki et. al., 2000; Maninder and Talwar, 2000; Ghosh et. al., 2001; Llyod and Lederman, 2002).

The present study reports on the growth status and nutritional status of scheduled caste children aged 6 to 12 years, belonging to Tehsil Nariangarh, District Ambala of Haryana.

MATERIAL AND METHODS

The present study is based on a cross-sectional sample of 299(154 boys and 145 girls) scheduled caste children ranging in age from 6 to 12 years.

The data were derived from the Government primary and Senior Secondary Schools at village Laha, Bhurewaland and proper Nariangarh tehsil of Ambala district of Haryana. The majority of parents of sample children were uneducated. The percentage of illiteracy was more among mothers (61.68%) than among fathers (38.00%). Majority of fathers were engaged in manual labour (85.40%) some worked as skilled workers like carpenter, driver, cobbler etc. (10.60%) and only 4.00% of them were engaged in agricultural work in their own fields. Most of mothers were housewives and were looking after the livestock. Only 15.00% mothers worked as labourers in the fields. Most of the subjects were living in kuchha houses and had no access to modern facilities. All subjects included in this sample were apparently normal and had not suffered from any chronic illness in the near past.

The anthropometric measurements taken on each subject included weight, stature, head circumference, chest circumference, upper arm circumference and triceps skinfold. All measurements were taken using standard instruments following Weiner and Lourie (1981). Besides, general information about the type of family, number of children, caste, education, occupation and income was collected. To have a rough estimate of food habits a 24 hour dietary recall method suggested by Weiner and Lourie (1981) was employed.

The nutritional assessment has been done with the help of anthropometric method using stature and weight as two basic measurements. The derived indices used here for assessing nutritional status are weight for age (wt/age), stature for age (st/age) and weight for stature (wt/st), upper arm circumference for age (ac/age) and triceps skinfold for age (tsf/age) following the recommendations of World Health Organization (WHO, 1986). Wt/age indicates disturbances in the linear growth and body proportions. Ht/age and wt/ht are indicators of past and current nutritional status, respectively. They are primary and useful indicators when used together for the assessment of nutritional status (Trowbridge et.al., 1980; WHO, 1986). The reference standards used for calculating these indices were those developed by National Centre for Health Statistics (NCHS) USA (Hamill et.al., 1979; Waterlow et.al., 1977; Jelliffe, 1966). The nutritional status was calculated as z scores or SD scores using NCHS reference data following Waterlow et.al., 1977. The cut off points for mild, moderate and severe malnutrition for the z scores of these indices were -1.1 to -2.0 SD, -2.0 to -3.0 SD and -3.1 to -4.0 SD respectively. Cut off points for upper arm circumference for age and triceps skinfold for age was less than 90%, 80% and 60% of the standard for mild, moderate and severe malnutrition following Jelliffe (1966), using the reference standards developed by Frisancho(1974). Triceps skinfold and upper arm circumference are useful in evaluating the relative deficits of fat vs. muscle and of calorie versus protein deficiency (Gurney and Jelliffe, 1973).

Age determination proved to be time consuming but considerable effort was made to ascertain age as accurately as possible. The date of birth of each subject was recorded from the school register and all doubtful cases were excluded. The ages were calculated from the dates of birth to the dates of examination using Decimal age calendar (Tanner et. al., 1966). The data were divided into seven yearly groups.

DIETARY HABITS

The 24 hour recall of types and frequency of food consumed revealed that the staple food of scheduled caste children was wheat. Their diet was mainly based on cereals, pulses, roots, tubers and vegetables. Rice was used in less frequency mainly at dinner time along with pulses. Milk was a part of the diet of many boys though in small quantity due to economic reasons but for majority of girls tea was the only beverage taken along with wheat chapattis made in the morning. During lunch they usually had chapattis with vegetables mostly potatoes. Eggs, meat and fruits were the least frequently consumed items. The frequency of protein rich food was very less in their diet due to being costly. Moreover, their calorie intake was found to be inadequate.

RESULTS

Growth Status

Table 1 presents the descriptive statistics of various anthropometric measurements of sample children with age and sex. As is evident from the table the bodily dimensions of sample children witnessed an increasing trend with advancing age except for triceps skinfold thickness which showed a fluctuating trend. Our results indicate that boys were heavier than girls at almost all ages but significantly greater differences were obtained at 6, 7, 9 and 12 years. ($p<0.05$) Sample boys were also taller than sample girls at all ages except for 8 and 10 years when girls report significantly higher mean values. Girls show inferior growth in head circumference than boys but significant differences were reported at 7, 8, 9 and 11 years. In chest circumference boys showed superior growth at all ages. Boys exhibited greater mean values than girls for upper arm circumference at 7, 9 and 12 years but the differences were not significant. Mean triceps skinfold thickness was significantly more in girls at all ages except for 9 and 11 years when boys report significantly higher values.

Nutritional Status

The nutritional status of scheduled caste children was assessed using various anthropometric indices namely weight deficit for age, stature deficit for age and weight for stature expressed as z scores below the reference median. Table 2 gives the age and sex specific mean z scores according to wt/age, st/age and wt/st.

Table 1
Means and SD of Various Anthropometric Measurements of Scheduled Caste Childern of Tehsil Naraingarh By Age and Sex

Measurements	*Sex*	*6 (N=23,20) MEAN+ SD*	*7 (N=22,22) MEAN+SD*	*8 (N=22,21) MEAN+SD*	*9 (N=22,22) MEAN+SD*	*10 (N=22,20) MEAN+SD*	*11 (N=22,20) MEAN+SD*	*12 (N=21,20) MEAN+SD*
Weight	M	16.80+2.43	19.75+2.03	21.11+2.73	23.54+3.02	25.34+4.42	27.92+3.67	31.30+5.44
	F	15.58+2.00	17.03+1.82	21.40+4.42	21.40+2.68	25.57+4.90	26.70+5.69	29.50+6.36
Height	M	107.16+6.43	115.63+4.73	118.86+6.19	126.40+4.76	131.33+7.18	136.04+7.44	140.23+5.16
	F	104.84+6.65	112.62+5.05	122.04+10.01	123.87+6.36	133.49+6.34	135.95+9.17	140.32+7.88
Head Circumference	M	48.16+2.21	49.22+1.70	48.46+1.82	50.04+2.16	50.61+2.19	51.10+1.64	50.98+1.76
	F	48.18+2.81	47.87+1.49	47.51+2.61	49.27+1.56	50.05+2.84	50.52+1.99	51.31+3.38
Chest Circumference	M	52.02+3.02	54.50+2.11	55.13+3.39	58.66+4.37	58.96+3.15	59.87+3.55	60.68+9.07
	F	50.32+2.51	50.72+2.69	53.23+3.30	52.51+2.99	56.83+5.25	56.56+4.64	56.44+3.51
Upper Arm Circumference	M	13.95+1.19	14.61+1.04	14.61+0.91	16.00+1.86	16.21+1.75	16.87+1.17	17.73+1.96
	F	14.31+0.91	14.19+0.94	15.41+1.77	15.25+0.97	16.40+2.14	16.89+2.15	17.04+2.06
Triceps Skinfold	M	5.88+1.21	5.30+1.14	5.25+0.59	6.52+1.82	6.61+1.41	7.16+1.08	6.60+1.71
	F	6.71+1.40	5.93+1.55	5.68+1.67	5.76+1.42	6.92+2.17	6.65+1.86	7.77+2.57

$p < 0.05$*

Table 2
Mean ±SD of Z-Scores by Age and Sex for Anthropometric Indicators of Nutritional Status in Scheduled Caste Children of Naraingarh Tehsil

Age Group (Yrs.)	*N*	*Weight/Age*		*Stature/Age*		*Weight/Stature*	
		Mean	*SD*	*Mean*	*SD*	*Mean*	*SD*
6	M 23	-1.69	1.05	-1.83	1.31	-0.75	0.56
	F 20	-1.61	1.21	-2.09	1.19	-0.82	1.36
7	M 22	-1.18	0.76	-1.19	0.89	-0.51	1.07
	F 22	-1.58	1.07	-1.51	0.86	-0.96	0.80
8	M 22	-1.35	0.88	-1.51	1.15	-0.42	0.82
	F 21	-0.99	1.29	-0.64	1.81	-1.44	0.91
9	M 22	-1.29	0.88	-0.85	1.01	-0.69	1.14
	F 22	-1.30	0.98	-1.09	1.19	-1.06	0.79
10	M 22	-1.32	0.96	-1.01	1.27	-0.96	1.26
	F 20	-1.61	0.61	-0.68	0.86	-1.55	0.84
11	M 22	-1.32	0.66	-1.09	1.11	-0.87	1.02
	F 20	-1.72	0.84	-1.26	1.31	-1.38	-0.78
12	M 21	-1.42	0.67	-1.25	0.68	-0.79	1.04
	F 20	-1.95	0.59	-1.54	1.19	-1.52	0.63

$p < 0.05^{*}$

It is clear from the table that majority of children have z scores between -1 and-2 SD below the reference median for wt/age and st/age. However at 6 years in st/age girls had z scores more than-2 SD below the reference median. The mean values for z scores for wt/st for scheduled caste boys range between -1 SD or below where as for girls it ranges between -1 SD and -1.55 from 8 to 12 years. However t values reveal significant differences between z scores of boys and girls for wt/age at 12 years and wt/st at 8 and 12 years respectively ($p<0.05$). Thus majority of children show some degree of malnutrition.

The percentage distribution of scheduled caste children in different z scores categories according to various indicators of malnutrition by sex has been presented in table 3. It is evident from the table that frequency of children classified as normal (with z scores of -1 SD or less) was maximum by weight for stature (43.20%) and minimum by weight for age (27.20%). Malnourished children with z scores of -2 SD or less showed percentages of 28.50%, 28.10% and 13.50% respectively, according to wt/age, st/age and wt/st. It is clearly indicated that the percentage of stunted children (28.10%) was more than those with wasting (13.50%). Regarding the sex differences it was found that the percentage of boys and girls classified as malnourished were 24.03%, 25.30%, 9.80% and 33.10%, 31.03% and 17.20% respectably according to wt/age, st/age and wt/st. The prevalence of both stunting and wasting is considerably more in girls of the same chronological age. They also show a higher incidence of under weight for age.

Malnutrition as defined by arm circumference for age occurred in about 95.60% of scheduled caste children. A majority of these children (68.00%)

Table 3
Prevalence (%) of Malnutrition in Scheduled Caste Children of Tehshil Naraingarh by Sex.

Anthropometric Index	*Males*		*Females*		*Sexes*	*Combined*
	N	%	N	%	N	%
Weight/Age						
>- IS.D. Scores	51	33.12	31	21.37	82	27.24
-1 To -2 S.D. Scores	66	42.85	66	45.52	132	44.18
-2 To -3 S.D. Scores	37	24.03	45	31.04	82	27.54
<-3 S.D. Scores	0	0.00	3	2.07	3	1.03
Stature/Age (Stunting)						
>- IS.D. Scores	66	42.86	55	37.93	121	40.39
-1 To -2 S.D. Scores	48	31.82	45	31.04	93	31.43
-2 To -3 S.D. Scores	26	16.88	36	24.82	62	20.85
<-3 S.D. Scores	13	8.44	9	6.21	22	7.32
Weight/Stature (Wasting)						
>-IS.D. Scores	92	59.70	38	26.72	130	43.21
-1 To -2 S.D. Scores	47	30.50	58	50.00	105	40.25
-2 To -3 S.D. Scores	14	9.10	18	15.52	32	12.31
<-3 S.D. Scores	1	0.70	2	1.72	3	1.21
ARM Circumference						
>90%	7	4.54	6	4.14	13	4.34
80-90%	46	29.87	34	23.45	80	26.66
60-80%	100	64.94	105	72.42	205	68.68
<60%	1	0.65	0	0.00	1	0.32
Triceps Skinfold						
>90%	13	8.44	1	0.69	14	4.56
80-90%	12	7.79	10	6.90	22	7.34
60-80%	62	40.26	35	24.14	97	32.20
<60%	67	43.59	99	62.28	166	55.89

were moderately malnourished and the rest (26.60%) were mildly malnourished. Incidence of moderately (72.40%) malnourished girls was higher than boys (64.90%).

Nearly 95.00% children showed malnutrition according to triceps skinfold for age. The percentage of severely malnourished children (55.90%) was significantly higher than those evaluated by other methods. Girls showed a higher incidence of malnutrition by this indicator (68.20%).

DISCUSSION

Changes in body dimensions reflect the overall health and welfare of individuals and populations. Child growth is determined primarily by food intake, genetic potential and the experience of infection and may be affected by other factors such as stress and exercise levels (Ferro-Luzzi, 1984; Mata, 1985). Growth assessment is the single measurement that best defines the health status of children because disturbances in health and nutrition, regardless of their aetiology, invariably affecs child growth.

To study the population differences in growth patterns mean heights and weights of scheduled caste children have been compared with NCHS standards and various Indian populations.

The weight curves of scheduled caste boys when compared with similar curves for NCHS coincide the 10th percentiles at almost all ages whereas these fluctuate between 5th and 10th percentiles in the case of girls (Fig. 1a, b).

Figure 1(a): Weight of Scheduled Caste Boys, Related to NCHS Percenties

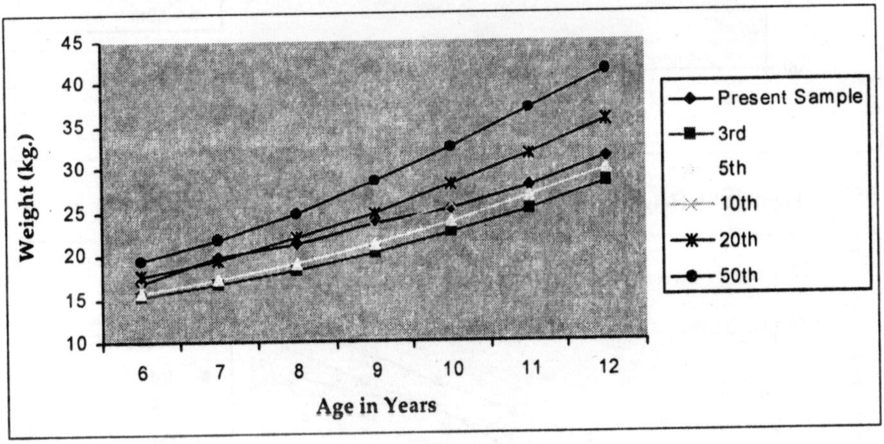

Figure 1(b): Weight of Scheduled Caste Girls, Related to NCHS Percenties

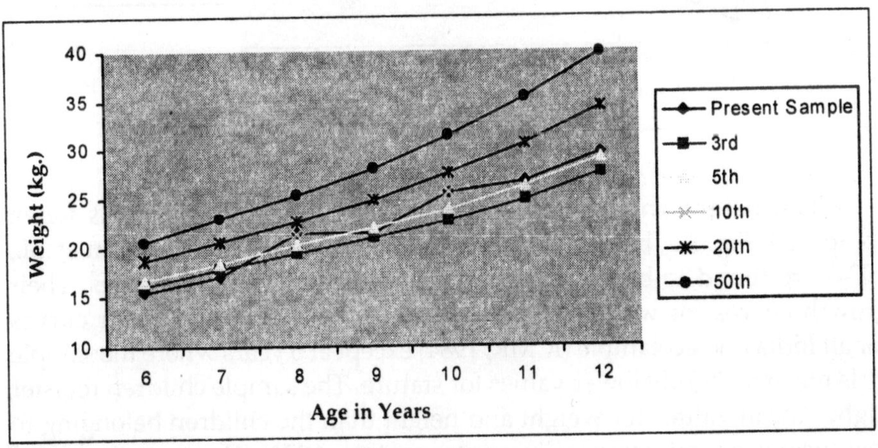

The height curve of scheduled caste boys and girls (Fig. 2a, b) start from 3rd percentile of NCHS curves at 6 years and fluctuate between 10th and 20th percentile to finally reach the 10th percentile at 12 years in case of boys and 5th percentile in case of girls. The inferior growth status of scheduled caste children may be attributed to the adverse socio-economic conditions and inadequate, faulty nutrition available to them.

Figure 2(a): Height of Scheduled Caste Boys, Related to NCHS Percenties

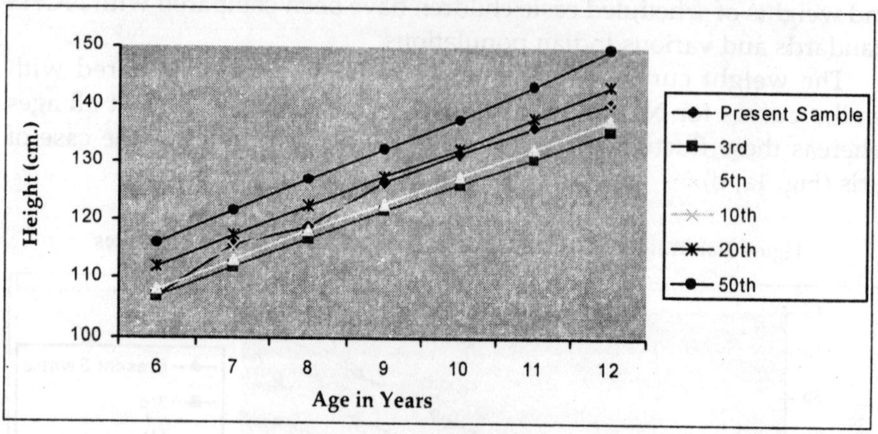

Figure 2(b): Height of Scheduled Caste Girls, Related to NCHS Percenties

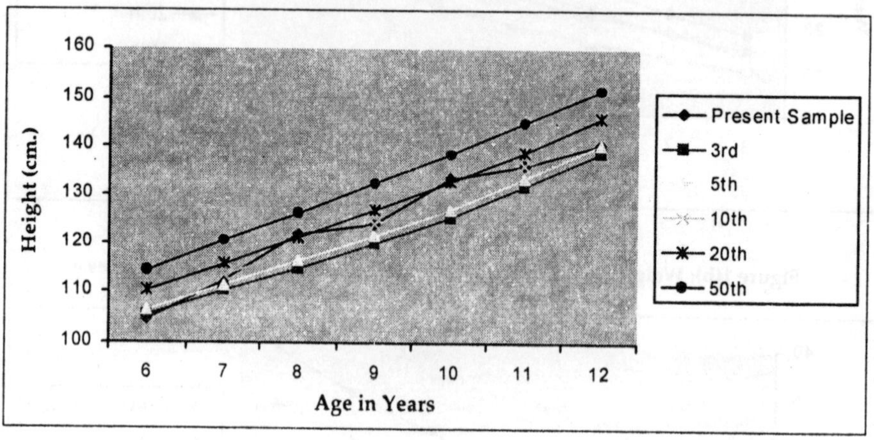

Mean height and weight of scheduled caste boys and girls when compared (Fig. 3 a, b; 4a, b) with well to do children (Vijayraghvan et. al., 1974) are found to be considerably shorter and lighter at all ages. Their growth curves for weight and height run well above the similar curves for all India pooled sample (ICMR, 1984) except at 6 years where the sample girls register slightly lower values for stature. The sample children register higher mean values for weight and height than the children belonging to low socio-economic status (Vijayraghvan et. al., 1974). Their weight curves run slightly above the weight curves of rural scheduled caste boys of Ropar District (Gaur, 1995) except for 11 years. Where as, for height sample boys register lesser mean values at 6, 7, 11 ands 12 years. The sample girls register slightly more values for weight at 7, 8 and 10 years and for height at 8 and 10 years than scheduled caste girls from Ropar. Thus population differences in height during adolescence in equal genetic constitution would reflect

Figure 3(a): Comparison of Weight of Scheduled Caste Boys of Nariangarh with well Nourished, Low Socioeconomic Inidan, Rural Ropar Boys

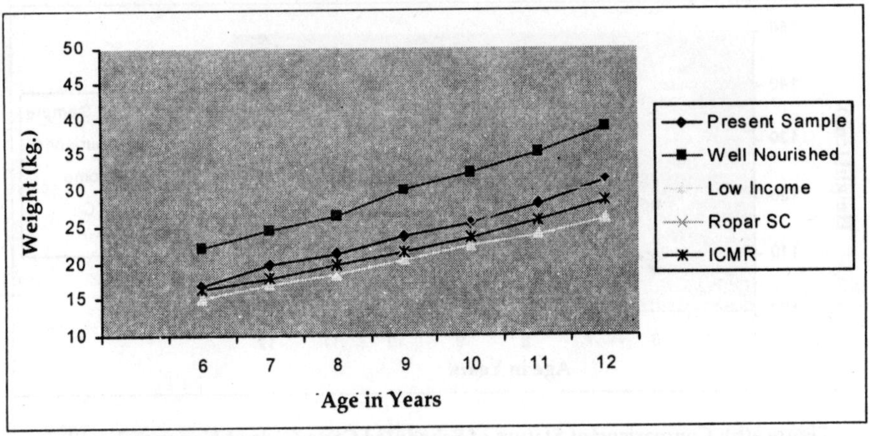

Figure 3(b): Comparison of Weight of Scheduled Caste Girls of Nariangarh with well Nourished, Low Socioeconomic Inidan, Rural Ropar Girls

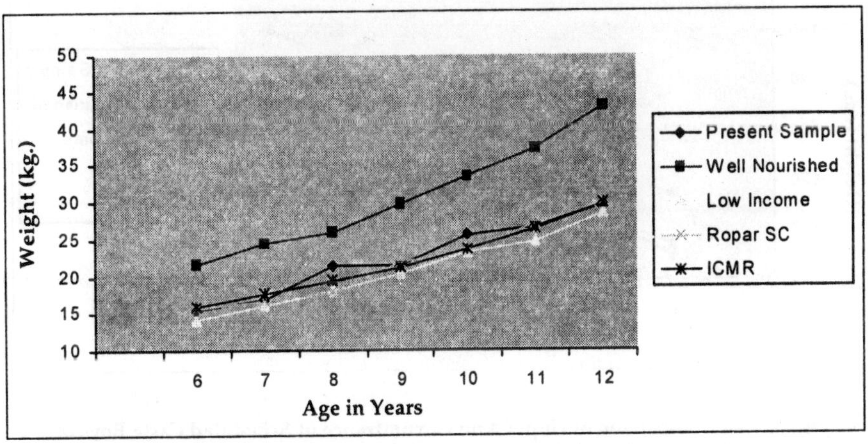

the effect of chronic under nutrition suffered during childhood and the role of genetic factors in growth is overridden by the influence of environmental factors (Frisancho et. al., 1975).

Comparison of mean upper arm circumference of scheduled caste boys and girls with the Standard reported for American Whites (Frisancho, 1974) and well to do Indians (Vijayraghvan et. al., 1974) reveals a poor performance of the sample children (Fig. 5a, b). Sample boys exhibit almost similar values but sample girls register lower mean values than their counterparts from low socio-economic status for upper arm circumference. When compared to scheduled caste boys and girls from Ropar District (Gaur et al., 1995) sample boys exhibit slightly lower mean values than them at almost all ages but girls exhibit almost similar values.

Figure 4(a): Comparison of Stature of Scheduled Caste Boys of Nariangarh with well Nourished, Low Socioeconomic Inidan, Rural Ropar Boys

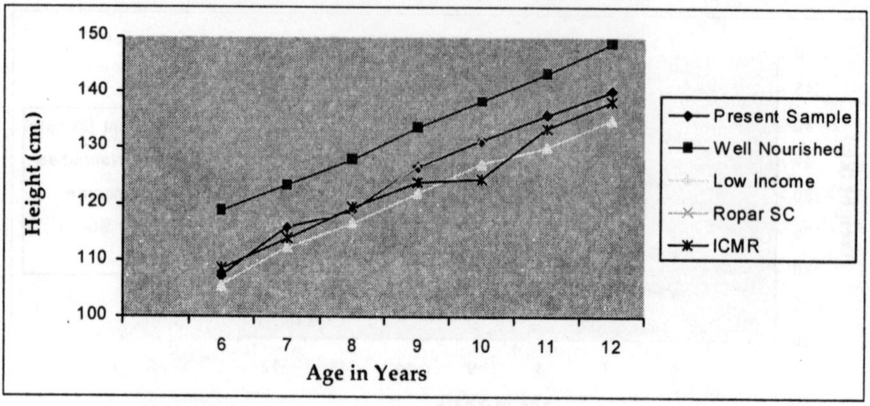

Figure 4(b): Comparison of Stature of Scheduled Caste Girls of Nariangarh with well Nourished, Low Socioeconomic Inidan, Rural Ropar Girls

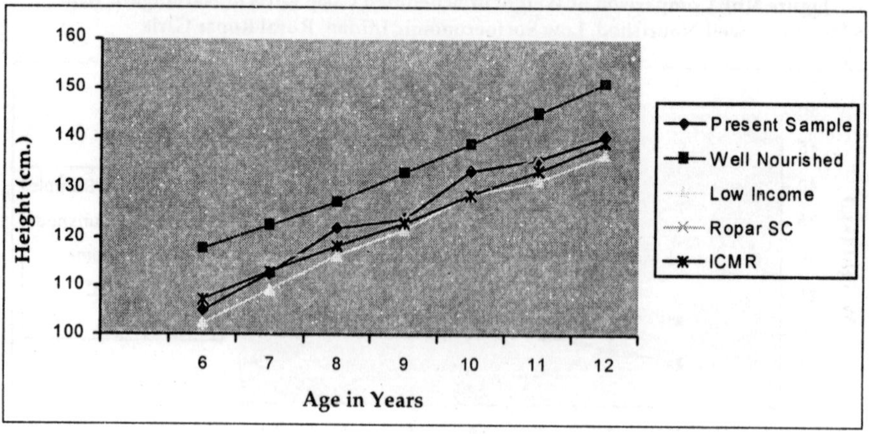

Figure 5(a): Comparison of Upper Arm Circumfrence of Scheduled Caste Boys of Nariangarh with Frisancho Standards and Rural Roper Boys

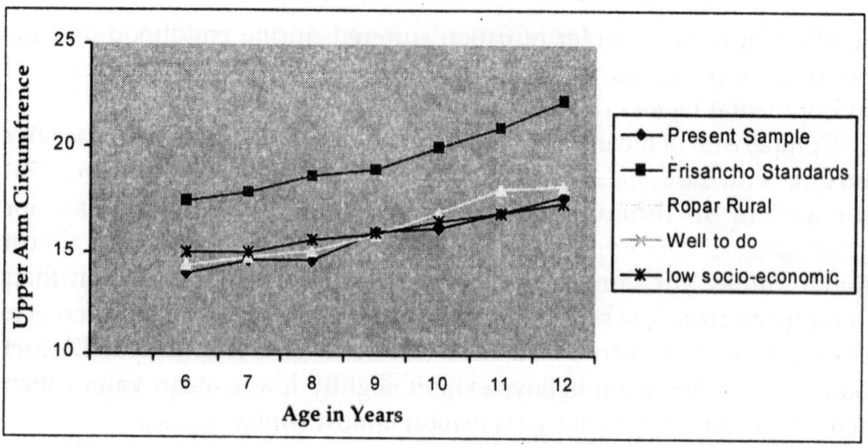

Figure 5(b): Comparison of Upper Arm Circumfrence of Scheduled Caste Girls of Nariangarh with Frisancho Standards and Rural Ropar Girls

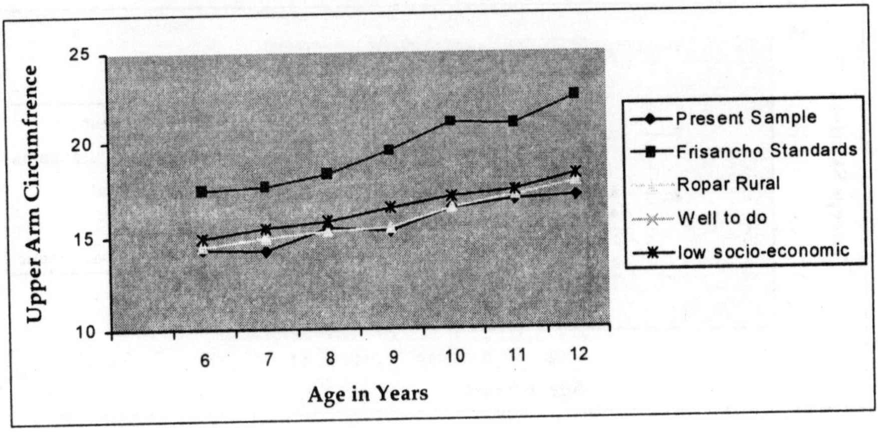

The mean values from triceps skinfold thickness of sample children were distinctly less than the Standard reported for American Whites (Frisancho, 1974) (Fig. 6a, b). The difference in subcutaneous fatness between sample children and well to do Indians suggest that different environmental agents are operating in children belonging to different socio-economic groups. The low fat resources in the present sample seem to have close relationships with their dietary intake. Under conditions of nutritional restrictions, body fat and muscles are utilized by the organism as sources of calories and amino acids for the production of protein. For these reasons the amount of body fat and muscles act as a proxy for protein and calorie reserve (Gurney and Jelliffe, 1973). Thus the children from higher socio-economic group have either more calorie intake or low energy expenditure and can be expected more advanced developmentally than a normal child.

Figure 6(a): Comparison of Triceps Skinfolds of Scheduled Caste Boys of Nariangarh with Frisancho Standards and Rural Ropar Boys

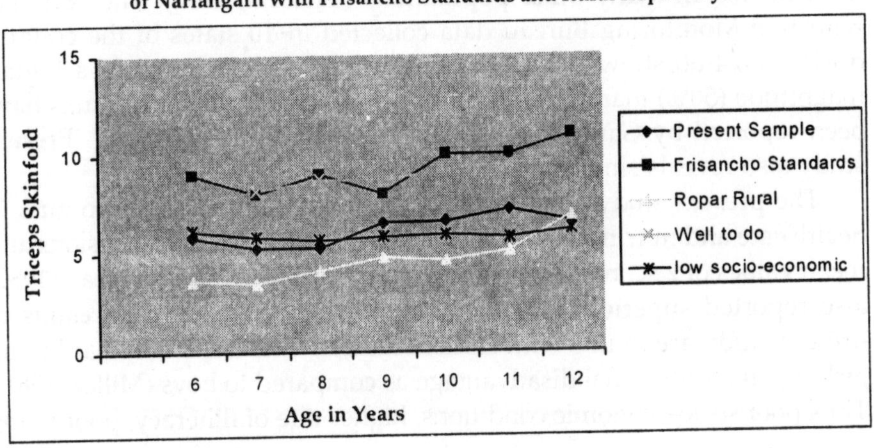

Figure 6(b): Comparison of Triceps Skinfolds of Scheduled Caste Girls of Nariangarh with Frisancho Standards and Rural Ropar Girls

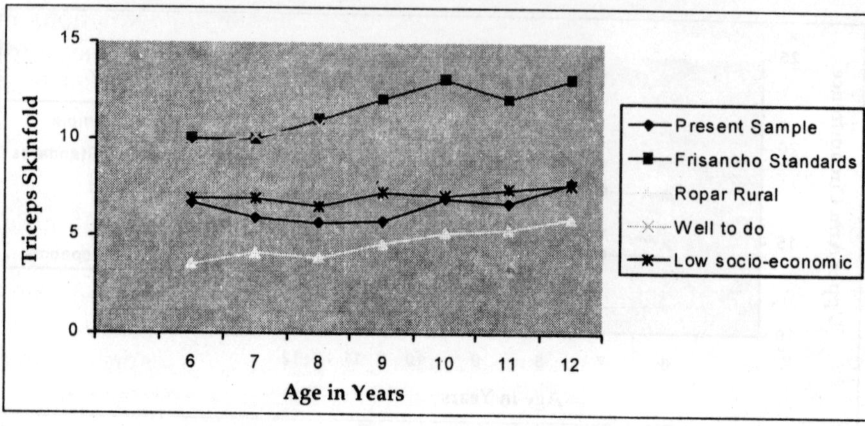

Biological, epidemiological and statistical evidence suggest that wasting and stunting represent different processes of malnutrition. As far as nutritional assessment was concerned the frequency of stunting was more than wasting in both boys and girls, but girls showed a higher incidence than boys. Stunting reflects long term growth faltering and wasting reflects an acute or recent growth disturbance. Wasting also indicates a deficit in tissue and fatness compared with the amount expected for a child of same height and may result either from weight loss or from failure to gain weight. Underweight children reflect a combination of disturbances in linear growth and body proportions. Sample children seem to be affected due to impaired nutrition during infancy and early childhood leading to deficit in attained stature. This is clearly linked to their inadequate dietary intake which was deficient in skeletal nutrients such as calcium, nitrogen, phosphorus and proteins required during growing periods and may be direct factors in growth in height.

A high prevalence of stunting with low prevalence of wasting has been documented in many other populations (Victoria, 1992). The National Nutrition Monitoring Bureau data collected in 10 states of the country during 1974-80 showed that the prevalence of stunting is of a higher magnitude (50%) than wasting (Sastry et al., 1989). Similar findings have been reported by Gaur, 1994 on Metei children from Manipur. Present study also reveals similar findings.

The present study suggests a differential treatment given to girls in health care and nutrition as is reflected in anthropometric dimensions and mean values of z scores for wt/age, st/age and wt/st. Brown et. al. (1982) also reported superior anthropometric indices for boys. The results of present study are in line with earlier studies which conclude that Indian girls are at a nutritional disadvantage as compared to boys (Miller, 1981). Thus poor socio-economic conditions, higher rate of illiteracy, poor living conditions, inadequate and impaired nutrition, lack of health and nutritional education seem to be the probable factors for the poor nutritional status of scheduled caste children. Significant reductions in child mortality and morbidity can be expected when appropriate measures are taken at younger ages by quickly identifying the degree of malnutrition and providing them with supplementation.

SUMMARY

Physical growth and nutritional status of 299 (154 boys and 145 girls) scheduled caste children from Naraingarh Tehsil, ranging in age from 6 to 12 years and belonging to low socio-economic backgrounds was evaluated with the help of selected anthropometric measurements. Information on 24 hour dietary recall was also obtained. Mean weight of sample children fluctuated between 5th and 10th percentiles of NCHS reference standard. Their mean stature coincided the 3rd percentiles of NCHS reference data at 6 years and fluctuated between 10th and 20th percentiles to finally reach 10th percentile at 12 years in case of boys and 5th percentile in girls. The percentage of malnourished children (having Z score of–2SD or below the NCHS median) was 28.5%, 28.1% and 13.5% according to weight for age, stature for age and weight for stature respectively. The incidence of stunting was substantially more than wasting. More boys than girls were classified as having normal weight/age, stature/Age and weight/height. The incidence of stunting and wasting was more in girls than in boys. Our results indicate that sample girls are at a nutritional disadvantage compared to boys.

REFRENCES

Brown K.H., R.E. Black, S. Becker, A. Hogue (1982), Patterns of Physical Growth in a Longitudinal Study of Young Children in Rural Bangladesh. *Am. J. Clin. Nutr.* 36: 294-302.

Fawzi, W.W., M.G. Herrera, D.L. Spigelman, A. El Amin, P. Nestel, K.A. Mohamed (1997), A Prospective Study of Malnutrition in Relation to Child Mortality in the Sudan. *American J. Clinical Nutrition.* 65: 1062-1069.

Ferro-Luzzi, A. (1984), Environment and Physical Growth. In Susanne C. (ed.): *Genetic and Environmental Factors During Growth Period.* New York: Plenum. pp. 169-198.

Frisancho, A.R. (1974), Triceps Skinfold and Upper Arm Muscle Size Norms for Assessment of Nutritional Status. *Am. J. Clin. Nutr.* 27: 1052-1058.

Frisancho, A.R., G.A. Borkan, J.E. Klayman (1975), Pattern of Growth of Lowland and Highland Peruvian Quechua of Similar Genetic Composition. *Am. J. Phys. Anthropol.* 32: 279-292.

Gaur, R. and N.Y. Singh (1994), Nutritional Status Among Rural Meitei Children of Manipur, India. *American Journal of Human Biology.* 6: 731-740.

Gaur, R., S. Dhingra, M. Lakhanpal (1995), Physical Growth and Nutritional Status of Rural Scheduled Caste Children of Kharar Tehsil, Ropar District, Punjab.

Ghosh, R., P.K. Dass, P. Bharti (2001), Health and Nutritional Status of Ho Preschool Children of Orissa. *J. Hum. Ecol.* 12 (2): 109-113.

Gurney, J.M. and D.B. Jelliffe (1973), Arm Anthropometry in Nutritional Assessment: Nomogram for Rapid Calculations of Muscle Circumference and Cross-sectional and fat areas. *Am. J. Clin. Nutr.* 26: 912.

Hamill, P.V.V., T.A. Drizd, C.L. Johnson, R.B. Reed, A.F. Roche, W.M. Moore (1979), Physical Growth: National Centre for Health Statistics Percentiles. *Am. J. Clin. Nutr.* 32: 607-629.

Indian Council of Medical Rearch (1972), *Growth and Physical Development of Indian Infants and Children*. Technical Report No. 18. New Delhi: ICMR.

Jelliffe, D.B. (1966), *The Assessment of Nutritional Status of the Community*. Geneva: World Health Organization. No. 53.

Llyod, Marry, E. and S.A. Lederman (2002), Anthropometry and Moderate Malnutrition in Preschool Children. *Indian Journal of Pediatrics.* 69: 771-774.

Maninder Kaur and Indu Talwar (2000), Physical Growth and Nutritional Status of Pre-school Slum Dewellers. In Vasishat, R.N. et. al. (eds): Anthropology at the turn of Century, pp. 81-89.

Mata, J. Leonardo (1985), *Environmental Factors Affecting Nutrition and Growth.* pp. 165-184 in M. Gracey and F. Falkner (eds): Nutritional Needs and Assessment of Normal Growth. New York: Raven Press.

Miller, B.D. (1981), *The Endangered Sex: Neglect of Female Children in Rural North India.* New York: Cornell University Press.

Monyeki, K.D., N. Cameron, B. Getz (2000), Growth and Nutritional Status of Rural South African Children 3-10 years old: The Ellisras Growth Study. Am. J. Hum. Biol. 12(1): 42-49.

Pelletier, D.C. (1994), The Relationship between Anthropometry and Child Mortality in Developing Countries: Implications for Policy, Programs and Future Research. *Journal of Nutrition.* 124(10 suppl): 2047s-2081s.

Rhode, J.E. (1996), Promoting Healthy Child Growth. National Institute of Primary Health. Case Document No.16, New Delhi.

Schroeder, D.G., K.H. Brown (1994), Nutritional Status as a Predictor of Child Survival: Summarizing the Association and Quantifying its Global Impact. *Bull WHO.* 72 (4): 569-579.

Schroeder, D.G , R. Martorell (1997), Enhancing Child Survival by Preventing Malnutrition. *Am. J. Clin. Nutrition.* 65: 1080.

Sharma, J.C. (1992), Nutrition Factor in Health, Physical Growth and Development and Politics. Sectional Presidential Address. Baroda: 79th Indian Science Congress: 1-32.

Tanner, J.M. (1966), Notes on the use of Height and Weight Standard Charts. London: Geasys, Herford.

Trowbridge, F.L., L. Newton, A. Houng, N. Staelhing, V. Vaiverde (1980), Evaluation of Nutrition Surveillance Indicators. Bull. *Pan Am. Health Org.* 14: 238-243.

Victoria, C.G. (1992), The Association between Wasting and Stunting: An International Perspective. *J. Nutr.* 122: 1105-1110.

Vijayaraghavan et.al. (1974), Arm Circumference and fat fold Triceps in well Nourished Indian School Childern. *Ind. J. Med. Res.* 62: 994-1001.

Waterlow, J.C. (1977), Classification and Definition of Protein Energy Malnutrition. In: G.H. Beaton, J.M. Bengo. (eds). Nutrition in Preventive Medicine, Monograph Series No. 62. WHO. Geneva.

Weiner, J.S. and J.A. Lourie (1981), *Practical Human Biology.* London: Academic Press.

WHO Working Group (1986), Use and Interpretation of Anthropometric Indicators of Nutritional Status. *Bull Wld. Hlth.* Org. 64: 924-941.

Yoon, P.W., R.E. Black, L.H. Moulton, S. Becker (1997), The Effect of Malnutrition on the Risk of Diarrhea and Respiratory Mortality in Children < 2 years of Age in Cebu, Philippines. *Am. J. Clin. Nutrition.* 65: 1070-1077.

11

PHYSICAL GROWTH AMONG ADOLESCENT BRAHMIN GIRLS OF BHIMTAL (UTTARANCHAL PRADESH)

Kusum Lata Thakur

INTRODUCTION

Growth implies increase in size; development involves change in form and function (Eveleth and Tanner, 1966). Growth studies in different populations are important to understand growth patterns as these may differ between regions and also between different segments of a population due to ecological factors such as nutritional and geographical conditions.

Human growth development is a function of both genetic and environmental factors. The height of an individual is also regulated by both genetic and environmental factors. Several studies (Kumar and Madhavilatha, 2000; Garg, 1974; Agarwal et al., 1992, 1995, 1998; ICMR, 1968) on Indian populations have suggested strong influence of socio-economic class on the rate of growth in height, weight and various body girths. It has also been found by some comparative studies that Europeans and American Indians exceed Indians in growth (Berry et al, 1965; 1968). Such social and economic influences on growth, have also been studied in various other studies from abroad (Rea, 1971).In view of the importance of the study and lack of information on Kumaon girls, the present study has been undertaken to investigate growth patterns in adolescent Brahmin girls from Kumaon region of Uttaranchal.

MATERIAL AND METHODS

The data were collected from 3 Government schools in Bhimtal (Uttranchal Pradesh). Cross sectional anthropometric data were collected on 269 Brahmin girls, aged 10-17 years. Age was verified from the school admission register and was converted into decimal age by using decimal age calendar (Tanner and Whitehouse, 1966). The subjects were asked to fill information regarding their socioeconomic status (place of residence, monthly income, and education, etc.).

Height vertex and body weight were taken using standard techniques (Weiner and Lourie, 1969). BMI was calculated as weight (in Kg/ht^2) (in meter) and Ponderal index was computed as weight (in Kg/ht^3) (in meters)

RESULTS

The results on growth trends in height and weight are presented in Table 1. The total increase from 10 to 17 years in stature is 27.22 cm. Significant differences in mean stature are observed in the three age groups. It is also noticed that the adolescent spurt takes place at the age group of 12 to 13 years where the gain is maximum.

Table 1
Mean, SD, t-Test, for Height and Weight of Adolescent Brahmin Girls of Bhimtal

Age (yrs)	*N*	*Stature (cm.)* Mean	S.D	t	*Weight (Kg.)* Mean	S.D	t
10	32	127.52	9.87	3.78**	25.33	6.89	0.77
11	33	136.93	10.35	1.71	28.54	6.07	5.55**
12	30	140.64	6.70	4.54**	29.55	4.28	1.37
13	40	147.80	6.38	2.14*	36.24	5.81	1.37
14	33	151.56	5.01	0.12	38.14	6.00	1.18
15	32	151.72	5.43	1.60	40.00	6.83	2.87**
16	35	153.98	6.06	0.60	44.50	5.94	0.67
17	34	154.74	4.24		45.26	2.98	

* Significant at 5%, ** Significant at 1%.

On stature measure, adolescent girls of present study are taller at ages 11-17 years when compared to all India ICMR. The average height of girls of NCHS sample is much higher at different age group as compared to average height of present study (see Table 2). The Table 3 indicates that the present sample of adolescent girls is relatively heavier when compared with ICMR, but weighed lesser when compared with NCHS standards. Weight show significant values at age group 11-12 and 15-16.

Table 2
Comparison of Height with other Studies

Age (yrs)	*Present sample*	*NCHS*	*ICMR*	*Kullu girls*	*Garhwal girls*
10	127.52	138.30	128.40	128.02	-
11	136.93	144.80	136.60	133.56	-
12	140.64	151.50	139.20	135.95	134.47
13	147.80	157.10	143.90	141.63	144.98
14	151.56	160.40	147.50	145.24	149.12
15	151.72	161.80	149.60	148.99	149.92
16	153.98	162.40	151.00	149.86	152.66
17	154.74	163.10	151.50	153.00	151.67

Table 3
Comparison of Weight (kg.) Measurement in Various Samples

Age (yrs)	*Present sample*	*NCHS*	*ICMR*	*Kullu girls*	*Garhwal girls*
10	25.33	32.80	23.60	24.61	-
11	28.54	37.00	26.40	26.79	-
12	29.55	41.50	29.80	27.80	24.19
13	36.24	46.10	33.30	31.18	25.77
14	38.14	50.30	36.80	34.09	27.67
15	40.00	53.70	58.80	38.24	28.12
16	44.50	55.90	41.10	39.73	28.80
17	45.26	56.70	42.40	42.26	29.06

DISCUSSION

The study clearly indicates that adolescent Brahmin girls in Bhimtal are lighter and shorter when compared with NCHS standards. The results of present study are compatible with studies conducted on other populations such as the Rajput girls of Kullu (Talwar, 1991) and Garhwal Rajput girls (Kapoor and Paul, 1995), but mean dimensions are found to be more in present study. In Rajput girls of Kullu and Garhwal, the adolescent spurt for height occurs at age group 12 to 13 years with weight age group of 14 to 15 years. In the present study, it occurs between 12 and 13 years for both height and weight.

Rosner et al, (1998) have documented significant ethnic variations in BMI. Well nourished Indian children over the past two decades are showing an increasing trend in somatic/physical growth dimensions (Aggarwal et al, 1992). The present study shows that Ponderal index did not change much during adolescence. Given that ethnic difference exist in BMI (Clarke et al, 1986), ethnic group specific standards would be more appropriate for comparing health compromised children, especially in India where the problem is more pronounced for under nutrition than over-nutrition. So far there are no available standards for BMI and Ponderal index percentiles for Indian affluent (well nourished healthy) children on an acceptable number of subjects. Kaur and Singh (1992) on a smaller sample of well nourished Delhi girls observed higher BMI values.

SUMMARY

Cross sectional anthropometric data on 269 adolescent Brahmin girls aged 10 to 17 years from Bhimtal (Uttaranchal) were collected. The pattern of growth show regular increase in the mean value with age through various age groups in Brahmin girls. The Brahmin girls of Bhimtal show greater mean weight at all ages, when compared to all India sample of ICMR, but much lighter at all age groups when compared to NCHS sample. Girls attain peak velocity for height and weight between 12 and 13.

REFERENCES

Agarwal D.K., Agarwal K.N., Upadhyay S.K., Mittal R., Prakash R. and Rai S. (1992), Physical and Sexual Growth Pattern of Affluent Indian Children from 5-18 years of Age. *Indian Pediatr* 29: 1203-1282.

Agarwal K.N., Agarwal D.K. and Upadhyay S.K. (1995), Impact of Chronic Undernutrition on Higher Mental Functions in Indian Boys Aged 10-12 year. *Acta Pediatr* 84: 1357-1361.

Agarwal K.N., Agarwal D.K. and Upadhyay S.K. (1998), Sequalae of Early Undernutrition on Reaction Time of Rural Children at 11-14 Year *Indian J. Med. Res.* 107: 98-102.

Berry J.N. (1957-58), Height and Weight of Male College Students in Central India. *Ind. J. Med.* Res. 53 (4): 323-333.

Clarke W.R., Woolson R.F. and Lauer R.M. (1986), Changes in Ponderosity and Blood Pressure in Childhood: The Muscatine Study. *Am. J. Epidemiol* 124: 195-206.

Corlett J.I. and Wollard E. (1988), Growth Patterns of Rural Children in the Kgalagadi Region of Bostwana. *Ann. Hum. Biol.* 15 (2): 153-159.

Davenort C.B. (1931), Individual Versus Man Studies in Child Growth. *Proc. Amer Phil. Soc.*, 70: 381.

Eveleth P.B. and Tanner J.M. (1966), *World wide Variation in Human Growth.* Cambridge University Press.

Garg S.K. (1974), The Physical Growth of Boys from the Urban area of Chandigarh. *The Anthropologist* 182 (22): 41-52.

Gupta R.K., Mittal R.D., Agarwal K.N. and Agarwal D.K. (1994), Muscular Sufficiency, Serum Protein, Enzymes and Bioenergetic Studies (31-phos-phorus Magnetic Resonance Spectroscopy) in Chronic Malnutrition. *Acta Pediatr* 83: 327-331.

ICMR (Indian Council for Medical Research) (1972), Growth and Physical Development of Indian Infants and Children. *Technical Report Series* No. 18, New Delhi.

Johnson T.O. (1972), The Physique of Urban Nigerians in the Adolescent Period. *Environmental Child Health* 18: 134-138.

Kaur B. and Singh R. (1992), Physical Growth and Age at Eruption of Deciduous and Permanent Teeth in well-nourished Indian Girls from Birth to 20 years. *Am. J. Hum. Biol.* 4: 757-766.

Kumar M. and Madhavilatha K. (2000), Physical Development of Rural Adolescent: A Cross Sectional Study in Andhra Pradesh. *Man in India* 80: 337-338.

Morley D.C., Woodland M., Martin W.J. et al. (1968), Height and Weight of West African Village Children from Birth to Age of Five. *West African Med. Journal* 1 7: 8-13.

Must A., Jacques P.F., Dallal G.E., Bajema C.J. and Dietz W.H. (1992), Long Term Morbidity and Mortality of Overweight Adolescent *N. Engl. J. Med.* 327: 1350-1355.

National Center of Health Statistics (1977), Growth Curve for Children 0-18 years, United States. Vital and Health Statistics, Series 11, No. 165, Health Resource Administration, Washington, D.C, United States: Govt. Printing Office.

Prentice A.M. (1998), Body Mass Index Standards for Children are Useful for Clinicians But not for Epidemiologists. *BMJ* 216: 1401-1402.

Paul K., Joyce and Satwanti K. (1995), Age Changes in Physiological Parameters and their Relationships with Physicals Traits Among Rajput Females. *Man in India* 75 (4): 379-383.

Rosner B., Prineas R., Loggie J. and Daniels S.R. (1998), Percentiles for Body Mass Index in US Children 5 to 17 Years of Age *J. Pediatr* 131: 211-222.

Srinivasan S.R., Freichs R.R., Webber L.S. and Berenson G.S. (1976), Serum Lipoprotein Profile in Children from a Biracial Community: The Bogalusa Heart Study. Circulation 54: 309-318.

Talwar I. (1991), Physical Growth and Development in Himachali Rajput Females Aged 6 to 17 years. *New Horizons in Hum Biol* 361-375.

Weiner J.S. and Lourie T.O. (1969), *A Guide to field Methods. Human Biology.* Handbook No. 9. Oxford: Blackwell Scientific Publication, 2.

Tanner J.M. and Whitehouse R.H. (1966), *Notes on the use of Height and Weight Standard Charts.* London: Creaseys, Herfford.

12

RESPIRATORY EFFICIENCY AS AFFECTED BY EXPOSURE TO TEXTILE DUST-HEALTH STATUS EVALUATION OF TEXTILE WORKERS OF DISTRICT VARANASI, UTTAR PRADESH

Ajeet Jaiswal

INTRODUCTION

India is a developing nation and presents the demographic features similar to the other developing nations of the world. Growing population is the major concern of the government and is considered as the principal obstacle to the economic growth of the country. Emerging occupational health problems are to be tackled along with communicable diseases, malnutrition, poor environmental sanitation and inadequate medical care. Globalization and rapid industrial growth about 7% annual economic growths in the last few years have further complicated the occupational health related issues.

Textile industry is one of the major growth industry for export purpose and which require large number of lab our i.e. Workers. Respiratory problem is one of the major health threats to Textile Workers. It leads to some systemic symptoms in exposed Workers, along with this they suffer from number of other physical problem like hearing loss or noise problem. (Shake, 1996; Chavalitsakulchai, 1989), low back pain (supplementary report, Industrial health 35, 1997); Respiratory symptoms and pulmonary function. (Mingih, et al, 2003; Ralf, 1998); Byssinosis diseases (Shamssain and Shamsian, 1996; Bhasker, et al, 2003) along with the respiratory problem there is colourvision dysfunction in long term solvent (Dye) exposure, but require long term exposure of dust (Ihrig, and Andrew, 2002). Occupational health (Shunichi,and Masotomo, 2002).

It has been observed that very few studies have been carried out on Textile worker by an anthropologist. Most of the studies were focused on Textile dust mediated pulmonary toxicity caused mainly through reactive intermediates. It appears that cause of causative might be many factors present in a complex dust, but the eventual consequence is more precarious.

In the present study an attempt has been made to study the respiratory efficiency as affected by exposure to Textile Dust with reference to Health and the evaluation of the Textile Workers with reference to anthropological and physiological variable of district Varanasi, Uttar Pradesh.

MATERIALS & METHODS

The field work was conducted in August to September 2004. A total no. of 162 Textile Workers (Cotton, wool, silk) from nine different factories i.e. study group. 56 persons residing in the same area but not working in the Textile Industries were taken as Non Textile Workers (NTW) i.e. control group. The Workers whose duration of work was less than 3 months were excluded from the present study; the study and control group were matched for age sex, and socioeconomic status.

Schedule Consists of:

- Collecting information about the personal history, occupational history & the state of health of every Textile Workers & Non Textile Workers.
- Anthropological and physiological measurements.

Measurements	*Parameter*	*Instrument used*	*units*
Linear Measurement	Stature	Martin's anthropometry (least count 0.1cm)	Cm
Weight Measurement	Body weight	Portable spring weighing machine (least count 0.5kg)	Kg
Skin fold thickness measurement	Biceps, triceps, subscapular, calf posterior, calf medial	Holton's skin fold caliper	Mm
Respiratory Measurement	Forced expiratory volume (FEV_1), Forced Vital Capacity (FVC), Forced Expiratory Ratio (FER), Peak Expiratory Flow Rate (PEFR).	Spirometer	L
Physiological Measurement	Heart rate, pulse rate, blood pressure, breath holding time	Sphygmomanometer, stethoscope, stopwatch	mm Hg. Sec
Derived Measurement	Body mass index, grand mean thickness		

Processing of Cotton/Wool Raw Material in Textile Industry with Reference Varanasi

UNIT - I *Disinfection of Raw Material*

1. *Raw Material:* (in the form of bales)

2. ***Blowing:*** In the modern factories bales are placed on the platform and the wool is carried automatically in the bolenopenner which is enclosed and provided with dust extracting apparatus. The purpose of all these machines is to open out the compressed raw material (Wool, Cotton, Silk) to spread it well and by a beating action aided by a powerful current of air to free it from high percentage of its impurities and at the same time ensure adequate mixing of different quality of raw material (Wool, Cotton & Silk).
3. ***Treatment in Fire Troughs:*** The raw material then moves slowly through succession of large trough by stainless steal prongs attached to harrow like frame. Each batch of raw material is treated for 10 minutes in each of fire trough. The first contain a 0.5% solution of sodium carbonate in water and second for 0.5% solution of soap in water containing free of sodium hydroxide. Both solutions are kept at the temp. of 102° F to 110° F. The solution is constantly agitated by the means of rates and between each trough passes through heavy squeeze rollers. The third and fourth trough contains 2% solution of formaldehyde in water at a temp from 102°F to 110°F. Finally the material is rinsed in clean water at the same temp. to remove excess. Formaldehyde. Passed again through squeeze rollers, dried in a current of air at a temp. of 160° F and I t is then pressed back into bales.
4. ***Seperation of Raw Fibre:***
   (a) *Teaseling:* In this process also there is mixing and separation of raw fiber.
   (b) *Carding:* Emerging from teaseling room, the raw fibre passes to card room. The carding process not only arrange the raw fibre in parallel order but also it carries out the final cleaning process by eliminating such impurities as have survived in the previous operation.
   (c) *Spinning:* These parallel arranged fibre get twisted during spinning for strength and then raw material (Wool, Silk and Cotton) gets change into raw thread.
   (d) *Dyeing:* Depending upon the colour required raw material's dyeing is done. The principle of raw material dyeing is based on the use of acid dye with basic mordents. In this process sulphuric acid is used which produce lanug i.e. acid in the raw material and this is the substance which is really dye free acid dye which is liberated from its salt (Sodium & Calcium) in the presence of acetic acid. The dye commonly used is lead and chrome salts.
   (e) *Treatment of Raw Material for Protection:* (Ulone process) these disinfected raw material i.e. bales are then treated with chemical (Ulone) 0.5% solution in water during dyeing for the protection against insect specially white ants.

(f) *Weaving:* Although now a days machine weaving is there but, at Bhadoi, Varanasi belt weaving is done by hands at weaver's cottage.

(g) *Cutting & Finishing:* In the last process of Textile (carpel, Sarees) making there is cutting of extra threads and finishing and this is again done at weavers cottage so, it is clear from the above that the places where teaseling, carding & the disinfection of raw material is done are the most dusty sites as compared to the places where spinning, weaving & cutting is done. During washing and dying the workers are exposed to high temperature, steam vapor with acid fumes & dyes.

These steps are there in modern factories but in factories which are not modernised.There are no process like disinfection and the raw material is directly put for carding.Then, for spinning by hand or foot. Spinning. Dye is not done in close tanks and thus, the worker in each factory is more likely to develop occupational hazards.

UNIT–II *Key Processing Units In Textile Industry*

1. Designing; 2. Dying; 3. Rolling; 4. Tana making; 5. Yarn weaving; 6. Cloth weaving; 7. Carpet weaving; 8. Carpet washing; 9. Carpet stretching; 10. Carpet finishing.

Processing of Cotton/Wool Raw Material in Textile Industry with Reference Varanasi

UNIT-I *Disinfection of Raw Material*

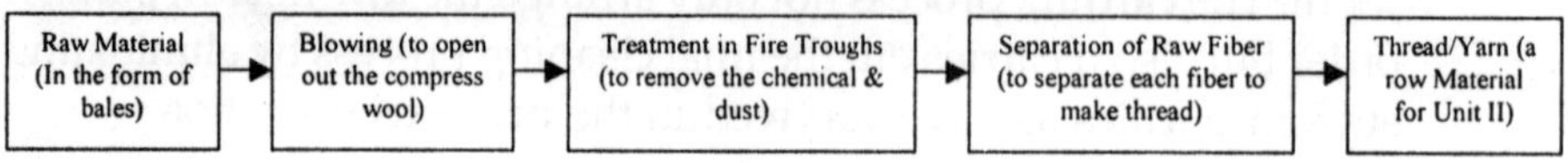

UNIT–II *Key Processing Units in Textile Industry*

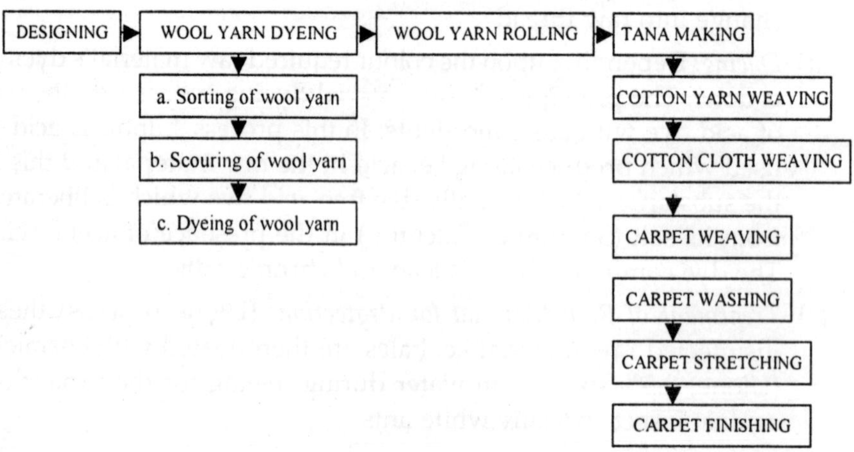

STUDY AREA–VARANASI, UTTAR PRADESH

Varanasi is most important city in eastern Uttar Pradesh. Varanasi also known as Benaras is one of the holiest pilgrimage sites in India. Situated on the west banks of sacred river Ganges. Varanasi has been a centre of learning and civilization for over 2000 years. Besides being a pilgrimage centre, it is considered as an auspicious place to die, ensuring an instant route to Heaven Apart from Hinduism it is also an important pilgrimage centre for Buddhists as it was at Sarnath (10 Km from Varanasi), Lord Buddha gave his Ist sermon after enlighten. It is only city in Asia with three Universities; it lies with in a 16 Km radius.

The population of Varanasi is 2508.11 Lakh (Census 1991) of which make is 1326.76 lakh and Female is 1181.35 lakh. Out of these, the rural population is 1450.14 lakh and urban population is 1057.97 lakh, Schedule cast population is 347 lakh, schedule tribe is .07 lakh. About the education the educated population is 1034.18 lakh of this Male is 708.67 and Female is 325.50 lakh (Census 1991). The percentage of Urban population of Varanasi is 42.2 9Census 1991). Density of Varanasi is 1618 per Km. Square (Census 1991). The Sex Ration 890 Female per thousand Male. In the educational sector 52.4% of population are educated of this 67.3% of Male and 35.3% of Female are educated. Percentage of Workers is 28.5% of the total population of this 29.8% are belongs to rural population and 26.7% are belongs to Urban Population (Census 1991).

RESULTS

In Table 1, it has been observed that the cough was the most common symptoms in both the groups but was significantly more common among Textile Workers (43.21%) as compared to Non Textile Workers (19.64%) Next common symptom was chest pain and this was more common among Textile Workers. Breathlessness along with fever was also more common among Textile Workers and the difference between the two groups was more i.e. 16.05% vs 8.93 for breathlessness and 6.07% Vs 3.57% for fever respectively in Textile Workers s and Non Textile Workers).

Table 1
Distribution of Symptoms Among Textile Workers & Non Textile Workers

Chest Ssymptoms	*Textile Workers (TW)*		*Textile Workers Non (NTW)*		χ^2 *(df=1)*	*P value*
	No.	%	No.	%		
Cough	70	43.21	11	19.64	27.83	<.001
Chest Pain	37	22.84	10	17.86	6.15	<.02
Fever	10	6.17	2	3.57	28.90	<.001
Breathlessness	26	16.05	5	8.93	-	-
Chest rightness	9	5.56	4	7.14	2.52	N.S.
Others (Normal)	10	6.17	24	42.86	22.39	<.001
Total	162	100	56	100		

Figure 1: Distribution of Symptoms Among Textile Workers & Non Textile Workers

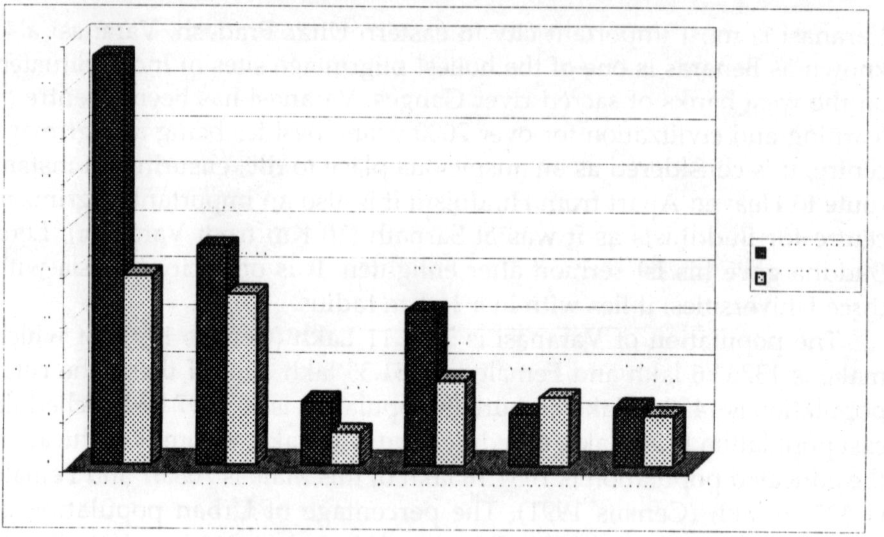

Religion and Sex wise Distribution

Table 2 shows 96 (70.59%) were Hindu Male, only 12 Textile Workers s were Hindu Female, 40 (29.41%) Textile Workers were Muslim Male, and 14 were Muslims Female. In Non-Textile Workers group, 36 (70.59%) persons were Hindu Male, 3 were Hindu Female, 15 (29.41%) were Muslim Male and 2 Muslim Female. As the number. of Female in both Hindu & Muslim, Textile Workers were quite less compare to that of the Male. Similar result was also found in the Non-Textile Workers group as Female are mostly engage in family work.

Table 2
Religion and Sex Wise Distribution

	Male				*Female*			
	Textile Workers (TW)		*Non Textile Workers (NTW)*		*Textile Workers (TW)*		*Non Textile Workers (NTW)*	
	No.	*%*	*No.*	*%*	*No.*	*%*	*No.*	*%*
Hindu	96	70.59	36	70.59	12	46.15	3	60.00
Muslim	40	29.41	15	29.41	14	53.85	2	40.00
Total	136	100	51	100	26	100.00	5	100.00

Age wise Distribution of Textile Workers and Non Textile Workers group

It has been observed from Table 3 as 21 (12.96%) Textile Workers were below 20 yrs of age. Maximum no. of Textile Workers 64 (39.51%) were between 21-30 yrs of age, 8 (4.94%) Textile Workers was above 51 yrs. Mean age of Textile Workers was 32.62±10.7 yrs. In Non Textile Workers,

Figure 2: Religion and Sex Wise Distribution of Textile Workers and Non Textile Worker s Group

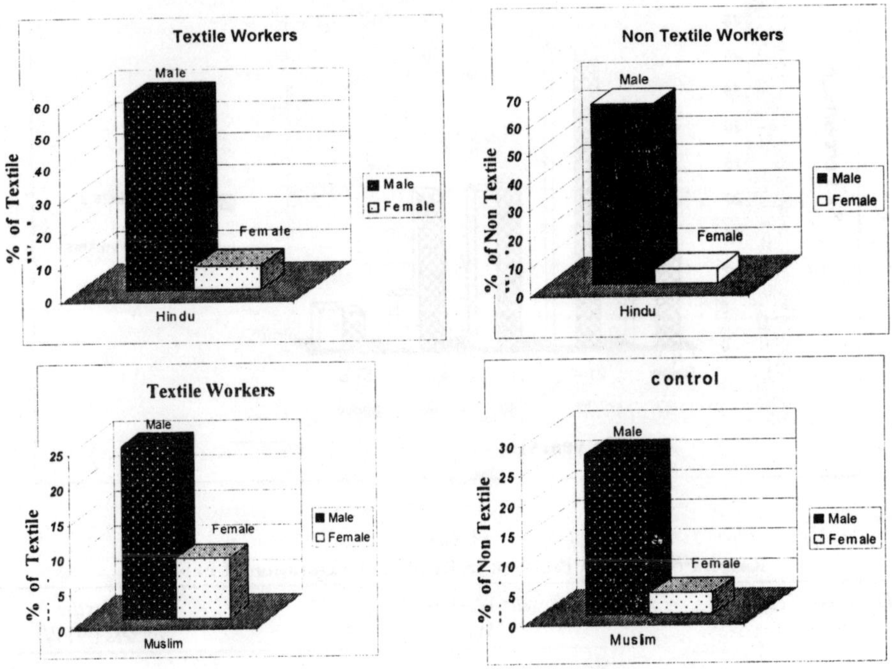

14 (25%) persons were below 20 years of age. Max, no. 23 (41.07%) was between 21-30 years of age and 3 (5.34%) persons were above 51 years and mean age of Non Textile Workers is 29.00±10.49 yrs.

Table 3
Age Wise Distribution of Textile Workers and Non Textile Worker s Group

Age in years	*Textile Workers (TW)*		*Non Textile Workers (NTW)*	
	No	*%*	*No*	*%*
Below 20	21	12.96	14	25.00
21 – 30	64	39.51	23	41.07
31 – 40	36	22.22	12	21.43
40 – 50	33	20.37	4	7.14
51 & above	8	4.94	3	5.36
Total	162	100	56	100
Mean age ± SD (in yrs)			32.62±10.80	29.00±10.49

Table 4 shows that maximum no. of Textile Workers 70% (43.21 %) were having duration of 0.25-9 years for working in Textile industry followed by 43 Textile Workers (26.5%) with 10-19 years 29 Textile Workers (17.9%) with 20-29 years and 19 (11.73%) with more than 30 years of putting in job. In Non Textile Workers group 30 (53.57%) persons were having their duration of work below 9 years and 4 (7.14%) above 30 years.

Figure 3 Age wise distribution of Textile Workers s and Non Textile Workers group

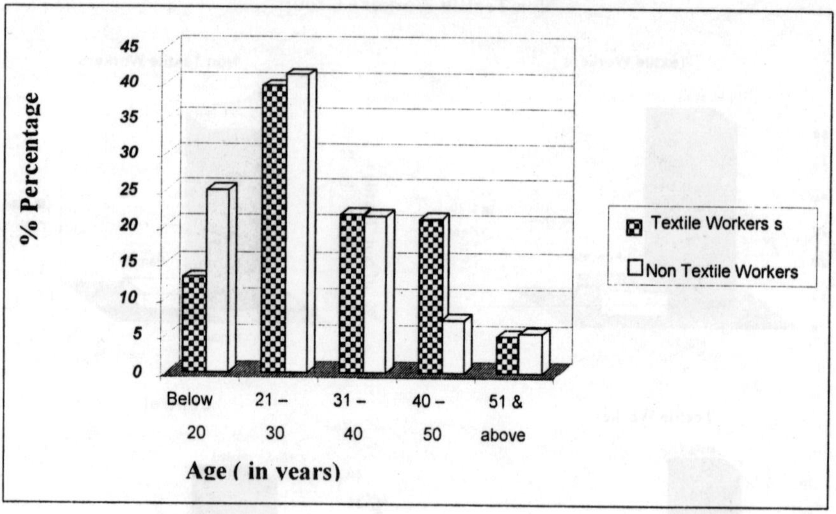

Table 4
Respiratory Health Problem In Relation To Duration of Exposure

Duration of exposure (in years)	*Textile Workers (TW)*		*Non Textile Workers (NTW)*	
	No.	*%*	*No.*	*%*
0.25-9	70	43.21	30	53.57
10-19	43	26.54	15	26.79
20-29	29	17.90	7	12.50
30+	20	12.35	4	7.14
Total	162	100	56	100

Figure 4: Respiratory Health Problem of Textile (TW) and Non Textile Worker (NTW) i.e. Control Group In Relation To Duration of Exposure

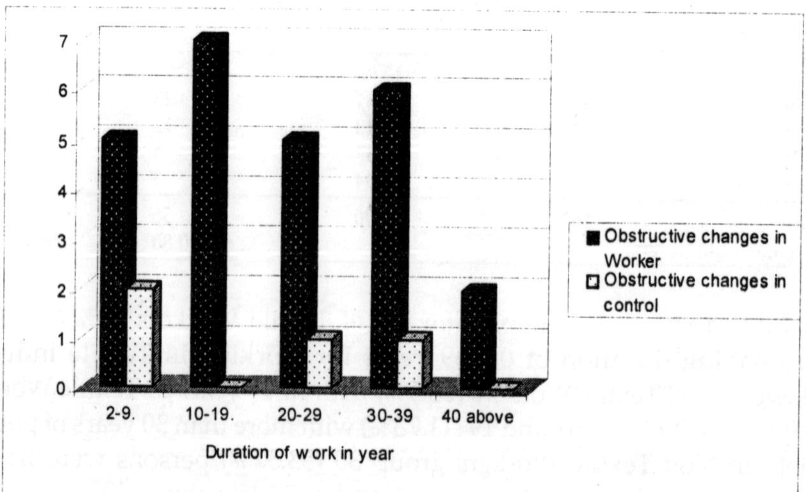

Table 5 depict that the maximum mean value of stature (156.3 cm) in case of Female Textile Workers in age group of 21-30 yrs & the minimum mean value (151.9 cm) in age group of 31-40 years, but in the case of Female Non Textile Workers the maximum mean value (161.51) and minimum (152. 4 cm) in age group of 31-40 yrs and 50 and above respectively. The maximum mean value of stature (171.7 cm) in case of Male Textile Workers in age group of below 20 yrs & the minimum mean value (164.4. cm) has been observed in age group of 51 and above years, but in the case of Male of the Non Textile Workers the maximum mean value (171.2) and minimum (165.3 cm) in age group of below 20 yrs. & 50 and above respectively. The "t" value has been to show statistically significant difference in Female Textile Workers age group41 -50yrs (p<0.05) as compared to Female Non Textile Workers but in the case of Male the "t" value has been to show statistically significant difference in Male Textile Workers age group of more than 50yrs (p<0.05) as compared to Male Non Textile Workers The overall picture of this table depict that the stature of Female Textile Workers is slightly less than the Non Textile Workers.

Table 5
Comparison of Stature between Textile Workers (TW) and Non Textile Workers (NTW)

Age-Group	*Female Textile Workers (TW)*			*Female Non-Textile Workers (NTW)*			*Value of 't' & level of significance*
	N	*Mean (cm)*	*± SD*	N	*Mean (cm)*	*± SD*	
Below 20	3	154.7	1.1	2	154.8	0.14	0.03
21 – 30	3	156.3	1.1	1	156.5	-	0.59
31 – 40	14	151.9	4.08	1	161.5	-	0.91
40 – 50	5	154.6	2.06	1	159.3	-	2.08*
51 & above	1	154.5	-	-	-	-	-
Total	26			5			

p< 0.05.

Age-Group	*Male Textile Workers (TW)*			*Male Non-Textile Workers (NTW)*			*Value of 't' & level of significance*
	N	*Mean (cm)*	*± SD*	N	*Mean (cm)*	*± SD*	
Below 20	18	171.7	8.84	12	171.2	5.95	0.02
21 – 30	61	169.7	6.81	22	170.8	7.51	0.42
31 – 40	21	169.8	7.90	11	169.8	6,87	0.36
40 – 50	29	165.7	8.55	3	168.2	5,26	1.13
51 & above	7	164.4	7.23	3	165.3	5.11	2.42*
Total	136			51			

Table 6 depict that the maximum mean value of body weight (59.90kg) in case of Female Textile Workers in age group of 21-30 yrs & the minimum mean value of body weight (48.3kg) in age group of < =20 years, but in the case of Female Non Textile Workers the maximum mean value (59kg) and minimum (49.6kg) has been observed in age group of 31 -40yrs and 50yrs and above respectively. The maximum mean value of body weight (68.5kg) in case of Male Textile Workers has been observed in age group of below 20 yrs & the minimum mean value (47.5kg) has been observed in age group of 51 and above years, but in the case of Male Non Textile Workers the maximum mean value (62.1kg) and minimum (59.9kg) has been observed in age group of below 20 yrs, 31 -40 and 41- 50 respectively. The "t" value shows statistically Non significant difference in Female Textile Workers) as compared to Female Non Textile Workers but in the case of Male the "t" value shows statistically significant difference in Male Textile Workers age group of more than 50yrs($p<0.01$) as compared to Male Non Textile Workers. The overall picture of depict that the body weight of Female and Male Textile Workers is slightly more than the Non Textile Workers but the difference is not very indicative as this may be because of continually working in sitting position without spending much energy. Although this is not very acceptable reason to explain the difference but still it has small impact on the body weight of the Textile Workers.

Table 6
Comparison of Body Weight between Textile Workers (TW) and Non Textile Workers (NTW)

Age-Group	*Female Textile Workers (TW)*			*Female Non-Textile Workers (NTW)*			*Value of 't' & level of significance*
	N	*Mean (cm)*	*± SD*	*N*	*Mean (cm)*	*± SD*	
Below 20	3	48.3	10.08	2	50.0	9.24	0.28
21 – 30	3	59.9	13.72	1	53.3	-	1.65
31 – 40	14	55.7	15.96	1	59.1	-	0.81
40 – 50	5	49.6	5.45	1	54.7	-	0.09
51 & above	1	50.6	-	-	-	-	-
Total	26			5			

Age-Group	*Male Textile Workers (TW)*			*Male Non-Textile Workers (NTW)*			*Value of 't' & level of significance*
	N	*Mean (cm)*	*± SD*	*N*	*Mean (cm)*	*± SD*	
Below 20	18	68.50	9.46	12	62.10	7.82	1.98
21 – 30	61	61.00	12.09	22	59.20	8.08	0.21
31 – 40	21	62.30	10.35	11	62.10	13.15	0.02
40 – 50	29	61.20	7.73	3	53.90	11.59	0.21
51 & above	7	47.50	4.39	3	59.90	8.65	5.07**
Total	136			51			

**$p < 0.01$.

Table 7 depict that the maximum mean value of biceps skinfold thickness (9.1 mm) in case of Female Textile Workers in age group of 21-

30 yrs and the minimum mean value (4.5 mm) in age group of 51 & above, but in the case of Female Non Textile Workers the maximum mean value (7.7 mm) and minimum (4.5 mm) has been observed in age group of 31-40 yrs and 20 and below respectively. The maximum mean value of biceps skinfold thickness (8.4 mm) in case of Male Textile Workers has been observed in age group of 31-40 yrs & the minimum mean value (3.4 mm) has been observed in age group of 51 and above years, but in the case of Male of the Non Textile Workers the maximum mean value (5.0mm) & minimum (3.4mm) has been observed in age group of below 31-40 yrs & 51 and above respectively. The "t" value shows statistically significant difference in Female Textile Workers age group 21-30yrs ($p<0.05$) as compared to Female Non Textile Workers. This is clearly shows that the biceps of the industrial Workers both Male & Female is more than the Non industrial Workers. The reason behind this may be because of more physical exertion done by these individuals.

Table 7
Comparison of Biceps Skin Fold Thickness between Textile Workers (TW) and Non Textile Workers (NTW)

Age-Group	*Female Textile Workers (TW)*			*Female Non-Textile Workers (NTW)*			*Value of 't' & level of significance*
	N	*Mean (cm)*	*± SD*	*N*	*Mean (cm)*	*± SD*	
Below 20	3	6.1	2.62	2	4.5	2.37	1.16
21 – 30	3	9.1	3.58	1	6.5	-	2.37*
31 – 40	14	6.6	3.49	1	7.7	-	1.7
40 – 50	5	6.4	2.46	1	7	-	1.75
51 & above	1	4.5	-	-	-	-	-
Total	26			5			

Age-Group	*Male Textile Workers (TW)*			*Male Non-Textile Workers (NTW)*			*Value of 't' & level of significance*
	N	*Mean (cm)*	*± SD*	*N*	*Mean (cm)*	*± SD*	
Below 20	18	4.9	1.58	12	5.6	2.58	0.55
21 – 30	61	4.5	2.42	22	4.9	1.52	0.66
31 – 40	21	8.4	3.6	11	5	2.11	1.35
40 – 50	29	5.7	2.59	3	4.6	3.24	0.07
51 & above	7	3.4	1.02	3	3.4	1.03	1.97
Total	136			51			

*$p < 0.05$.

Table 8 depict the maximum mean value of triceps skinfold thickness (12.4 mm) in case of Female Textile Workers in age group of 31-40 yrs & the minimum mean value (8.4 mm) in age group of 41-50yrs, but in the case of Female Non Textile Workers the maximum mean value (14.5mm) & minimum (8.3mm) in age group of 21-30 yrs & 20 and below respectively.

The maximum mean value of triceps skinfold thickness (8.6 mm) in case of Male Textile Workers has been observed in age group of 20 and below, and the minimum mean value (8.4) mm) has been observed in age group of 41-50 & 51 and above years, but in the case of Male of the Non Textile Workers the maximum mean value (9.2 mm) & minimum mean value (6 mm) in age group of below 20 & below & 41-50 yrs. respectively. The "t" value to shows a statistically significant difference in Female Textile Workers age group 31-40 yrs ($p<0.05$) as compared to Female Non Textile Workers, but in the case of Male the "t" value to shows a statistically significant difference in Male Textile Workers age group of more than 41-50 yrs ($p<0.001$) as compared to Male Non Textile Workers.

Table 8
Comparison of Triceps Skin Fold Thickness between Textile Workers (TW) and Non Textile Workers (NTW)

Age-Group	*Female Textile Workers (TW)*			*Female Non-Textile Workers (NTW)*			*Value of 't' & level of significance*
	N	*Mean (cm)*	*± SD*	*N*	*Mean (cm)*	*± SD*	
Below 20	3	11.7	5.99	2	8.3	3.55	1.52
21 – 30	3	11.8	4.59	1	14.5	-	1.55
31 – 40	14	12.4	4.69	1	12.1	-	2.31*
40 – 50	5	8.4	3.33	1	11.2	-	0.06
51 & above	1	11.9	-	-	-	-	-
Total	26			5			

Age-Group	*Male Textile Workers (TW)*			*Male Non-Textile Workers (NTW)*			*Value of 't' & level of significance*
	N	*Mean (cm)*	*± SD*	*N*	*Mean (cm)*	*± SD*	
Below 20	18	8.6	3.92	12	9.2	3.6	0.45
21 – 30	61	8.5	8.25	22	7.8	4.24	1.67
31 – 40	21	8.5	5.45	11	8.4	3.1	0.82
40 – 50	29	8.4	2.78	3	6	2.19	4.02**
51 & above	7	8.4	4.82	3	6.2	2.96	2.1*
Total	136			51			

*$p<0.05$ **$p<0.01$.

Table 9 depict the maximum mean value of sub scapular skinfold thickness (12.8 mm) in case of Female Textile Workers in age group of 31-40 yrs and the minimum mean value (7.2 mm) in age group of 20 and below yrs, but in the case of Female Non Textile Workers the maximum mean value (14.5 mm) and minimum mean value (7.6 mm) in age group of 21-30 yrs and 41 & 50 and below respectively. The maximum mean value of sub scapular skinfold thickness (14.5 mm) in case of Male Textile Workers has been observed in age group of 20 and below, and the minimum mean value (6.5 mm) in age group of 51 & above years, but in the case of Male Non Textile Workers the maximum mean value (12.5mm) & minimum (8 mm) has been observed in age group of below 20 & below & 51 & above yrs. respectively. The "t" value has been found to show statistically significant difference in Female Textile Workers age group 20 & below yrs ($p<0.01$) as compared to Female Non Textile Workers, but in the case of Male the "t" value shows statistically significant difference in Male Textile Workers age group of 20 & below and 51 & above ($p<0.05$) as compared to Male Non Textile Workers. So, the sub scapular of Female Non Textile Workers were more than that of Female Textile Workers but in the case of Male the result is opposite except at certain age group but overall sub scapular skin fold thickness followed on irregular trend. The inconsistency of an particular trend may be attributed to the nutritional status, physical activity level, energy expenditure, fat intake etc. the "t" value has been found to show significant statistically difference a only certain groups between Textile Workers & Non Textile Workers in both Male & Female.

Table 9
Comparison of Sub Scapular Skinfold Thickness between Textile Workers (TW) and Non Textile Workers (NTW)

Age-Group	*Female Textile Workers (TW)*			*Female Non-Textile Workers (NTW)*			*Value of 't' & level of significance*
	N	*Mean (cm)*	*± SD*	*N*	*Mean (cm)*	*± SD*	
Below 20	3	7.2	2.64	2	13.3	3.03	3.36**
21 – 30	3	11.3	5.86	1	14.5	-	0.77
31 – 40	14	12.8	2.51	1	8.3	-	0.28
40 – 50	5	9.8	5.91	1	7.6	-	1.61
51 & above	1	9.7	-	-	-	-	-
Total	26			5			

*p<0.05 **p<0.01.

Age-Group	*Male Textile Workers (TW)*			*Male Non-Textile Workers (NTW)*			*Value of 't' & level of significance*
	N	*Mean (cm)*	*± SD*	*N*	*Mean (cm)*	*± SD*	
Below 20	18	14.5	7.76	12	12.4	6.54	2.17*
21 – 30	61	12.6	6.78	22	11.5	4.38	0.07
31 – 40	21	12	3.22	11	10.2	5.97	0.34
40 – 50	29	9.6	5.55	3	7.4	2.09	1.15
51 & above	7	6.5	5.69	3	8	5.42	2.65*
Total	136			51			

*p < 0.05.

Table 10 depict the maximum mean value of calf posterior skinfold thickness (12.6 mm) in case of Female Textile Workers in age group of 31-

40 yrs & the minimum mean value (9.8mm) in age group of 51 & above yrs, but in the case of Female Non Textile Workers the maximum mean value (12.1mm) & minimum (8.5mm) has been observed in age group of 21-30 yrs & 31-40 yrs respectively. The maximum mean value of calf posterior skinfold thickness (10.8 mm) in case of Male Textile Workers has been observed in age group of 31-40 yrs and the minimum mean value (4.27 mm) has been observed in age group of 51 & above years, but in the case of Male Non Textile Workers the maximum mean value (9.5mm) & minimum (6.1 mm) has been observed in age group of 31-40 yrs and 41-50 yrs respectively. The "t" value has been found to be statistically significant in Male Textile Workers age group above 51 yrs (p<0.05) as compared to Male Non Textile Workers.

Table 10
Comparison of Calf Posterior Skinfold Thickness between Textile Workers (TW) and Non Textile Workers (NTW)

Age-Group	*Female Textile Workers (TW)*			*Female Non-Textile Workers (NTW)*			*Value of 't' & level of significance*
	N	*Mean (cm)*	*± SD*	N	*Mean (cm)*	*± SD*	
Below 20	3	12.3	4.55	2	9.7	3.56	1.24
21 – 30	3	10.4	4.85	1	12.1	-	0.34
31 – 40	14	12.6	2.77	1	8.5	-	1.14
40 – 50	5	10.7	2.96	1	10.2	-	0.24
51 & above	1	9.8	-	-	-	-	-
Total	26			5			

Age-Group	*Male Textile Workers (TW)*			*Male Non-Textile Workers (NTW)*			*Value of 't' & level of significance*
	N	*Mean (cm)*	*± SD*	N	*Mean (cm)*	*± SD*	
Below 20	18	9.4	3.33	12	8.9	3.25	0.26
21 – 30	61	7.3	3.15	22	6.3	2.91	0.81
31 – 40	21	10.8	3.78	11	9.5	3.65	1.05
40 – 50	29	10	2.54	3	6.1	2.6	0.64
51 & above	7	4.27	1.56	3	7.72	5.04	2.59*
Total	136			51			

*p<0.05 **p<0. 01.

Table 11 depict the maximum mean value of calf medial skinfold thickness (12.1 mm) in case of Female Textile Workers in age group of 31-40 yrs & the minimum mean value (7.3mm) in age group of 51 & above yrs, but in the case of Female Non Textile Workers the maximum mean value (11.2mm) & minimum (7.3mm) has been observed in age group of

21-30 yrs & 41-50 yrs respectively. The maximum mean value of calf medial skinfold thickness (9.0 mm) in case of Male Textile Workers in age group of 31-40 yrs and the minimum mean value (3.3 mm) in age group of 51 & above years, but in the case of Male Non Textile Workers the maximum mean value (7.7mm) & minimum (5.2 mm) has been observed in age group of below 20 yrs and 41-50 yrs respectively. The "t" value has been found to be statistically significant difference in Male Textile Workers age group above 51 yrs ($p<0.05$) as compared to Non Textile Workers.

Table 11
Comparison of Calf Medial Skinfold Thickness Between Textile Workers (TW) and Non Textile Workers (NTW)

Age-Group	*Female Textile Workers (TW)*			*Female Non-Textile Workers (NTW)*			*Value of 't' & level of significance*
	N	*Mean (cm)*	*± SD*	*N*	*Mean (cm)*	*± SD*	
Below 20	3	8.9	3.42	2	9.1	4.27	0.07
21 – 30	3	10.1	6.07	1	11.2	-	0.41
31 – 40	14	12.1	2.54	1	9.9	-	1.95
40 – 50	5	9.4	4.88	1	7.3	-	0.06
51 & above	1	7.3	-	-	-	-	-
Total	26			5			

Age-Group	*Male Textile Workers (TW)*			*Male Non-Textile Workers (NTW)*			*Value of 't' & level of significance*
	N	*Mean (cm)*	*± SD*	*N*	*Mean (cm)*	*± SD*	
Below 20	18	7.1	2.63	12	7.7	2.19	0.32
21 – 30	61	5.8	2.05	22	6.7	3.46	1.07
31 – 40	21	9	3.46	11	7	2.35	0.99
40 – 50	29	6.9	2.17	3	5.2	1.77	0.41
51 & above	7	3.3	1.14	3	6.5	3.95	2.67*
Total	136			51			

*$p<0.05$ **$p<0.01$.

Table 12 depict the maximum mean value of heart rate (81.5 b/m) in case of Female Textile Workers in age group of 21-30 yrs and the minimum mean value (69.5 b/m) in age group of 51+ yrs, but in the case of Female Non Textile Workers the maximum mean value (78.7 b/m) & minimum (77.2 b/m) has been observed in age group of 31-40 yrs & 41-50 The maximum mean value of heart rate (84.5 b/m) in case of Male Textile Workers, age group of 21-30 yrs and the minimum mean value (77.7 b/m) in age group of 41-50 years, but in the case of Male Non Textile Workers the maximum mean value (82.5 b/m) & minimum (75.5 b/m) has been observed in age group of 41-50 yrs and 21-30 yrs respectively. So, the heart rate does not show much variation between Male Textile Workers and Female Textile because they share more or less similar ecological condition and hence adopt almost similar kind of attributes such as nutrition, water, health status etc but there is very slight difference observe between Textile Workers and Non Textile Workers i.e. less variation is observed.

Table 12
Comparison of Heart Rate between Textile Workers (TW) and Non Textile Workers

Age-Group	*Female Textile Workers (TW)*			*Female Non-Textile Workers (NTW)*			*Value of 't' & level of significance*
	N	*Mean (cm)*	*± SD*	*N*	*Mean (cm)*	*± SD*	
Below 20	3	79	7.63	2	78.5	9.31	0.12
21 – 30	3	81.5	9.05	1	78.5	-	0.54
31 – 40	14	78.5	5.21	1	78.75	-	0
40 – 50	5	79.2	8.41	1	77.2	-	0.15
51 & above	1	69.5	-	-	-	-	-
Total	26			5			

Age-Group	*Male Textile Workers (TW)*			*Male Non-Textile Workers (NTW)*			*Value of 't' & level of significance*
	N	*Mean (cm)*	*± SD*	*N*	*Mean (cm)*	*± SD*	
Below 20	18	79.2	4.52	12	79.7	8.71	0.73
21 – 30	61	84.5	17.26	22	75.5	5.42	0.62
31 – 40	21	78.5	4.24	11	76.7	5.84	0.03
40 – 50	29	77.7	5.8	3	82.5	7.98	0.51
51 & above	7	79.7	3.77	3	76.7	7.08	0.96
Total	136			51			

Table 13 depict the maximum mean value of pulse rate (84.0 b/m) in case of Female Textile Workers in age group of 41-50 yrs & the minimum mean value (73.7 b/m) in age group of 31-40 yrs, but in the case of Female of the Non Textile Workers the maximum mean value (74.5 b/m) has been observed in the age group of 31-40 & 41-50 yrs & minimum (73.5 b/m) has been observed in age group of 21-30 yrs respectively. The maximum mean value of pulse rate (81.0 b/m) in case of Male Textile Workers has been observed in age group of 21-30 yrs and the minimum mean value (74.7 b/m) has been observed in age group of 41-50 years, but in the case of Male Non Textile Workers the maximum mean value (78.0 b/m) & minimum (73.0 b/m) has been observed in age group of 41-50 yrs and 21-30 yrs respectively. So, Table clearly shows the pulse rate of both Female and Male Textile Workers is less than that of Non Textile of both Female and Male. Although the pulse rate followed an irregular trend.

Table 13
Comparison of Pulse Rate between Textile Workers (TW) and Non Textile Workers (NTW)

Age-Group	*Female Textile Workers (TW)*			*Female Non-Textile Workers (NTW)*			*Value of 't' & level of significance*
	N	*Mean (cm)*	*± SD*	*N*	*Mean (cm)*	*± SD*	
Below 20	3	75.6	6.67	2	74.2	5.51	0.45
21 – 30	3	77.5	7.98	1	73.5	-	0.17
31 – 40	14	73.7	5.81	1	74.5	-	0.13
40 – 50	5	84	34.3	1	74.5	-	1.05
51 & above	1	74.5	-	-	-	-	-
Total	26			5			

Age-Group	*Male Textile Workers (TW)*			*Male Non-Textile Workers (NTW)*			*Value of 't' & level of significance*
	N	*Mean (cm)*	*± SD*	*N*	*Mean (cm)*	*± SD*	
Below 20	18	77	1.85	12	75.5	5.52	0.65
21 – 30	61	81	14.89	22	73	4.14	0.91
31 – 40	21	76	4.27	11	75.2	4.26	0.39
40 – 50	29	74.7	7.47	3	78	8	0.22
51 & above	7	76.5	3.33	3	75.7	7.74	0.62
Total	136			51			

Table 14
Comparison of Blood Pressure Systolic between Textile Workers (TW) and Non Textile Workers (NTW)

Age-Group	*Female Textile Workers (TW)*			*Female Non-Textile Workers (NTW)*			*Value of 't' & level of significance*
	N	*Mean (cm)*	*± SD*	*N*	*Mean (cm)*	*± SD*	
Below 20	3	124.5	12.82	2	121.8	9.16	1.03
21 – 30	3	138.1	21.53	1	131.8	-	2.26*
31 – 40	14	138.7	10.6	1	138.1	-	3.21*
40 – 50	5	141.2	24.06	1	133.1	-	2.66*
51 & above	1	137.1	-	-	-	-	-
Total	26			5			

Age-Group	*Male Textile Workers (TW)*			*Male Non-Textile Workers (NTW)*			*Value of 't' & level of significance*
	N	*Mean (cm)*	*± SD*	*N*	*Mean (cm)*	*± SD*	
Below 20	18	128.7	8.76	12	127.8	6.57	1.05
21 – 30	61	132.5	17.7	22	130.6	10.5	0.75
31 – 40	21	143.1	12.8	11	137.5	12.24	0.96
40 – 50	29	148.8	17.3	3	145.2	16.2	1.96
51 & above	7	136	6.61	3	135.6	91.87	0.1
Total	136			51			

*$p < 0.05$.

Table 14 depict the maximum mean value of systolic blood pressure (141.2 mmHg) in case of Female Textile Workers in age group of 41-50 yrs & the minimum mean value (124.5) in age group of below 20 yrs, but in the case of Female Non Textile Workers the maximum mean value (138.1mmHg) & minimum (121.8mmHg) has been observed in age group of 31-40 yrs & below 20 yrs respectively. The maximum mean value of systolic blood pressure (148.8 mmHg) in case of Male Textile Workers in age group of 41-50 and the minimum mean value (128.7 mmHg) in age group of below 20 years, but in the case of Male Non Textile Workers the maximum mean value (145.2mmHg)and minimum (127.8mmHg) has been observed in age group of 41-50 and below 20 yrs. respectively. The "t" value shows a statistically significant difference in Female Textile Workers age group 21-30 to 41-50 yrs (p<0.05) as compared to Female Non Textile Workers.

Table 15
Comparison of Blood Pressure Diastolic between Textile Workers (TW) and Non Textile Workers (NTW)

Age-Group	*Female Textile Workers (TW)*			*Female Non-Textile Workers (NTW)*			*Value of 't' & level of significance*
	N	*Mean (cm)*	*± SD*	*N*	*Mean (cm)*	*± SD*	
Below 20	3	82.1	10.97	2	81.2	11.32	0.19
21 – 30	3	89.3	11.16	1	86.7	-	1.65
31 – 40	14	92.7	9.23	1	90.5	-	2.37*
40 – 50	5	88.2	34.91	1	86.7	-	0.58
51 & above	1	101.2	-	-	-	-	-
Total	26			5			

Age-Group	*Male Textile Workers (TW)*			*Male Non-Textile Workers (NTW)*			*Value of 't' & level of significance*
	N	*Mean (cm)*	*± SD*	*N*	*Mean (cm)*	*± SD*	
Below 20	18	86.5	5.3	12	83.7	3.72	1.47
21 – 30	61	86.8	12.79	22	86.8	5.58	0.85
31 – 40	21	98.1	6.51	11	91.2	6.94	3.96**
40 – 50	29	97.5	8.86	3	95	13.88	3.78**
51 & above	7	91.8	7.52	3	91.8	12.79	1.78
Total	136			51			

*p<0.05 **p<0.01.

Table 15 depict the maximum mean value of diastolic blood pressure (101.2 mmHg) in case of Female Textile Workers in age group of 51+ yrs & the minimum mean value (82.1) in age group of below 20 yrs, but in the case of Female Non Textile Workers the maximum mean value

(90.5mmHg) and minimum (81.2mmHg) has been observed in age group of 31-40 yrs and below 20 yrs respectively. The maximum mean value of diastolic blood pressure (98.1mmHg) in case of Male Textile Workers has been observed in age group of 31-40 and the minimum mean value (86.5 mmHg) has been observed in age group of below 20 years, but in the case of Male Non Textile Workers the maximum mean value (91.2 mmHg) and minimum (83.7mmHg) has been observed in age group of 31.40 and below 20 yrs. respectively. The "t" value shows a statistically significant difference in Female Textile Workers age group 31.40 yrs (p<0.05) as compared to Female Non Textile Workers, but in the case of Male the "t" value has been to show statistically significant difference in Male Textile Workers age group of 31-40 and 41-50 (p<0.05) as compared to Male Non Textile Workers. The blood pressure of both Male and Female Textile Workers is more than that Male and Female Non Textile Workers. The probable reason of this could be loss of elasticity of blood vessel, with pollution, due to which the walls of blood vessels become more rigid hence high pressure, is required for the regular and constant flow of blood.

Table 16
Comparison of Breath Holding Time between Textile Workers (TW) and Non Textile Workers (NTW)

Age-Group	*Female Textile Workers (TW)*			*Female Non-Textile Workers (NTW)*			*Value of 't' & level of significance*
	N	*Mean (cm)*	*± SD*	*N*	*Mean (cm)*	*± SD*	
Below 20	3	11	4.62	2	18.7	6.51	0.25
21 – 30	3	15.6	6.61	1	19.5	-	0.98
31 – 40	14	27.2	22.6	1	24.1	-	1.12
40 – 50	5	11.2	4.52	1	13.6	-	2.15*
51 & above	1	15.1	-	-	-	-	-
Total	26			5			

Age-Group	*Male Textile Workers (TW)*			*Male Non-Textile Workers (NTW)*			*Value of 't' & level of significance*
	N	*Mean (cm)*	*± SD*	*N*	*Mean (cm)*	*± SD*	
Below 20	18	32.5	11.08	12	28.5	16.25	1.22
21 – 30	61	29.8	16.67	22	30.8	14.61	0.16
31 – 40	21	30.3	10.78	11	32.2	19.87	0.13
40 – 50	29	16.8	22.51	3	20.3	9.69	0.22
51 & above	7	14.8	10.82	3	15	4.99	1.84
Total	136			51			

*p<0.05 **p<0.01

Table 16 shows that the maximum mean value of breath holding time (27.2 sec) in case of Female Textile Workers in age group of 31-40 yrs & the minimum mean value (11.0) in age group of below 20 yrs, but in the case of Female Non Textile Workers the maximum mean value (24.1 sec) & minimum (13.6 sec) has been observed in age group of 31-40 yrs & 41-50 yrs respectively. The maximum mean value of breadth holding time (32.5 sec) in case of Male Textile Workers in age group of below 20 and the minimum mean value (14.8 sec) has been observed in age group of 51+ years, but in the case of Male Non Textile Workers the maximum mean value (32.2 sec) & minimum (15.0 sec) has been observed in age group of 31.40 and 51+ yrs. respectively. The "t" values show statistically significant difference in Female Textile Workers age group 41-50 yrs ($p<0.01$) as compared to Female Non Textile Workers. The irregular trend in both Textile and Non Textile groups. This may be attributed to the high level of intoxication especially Textile dust or others like cigarettes, biddy, tobacco etc.

Table 17
Compaeision of Forced Expiratory Volume$_{1.0}$ between Textile Workers (TW) and Non Textile Workers (NTW)

Age-Group	*Female Textile Workers (TW)*			*Female Non-Textile Workers (NTW)*			*Value of 't' & level of significance*
	N	*Mean (cm)*	*± SD*	*N*	*Mean (cm)*	*± SD*	
Below 20	3	0.9	0.68	2	1.1	0.39	0.49
21 – 30	3	1.5	0.61	1	0.9	-	1.75
31 – 40	14	0.8	0.41	1	1.7	-	1.25
40 – 50	5	0.8	0.57	1	1.1	-	0.66
51 & above	1	0.8	-	-	-	-	-
Total	26			5			

Age-Group	*Male Textile Workers (TW)*			*Male Non-Textile Workers (NTW)*			*Value of 't' & level of significance*
	N	*Mean (cm)*	*± SD*	*N*	*Mean (cm)*	*± SD*	
Below 20	18	1.8	0.76	12	2	0.95	0.51
21 – 30	61	1.7	0.48	22	1.9	0.74	0.4
31 – 40	21	1.1	0.79	11	1.9	3.62	0.93
40 – 50	29	1.2	1.06	3	0.7	0.43	1.23
51 & above	7	0.7	0.43	3	0.7	0.38	0.97
Total	136			51			

Table 17 depict the maximum mean value of forced expiratory volume$_{1.0}$ (1.5 lit.) in case of Female Textile Workers in age group of 21-30 yrs & the minimum mean value (0.8) in age group of 31-40, 41-50 and 51+

yrs, but in the case of Female Non Textile Workers the maximum mean value (1.7 lit.) and minimum (1.1 lit.) has been observed in age group of below 20 and 41-50 yrs respectively. The maximum mean value of forced expiratory volume$_{1.0}$ (1.8 lit.) in case of Male Textile Workers in age group of below 20 and the minimum mean value (0.7lit) has been observed in age group of 51+ years, but in the case of Male Non Textile Workers the maximum mean value (2.0 lit.) of below 20 yrs & minimum (0.7 lit.) has been observed in age group of 41-50 and 51+ yrs. respectively.

Table 18 depict the maximum mean value of forced vital capacity (1.5 lit.) in case of Female Textile Workers in age group of 31-40 yrs & the minimum mean value (1.1) in age group of 41-50 and less than 20 yrs, but in the case of Female Non Textile Workers the maximum mean value (1.4 lit.) of 31-40 years and minimum (1.2 lit.) has been observed in age group of below 20 and 21-30 yrs respectively. The maximum mean value of forced vital capacity (2.0 lit.) in case of Male Textile Workers in age group of 41-50 and the minimum mean value (0.81lit) has been observed in age group of >20 years, but in the case of Male of the Non Textile Workers the maximum mean value (1.4 lit.) & minimum (1.1 lit.) has been observed in age group of 31-40 and 51+ yrs. respectively.

Table 18
Comparison of Forced Vital Capacity between Textile Workers (TW) and Non Textile Workers (NTW)

Age-Group	*Female Textile Workers (TW)*			*Female Non-Textile Workers (NTW)*			*Value of 't' & level of significance*
	N	*Mean (cm)*	*± SD*	*N*	*Mean (cm)*	*± SD*	
Below 20	3	1.1	0.63	2	1.2	0.54	0.45
21 – 30	3	1.3	0.46	1	1.2	-	0.63
31 – 40	14	1.5	0.43	1	1.4	-	0.63
40 – 50	5	1.1	0.64	1	1.3	-	0.42
51 & above	1	1.2	-	-	-	-	-
Total	26			5			

Age-Group	*Male Textile Workers (TW)*			*Male Non-Textile Workers (NTW)*			*Value of 't' & level of significance*
	N	*Mean (cm)*	*± SD*	*N*	*Mean (cm)*	*± SD*	
Below 20	18	0.81	0.47	12	1.2	0.54	0.14
21 – 30	61	1.2	1.05	22	1.2	0.46	0.11
31 – 40	21	1.4	0.78	11	1.4	0.65	0.79
40 – 50	29	2	0.56	3	1.3	0.51	0.24
51 & above	7	1.9	0.81	3	1.1	0.64	0.68
Total	136			51			

*p<0.05 **p<0.01T.

Table 17 and 18 the forced expiratory valume$_{1.0}$ and force vital capacity shows decreasing trend with increasing age in the Non Textile Workers group but this declining trend is more in case Textiles Workers. The marked decline with age might be due to the impairment of pulmonary elasticity & decrease mobility of chest cage and also may be the exposure to Textile dust is responsible for consistent decrease in lung functions as well as slight increase in air way reactivity.

Table 19 depict the maximum mean value of forced expiratory ratio (90.5 %) in case of Female Textile Workers in age group of 31-40 yrs & the minimum mean value (77.5 %) in age group of 41-50 yrs, but in the case of Female Non Textile Workers the maximum mean value (99%) of 31-40 years and minimum (79.2 %) has been observed in age group of 21-30 yrs respectively. The maximum mean value of forced expiratory ratio (89.7%) in case of Male Textile Workers has been observed in age group of 21-30 and the minimum mean value (74.5%) has been observed in age group of 31-50 years, but in the case of Male Non Textile Workers the maximum mean value (92.8%) & minimum (64.0%) has been observed in age group of 21-30 and 41-50 yrs. respectively. The "t" value shows a statistically significant difference in Male Textile Workers age group of 41-50 yrs ($p<0.05$) as compared to Male Non Textile Workers.

Table 19
Comparison of Forced Expiratory Ratio between Textile Workers (TW) and Non Textile Workers (NTW)

Age-Group	*Female Textile Workers (TW)*			*Female Non-Textile Workers (NTW)*			*Value of 't' & level of significance*
	N	*Mean (cm)*	*± SD*	N	*Mean (cm)*	*± SD*	
Below 20	3	78.6	24.66	2	87.3	16.17	1.26
21 – 30	3	85.7	15.73	1	79.2	-	1.2
31 – 40	14	90.5	13.85	1	99	35.77	2.6*
40 – 50	5	77.5	20.12	1	81.5	15.46	1.09
51 & above	1	86.8	-	-	-	-	-
Total	26			5			

Age-Group	*Male Textile Workers (TW)*			*Male Non-Textile Workers (NTW)*			*Value of 't' & level of significance*
	N	*Mean (cm)*	*± SD*	N	*Mean (cm)*	*± SD*	
Below 20	18	88.6	15.78	12	80.6	8.84	1.04
21 – 30	61	89.7	17.37	22	92.8	9.84	0.39
31 – 40	21	74.5	23.71	11	91.1	16.71	1.74
40 – 50	29	83.8	12.72	3	64	26.91	2.06*
51 & above	7	82.3	8.94	3	75.7	19.99	0.46
Total	136			51			

*p<0.05 **p<0.01.

Table 20 depict the maximum mean value of peak expiratory flow rate$_0$ (131.2 l/min) in case of Female Textile Workers in age group of 21-30 yrs & the minimum mean value (75.8 l/min) in age group of 41-50 yrs, but in the case of Female Non Textile Workers the maximum mean value (158 l/min) of 31-40 years and minimum (87 l/min) has been observed in age group of >20 yrs respectively. The maximum mean value of peak expiratory flow rate$_0$ (188.62 l/min) in case of Male Textile Workers in age group of less than 20 yrs. and the minimum mean value (56.87 l/min) in age group of 51+ years, but in the case of Male Non Textile Workers the maximum mean value (211.12 l/min) & minimum (61.25 l/min) has been observed in age group of 21-30 and 51+ yrs. respectively. So, the forced expiratory ratio initially showed an increasing trend followed by decreasing trend is Female Textile Workers and Female Non Textile Workers also in Male Textile Workers and Non Textile Workers and the value of Male Non Textile Workers is more than that of Male Textile Workers but in the case of Female the difference is not very indicative. In the case peak expiratory flow rate the difference is very minimal between Textile Workers and Non Textile Workers.

Table 20
Comparison of Peak Expiratory Flow Rate$_0$ between Textile Workers (TW) and Non Textile Workers (NTW)

Age-Group	*Female Textile Workers (TW)*			*Female Non-Textile Workers (NTW)*			*Value of 't' & level of significance*
	N	*Mean (cm)*	*± SD*	*N*	*Mean (cm)*	*± SD*	
Below 20	3	85	57.73	2	87	35.77	0.05
21 – 30	3	131.2	74.13	1	102.1	-	1.76
31 – 40	14	107.2	49.03	1	158	-	1.18
40 – 50	5	75.8	51.88	1	101.8	-	0.51
51 & above	1	109.1	-	-	-	-	-
Total	26			5			

Age-Group	*Male Textile Workers (TW)*			*Male Non-Textile Workers (NTW)*			*Value of 't' & level of significance*
	N	*Mean (cm)*	*± SD*	*N*	*Mean (cm)*	*± SD*	
Below 20	18	188.62	38.62	12	65.24	38.88	0.65
21 – 30	61	172.75	74.41	22	211.12	63.24	0.89
31 – 40	21	120.87	82.63	11	173	11.59	1.35
40 – 50	29	102.38	65.29	3	161.25	65.32	1.8
51 & above	7	56.87	25.14	3	61.25	26.65	0.31
Total	136			51			

Table 21 depict the maximum mean value of body mass index (24.54 kg/m^2) in case of Female Textile Workers in age group of 21-30 yrs & the minimum mean value (20.2 kg/m^2) observed in age group of below 20 yrs, but in the case of Female of the Non Textile Workers the maximum mean value (22.73 kg/m^2) of 31-40 years and minimum (20.92kg/m^2) has been observed in age group of >20 yrs respectively. The maximum mean value of body mass index (23.45 kg/m^2) in case of Male Textile Workers in age group of less than 20 yrs. and the minimum mean value (17.72kg/m^2) in age group of 51+ years, but in the case of Male Non Textile Workers the maximum mean value (22.02 kg/m^2) of 31-40 yrs and 51+ and minimum (19.11 kg/m^2) has been observed in age group of 41-50 yrs. respectively. So in this table both Female on well on Male Textile Workers and Non Textile Workers a gradual increase is observed up to 50 yrs after which 9 decrease is seen the Female Textile Workers of middle age group have been found to posses more BMI.

Table 21
Comparison of to Body Mass Index (BMI)' Between Textile Workers (TW) and Non Textile Workers (NTW)

Age -Group	*Female Textile Workers (TW)*		*Female Non-Textile Workers (NTW)*	
	N	*Mean kg/m^2*	*N*	*Mean kg/m^2*
Below 20	3	20.2	1	20.92
21 – 30	3	24.54	1	21.84
31 – 40	14	24.21	1	22.73
40 – 50	5	20.75	1	21.62
51 & above	1	21.6	1	21.2
Total	26		5	

Age -Group	*Male Textile Workers (TW)*		*Male Non-Textile Workers (NTW)*	
	N	*Mean kg/m^2*	*N*	*Mean kg/m^2*
Below 20	18	23.45	12	21.26
21 – 30	61	21.4	22	20.48
31 – 40	21	21.85	11	22.02
40 – 50	29	22.5	3	19.11
51 & above	7	17.72	3	22.02
Total	136		51	

Table 22 Shows that the maximum mean value of grand mean thickness (11.3 mm) in case of Female Textile Workers in age group of 31-40 yrs & the minimum mean value (8.64 mm) in age group of 51+ yrs, but in the case of Female Non Textile Workers the maximum mean value (11.01mm)

of 21-30 years and minimum (8.66 mm) has been observed in age group of 41-50 yrs respectively. The maximum mean value of grand mean thickness (8.9 mm) in case of Male Textile Workers in age group of less than 20 yrs. and the minimum mean value (5.11 mm) in age group of 51+ years, but in the case of Male Non Textile Workers the maximum mean value (9.74 mm) of 31-40 yrs and minimum (5.17 mm) has been observed in age group of 51+ yrs. respectively.

Table 22
Comparison of Total Grand Mean Thickness between Textile Workers (TW) and Non Textile Workers (NTW)

Age -Group	*Female Textile Workers (TW)*		*Female Non-Textile Workers (NTW)*	
	N	*Mean kg/m²*	*N*	*Mean kg/m²*
Below 20	3	9.24	1	8.98
21 – 30	3	10.54	1	11.01
31 – 40	14	11.3	1	9.3
40 – 50	5	8.94	1	8.66
51 & above	1	8.64	1	10.88
Total	26		5	

Age -Group	*Male Textile Workers (TW)*		*Male Non-Textile Workers (NTW)*	
	N	*Mean kg/m²*	*N*	*Mean kg/m²*
Below 20	18	8.9	12	8.76
21 – 30	61	8.02	22	7.44
31 – 40	21	5.86	11	9.74
40 – 50	29	6.36	3	8.12
51 & above	7	5.11	3	5.17
Total	136		51	

DISCUSSION

Pulmonary disability resulting from textile (wool carpet – silk- cotton) industries always remains an important problem in occupation medicine. Production of textile (carpet in Bhadoi and silk product in Varanasi, Mirza Pur belt) account for nearly 90-95% of the total production textile. The Textile Workers studied were mostly Hindu male (59.26%). The mean age of the Textile Workers was 32.62 ± 10.79 year. It was observed that the two groups i.e. Textile worker and Non Textile worker of both male and female did not differ statistically on to height, weight & also the BMI.

As far as the symptoms among Textile Workers and Non Textile Workers concern cough is most common symptom in the both groups but higher in Textile group (43.21%) .The next common symptom was chest pain and breathlessness (22.84%) i.e. pulmonary defect. K. C. Gupta (1963 has also found the similar result i.e. higher prevalence of cough (54.32%) and pulmonary defect (38.25%) among workers working in Textile Industry.

Chest symptoms were more common and statistically more significant among Textile workers both in male and female (56.17%) had chest symptoms (chest pain(22.84%), breathlessness(16.05%), chest tightness(5.56%) and fever (6.17%) as compared with 14 out of 56 (25.00%) in non textile worker group.

Jordeczka et al. (1970) had also found the prevalence of chest symptoms in (18.15%) Textile Workers. Jordeezka et al. (1973) showed the prevalence of respiratory symptoms among textile (wool) Textile Worker again more among fur Textile Workers (28.76%). Jorkeezka et al. (1976) found that among jute and hemp Textile Workers that cough was the most common symptoms (in 85.4 % of Textile Workers). And shortness of breath in 52.9% of Textile Workers, similarly Kurilora (1977) also found the higher prevalence of chest symptom and short respiratory illness among wool Textile Workers and specially more among Textile Worker at dusty vocation. Heart Rate, Blood Pressure (Systolic, Diastolic) and Breath Holding time of Textile Workers was more than the Non Textile Workers showing statistically significant differences may be because of elasticity of blood vessel with pollution due to which the walls of blood vessels become more rigid hence high pressure is required for the regular and constant flow of blood, Zuskin et al., (1976) also found the similar results focusing the effect of dust on their health.

The forced expiratory valume$_{1.0}$ and force vital capacity shows decreasing trend with increasing age in the Non Textile Workers group but this declining trend is more in case Textiles Workers. The marked decline with age might be due to the impairment of pulmonary elasticity & decrease mobility of chest cage and also may be the exposure to Textile dust is responsible for consistent decrease in lung functions as well as slight increase in air way reactivity. Bresiewiz et al. (1970) showed the similar result. It has been concluded that the significant decrement in Forced Vital Capacity across the shift among the Textile Workers having respiratory illness. Prevalence of higher tension, Hearing impairments, visual disturbance & many other problems is also faced by these Textile Workers (Ihrig & Andreas 2002).

CONCLUSIONS

It has been observed that very few studies have been conducted on Textile Workers by an anthropologist most of the studies had been conducted mostly by either medical professional or a person belongs to a life science field and it is altogether require a multi field support to complete this work. So at last the present pilot survey report suggest that the Textile

Dust Exposure had not affected the body structure significantly but the effect of exposure is noticeable in cardiorespiratory function.

ACKNOWLEDGEMENTS

The study was supported by UGC in the form of Junior Research Fellowship (Letter No. 15-9 (JUNE 2003/2003 (NET) UGC-REF. No. 101 (NET-JUNE 2003)). I would like to thanks textile worker and their family, factory owners & medical professionals for their wonderful cooperation during my field work.

I am highly indebted to Prof. Satwanti Kapoor & Prof. A.K. Kapoor, Department of Anthropology, University of Delhi, Delhi-110007 for guidance and valuable advice during my field work.

REFERENCES

Bhasker P. Chattopadhyay, Habibullah N. Saiyed and Mukherjee A.K. (2003), Byssinosis Among Jute Mill Workers. *Industrial Health.* 41: 265-272.

Brysiewiz K., Buluk H., Cesry-Fro-Nozyk M., Kordeoka L., Leszeynski B., Lukjan Z. and Sadokiersha H. (1970), The Effect of Occupation in Dustiness on the Prevalence of Chronic Bronchitis Among the Workers of the *Sierzan's Establishments* of Wool Industry at Bialystok. *Gruzlica* 38: 657-661.

Chavalitsakulchai, P. (1989), Noise Expose and Permanent Hearing Loss of Textile Workers in Thailand. *Industrial Health.* 27: 165-173.

Flechsig, Ralf (1998), Pros and Cons of Dust Induce Bronchitis as an Occupational Disease. *Industrial Health.* 27: 27-30.

Gupta K.C. and Kulkarni P.S. (1963), Byssinosis in Textile Industry of Ahmedabad. *Ind. J. Chest. Dis.* 5, 136 IIIrd Ed. 686-699.

Ihrig, Andreas (2003), Pilot Survey on Prevalence of Colour Vision Dysfunction in Long Term Solvent Exposed Painter. *Industrial Health.* 41: 39-42.

Jordeozka S., Basa S., Basa B. (1976), Chronic Non- specific Respiratory Diseases in Workers of the Flex, Jute and Hemp Industry. *Pneumonol, Pul.* 44/89: 809-816.

Kurilova L.N. (1977), Workers Morbidity in Wool Processing Enterprises. *Sov. Zdra Vookhr.* 7: 42-7.

Mathur K.C., Mishra S.N. (1972), Incidence of Pulmonary Diseases Among Wool Workers. *Ind. J. Chest. Dis.* 14 (2): 172.

Ming Yih, Rong S.U. Jenn, Sheu Jia-Yih, Loh ching-hui and LTOU Saou Hsing (2003), Additive Effect of Smoking and Cotton Dust Exposure on Respiratory Symptoms and Pulmonary Function of Cotton Textile Workers. *Industrial Health.* 41: 109-115.

Shake G.H. (1996), Noise Problem in a Polyester Fiber Plant in Pakistan. *Industrial Health.* 427-431.

Shamssain, M.H. and Shamssian, N. (1996), Respiratory Symptoms and Pulmonary Function in a Group of Women Weavers in South Africa. *Annual of Human Biology* 24. 4: 299-306.

Shunichi A., Masatomo T. (2002), National Occupational Health Research Priorities, Agenda & Strategy of Japan : Invited Report in NORA system USA. *Industrial Health.* 41: 49-54.

Supplement Report (1997), Guidelines on Worksite Prevention of Low Back Pain. Explanatory Remarks for Guidelines on Worksite Prevention of Low Back Pain: Measures by Types of Work. *Industrial Health.* 35: 143-172.

Zuskin E. (1976), Effect of Wool Dust on Respiratory Functions. *Amn. Rev. Resp. Dis.* 144 (4): 705-709.

13

PALMAR MAINLINE INDEX, a – b RIDGE COUNT AND atd ANGLE AMONG THE MADIGAS OF ANDHRA PRADESH

K. Rajasekhara Reddy

INTRODUCTION

Plamar dermatoglyphic features are very important to know the biological variation in man. Mainline index is an estimate of the degree of transversality of ridge direction over the palm obtained by the sum of the value of two numbers corresponding to the termination of line A and D (Cummins and Midlo, 1961). Ridge count scores between various interdigital triradii of palmar surfaces are an interesting dermatoglyphic marker in the population variation studies due to their non–adaptiveness and variability. The published literature on correlations between palmar inter digital ridge counts particularly *a–b* ridge count shows clear and wide variations among different population groups (Holt, 1968; Knussmann, 1969; Mate, 1975; Mandal and Sharma,1980 and others). The nature of inheritance of the *atd* angles also gives much information in the discrimination of the population groups (Penrose, 1954 and 1970). The present study is concerned with *mainline index, a–b ridge count and angle atd* of the palm among the two groups of Madigas i.e., Madigas of Cuddapah district (MDCDP) and Madigas of Chittoor district (MDCTR).

The Madigas, the great leather working scheduled caste of Andhra Pradesh, correspond to Chakkiliyan of Tamil Nadu, Karnataka and Kerala; Madiga of Maharashtra and Orissa; Madig of Gujarat and Rajasthan States. They are found distributed almost all over the state, including Cuddapah and Chittoor districts, where the investigation was carried out. They are called by a number of terms such as Arundhatiyulu, Asprughyulu, Jambavulu, Gosangis, Matangas, Muttaranivaru, Harijans, Ettivaru, Tegavaru, Masthigalu, Pedda Intivaru etc. However, the terms like Arundhatiya, Gosangi, Jambavaulu etc. are included separately in the list of other scheduled castes (Census of India, 1971).

The Madigas are a short to medium-statured people with prominent cheek bones, oval-elliptical face and hard constitution, dark brown skin colour, straight nose, black hair and brown eye. An economically distressed community, Madigas occupies the lowest position in the Hindu caste hierarchy of the country. Their settlement is generally situated outside the main village. They mainly earn their livelihood by working as labourers on the farm lands of the so called upper castes, besides they thrive on their traditional occupation of tanning of skin and making of leather articles such as shoes, buckets, belts etc. Their family descent is Patriarcheal, Patrilineal and Patrilocal type. The Basavi system is prevalent among them.

There are about fifteen main endogamous sub-divisions or sub-castes among which the Gampadhompti, Chataladhompti, Bhumidhompti. Ginnedhompti Madigas are the most predominant groups in the state, including both Cuddapah and Chittoor districts, where the study was conducted. The remaining sub-divisions are very few in number and scattered in different places. The Madigas strictly follow the endogamous rules. They do not marry outside their own endogamous sub-division. The present study has been undertaken on a single endogamous group, i.e., Gampadhompti Madigas from two different revenue districts of Cuddapah and Chittoor districts.

MATERIAL AND METHODS

The data for the present study were chosen from Cuddapah and Chittoor districts of Andhra Pradesh. Bilateral palm prints of 400 unrelated Madiga individuals (Males: 200; Females: 200;) were collected and analysed according to the methods and techniques given by Cummins and Midlo (1961). Appropriate statistical treatment was extended.

RESULTS AND DISCUSSION

Mainline Index (MLI)

Table 1 lists the mainline index (MLI) values among the Madiga groups. The mean value of MLI is found to be relatively higher in males (R: 8.51, L: 7.89) than in females (R: 8.30, L: 7.82) of the pooled group. However in both the sexes higher incidence of mean values are observed on right hand than on left hand. Thus the transversality as measured by their index is more pronounced on the right palm than the left.

The MDCDP female MLI values (R: 8.32, L: 7.72 constitute higher proportions than those of males (R: 8.14, L: 7.13) while the MDCTR presents a reverse trend. However, either sex of the both groups indicates the higher proportion of values on right hand than on the left hand. But the intergroup difference is significant in both right and left palm of the male series only as evidenced by t-test.

Table 1
Mainline Index

Madiga groups	*Sex*	*Hand*	*Mainline index*			*t – value (d.f. = α)*		
			Mean ± S.E.	*S.D.*	*C.V.*	*Bilaterality*	*Sex difference*	*Inter group difference*
MDCDP	M	R	8.14 ± 0.22	2.20	27.00	5.06***	0.57	
	(100)	L	7.13 ± 0.21	2.13	29.88		1.85	
	F	R	8.32 ± 0.23	2.34	28.17	3.15**		
	(100)	L	7.72 ± 0.24	2.38	30.87			
MDCTR	M	R	8.87 ± 0.20	1.98	22.24	2.56*	2.25*	
	(100)	L	8.65 ± 0.20	1.97	22.73		2.49*	
	F	R	8.28 ± 0.17	1.69	20.46	3.37**		
	(100)	L	7.91 ± 0.22	2.21	27.96			
POOLED	M	R	8.51 ± 0.15	2.09	24.55	4.23**	1.02	2.46*
	(200)	L	7.89 ± 0.14	2.05	25.98		0.33	5.24***
	F	R	8.30 ± 0.14	2.01	24.22	3.06**		0.14
	(200)	L	7.82 ± 0.16	2.29	29.28			0.58

* Significant at 5% probability level.
** Significant at 1% probability level.
*** Significant at 0.1% probability level.

The bilateral differences for MLI are found to be statistically significant by paired t–test in all the series of the Madigas, while sex differences are significant in right and left hand of MDCTR only as shown by t–test.

a–b Ridge Count

Table 2 represents the mean values of palmar *a–b* ridge count among the Madiga groups. It is interesting to not that among the male series right hand (35.58) shows relatively higher values than the left hand (35.46) whereas among female series left hand (35.40) shows higher values than the right hand (35.07) in the pooled Madigas. This trend is noticed in both the Madiga groups.

The MDCDP males (R: 36.73 and L: 36.57) show relatively higher number of ridges than the females (R: 34.28 and L: 34.61), while in the MDCTR this trend is just reversed with higher female values (R: 35.86 and L: 36.19) than these of males (R: 34.43 and L: 34.35). The inter group differences are significant in either hand of the both sexes as revealed by t–values.

The bilateral differences for *a–b* ridge count are not significant in any Madiga series as evidenced by paired t–test. But there is significant sex dimorphism in either hand of both MDCDP and MDCTR.

atd Angle

The mean atd-angle values in the Madiga groups listed in table 3 are of higher proportion in females (R: 43.88 and L: 43.84) than in males (R: 41.89 and L: 41.49) and right than the left hand in both sexes of the general population. While the MDCDP males agree with the above trend, a reverse trend is observed in their females. But both sexes of MDCTR show a trend observed in the pooled group. However, 't' test fails to show significant inter group difference in either hand of both the sexes.

Table 2
Palmar a–b Ridge Count

Madiga groups	*Sex*	*Hand*	*Mainline index*			*t – value (d.f. = α)*		
			Mean ± S.E.	*S.D.*	*C.V.*	*Bilaterality*	*Sex difference*	*Inter group difference*
MDCDP	M	R	36.73 ± 0.46	4.57	12.44	0.59	3.65***	
	(100)	L	36.57 ± 0.52	5.17	14.13		2.69**	
	F	R	34.28 ± 0.49	4.95	14.44	1.14		
	(100)	L	34.61 ± 0.51	5.15	14.87			
MDCTR	M	R	34.43 ± 0.49	4.94	14.34	0.27	2.04*	
	(100)	L	34.35 ± 0.39	3.90	11.35			
	F	R	35.86 ± 0.50	4.99	13.91	1.32	3.09**	
	(100)	L	36.19 ± 0.45	4.54	12.54			
POOLED	M	R	35.58 ± 0.34	4.76	13.36	0.22	1.05	3.42***
	(200)	L	35.46 ± 0.32	4.54	12.79		0.13	3.42***
	F	R	35.07 ± 0.35	4.97	14.17	0.96		2.26*
	(200)	L	34.40 ± 0.34	4.85	13.69			2.32*

* Significant at 5% probability level.
** Significant at 1% probability level.
*** Significant at 0.1% probability level.

Table 3
atd Angle

Madiga groups	*Sex*	*Hand*	*Mainline index*			*t – value (d.f. = α)*		
			Mean ± S.E.	*S.D.*	*C.V.*	*Bilaterality*	*Sex difference*	*Inter group difference*
MDCDP	M	R	41.86 ± 0.58	5.76	13.75	1.08	2.46*	
	(100)	L	41.55 ± 0.55	5.55	13.36		3.21**	
	F	R	44.45 ± 0.88	8.83	19.89	0.46		
	(100)	L	44.72 ± 0.82	8.22	18.38			
MDCTR	M	R	41.92 ± 0.68	6.84	16.32	1.40	1.36	
	(100)	L	41.43 ± 0.66	6.60	15.92		1.51	
	F	R	43.30 ± 0.75	7.47	17.24	1.12		
	(100)	L	42.95 ± 0.76	7.56	17.60			
POOLED	M	R	41.89 ± 0.45	6.30	15.04	1.02	2.71**	0.07
	(200)	L	41.49 ± 0.43	6.08	14.64		3.33***	0.14
	F	R	43.88 ± 0.58	8.15	18.58	0.08		0.99
	(200)	L	43.84 ± 0.56	7.89	18.00			1.58

* Significant at 5% probability level.
** Significant at 1% probability level.
*** Significant at 0.1% probability level.

Bilateral differences are not found to be significant in any series of the Madigas as revealed by the paired't' test. t-values show significant sex differences in MDCDP and pooled group, but not in MDCTR.

SUMMARY

The study reports on bilateral palm prints among 400 unrelated individuals (200 Males and 200 Females) of Madigas in two revenue districts of Cuddapah and Chittoor in Andhra Pradesh were collected and analysed. The mean mainline index values are highly variable in both MDCDP and MDCTR groups. Further right hand shows higher variable than the left in all the Madiga series indicating a more pronounced transversality on the right palm than the left. The mean values of *a–b* ridge counts among male (R: 35.58, L: 35.46) and female (R: 35.07 and L: 35.40) series have not deviated much in the pooled Madigas, though higher values figured in males of MDCDP and females of MDCTR. The mean atd angle values are relatively higher in female (R: 43.88, L: 43.48) than male (R: 41.89, L: 41.49) series in both MDCDP and MDCTR groups.

REFERENCES

Census of India (1971), *Series 2–Andhra Pradesh Part V–A Town Directory.* Andhra Pradesh: Director of Census Operations.

Cummins H. and Midlo C. (1961), *"Finger prints, Palms and Soles",: An Introduction to Dermatoglyphics.* New York: Dover.

Holt S.B. (1968), Palmar Ridge Counts. *The Anthropologist* (Special Volume): 117–120.

Knussmann R. (1969), Biostatistische Familie Nunter–Suchungen Zur Hauleisten Variabilitatdes Menschen. *Humangenetik,* 8: 208–216.

Mandal B.K. and Sharma K.K.N. (2000), A Study on Palmar Inter Digital Ridge Counts Among the Lodha of West Bengal. *Man in India,* 80 (3 and 4): 359–265.

Mate M. (1975), The Ridge Counts of the Inter Digital *a–b, b–c and c–d* areas in a Normal Sample and in Cerebrally Damaged Patterns of Thuringia, G.D.R. (East Germany). *Am. J. Phys. Anthrop* 42: 233–235.

Penrose L.S. (1954), The Digital Triradius on the Hands of Parents and Sibs of Mangol Imbeciles, *Ann. Eugen (Lond)* 19: 10.

Penrose L.S. (1970), Measurement in Mental Deficiency. *Brit. J. Psycych* 116: 369–375.

Part-III

GENETIC STUDIES

14

HUMAN GENETICS IN COMMUNITY HEALTH PRACTICE IN INDIA: AN URGENT NEED OF ACTION

R.S. Balgir

INTRODUCTION

In this paper, human genetics in relation to community health and practices, i.e. population health have been discussed with a view and over emphasis on the action strategies for the well-being of the people against the common prevalent genetic diseases in India.

HUMAN HEALTH

Health is wealth, goes the popular adage. Health is also a source of happiness and comfort in life. The general health of each individual is basically assessed through two components, the mental and the physical health. An individual is considered to be healthy with the perfection of mental and physical conditions.

The mental and physical elements of health complement each other. They form the basic component of health and well-being of each individual and depend on the body constitution, the life-style and self-discipline one adopts, the food habits and the environment in which one lives.

A human being endowed with an absolutely perfect constitution does not normally contact illness except for the minor ailments due to external factors. The body is generally insulated within to avoid any illness and work perfectly. It is only hampered by the external factors like unhealthy lifestyle and the environment.

It is, therefore vital on the part of each individual to keep fit mentally as well as physically to lead a happy and comfortable life. While the genetic constitution provides all the necessary impetus and feedback right from conception to enable one to grow physically and mentally, the external feedback provided by the intake of nutritious food and physical exercise help the inner body mechanism to sustain health. Hence it should be kept in mind that the mysterious inner body mechanism granted by virtue of genes should be guarded and nurtured with healthy food and proper exercise.

The functioning of the human body system as such is so sensitive that the slightest impairment caused to any part of the system would affect the entire body. The human body and mind are set to act in tandem. As far as the individual is genetically fit, there is absolutely no reason why one should fall prey to the social/environmental evils that would ultimately hamper the whole system.

PUBLIC HEALTH

The dictionary meaning of public health is the science and practice of protecting and improving the health of a community, as by preventive medicine, health education, control of communicable diseases, application of sanitary measures, and monitoring of environmental hazards. In medical term, public health is community health. It has been said, "Health care is vital to all of us some of the time, but public health is vital to all of us all the time". The mission of public health is to fulfill the interest of society in assuring conditions in which people can be healthy. The three core public health functions are:

1. The assessment and monitoring of the health of communities and populations at risk to identify health problems and priorities;
2. The formulation of public policies designed to solve identified local and national health problems and priorities;
3. To assure that all populations have access to appropriate and cost-effective care, including health promotion and disease prevention services, and evaluation of the effectiveness of that care.

Public health professionals monitor and diagnose the health concerns of entire communities and promote healthy practices and behaviors to assure that populations stay healthy.

HUMAN GENETICS

Human genetics is the biological science, which deals with inherited characteristics, human origin and variations, application of genetic knowledge for genetic/marriage counseling, community health, prevention and control of genetic diseases, and promotion of health strategies for amelioration of human sufferings.

The dimensions of human diseases are being perceived in genetic terms today and the effects of genetic variation are being discovered as the root of many illnesses in the modern society. Human diseases with a genetic component are quite prevalent and the frequency varies with ethnic group, endogamy and geographical region in India. As a result of founder effect, genetic drift or selection of particular Mendelian conditions may occur at unusually high frequency in specific ethnic group, caste or tribe or locality (Balgir 1994).

GENETICS IN HEALTH AND DISEASE

Human genetic variability proposes a genetic paradigm of health and disease such that the health is viewed as a state of equilibrium and disease as disequilibrium in relationship between man and the environment. Any biological function involved is ultimately dependent on environment; a gene product controls the interaction between environment and the function, called phenotype. The interaction results either when the environment component is changed significantly or when the gene product is modified by mutation. The genetic paradigm recognizes the role of intrinsic (genetic) factors for individual disease susceptibility or resistance; the medical paradigm emphasizes the importance of extrinsic (environmental) factors in the etiology of a disease (Balgir 1999a).

Since individuals have their own genetic signatures, it follows from the genetic paradigm that each person is at his/her own specific risk for a particular disease. Each person is adjusted in a different manner to the environment and every one has a different and relative state of health. Thus, the traditional medical paradigm is effective in preventing and curing diseases when the environment plays the primary role in pathogenesis. However, for diseases involving prominent genetic component such as cardiac vascular disease, hyper-tension, duchenne muscular disease, Huntington's chorea, hemoglobinopathies, glucose-6-phosphate dehydrogenase (G-6-PD) deficiency, schizophenia, manic depressive psychosis, etc., their control requires a different approach (Balgir 2004a and b). It has become imperative for the practicing clinicians to detect the different disorders affecting the human being due to genetic origin. The treatment and prognosis of a malady depends on a correct diagnosis and also for its possible prevention.

The genetic paradigm recognizes disease as a spectrum. The position of a particular illness on the spectrum is relevant in planning of its prevention and treatment. There are some diseases in which the expression of a particular gene or genes in a specific environment is responsible for precipitating the illness, e.g. schizophrenia, manic-depressive psychosis, etc. The pharmacogenetic disorders and multifactorial diseases have this character, e.g. coronary artery disease, diabetes mellitus, etc. There are diseases whose origins lie in the interaction of specific environment with the genotype. Modern epidemics of non-communicable diseases fall in this category.

CURRICULUM IN GENETICS

Medical genetics is one of the most advancing fields of medicine. Since a few numbers of genetic centers exist in India, it is, therefore, expected that the primary health physicians should deal with common genetic disorders prevalent in the country. It is also desirable that they should be aware of the basic principles of genetics, available molecular techniques, and their applications in molecular diagnosis, carrier screening genetic counseling, and prenatal diagnosis (Balgir 2004b). At present, the undergraduate medical curriculum in India imparts practically no training in medical genetics; hence the knowledge among the clinicians is inadequate. The objective of teaching medical genetics is to train all clinicians in identifying genetic disorders and providing counseling for common genetic diseases. They should be able to identify the genetic abnormality for referral purpose to genetic clinics, accuracy and limitation of techniques and know about the indications and interpretation of various tests in genetics. The Medical Council of India needs to ensure adequate knowledge to be imparted to undergraduates and postgraduates in genetics about the basic and clinical aspects. Short-term training courses, lectures, workshops, conferences, etc. will be quite fruitful to improve the knowledge about genetics among the students, practicing clinicians and the medical fraternity as a whole (Balgir 2004b).

It is desirable that the government and the planning wings of the central and state governments must develop a long-term goal for the establishment and development of clinical laboratory for genetic services all over the country. It is highly essential because, if the genetic diagnosis is done without quality control and is incorrect, it can cause immense damage to the user of this service.

As the education is a state subject, the state government can review its resources in imparting training in medical genetics for faculty in different medical colleges, hospitals, community health centers, primary health centers, etc. to serve effectively for the betterment of the affected society. The population in the rural sectors harbours many genetic diseases in India.

GENETIC BURDEN

There is a heavy risk and load of genetic diseases in India because of the high birth rate, practice of consanguinity, territorial and caste/tribe endogamy and lack of rehabilitative facilities to poverty stricken rural masses. The cumulative allele frequency of the three most predominant abnormal hemoglobins, i.e. sickle cell, hemoglobin D and hemoglobin E has been found to be 5.35% in India (Balgir 1999b, 2000). The average allele frequency of hemoglobin D, sickle cell and hemoglobin E in India has been observed to be 0.86%, 4.3%, and 10.9%, respectively (Balgir 1996a). Every year 80,000 infants with congenital malformation, 27,200 infants with Down's syndrome, 5,000 infants with hereditary anemia, over 12,000 thalassemia children and 4,3 00 babies with Duchenne muscular dystrophy are born with high morbidity and mortality in India (Verma 1991). There are about 45 million people carriers of beta-thalassemia gene in India (Balgir 2000). It is alarming to note that on the whole, at least one child with genetic disease is born in every 40 seconds in India.

Thus, due to the huge population and a high birth rate, there are a large number of patients with genetic diseases in India. High rate of consanguinity (marriage among blood relatives) among many communities further increase the burden of genetic disorders, while lack of rehabilitative facilities escalates the burden of genetic disorders (Balgir 1995a, Balgir 2005a).

BIODIVERSITY AND HEALTH

Biodiversity refers to the totality of all heritable variations in the world, which means variety of all life forms–the different plants, animals and microorganisms, the genes they contain, and the ecosystems of which they form a part:

1. Genetic diversity–the variety of genetic material contained in all species that inhabit a region, including the variation within and between populations of species,
2. Species diversity–the variety of species,
3. Ecosystem diversity–the variety of habitats, biological communities (groups of organisms that co-occur and interact within a habitat), and ecological processes, and
4. Cultural diversity–the variation in behavior or customs among different groups of the same species.

Humans also derive aesthetic, cultural, intellectual and spiritual values from the Nature. Conservation of these natural ecosystems is essential for the very survival of humans as a species on the earth. Human health and well-being directly reflect the health of biodiversity of a region (Balgir 2004c).

About 80% of the world's population depends on plant-based medicines for primary healthcare. It is estimated that over 50% of commercially available drugs depend on bioactive compounds extracted/ patterned from non-human species. Currently 80,000 species are used for drug formulations. In fact, the first Symposium on Medicinal Plants in the world was held as early as 500 BC in India. The Ayurveda and Unani Systems, which treat a human being as a whole, are slow science today. Although known for centuries, as nothing existed in written form; the knowledge was passed on orally to next generation. Herbal medicine is the oldest system for human health and even today 80% of the Indians use herbs for treatment of ailments. Drugs or plant products routinely used by us for centuries together such as triphala, yashthimadha, pipari, vasaka, ashwagandha, motha (Methi), tinospora, etc. are commercially now exploited in India and abroad by the pharmaceutical companies. Nature's storehouse is still the largest (Balgir 2002a). Most of the chemically diverse sources of unique molecular architecture and of the genes that encode for them exist in nature. So far, less than 1% of flowering plants have been screened for their beneficial pharmaceutical properties.

Anthropogenic activities to meet the growing demand of a burgeoning population have increased (non-sustainable) resource use per capita, cultural homogenization, agricultural development, habitat fragmentation, environmental pollution, introduction of alien species and genes (through genetically modified organisms), and diseases, resulting in rapid climate change and natural habitat destruction. This has contributed to the degradation of the ecosystem or eco-degradation and lowering of its productivity and increase in pests, invasive species, etc.

Higher pollution levels in the environment have led to asthma, constriction of blood vessels, and increase in the incidence of heart disease/ cardiopulmonary disease, and lung cancer in human population.

Science is an adventure, and adventure stories need to be told, retold and expanded. The struggle of tribals explains the linkages between environment and health. Environmental health comprises aspects of human health including quality of life as determined by physical, biological, social and psychological constraints of environment (Balgir 2005a and b). In India, several tribal communities such as Saharia tribe of Rajasthan, Kutia Kondh of Belghar (Balgir 2004c) and Bonda tribe in Orissa, Muslim Gujjars of Himachal Pradesh (Balgir 1995b, 1999c), etc. are struggling for survival due to harsh environmental conditions, susceptibility to health hazards, nonavailability of potable water, inadequacy of nutrition and vulnerability to deleterious diseases like AIDS, syphilis, etc.

Today, several health-related issues of humans are crying for attention. The spread of HIV infection, the continuing surge of lifestyle illnesses, the perceived threat of bio-terrorism, the continuing scourge of malnutrition and infectious diseases afflicting children in the developing countries and the under-privileged sections the world over finding the healthcare system inaccessible, are some of the most prominent issues amongst them (Balgir 2005c). Rapid proliferation and multiplication of genetic disorders is one of such issues that has the potential of diminishing, if not nullifying, the benefits that mankind has reaped through the knowledge of anthropology for betterment, through different stages of development, and public welfare for the larger interests of human society.

ANTHROPOLOGICAL PERSPECTIVES

What makes anthropology? What does it mean to be human? What makes a human being? Why do people behave in particular ways? What are the historical and environmental pressures that helped shape the experience and behavior of a specific group of people? What are universal facts of human life?

The answers to above questions constitute the anthropology—the study all about. Anthropologists maintain intense curiosity and are careful observers of humans and their behavior. They consider such fascinating questions as how peoples' behavior changes over time, how people move about the world, why and how people from distant parts of the world and dissimilar cultures are different and similar, how the human species has evolved over millions of years, and how individuals understand and operate successfully in distinct cultural settings (Balgir 2002b). They explore variations in time and space to improve our understanding on the basics of human biology, society, and culture.

Human migration is as old as human history. For over three millennia, this land of ours, i.e. India, has drawn people from all over the world: itinerant traders, inveterate travelers, passionate proselytizers, sundry adventurers, foreign diplomats and conquering armies. Beginning with the arrival of Aryan-speaking people from the plains of Central Asia more than 3,000 years ago, this steady influx has made India the rich civilization, the palimpsest that it is. Alongside this ceaseless cross-border flow of communities and cultures, India has had an equally long history of internal migration, displacement and re-location. Marathas, Gujaratis, Marwaris, Tamils, Telugus and Bengalis, there is not a single linguistic, ethnic or religious community in India that has not seen substantial migration in history (Balgir 1995a, 1996b). Just as many present day Brahmin clans in Tamil Nadu trace their genealogy to ancient North Indian sages, so do the Saraswat Brahmins of the Konkan region, locating their ancestral roots in far away Kashmir. In more modern times, the movement of Marwaris to Kolkata and the North-east, the Bengalis to the plains of Northern India, the Gujaratis to Maharashtra and the Marathas to places as far a field as Tamil Nadu, Madhya Pradesh has been as substantial as it is well-documented.

The reasons for this migration may have been many, but the effect has been much the same. The emergence of a bewilderingly complex cultural mosaic-what Tagore, and later Nehru referred to as our essential unity in diversity.

> *"No one knows whence and at whose call*
> *came pouring endless inundations of men*
> *rushing madly along—to loose themselves in the sea:*
> *Aryans and non-Aryans, Dravidians and Chinese*
> *Scythians, Huns, Pathans and Moghuls—*
> *all are mixed, merged and lost in one body.*
>
> *Now the door has opened to the West*
> *and gifts in hand they beckon and they come —*
> *they will give and take, meet and bring together,*
> *none shall be turned away*
> *from the shore of this vast sea of humanity*
> *that is India."*

—*Rabindranath Tagore*

What is remarkable too is that, apart from the odd case, the people of this country have been, through the ages, welcoming of outsiders in their midst. Ironically, it is only with the onset of democracy that several Indian states have seen the growth of anti-outsider movements with the slogan of nativism. This has affected biological endowment of anthropology towards betterment, society welfare, and development in India (Balgir 1995a).

Biomedical anthropology is disease-centered and its investigations inquire into the impact of the disease (or condition) upon biological processes of individuals or the populations to which they belong (Balgir 2002a, 2005c).

In constitutional medicine, the study of morphological variability among individuals and groups is a factor in disease, has long reflected the input of anthropologists especially in clinical settings and maintaining secular trends of particular ethnic group or population.

In large part, the involvement of physical or biological anthropology from its inception with studies of disease is due to the interest of many early researchers in the relationship between anatomical form and function, the relationship between variations in form and abnormalities in function in different ethnic groups and populations.

The study of the disease process received its greatest impetus with two developments within biological sciences. The first was the rise of population biology, particularly population genetics, a conceptual approach to human variation, based on natural selection, genetic drift and consequences of adaptive significance. Intensive search for relationships between genetic polymorphisms and disease by population geneticists have come up. The second major development was rise of human ecology as an approach to understanding the complexity of population and environment interactions.

Thus human ecology seeks to understand humans and their problems by studying individuals and populations as biological entities profoundly modified by culture and by studying the effects of environment on man and those of man upon his environment (Balgir 1996b). Explosion of population has not only affected the quality of human life but the survival also in terms of demand of requirements, needs and necessities of daily life under the shrinking resources.

A natural outgrowth of this development is the rise of health ecology leading to basic and applied studies in medical ecology, epidemiology, medical anthropology, health and nutrition. The integration of issues related to health, disease and nutrition, named as nutritional anthropology, but I would like to add here in nutrition the various aspects of human diets or dietetrics due to one's liking and disliking, and differential absorption of nutrients, which is a highly flourishing field in anthropology because of biological components involved in it including the ecosystems. Human behavior, habits, habitats, occupation, daily biological and physiological activities, all amply has contribution towards human health.

Most interesting and rewarding field that has come in the forefront is the human developmental (gestational or intra-uterine period) anthropology and psychological (occupational causes) stress, which has profound effects upon the human physiology, personality and human (predictive) behavior throughout the life of an individual (Balgir 2002a).

Decision-making role of the patient and family members regarding affordability of treatment, side effects of allopathic drugs, side effects of birth control pills, body changes and differences in menstrual flow, are perceived as very important health related issues for the well-being of individual.

Your food habits could be your worst enemies. The kind of food we eat is instrumental in endowing us with qualities such as a sense of well-being, concentration, alertness and different energy levels (Balgir 2002a). The food you eat can have a huge impact on your mood and your energy levels. All human beings have chemicals in our brains called the neurotransmitters. Certain neurotransmitters excite us while others make us calm. Three of these chemical neurotransmitters, namely, Dopamine, Norepinephrine and Serotonin, are made in the brain from byproducts of the food we eat. Dopamine and Norepinephrine are the alertness chemicals. When your brain is producing these, you have a tendency to think and react more quickly, and feel more motivated, attentive and mentally energetic. Serotonin is the calming and relaxing chemical. When the brain is using serotonin, feelings of stress and tension decrease and the mind can concentrate and focus better. Your mind is not going "a million miles an hour" in all directions. Serotonin also reduces reaction time and, depending on what time of day it is, you can feel sleepy or sluggish. Proteins encourage the production of Dopamine and Norepinephrine, which produces alertness, mental energy and faster reaction time for the duration of two-three hours. The monitoring of these chemicals is genetically determined.

INNOVATIVE DEVELOPMENTS

One of the very first biological questions a child asks is why there are boys and girls–or some variation thereof. I suspect that the way a parent handles this question has a profound effect on a child's future scientific curiosity. Certainly it is one that I pestered my father with until he said, "When you grow up, you figure it out". Many current scientific findings make it useful and very enjoyable for an individual with a basic biological education and a sense of humor. Historical discoveries and medical advancements, which made genes encoded on the X chromosome, are extremely important to scientists' understanding of gene regulation. Some of the genetic characters are specific only to females, which influence the human behavior.

There are discrepancies of immunological disorders in human females and males. Understanding why, in certain diseases, there are major differences in rates of incidence between the sexes will be one of our biggest scientific challenges.

Sound Sleep, Sound Body

The people who get a good night's sleep have a better immune system than those with sleep problems. Researchers studied patients who had received Hepatitis-A vaccinations. After four weeks, those patients who slept well had developed twice as many anti-bodies in their blood system than those who had sleeping problems. The researchers concluded that people who sleep badly have a much more lethargic reaction in the battle against viruses and so are less protected against infections.

Technologies that Deliver

A diabetic who is fed up with using syringes and hates injections daily need not wait for long to do away with syringes and needles. There are 30 to 40 million Indians out of 200 millions in the world who suffer from diabetes. There are 10 million diabetics neglect the insulin treatment, many of them because of just such an aversion to needles. Soon they will be able to sniff insulin through the nose or spray a clear insulin mist directly into the mouth and lungs. The inhaled insulin product, Exubera, generates an aerosol cloud from insulin by compressing air and crushing the drug into tiny particles that disperse throughout the lungs is expected to hit the market. The synthesis of the medicine is only one part of the drug. Without delivery you just won't have a successful treatment. Researchers scrutinize every part of the body–including the skin, nose, lungs, intestine and back of the eye–to transport a drug precisely to its target. A therapeutic agent often thwarts a disease only when it is delivered accurately, timely and at a precise dose rate.

Cure for Male Infertility

In what could be a cure for male infertility, scientists have completed a laboratory experiment with artificial sperm capable of fertilizing an egg for the first time. The new research is seen as also aiding efforts to produce artificial eggs from stem cells. The scientists have successfully coaxed embryonic stem cells from mice to mature into primitive sperm, which were then injected into eggs to form normal embryos. The advance opens a new frontier in infertility research, suggesting it will be possible to manufacture sperm for men who make none of their own.

Fertility's New Frontier takes Shape in the Test Tube

It is day seven of a young woman's menstrual cycle. More than a dozen small follicles in her ovaries respond to the surge of hormones, releasing estrogen, filling with blood and growing faster than any other structure in the body. Within a couple of days, one among them becomes dominant, growing even larger and protecting and nourishing the egg it carries. The others shrink rapidly, stop secreting estrogen and disappear. But if you could capture those young follicles before they shrink into oblivion, and you could allow each to fulfill its destiny and release an egg capable of fertilization. Scientists have started clinical trials to collect immature follicles from young women with polycystic ovary syndrome–who have many more follicles than average, and bathe the cells in a nourishing mixture of growth factors, proteins, vitamins and amino acids. The technique, called in vitro maturation (IVM), has already been successful in some East Asian nations, in Australia and in Canada. Nearly 200 babies have been born and, so far, all appear perfectly healthy. IVM is one of many new advances in the booming field of assistive reproductive technology (ART), which burst into fame with the birth of the first "test tube" baby in 1978. Today, there are more than a million babies born by in vitro fertilization (IVF). This IVM technique allows women to bypass hormone treatment and offers women with polycystic ovary syndrome a safe alternative to IVF. However, contrary to these developments, some are of the view that babies born by ART might be at greater risk of birth defects, low birth weight and genetic diseases.

Approval of Human Embryo Research

In theory, therapeutic cloning is simple. It involves taking a donor egg from which the nucleus has been removed and replacing it with the nuclear DNA material from the cell of another organism. The result is a blastocyst, a stage of development of an embryo when it's about five days old. This is when embryonic stem cells can be extracted. Such cells are the stuff of biotech dreams since they can be transplanted to grow into almost any of the body's cell types and combat or cure diseased tissues and organs. In practice, however, the process is dicey, at least at the current level of understanding and technology available. So when a South Korean team announced recently that it had successfully managed to create patient-specific, tailor-made stem cells from such cloned embryos, which would not be immediately rejected by the recipient's immune system, it made headline news around the world. Especially since the Koreans also managed to create up to 11 batches of these cells, which could potentially replace those, damaged by spinal cord injuries, diabetes, Parkinson's and other diseases.

The use of human frozen embryos for research with the consent of parents to derive new stem cell lines has been approved in many countries.

Accordingly, the spare embryos are to be frozen throughout the full fertility period of the woman for subsequent use in transplantation in the defective individuals.

The United States, usually at the forefront of hi-tech innovation, has managed to emasculate itself for embryonic stem cell research in 2001, limiting it to only some 70-odd stem cell batches in existence. About 8-10 of these were in India, which, along with countries like the UK, Belgium, Sweden, Israel, China, Japan and South Korea, have a far more liberal and supportive system. With more than 15 laboratories in India involve in this work and Rs.500 crores of Department of Biotechnology (DBT) budget, of which 30% is allocated for stem cell related study in India (May 2005) today has the potential to become a global hub for this kind of research.

What are stem cells? Most adult cells in the body are developed to perform specific functions and cannot be transformed to suddenly take on another role. For example, a living cell cannot take on the role of a heart cell. But stem cells can. They are still at an early stage of development and retain the potential to turn into many different types of cell.

Why are they so useful? When a stem cell divides, each new cell has the potential to either remain a stem cell or become another type of cell with a more specialized function. It should be possible to turn stem cells into a super "repair kit" for the body to treat Parkinson's disease, Alzheimer's disease, heart disease and many others.

Are there different types of stem cells? Yes. The most useful stem cells come from the tissue of embryos, as they are pluripotent - having the ability to become virtually any type of cell within the body. Stem cells are also found within adult organs.

Can they be grown in the lab? Large numbers of embryonic stem cells can be relatively easily grown in culture. But adult stem cells are rare in mature tissues and science is still working on ways to grow them in the lab in sufficient numbers.

Is the use controversial? Very well. Particularly the use of embryonic stem cells as they are typically taken from lab created embryos that are just four or five days old and are little more than a microscopic ball of cells.

Are there safety concerns? Yes. It is feared that stem cell therapy could pass viruses and other disease causing agents to people who receive cell transplantations. They may also turn cancerous.

The human genome contains a large amount of highly repetitive DNA sequences including many variable number of tandem repeats (VNTRs). Minisatellites are the loci composed of tandemly repeated sequences between 10 and 100 base pairs (bp) and show substantial allelic variability in the number of repeat units. The VNTR markers have been used for different applications, including linkage analysis, forensic identification, paternity testing, anthropological research and phylogenetic studies.

Indian population needs to be studied with a view to define the distribution of various polymorphic DNA markers, e.g. VNTR, Minisatellite, Microsatellite, STR, etc.

HUMAN GENETICS IN CLINICAL PRACTICE

The clinician plays an important role in genetic studies by determining phenotypically pure categories of disease, detecting mild manifestations (carrier status), in relatives and pointing out the features which suggest further investigations in cytological, biochemical, pedigree analysis, and other specific tests.

There are three levels of intervention, i.e. primary (individual or propositus), secondary (relatives) and tertiary (community or population) at which the genetic problems can be handled (Balgir 1999a). When an individual is affected, it is likely that his/her sibling will either be affected; carrier or normal and he/she will transmit the abnormal genes to his/her offspring like his/her parents. It would be desirable that the person suffering from serious hereditary disease, carrying high (theoretical or empirical) risk of transmission is to be encouraged to refrain from having children. This may be achieved by education and counseling, but may never be enforced.

Accentuation of any abnormality, other than the infections, in the family members (including the first degree relatives, i.e. father, mother, brother/sister, son/daughter and both at paternal or maternal side), indicates the involvement of genetic disorder. Once the accurate diagnosis is made, it is the responsibility of a clinical practitioner to suspect the segregation of the disease among the other family members. Genetic disorders can be detected at birth (even before birth during antenatal period), during manifestations of signs and symptoms or precipitating factor, irrespective of the age/sex of the individual. However, some genetic disorders, e.g. Huntington's disease, Duchenne muscular dystrophy, etc. are age/sex specific depending upon the involvement of type, number and side of chromosome of genes.

At tertiary level, community or population screening will provide useful information about the prevalence of a disease. Community participation will help to completely eradicate the disease, which is creating havoc in some communities. Community sensitization, motivation and imparting of health education through well organized preventive program is highly desirable (Balgir 1999b).

The advent of molecular testing has been a great boon for the people, as this has enabled antenatal diagnosis of many burdensome disorders, which were earlier not identifiable in the fetus. Molecular diagnosis is now possible for a large number of genetic disorders. For the strategy of management of genetic diseases, the intake of patients into the programme will occur by two routes: through planned genetic screening and through individual referrals for medical diagnosis and genetic counseling (Balgir 1999a and b). Genetic screening has three major objectives:

(a) To provide opportunity for medical intervention (treatment)

(b) To provide opportunity for counseling about reproductive options; and

(c) To collect research data pertinent to public health policy and basic knowledge.

At present, there are several institutes/centers throughout India especially in Metro-cities where sufficient technological facilities are available for the detection/diagnosis of various genetic diseases along with the detailed investigations as well as genetic/marriage counseling (Balgir 1999a and b).

The accumulated genetic data have enhanced the rapid advancement of clinical genetics in India. Basically, the practice of genetic medicine seeks the answer to three questions:

1. ***What is wrong***—The answer is accurate diagnosis, which is aided by pedigree analysis, biochemical tests, cytogenetics and chromosomal studies of cultured fibroblast and leucocytes for pinpointing the gene or chromosome responsible for a change. Additional factors involved are the environmental ones—internal, external or social.
2. ***What will happen***—The answer is prognosis, which is the basis of genetic counseling, to be helped by prenatal diagnosis, family history and pedigree studies.
3. ***What can be done about it***—The answer is treatment–palliative and/or curative. Prevention is better than cure in some instances, when the parents are carriers. Stem cell implantation or gene therapy is the other option, although limited in India. For both these alternatives, exhaustive knowledge about the basic defect is a must. For the prevention of recessive diseases, identification of carriers will help to impart prospective counseling and gene therapy in future.

Currently in India, the emphasis is on the small family norms and the socio-economic constraints have created a desired in all the eligible couples that every child born should be normal. Thus, it has been emphasized that medical genetics play a pivotal role in the clinical practice, therapy, innovative developments, prevention, and the management of genetic diseases.

Any community must be encouraged to organize itself in order to take advantage of the programmes designed for its development and health in the light of human genetics, socio-cultural traditions and eco-friendly environment. The foregoing discussion confirms that unless appropriate biotechnological approaches like locality specific, community specific and need-based health care delivery system is evolved which is appropriate, acceptable, accessible, and affordable, the goal of health for all would remain a Utopian dream!

No doubt, other sectors have a role to play. But, there is no running away from the fact that healthcare providers will have to play a pivotal role. It is better if the anthropologists begin with analyzing their own behavior before inviting and goading other disciplines to act. Small steps such as changing one's own practices and guidelines could be the first step. This could be followed with other avenues for action. The action anthropology era began several decades ago. Let us not write its obituary so soon.

ACKNOWLEDGEMENTS

Author is grateful to the Director General, Indian Council of Medical Research, New Delhi for providing the necessary facilities.

REFERENCES

Balgir R.S. (2005a), Genetic Disease Burden, Nutritional Status and Tribal Health Care in Chhattisgarh of Central-East India: A Status Paper. In Pati R.N. (ed.): *Tribes of Chhattisgarh: Needs, Problems and Development Perspectives.* New Delhi: IK Foundation of India (Bhubaneswar) in Press.

Balgir R.S. (2005b), Emerging Trends in Genetic Epidemiology of Hemoglobinopathy in the Seven Sister States of North Eastern India. In Das Rajat Kanti & Basu Debashish (eds.). *North East India in Perspectives: Biology, Social Formation and Contemporary Problems.* New Delhi: Akansha Publishing House, pp.17-37.

Balgir R.S. (2005c), Biomedical Anthropology in Contemporary Tribal Society of India. In Behera Deepak Kumar & Pfeffer Georg (eds).*Contemporary Society: Tribal Studies (Tribal Situation in India).* Vol.6. New Delhi: Concept Publishing Company. pp. 292-301.

Balgir R.S. (2004a), Health Care Strategies, Genetic Load, and Prevention of Hemoglobino-pathies in Tribal Communities in India. *South Asian Anthropologist* 4: 189-198.

Balgir R.S. (2004b), Medical Genetics in Orissa: An Urgency in Health and Disease. *Proceedings of the 8th Orissa Bigyan Congress on Science for Sustenance* Held During 11-12th December 2004, Bhubaneswar, pp. 20-23.

Balgir R.S. (2004c), Dimensions of Rural Tribal Health, Nutritional Status of Kondh Tribe and Tribal Welfare in Orissa: A Biotechnological Approach. *Proceedings of the UGC Sponsored National Conference on Human Health and Nutrition: A Biotechnological Approach* (Lead Lecture), 12-13th December 2004, Thane. pp. 47-57.

Balgir R.S. (2002a), Biomedical Anthropology in the Service of Mankind in the New Millennium: Are we Ready? In Bhasin M.K. and Malik S.L. (eds.). *Anthropology: Trends and Applications.* New Delhi: Kamala Raj Enterprises. pp. 141-147.

Balgir R.S. (2002b), Academic Curricula of Anthropology Need Overhauling:An Observation. *Man in India* 82: 407-412.

Balgir R.S. (2000), The Burden of Hemoglobinopathies in India and the Challenges Ahead. *Curr. Sci.* 79: 1536-1547.

Balgir R.S. (1999a), Medical Genetics in Clinical Practice in India.*Curr. Med. Trends* 3: 567-572.

Balgir R.S. (1999b), Control and Prevention of Genetic Load of Hemoglobinopathies in India. *Natl. Med. J. India* 12: 234-238.

Balgir R.S. (1999c), Biomedical Anthropology and Health Status of the Tribal Muslim Gujjars of Himachal Pradesh, India. In Sengupta Sarthak (ed.): *Health, Healers and Healing: Studies in Medical Anthropology*. Dibrugarh: National Library Publishers. Chapter I, pp. 1-19.

Balgir R.S. (1996a), Genetic Epidemiology of the Three Predominant Abnormal Hemoglobins in India *J. Assocn. Phys. India*, 44: 25-28.

Balgir R.S. (1996b), Biomedical Anthropological Approaches in North Eastern India: A Synthesis of the Tea Garden Population of Assam. In Sengupta Sarthak (ed.). *Peoples of North East India: Anthropological Perspective*. New Delhi: Gyan Publishing House. pp. 91-104.

Balgir R.S. (1995a), Genetic Markers in the Tribal Health, Development and Welfare with Special Reference to North Eastern India. In Sharma J.C. (ed). *Anthropology, Population and Development*. New Delhi: Inter-India Publications. pp. 151-171.

Balgir R.S. (1995b), Environmental Constraints, Health and Population Trends Among the Muslim Gujjars of Himachal Pradesh, India *J. Hum. Ecol.* 6: 191-196.

Balgir R.S. (1994), Human Genetics in Tribal Health. *Curr. Med. Trends* 9:1.

Verma I.C. (1991), Human Genetics on the Crest of Development. *Bull Hum Genet* 16:1-6.

15

GENETIC AND ENVIRONMENTAL FACTORS IN MENSTRUAL CHARACTERISTICS AND PREMENSTRUAL SYNDROME: A TWIN STUDY

Krishan Sharma

INTRODUCTION

The development and variability of menstrual patterns are of considerable clinical interest. These patterns are studied with reference to chronological and gynecological ages. Rates and patterns of the adolescent growth spurt and sexual maturation are apparently under genetic control. This is borne out of twin research (Fischbein, 1977; Sharma, 1983; Wilson, 1986; Treloar and Martin, 1990).

Premenstrual syndrome (PMS) is experienced after menarche, and is defined as the recurrence of symptoms limited to the premenstruum with their complete absence at least seven days in the postmenstruum (Dalton, 1984). PMS usually affects females in the age range of 25 to 35 years (Wyatt et al., 2000; Dickerson et al., 2003). It is characterized by a series of physical and emotional symptoms that some women experience on a regular basis by the cyclical recurrence of symptoms during the luteal phase of the menstrual cycle. A large number of symptoms are associated with PMS. List runs over 150 symptoms. Estimates of prevalence of premenstrual symptoms vary substantially, partly because of differences in definitions, instruments and populations (Woods et al., 1982; Johnson et al., 1988; River-Tovar and Frank, 1990). Studies show that many women experience no PMS, a substantial number experiences mild symptoms and a few women report severe or disabling symptoms (Severino and Molina, 1989).

The etiology of PMS remains an enigma. It is complex and multifactorial. Research suggests that altered regulation of neurohormones and neurotransmitters is involved (Kessel, 2000; Wyatt et al., 2000). Lombard et al. (2004) have found significantly lower levels of allopregnanolone hormone during luteal phase in PMS group women.

Several family and twin studies suggest significant familial and hereditary components of variation to explain individual differences in the vulnerability to PMS symptoms (Kantero and Widholm, 1971; Dalton et al., 1987; Van den Akker et al., 1987; Merikangas et al., 1993; Condon, 1993; Kendler et al., 1998). These inferences have been contradicted by a few other studies (Glick et al., 1993).

The present study was undertaken to evaluate PMS symptoms in a sample of relatively young twin females. The major objective was to examine etiological importance of genetic and environmental factors in retrospectively reported patterns of menstrual characteristics, age at menarche and PMS.

MATERIAL AND METHODS

Twin registry at Panjab University, Department of Anthropology, was formed in the year 1975. It has been updated from time to time. The twins belong to urban Punjabi population of Chandigarh. The zygosities of the same-sexed twin pairs were determined by the similarity for various genetic markers: A1A2BO, Rh, MN, Kell and Duffy blood groups, ABH secretion, PTC tasting ability, dermatoglyphics and photographs. This criterion gives a probability of error of less than 3% (see Sharma, 1999; 2005).

The data of the present report were collected on a sample of 14 MZ and 12 DZ female twin pairs in the age range of 14 to 24 years. The subjects were quizzed to get detailed information on their menstrual characteristics by using a structured interview schedule. The term menstrual cycle length in the study meant the number of days from the first day of the menstrual flow up to the day preceding the day of the next menstrual flow. The term, duration of menstrual flow, was defined as the number of the days the bleeding was recorded by the girl for the each menstrual cycle. The intensity of bleeding was rated on a three-point-scale. The term gynecological age referred to the number of years after the age of menarche. The list of premenstrual symptoms was prepared following standard books (Severino and Moline, 1989; Stewart, 1989). Two different types of approaches are used in the literature for assessing PMS. The first uses retrospective method through questionnaire asking women to report their experiences on either their last cycle or a typical cycle. The second uses prospective method asking women to record their daily ratings in menstrual diaries of symptoms experienced throughout one or more cycles. The latter approach is costly, cumbersome and requires complex mathematical handling, such as sine-wave fitting (Sampson and Jenner, 1977). Retrospective questionnaire approach is potentially contaminated by retrospective falsification and over reporting. Some studies used both these approaches and found poor agreement between them (Christensen and Oei, 1989). A number of studies have presented a defence of the retrospective approach (Halbreich et al., 1982; Hart et al., 1987). In this study too, retrospective approach was used to assess PMS. The subjects were asked to record the presence of symptoms if these were experienced about one-week prior to the menstrual period along with the extent of symptoms. The three key elements of the diagnosis were: (i) Consistent occurrence of symptoms, (ii) occurrence of these symptoms about one week prior to the menstrual flow period, and symptom free phase following menses (iii) severity of the symptoms on a three-point-scale. Symptoms occurring during the menstrual flow like stomach cramps, abdomen pain, or nausea were not included as PMS symptoms.

Intraclass correlations for MZ and DZ twins were calculated and these were used to calculate to Holzinger's heritability estimate by using the formula; $h^2= r_{MZ}- r_{DZ} /1-r_{DZ}$ (Holzinger, 1929).

RESULTS

Prevalence, severity and frequency of various PMS symptoms are given in Table 1. Prevalence is higher in DZ (77.27%) than MZ (64.29%) twins. 18% of DZ twins experienced severe PMS, against none in MZ twins. The most commonly reported symptoms are fatigue, irritability, nervous tension, mood swings and increased physical activity.

Table1

Premenstrual Syndrome (PMS) in MZ and DZ Twins: Prevalence and Symptoms

	MZ (N=28)		*DZ (N=22)*	
	N	%	N	%
1. Prevalence/Severity				
Absent	10	35.71	5	22.73
Present	18	64.29	17	77.27
Mild	8	28.57	5	22.73
Moderate	10	35.71	8	36.36
Severe	-	-	4	18.18
2. Symptoms of PMS				
(i) PMT-A. Anxiety				
Nervous tension	9	32.14	7	31.82
Mood swings	10	35.71	7	31.82
Irritability	9	32.14	4	18.18
Anxiety	5	17.86	5	22.73
(ii) PMT-H. Heaviness/Headache/ Physical				
Weight-gain	-	-	3	13.64
Swelling of extremities	1	3.57	2	9.09
Breast tenderness	2	7.14	1	4.54
Abdominal pain/bloating	2	7.14	6	27.27
Headache	3	10.71	3	13.64
Heart pounding	1	3.57	2	9.09
Fatigue	11	39.28	7	31.82
Dizziness or fainting	3	10.71	-	-
Heavy/aching legs	2	7.14	5	22.73
Generalized aches	5	17.86	1	4.54

Contd...

	MZ (N=28)		DZ (N=22)	
	N	%	N	%
(iii) PMT-C. Cravings				
Craving for sweets	8	28.57	3	13.64
Increased appetite	4	14.28	3	13.64
(iv) PMT-D. Depression				
Depression	4	14.28	5	22.73
Forgetfulness	4	14.28	5	22.73
Crying/tearfulness	3	10.71	3	13.64
Confusion	7	25.00	4	18.18
Insomnia	2	7.14	1	4.54
Disorientation	-	-	1	4.54
Clumsiness	1	3.57	1	4.54
Thought of suicide	-	-	2	9.09
Agoraphobia	3	10.71	4	18.18
(v) Other symptoms				
Increased physical activity	6	21.43	7	31.82
Bad breath	-	-	2	9.09
Sensitivity to light	1	3.57	2	9.09
Excessive thirst	5	17.86	5	22.73

Frequency distribution of various menstrual characteristics is given in Table 2. Severe intensity of menstrual flow was reported by 21.43% of MZ and 4.17% of DZ twins. Table 2 shows that greater the intensity of menstrual flow, higher is the mean gynecologic age, both in MZ and DZ twins. But no such trend is observed for the duration of the menstrual flow. Higher numbers of DZ twins (41.67%) have 3-4 days of menstrual flow period as compared to the MZ twins (14.28%).Converse is the position for 5-6 days of duration period, where 20.84% of DZ twins have this duration compared to 35.71% of MZ twins. Majority of MZ (60.71%) and DZ (62.5%) twins have 29-31 days of menstrual cycle length. Table 2 shows that highest mean gynecologic age is observed in the middle categories of the duration of flow and length of menstrual cycle traits.

Results of genetic analysis of various menstrual characteristics are given in Tables 3 and 4. It is evident from the Table 3 that DZ twins (4.59) have slightly higher PMS score than MZ twins (3.96), but the differences between them are not statistically significant. Significant differences are observed between zygosities for mean duration of menstrual flow. The mean value is about 4 days in DZ twins and 5 days in MZ twins. Mean length of menstrual cycle is slightly greater in MZ than in DZ twins, but the differences are not statistically significant.

Within pair F ratios between zygosities are insignificant for PMS scores, duration of menstrual flow and length of menstrual cycle indicating insignificant genetic component of variation for these traits. Similarly, concordance rates (see Table 4) in MZ twins for these characteristics in MZ twins are lower than DZ twins except for intensity of menstrual flow.

These results also do not favor genetic hypothesis to explain individual differences for these four menstrual characteristics. On the contrary, significant within-pair F-ratio between zygosities for age of menarche reveals significant genetic component of variation for this characteristics.

Table 2
Frequency of Various Types of Menstrual Characteristics with Reference to Mean Gynecological Age

Trait	*MZ (N=14)*				*DZ (N=12)*			
	Frequency		*Gynecological age*		*Frequency*		*Gynecological age*	
	N	%	*Mean (Yrs)*	*SD*	N	%	*Mean (Yrs)*	*SD*
1. Intensity of menstrual flow								
Mild	3	10.71	4.93	0.90	3	12.50	3.67	0.58
Moderate	18	64.28	2.54	1.85	20	83.33	3.98	3.39
Severe	6	21.43	7.32	2.91	1	4.17	5.00	-
Irregular	1	3.57	4.00	-	-	-	-	-
2. Duration of menstrual flow (Days)								
3	1	3.57	2.40	-	6	25.00	5.25	4.08
3-4	3	10.71	3.90	0.85	4	16.67	2.58	2.80
3-7	-	-	-	-	1	4.17	1.00	-
4	4	14.28	4.70	2.20	7	29.17	4.67	3.59
4-5	5	17.86	1.28	1.65	1	4.17	2.00	-
4-7	1	3.57	10.00	-	-	-	-	-
5	5	17.86	5.46	2.12	4	16.67	3.50	0.58
5-6	3	10.71	1.97	1.91	-	-	-	-
6	2	7.14	3.00	2.83	1	4.17	4.00	-
7	2	7.14	7.50	3.54	-	-	-	-
8	1	3.57	0.90	-	-	-	-	-
Irregular	1	3.57	4.00	-	-	-	-	-
3. Length of menstrual cycle (Days)								
22	-	-	-	-	1	4.17	0.5	-
24	1	3.57	10.0	-	-	-	-	-
25-26	1	3.57	10.0	-	-	-	-	-
26	-	-	-	-	2	8.33	10.0	2.83
26-27	1	3.57	8.5	-	-	-	-	-
28	5	17.86	4.36	2.58	5	20.83	4.4	2.22
28-34	-	-	-	-	1	4.17	5.0	-
29-30	1	3.57	2.40	-	-	-	-	-
30	14	50.00	3.47	1.76	15	62.50	3.2	2.62
31	2	7.14	0.20	-	-	-	-	-
30-40	2	7.14	1.35	0.49	-	-	-	-
Irregular	1	3.57	4.00	-	-	-	-	-

Results of intraclass correlation analysis and heritability estimates are presented in Table 5. Heritability for age of menarche is significantly high with a value of 0.67. Heritability estimates for other traits are substantially low.

Table 3
Mean, SD, and F-tests Contrasting within and between-zygosities Mean Squares for Menstrual Characteristics

	MZ	DZ	Test statistics value
1. PMS Score			
Mean score	3.96	4.59	-
S.D.	3.69	3.96	-
t-test	-	-	1.13
WMS	7.18	9.14	-
AMS	20.50	22.88	-
F-ratio (WDZ/WMZ)	-	-	1.27
F-ratio (TMZ/TDZ)	-	-	0.86
2. Age at menarche			
Mean (Yrs)	12.95	13.07	-
S.D.	0.87	0.93	-
t-test	-	-	0.48
WMS	0.15	0.51	-
AMS	1.44	1.27	-
F-ratio (WDZ/WMZ)	-	-	3.46*
F-ratio (TMZ/TDZ)	-	-	0.89
3. Duration of menstrual flow			
Mean (days)	4.93	3.98	-
S.D.	1.17	0.84	-
t-test	-	-	3.28*
WMS	0.56	0.34	-
AMS	2.01	1.10	-
F-ratio (WDZ/WMZ)	-	-	0.61
F-ratio (TMZ/TDZ)	-	-	1.70
4. Length of menstrual cycle			
Mean (days)	29.56	28.96	-
S.D.	2.28	1.99	-
t-test	-	-	1.00
WMS	3.11	2.54	-
AMS	7.86	5.50	-
F-ratio (WDZ/WMZ)	-	-	0.82
F-ratio (TMZ/TDZ)	-	-	1.36

* $P < 0.05$.

Table 4
Concordance for Menstrual Characteristics

	Concordance			
	MZ (N=14)		DZ (N=12)	
	N	%	N	%
1. Intensity of menstrual flow	3	21.43	2	16.67
2. Duration of menstrual flow	4	28.57	4	33.33
3. Length of menstrual cycle	8	57.14	7	58.33
4. Premenstrual syndrome	8/10	80.00	8/9	88.89

Table 5
Intraclass Correlation in MZ and DZ Twins and Holzinger's Heritability Estimate for Various Menstrual Characteristics

Trait	*Intraclass correlation coefficients*		*Holzinger's heritability estimate h^2*
	MZ	*DZ*	
PMS	0.48	0.43	0.09
Age of menarche	0.81	0.43	0.67*
Duration of menstrual flow	0.56	0.53	0.06
Length of menstrual cycle	0.43	0.37	0.10

*P<0.05

DISCUSSION

Our findings reinforce the view that there is a substantial genetic effect on individual differences in age at menarche reported by earlier studies (Chen et al., 1980; Kantero and Widholm 1971; Van den Akker et al., 1987; Martin and Treloar, 1991). Genetic variance and heritability estimates for the other menstrual and premenstrual symptoms/patterns have been found to be much lower in this study. Kendler et al. (1992) reported the presence of nonadditive genetic influences for menstrual flow with an overall heritability of 0.34. Studies by Silberg et al. (1987) and Treloar et al. (1998) have reported heritability of 0.22, 0.19 for 1981 sample and 0.20 for 1989 data respectively. These reports indicate that both genetic and environmental factors undoubtedly affect individual variations for menstrual flow and other menstrual patterns. Kantero and Widholm (1971) have studied correlations of menstrual patterns of mothers and their daughters. They have found correlation coefficients of 0.198 for length of cycle, 0.242 for duration of menses, and 0.240 for premenstrual tension. Treloar et al. (1998) investigated relative contribution of gene and environment to individual differences in menstrual symptomatology over 8 years of longitudinal Australian twin study on 728 twin pairs. They observed that genetic factors accounted for 39% of the longitudinally stable variation in menstrual flow, and the remaining stable variance was due to environmental factors (61%) and hence stable variance over the 8-year interval was largely environmentally influenced for menstrual flow.

Our results further reveal that onset of PMS may take place right after menarche, and not necessarily in the age range of 25 to 35 years. However, there may be individual differences in age at onset of PMS, because the proportion of females expressing PMS in this study is lower than other reports (Steiner and Born, 2000). There are variations in the type of symptoms from month to month and even with age changes. Treloar et al. (2002) observed that most frequently reported symptoms of PMS in a sample of 720 Australian twin pairs were breast tenderness/pain and bloating/weight gain.

The results of the present study on heritability of PMS are compared with other published reports in Table 6. The studies of Van den Akker et al. (1987) and Dalton et al. (1987) give very high heritability estimates (0.80 and 0.88), while other studies give moderately lower heritability in the range of 30%-35%. Our study gives lowest heritability estimate (0.09). The differences may be attributed to a number of factors: different methodologies, age differences in the sampled twins, low sample size in the present study, etc. Kendler et al. (1998) analyzed the role of measurement error in the assessment of the PMS. They observed that heritability of PMS rose substantially after incorporating data unreliability into twin modeling. They found estimates of common environment as zero and thereby rejected any significant role of family environmental factors in influencing PMS. Treloar et al. (2002) found that 44% of the total variance for PMS in an Australian sample of twins was due to additive genetic influences and supported the existence of genetic influences in PMS. The mean age of responding twin pairs from the Virginia Twin Register was 30±8 years (Kendler et al., 1992) and that Australian sample was 35±6 years (Treloar et al., 1998).

Table 6
Comparison of Heritability of PMS in the Present Study with other Published Reports from Different Nationalities

Population/Country	*No. of twin pairs*	*Heritability (h^2)*	*Reference*
1. London (England)	364	0.30	Van den Akker et al. (1987)
2. Birmingham (England)	98	0.80	Van den Akker et al. (1987)
3. London (England)*	31	0.88	Dalton et al. (1987)
4. Virginia (USA)	827	0.35	Kendler et al. (1992)
5. Australia	300	0.38	Condon (1993)
6. Australia	720	0.44#	Treloar et al. (2002)
7. Chandigarh (India)	25	0.09	Present study

* Heritability derived from concordance rates in MZ and DZ twins.
\# Additive genetic variance.

In conclusion, individual variations in age at menarche are substantially genetically determined. But, other menstrual or premenstrual characteristics like flow, length of cycle, duration of menses and PMS are less influenced by genetic factors and more by environmental factors in the present study. Apart from other genetic and environmental factors, the differences in results from different studies can also be due to age differences in twin samples.

SUMMARY

The study was based on data from a sample of 14 MZ and 12 DZ female twin pairs ranging in age from 14 to 24 years. The twins sample was drawn from an urban Punjabi population of Chandigarh. Prevalence of premenstrual syndrome (PMS) was higher in DZ twins (77.27%) than in MZ twin pairs (64.29%). 18% of DZ twins experienced severe PMS against none in DZ twins. The data did not support the known hypothesis that intensity of menstrual flow was higher in young females with lower gynecological age. Mean duration of menstrual flow was statistically significantly lower ($p<0.05$) in DZ twins (3.98 days) than in MZ twins (4.93 days). But difference in the mean length of the menstrual cycle between MZ (29.56 days) and DZ (28.96 days) twin pairs was not statistically significant. Genetic analysis revealed insignificant genetic component of variation for PMS scores, duration of menstrual flow and length of menstrual cycle. Concordance rates in MZ twins were also generally lower than that in DZ twins for these measures. However, results showed significant genetic component of variation for age at menarche with a heritability of 0.67 ($p<0.05$). These results were compatible with known hypothesis that age at menarche is substantially under genetic control.

REFERENCES

Chern M.M., Gatewood L.C. and Anderson V.E. (1980), The Inheritance of Menstrual Traits. In Dan A.J., Graham E.A. and Beecher C.P. (eds): *The Menstrual Cycle: A Synthesis of Interdisciplinary Research, 1*. New York: Springer, pp. 123-130.

Christensen A.P. and Oei T.P.S. (1989), Correlates of Confirmed Premenstrual Dysphoria. *J. Psycholsomatic Res.* 33: 307-313.

Condon J.T. (1993), The Premenstrual Syndrome: A Twin Study. *Br. J. Psychatry* 162: 481-486.

Dalton K. (1984), *Premenstrual Syndrome and Progesterone Therapy*. 2nd ed. London: Heinemann Medical.

Dalton K., Dalton M.E. and Guthrie K. (1987), Incidence of the Premenstrual Syndrome in Twins. *Br. Med. J.* 295: 1027-1028.

Dickerson L.M., Mazyck P.J. and Hunter M.H. (2003), Premenstrual Syndrome. *Am. Family Physician* 67: 1743-1752.

Fischbein S. (1977), Intra-pair Similarity in Physical Growth of Monozygotic and of Dizygotic Twins During Puberty. *Ann. Hum. Biol.* 4: 417-430.

Glick H., Endicott J. and Nee J. (1993), Premenstrual Changes: Are they Familial? *Acta Psychiatr Scand (Suppl)* 14: 30-36.

Halbreich U., Endicott J., Schacht S., et al. (1982), The Diversity of Premenstrual Changes as Reflected in the Premenstrual Assessment form. *Acta. Psychiatr Scand* 65: 46-65.

Hart W.G., Coleman G.J. and Russell J.W. (1987), Assessment of Premenstrual Symptomatology: A Revaluation of the Predictive Validity of Self Report. *J. Psychosomatic Res.* 31: 185-190.

Holzinger K.J. (1929), The Relative Effect of Nature and Nurture on Twin Differences. *J. Educational Psychol* 20: 241-248.

Johnson S.R., McChesney C. and Bean J.A. (1998), Epidemiology of Premenstrual Symptoms in a Non Clinical Sample 1: Prevalence, Natural History and Help Seeking Behavior. *J. Reproduct Med.* 33: 340-346.

Kantero R.L. and Widholm O. (1971), Correlation of Menstrual Traits between Adolescent Girls and their Mothers. In a Statistically Analysis of the Menstrual of 8000 Finnish Girls and their Mothers IV. *Acta Obstet Gynecol Scand (Suppl)* 14: 30-36.

Kendler K.S., Karkowski L.M., Corey L.A. and Neale M.C. (1998), Longitudinal Population-based Twin Study of Retrospectively Reported Premenstrual Symptoms and Lifetime Major Depression. *Am. J. Psychiatry* 155: 1234-1240.

Kendler K.S., Silberg J.L., Neale M.C., Kessler R.C., Heath A.C. and Eawes L.J. (1992), Genetic and Environmental Factors in the Aetiology of Menstrual, Premenstrual and Neurotic Symptoms-A Population-based Twin Study. *Psychol. Med.* 22: 85-100.

Kessel B. (2000), Premenstrual Syndrome: Advances in Diagnosis and Treatment. *Obstet Gynecol Clin North Am.* 27: 625-639.

Lombard I., Luisi S., Quirici B., Monteleone P., Bernardi F., et al. (2004), Adrenal Response to Adrenocorticotropic Hormone Stimulation in Patients with Premenstrual Syndrome. *Gynecol Endocrinol* 18: 79-87.

Martin N.G. and Treloar S.A. (1991), Age at Menarche as a Fitness Trait: Further Considerations. *Am. J. Hum. Genet* 48: 420-421.

Merikangas K.R., Foeldenyi M. and Angst J. (1993), The Zurich Study. XIX: Patterns of Menstrual Disturbances in the Community Results of the Zurich Cohort Study. *Eur. Arch. Psychiatry Clin Neurdsci* 243: 23-32.

River-Tovar A.D. and Frank E. Luteal Phase Dysphoric Disorder in Young Women. *Am. J. Psychiatry* 49: 469-474.

Sampson G.A. and Jenner F.A. (1977), Studies of Daily Recordings from the Moos Menstrual Distress Questionnaire. *Br. J. Psychiatry* 130: 265-271.

Severino S.K. and Moline M.L. (1989), *Premenstrul Syndrome: A Clinician's Guide.* New York: Guilford Press.

Sharma J.C. (1983), The Genetic Contribution to Pubertal Growth and Development Studied by Longitudinal Growth Data on Twins. *Ann. Hum. Biol.* 10: 163-172.

Sharma K. (1999), Dynamics of Permanent Tooth Emergence in North-West Indian Twins. *Acta Genet Med Gemellol* 48: 17-29.

Sharma K. (2005), Genetic Epidemiology of Epilepsy: A Twin Study. *Neurology India* 53: 93-98.

Silberg J. L., Martin N.G. and Heath A.C. (1987), Genetic and Environmental Factors in Primary Dysmenorrhea and its Relationship to Anxiety, Depression and Neuroticism. *Behav. Genet* 17: 363-383.

Steiner M. and Born L. (2000), Diagnosis and Treatment of Premenstrual Dysphoric Disorder: An update. *Int. Clin Psychopharmacol* 15 (Suppl 3): 55-517.

Stewart M. (1989), *Beat PMT Through Diet: The PMT Advisory Service Programme Based on Medically Proven Treatment.* London: Ebury Press, pp. 239.

Treloar S.A. and Martin N.G. (1990), Age at Menarche on a Fitness Trait: Nonadditive genetic variance detected in a large twin sample. *Am J Hum Genet* 47: 137-148.

Treloar S.A., Martin N.G. and Heath A.C. (1998), Longitudinal Genetic Analysis of Menstrual flow, Pain and Limitation in a Sample of Australian Twins. *Behav Genet* 28: 107-116.

Treloar S.A., Heath A.C. and Martin N.G. (2002), Genetic and Environmental Influences on Premenstrual Symptoms in an Australian Twin Sample. *Psychol Med.* 32: 25-38.

Van den Akker, O.B.A., Stein G.S., Neale M.C. and Murray R.M. (1987), Genetic and Environmental Variation in Menstrual Cycle Histories of Two British Twin Samples. *Acta Genet Med Gemellol* 36: 541-548.

Wilson R.S. (1986), Genetic Effect on Twin Growth at Adolescence, In Demirjian A (ed.): *Human Growth: A Multidisciplinary Review*. London: Taylor and Francis, pp. 193-202.

Woods N., Most A. and Dery G.K. (1982), Prevalence of Premenstrual Symptoms *Am. J. Public Health* 72: 1257-1264.

Wyatt K., Dimmock P.W. and O'Brien P.M. (2000), Premenstrual Syndrome. In Barton S. (ed.): *Clinical Evidence*, 4th Issue. London: BMJ Publishing Group, pp. 1121-1133.

16

GENETIC SUSCEPTIBILITY TO PERIODONTAL DISEASES: A TWIN STUDY

Krishan Sharma

INTRODUCTION

Dental caries is primarily a sugar dependent microbial disease affecting human populations across all countries. Anthropological research reveals increased prevalence of caries with the rise of agriculture during Neolithic period due to adoption of carbohydrate staple diet (see Cohen, 1989; Lukacs and Minderman, 1992). However, susceptibility to periodontal diseases including caries has a complicated etiology. It is now becoming increasingly realised that besides environmental factors, susceptibility to infectious diseases is dependent, to a variable degree, upon host's genetic factors (Abel and Dessien, 1998).

Genetic susceptibility to periodontal diseases has been investigated following three major approaches as for other multifactorial traits. The familial studies are undertaken to determine whether disease clusters within families (Klein and Palmer, 1938; Klein, 1946; Book and Grahnen, 1953; Dowsett et al, 2002). Population studies have been carried to compare caries resistant and caries susceptible people to explore role of genetic factors in the phenotypic expression (Mandel, 1994). Twin studies (Horowitz et al., 1958; Goodman et al., 1959; Finn and Caldwell, 1963; Fairpo, 1979; Borass et al., 1988) have also been conducted to study the relative role of heredity and environment in dental diseases. DNA-based studies to elucidate genetic determinants have proposed that genetic susceptibility to chronic periodontitis is related in part to allelic variations of polymorphic genes in the interleukin-1 (IL-1) gene cluster (Kornman et al., 1997; Gore et al, 1998). However, studies in this area are still in their infancy and contradictory.

Human populations across various cultures and geographic regions differ in their allele frequencies, genetic susceptibilities and environmental factors. So there is need to undertake studies examining genetic susceptibility to disease among different human populations across various cultures. With this aim in view, the present twin study was undertaken.

MATERIAL AND METHODS

The data on oral pathology were collected on sample of 57 pairs of twins (114 subjects) ranging in age from 11 to 28 years. Their mean age at the time of clinical observations was 18.15 years (S.D. 4.15) in MZ and 16.84 years (S.D. 4.06) in DZ twins. Twin zygosity was determined by the similarity method for A_1A_2BO, Rh, MN, Kell and Duffy blood groups, ABH secretion, PTC tasting ability, dermatoglyphics and photographs. The zygosity analysis resulted in 26 MZ and 31 DZ twin pairs. Dental examination was conducted either under natural light or at the best-lighted place in the room by the author himself. Presence of calculus, caries and gingivitis were recorded using dental probes following methods recommended by WHO (1987). Caries were considered to be present in a tooth when any lesion had a detectably softened floor, undermined enamel or softened wall. No attempt was made to categorize caries by its size. The intensity or extent of dental caries in terms of number of teeth affected per person was measured through DMF index/score. The DMF index was defined as the number of permanent teeth per person which were decayed, missing (extracted) because of caries or filled.

The twin pair was considered concordant if both members of the twin pair had the dental pathological condition under investigation. If only one member of the pair had the condition, the pair was classified discordant. Pairwise concordance rate was estimated as: C/C+D, where C and D were the number of concordant and discordant twin pairs. Case-wise concordance was calculated as: 2C/2C+D. Pairwise concordance rates in MZ and DZ twins were used to calculate the heritability index following Holzinger (1929): (CMZ-CDZ)/(1-CDZ). The DMF scores data were analysed for calculating means and variances. Within-pair means squares (WMS) between zygosities were contrasted by F-test.

RESULTS

Table 1 show that concordance rates in MZ twins were higher than those in DZ twins. Heritability of gingivitis condition was highest, while that of calculus was the lowest. Prevalence rate of gingivitis was higher in MZ twins than DZ twins, while for calculus and caries the prevalence was higher in DZ twins than MZ twins.

Table 2 shows that mean DMF index was slightly lower in MZ twins (1.90) than DZ twins (2.03). F-ratio contrasting within MZ and within DZ mean squares was statistically insignificant. These results indicate no significant genetic component of variance in the intensity of dental caries.

Table 1
Concordance Rates, Prevalence and Heritability of Dental Pathology in Twins

	Gingivitis		*Calculus*		*Caries*	
	MZ	*DZ*	*MZ*	*DZ*	*MZ*	*DZ*
No. of Pairs	26	31	26	31	26	31
Concordant Pairs	10	6	11	13	13	13
Discordant Pairs	1	6	3	7	3	10
Pair-wise Concordance Rate	0.91	0.5	0.79	0.65	0.81	0.57
Case-wise Concordance Rate	0.95	0.67	0.88	0.79	0.90	0.72
Pair-wise Prevalence Rate (%)	42.31	38.71	53.85	64.52	61.52	74.19
Case-wise Prevalence Rate (%)	40.38	29.03	48.08	53.23	55.77	58.06
Holzinger's Heritability Estimate	0.82		0.40		0.56	

Table 2
Mean, Variance, within-pair Variance (WPV) and F-ratio of WPVs between Zygosities for DMF Scores

Variable	*MZ twins*			*DZ twins*			*F-ratio*	
	Mean	*Variance*	*WPV*	*Mean*	*Variance*	*WPV*	*Value*	*Probability*
DMF Score	1.9	7.66	1.92	2.03	8.75	3.21	1.672	>0.05

DISCUSSION

The study indicates substantial heritability for gingivitis (0.82), moderate for caries (0.56) and relatively low for calculus (0.40). Heritability of a trait is affected by the amount of genetic variation present for that trait if the trait is determined by both genetic and environment factors of variation. Genetic variance would depend upon gene frequencies of the alleles underlying the phenotypic variation. Since the study reveals significant genetic component of variation, it can be hypothesized that there exist substantial genetic variation for gingivitis and dental caries. It is known that genes contribute much more variance when at intermediate frequencies (Falconer, 1981).The science of population genetic tells that gene frequencies differ between populations. So different heritability estimates in different human populations would indicate population variations for genetic and environmental factors underlying susceptibility to periodontal diseases.

The findings of this study support previous findings of twin studies in reporting presence of genetic factors in the expression of periodontal diseases (Corey et al., 1993; Conry et al., 1993; Michalowicz, 1994; Michalowicz et al., 2000). Conry et al. (1993) demonstrated significant genetic variance for dental caries ($h^2 = 0.64$) on the basis of study on adult twins. The studies on younger twins (Goodman et al., 1959; Fairpo, 1979) have reported a smaller genetic contribution (≈ 44%) to dental caries. The heritability estimates from twin studies ranged from 0.44 to 0.64. The heritability estimates based on studies on adult twins reflect cumulative effects of caries.

Family and sibling studies found low heritabilities in periodontal disease expression. Chung et al. (1977), using path analysis failed to detect significant heritabilities for periodontal diseases in a number of different racial groups living in Hawaii. Rao et al. (1979) identified high marital correlation for periodontal diseases suggesting post-marital resemblance highlighting shared environmental component resulting in familial clustering of disease. Dowsett et al. (2002) also reported low heritability estimates for mean gingival index, and probing depth. They attributed this to an underlying lack of genetic variation within the sampled population from Guatemala or to the miner role of genetic factors compared with environmental factors. However, they found high heritability for mean plaque score (0.67) and mean recession score (0.51). A statistically significant effect of familial factors has also been shown for mean plaque index by Beaty et al. (1993) and Vandervelden et al. (1993).

The current knowledge on the topic implicates both genetic and environmental factors in the etiology of periodontal disease. The results of the present study also affirm such a decision. The capacity of humans to select their own environment may be of special relevance to a multifactorial disease like dental caries. If the genetic factors are involved in variables such as food habits, oral hygiene, reaction to stress, etc, then environmental covariance will be higher in MZ twins than DZ twins and heritabilities will be inflated compared to family and sibling studies. A similarity in food favouritism has been reported in MZ twins reared together (Forrai and Bankovi, 1984). On the contrary, it can be argued that within a family, such habits are determined by modelling on parents or other family members or the cotwin. In view of above, the zygosity of twins may not be of much consequence in determining food and oral habits, and the heritability estimate from the twin studies would be valid to draw conclusion on the relative role of heredity and environment.

In the present sample, moderate heritability was found for the prevalence of dental caries. However, the twin data also demonstrated that an insignificant proportion of variance for the number of teeth affected by caries (DMF index) was attributable to genetic variance. It may be concluded that though susceptibility to caries seems to be under moderate genetic control factors, yet the intensity of caries does not seem to have significant genetic variance. These results provide evidence to the hypothesis that dental caries is a multifactorial disease.

SUMMARY

Fifty-seven twin pairs (114 subjects) ranging in age from 11 to 28 years were examined for dental caries, calculus and gingivitis. Zygosity analysis resulted in 26 monozygotic (MZ) and 31 dizygotic (DZ) twin pairs. Prevalence rates of caries and calculus were marginally higher in DZ twins (58.06% and 53.23% respectively) than in MZ twins (55.77% and 48.08%

respectively). Prevalence of gingivitis was higher in MZ twins (40.38%) than in DZ twins (29.03%). Heritability estimate of gingivitis was high (0.82). This estimate was moderate for caries (0.56) and low for calculus (0.40). Analysis of variance of DMF scores revealed higher within- pair mean squares (WMS) in DZ twins (3.21) than in MZ twins (1.92) as expected under genetic control hypothesis. But F-ratio contrasting these variances was statistically insignificant; revealing that genetic component of variation for the intensity of dental caries was not substantially high. The study, however, revealed presence of within- population genetic variance for periodontal disease phenotypes.

REFERENCES

Able L. and Dessein A.J. (1998), Genetic Epidemiology of Infectious Diseases in Human: Design of Population Based Studies. *Emerge Infect Dis* 4: 593-603.

Beaty T.H., Colyer C.R., Chang Y.C., Liang K.Y., Graybeal J.C., Muhammad N.K. and Levin L.S. (1993), Familial Aggregation of Periodontal Indices. *J. Dent Res.* 72: 544-551.

Book J.A. and Grahnen H. (1953), Clinical and Genetical Studies of Dental Caries II. Parents and Sibs of Adult High Resistant (caries-free) Propositi. *Odontol Rev.* 4: 1-53.

Borass J.C., Messer L.B. and Till M.J. (1988), A Genetic Contribution to Dental Caries, Occlusion and Morphology as Demonstrated by Twins Reared Apart. *J. Dent Res.* 67: 1150-1155.

Chung C.S., Kau M.C.W., Chung S.C.C. and Rao D.C. (1977), A Genetic and Epidemiologic Study of Periodontal Disease in Hawaii. II. Genetic and Environmental Influence *Am. J. Hum. Genet* 29: 76-82.

Cohen M.N. (1989), *Health and Rise of Civilization*. New Haven: Yale University Press.

Conry J.P., Messer L.B., Boraas J.C., Aeppli D.P. and Bouchard T.J., Jr. (1993), Dental Caries and Treatment Characteristics in Human Twins Reared Apart. *Arch. Oral Biol.* 38: 937-943.

Corey L.A., Nance W.E., Hofstede P. and Schenkein H.A. (1993), Self Reported Periodontal Disease in Virginia Twin Population. *J. Periodontol* 64: 1205-1208.

Dowsett S.A., Archila L., Foround T., Koller D., Eckert G.J. and Kowolik M.J. (2002), The Effect of Shared Genetic and Environmental Factors on Periodontal Disease Parameters in Untreated Adult Siblings in Guatemala. *J. Periodontol* 73: 1160-1168.

Fairpo C.G. (1979), Total Caries Experience in Monozygotic and Like-sexed Dizygotic Twins of Caucasoid Origin Age 5 to 15 years. *Arch. Oral Biol.* 24: 491-494.

Falconer D.S. (1981), *Introduction to Quantitative Genetics*. 2nd ed. London: Longman.

Finn S.B. and Caldwell R.C. (1963), Dental Caries in Twins I. A Comparison of the Caries Experience of Monozygotic Twins and Unrelated Children. *Arch. Oral Biol.* 8: 571-585.

Forrai G. and Bankovi G. (1984), On the Food Favouritism of Twins *Acta. Physiol Hung* 64: 25-32.

Goodman H.O., Luke J.E., Rosen S. and Hackel E. (1959), Heritability in Dental Caries, Certain Oral Microflora and Salivary Components. *Am. J. Hum. Genet* 11: 263-273.

Gore E.A., Sanders J.J., Pandey J.P., Palesch Y. and Galbraith G.M.P. (1998), Interleukin-1B+3953 Allele 2: Association with Disease Status in Adult Periodontitis. *J. Clin Periodontol* 25: 781-785.

Holzinger J.J. (1929), The Relative Effect of Nature and Nurture on Twin Differences. *J. Educ. Psychol* 20: 241-248.

Horowitz S.L., Osborne R.H. and De George F.V. (1958), Caries Experience in Twins *Science* 128: 300-301.

Klein H. (1946), Family and Dental Disease. IV. Dental Disease (DMF) Experience in Parents and Offspring. *JADA* 33: 735-743.

Klein H. and Palmer C.E. (1938), Studies on Dental Caries: V. Familial Resemblance in the Caries Experience of Siblings. *Public Health Rep.* 53: 1353-1364.

Kornman K.S., Crane A., Wang H., di Giovine F.S.; Newman M.G., Pirk F.W., Wilson T.G., Higginbottom Fl Duff G.W. (1997), The Interleukin-1 Genotype as a Severity Factor in Adult Periodontal Disease. *J. Clin Periodontol* 24: 72-77.

Lukacs J.R. and Minderman L. (1992), Dental Pathology and Agricultural Intensification from Neolethic to Chalcolethic Periods of Mehrgarh (Baluchistan, Pakistan). In Jarrige C. (ed.): *South Asian Archaeology*. Madison: Prehistory Press, pp. 167-179.

Mandel I.D. (1994), Nature vs Nurture in Dental Caries. *JADA*. 125: 1345-1351.

Michalowicz B.S. (1994), Genetic and Heritable Risk Factors in Periodontal Disease. *J. Periodontol* 65: 479-488.

Michalowicz B.S., Diehl S.R., Gunsolley J.C., Sparks B.S., Brooks C.N., Koertge T.E., Califano J.V., Burmeister J.A. and Schenkein H.A. (2000), Evidence of Substantial Genetic basis for Risk of Adult Periodontitis. *J. Periodontol* 71: 1699-1707.

Rao D.C., Chung C.S. and Morton N.E. (1979), Genetic and Environmental Determinants of Periodontal Disease. *Am. J. Med. Genet* 4: 39-45.

Vandervelden U., Abbas F., Armand S., Degraaff J., Timmerman M.F., Vanderweijden G.A., Vanwinkelholm A.J. and Winkel E.G. (1993), The Effect of Sibling Relationship on the Periodontal Conditions. *J. Clin Periodontol* 20: 683-690.

WHO (1987), *Oral Health Surveys: Basic Methods*. Third ed. Geneva: WHO.

17

ABO BLOOD GROUPS, SECRETOR STATUS AND DENTAL CARIES SAMONG ADOLESCENT CHILDREN

Krishan Sharma and Tripta

INTRODUCTION

The search for association between blood groups and susceptibility to disease had started immediately after the discovery of ABO blood groups by Landsteiner in the year 1900. But the early literature on these associations was rampant with inadequate controls, controversial data, incorrect analysis etc. Meaningful scientific research in this field started in 1950s. Since then, the literature has grown voluminous as there are thousands of publications analyzing associations of various blood group and other genetic markers with diseases. There are many excellent reviews on the topic (Clarke, 1961; Mourant, 1973; Rios and Bianco, 2000). Though ABH secretion polymorphism is closely related to the ABO blood group system, yet they are under the control of separate genetic factors. Secretors secrete into their saliva and other body fluids water soluble substances having antigenic properties similar to the ABH antigens on their red blood cells. The secretor gene is dominant over the non-secretor allele.

Associations between ABO blood types and infectious diseases have been explained on the basis of presence of substances similar to ABO antigens on the relevant pathogens (Schiff, 1934; Springer et al, 1961; Bogitsh, 1993). Bacteria are considered the primary extrinsic etiologic agent in dental caries. Adherence of bacteria to teeth is inhibited by secretory IgA which is a part of the oral immunologic defence system (Williams and Gibbons, 1972). It is hypothesized here that ABO blood group and secretor gene polymorphisms may also be associated with the susceptibility to dental caries. Since O blood group person can secrete both anti-A and/or anti-B antibodies in their saliva (Hummel and Schoch, 1967; Bell and Fortwengler 1971), the former would tend to have lower prevalence of dental caries than the latter. Likewise, persons with AB blood group would show the highest prevalence of dental caries because of absence of naturally occurring agglutinins. It was also hypothesized that ABH secretors would tend to have higher caries prevalence than non-secretors. The present study was undertaken to test these hypotheses.

MATERIALS AND METHODS

Blood and saliva samples of 202 subjects (117 males and 85 females) were collected. The subjects belonged to Brahmin (102 subjects) and Rajput (100 subjects) castes. They were apparently physically and mentally healthy school going children living in and around Theog (Shimla), Himachal Pradesh. They ranged in age from 14 to 18 years.

The ABO blood grouping was done by the slide method using standard antisera and 2% suspension of washed red cells in normal saline. Saliva samples were collected in glass tubes and placed in boiling water bath for 10 minutes within two hours after their collection. Each sample was centrifuged for 10 minutes at about 1500g. The supernatant clear fluid was tested for ABH secretion by the haemoagglutination-inhibition method. Anti-A, anti-B and anti-H sera was titrated and diluted to have a uniform titre of 1:4. Equal amounts of saliva and diluted relevant antiserum were mixed. After half an hour at room temperature, an equal amount of 2% suspension of relevant washed red cells was added and 15 minutes later the test was read. Controls were set in each test series.

Clinical dental examination was performed making use of direct and indirect natural sunlight in the school building. Each subject was examined sitting in a regular chair or on a stool. The teeth were carefully examined for the presence of caries with a probe and a dental mirror. Caries were considered to be present in a tooth when any lesion had detectably softened floor, undermined enamel or softened wall. Missing teeth were recorded missing due to dental caries and the subject was quizzed for the cause of missing teeth.

The data was subjected to statistical treatment to draw inferences. The χ^2 test for 2 x 2 contingency tables was used without continuity correction (Yates's correction) as this correction makes the test too conservative (Grizzle,1967). The relative risk was calculated to measure the strength of an association and significance of the risk was tested by the Chi-square test.

RESULTS

Prevalence of dental caries according to sex and caste groups is given in Table 1. Caries prevalence is slightly higher among males than females in Brahmins and among females than males in Rajputs, but sex and ethnic differences are not statistically significant. Consequently, data from two sexes and castes were pooled to study caries prevalence with reference to ABO blood group and ABH secretion. These results are presented in Table 2.

Table 1
Sex, Ethnicity and Prevalence of Dental Caries

Caste & Sex	*Sample Size* N	*Dental Caries* C	%	χ^2
Brahmins				
Male	57	38	66.7	0.21
Female	45	28	62.2	NS
Rajputs				
Male	60	37	61.7	0.12
Female	40	26	65.0	NS
Total Sample				
Male	117	75	64.1	0.01
Female	85	54	63.5	NS
Brahmins	102	66	64.71	0.04
Rajputs	100	63	63.00	NS

Table 2
ABO Blood Group, Secretor Status and Caries Prevalence

ABO Blood Group	*Status*	*ABH Secretion* N	%	*Caries Prevalence* N	%	χ^2	*Relative Risk in secretors vs. non-secretors*
A	Secretor	38	62.30	28	73.68	1.92	1.304
	Non-Secretor	23	37.70	13	56.52		
	Total	61	30.20	41	67.21		
B	Secretor	52	65.00	28	53.85	6.31*	0.656
	Non-Secretor	28	35.00	23	82.14		
	Total	80	39.60	51	63.75		
O	Secretor	33	78.57	19	57.58	0.23	0.864
	Non-Secretor	9	21.43	6	66.67		
	Total	42	20.79	25	59.52		
AB	Secretor	12	63.16	7	58.33	0.33	0.817
	Non-Secretor	7	36.84	5	71.43		
	Total	19	9.41	12	63.16		
Pooled	Secretor	135	66.83	82	60.74	1.72	0.866
	Non-Secretor	67	33.17	47	70.15		

*p<0.005.

Table 2 shows that blood group A subjects manifest highest prevalence of caries (67.21%), while group O subject manifest lowest caries prevalence (59.52%). However, the differences among various ABO blood groups for caries prevalence are statistically not significant (X^2 = 0.64). With reference to secretor status, blood group A secretors show higher caries prevalence (73.68%) than their non-secretor counterparts (56.52%), but differences are not statistically significant. On the contrary, B, O and AB secretors show reverse trend by manifesting lower caries prevalence. Statistically significant differences between secretors and non-secretors for caries prevalence are observed only in B blood group (X^2 =

6.31, $p<0.005$). In the total sample, non-secretors suffer from higher caries prevalence (70.15%) than secretors (60.74%). The relative risk (RR) of dental caries in secretors compared to non-secretors is more than 1 in only one of four ABO phenotypes, i.e. in A versus others, though the ratio is not statistically significant. While in other three categories, RR is lower in secretors.

DISCUSSION

Results of the present study support the hypothesis that ABO blood groups and secretor status may be associated with the susceptibility to dental caries. As hypothesized, O blood group individuals have been found to have lower caries prevalence than groups A and B individuals. However, differences do not reach statistically significant level. The literature review reveals that anti-A and anti-B isohaemagglutinins have been detected more frequently in saliva of group O individuals than groups A and B individuals (Jakobowicz at al, 1966; Boettcher 1967; Denborough et al, 1967). Bell and Fortwengler (1971) have detected anti-A agglutinins in 98% and anti-B in 96% of group O individuals. Salivary IgA anti-A and anti-B aglutinins would offer some protection against dental caries by preventing bacteria adherence to gingiva and teeth. Without bacterial adherence, colonization and plaque formation cannot take place and thus blocking an essential step in the pathogenesis of dental pathology (Van Houte et al, 1970; Gibbons and Van Houte, 1971; Williams and Gibbons, 1972; Hardman and Hardman, 1983).

The results of the present study do not support the other two hypotheses. First hypothesis was that AB blood group individuals would have the highest prevalence of caries, but caries prevalence has been found to be of similar magnitude in A, B and AB individuals. Second framed hypothesis was that ABH secretors would tend to have higher caries prevalence than non-secretors. Only group A secretors show higher caries prevalence (73.68%) than non-secretors (56.52%). While in all other groups, secretors have lower caries prevalence than non-secretors. In the total pooled sample, secretors have lower caries prevalence (60.74%) than non-secretors (70.15%). Incidentally among non-secretors, B blood group individuals show the highest incidence of caries (82.14%).

These results clearly show that no simple explanation can explain the observed differential caries prevalence rates in secretors and non secretors with reference to ABO blood groups. A possible explanation that can be forwarded is that many of the bacteria implicated in dental caries may have surface antigens which are not A-like or B-like. Scott and Corry (1980) have reported more than 150 known naturally occurring monosaccharide antigenic determinants. Moreover, the amount of salivary agglutinin has been found to vary from one individual to another. Incidence of agglutinin secretors has also been reported to vary with ABO blood type. O blood group individuals have been reported to have higher incidence of agglutinin secretors than A and B blood group individuals (Roy and Bhalla, 1977; Chattopadhyay and Ganeson, 1983). Hence, partly lower incidence of dental caries in O blood group persons may be attributed to above finding. With reference to ABH secretion, no difference has been reported in the incidence of salivary agglutinins between secretors and non-secretors (see Chattopadhyay and Ganeson, 1983). In view of above, there should not be any differences in caries prevalence between secretors and non-secretors. But we do find some evidence of significant differences in caries prevalence between secretors and non-secretors at least in blood group B individuals.

In conclusion, the ABO blood antigens and secretor phenotypes appear to influence binding of bacteria to gingiva and tooth surfaces and thereby resulting in differential caries risk with reference to these genetic markers. Pradhan et al (1971) and Gawrzewska (1975) have also found significant association between ABO blood groups and severity of periodontal disease. On the contrary, Carmichael (1965) and Kaslick et al (1980) have found insignificant differences among ABO blood groups for dental pathology. Such contradictory reports lend support to the hypothesis that several defence mechanisms exist in the mouth and interactions between these and cariogenic factors determine differential prevalence rates of dental caries in different human population groups.

SUMMARY

Prevalence of dental caries in relation to ABO blood groups and ABH secretion was studied on a sample of 202 children (117 males and 85 females) ranging in age from 14-18 years. No significant differences in dental caries were observed between sexes and between caste groups. O blood group individuals had lower prevalence of caries (59.52%) than blood group A individuals (67.21%). But the differences among various ABO blood group persons for caries prevalence were statistically insignificant. ABH secretors had lower prevalence of caries (60.74%) than non-secretors (70.15%). 'A' blood group secretors had higher caries prevalence (73.68%) than their non-secretor counterparts (56.52%), giving a relative risk value of 1.3 in secretors versus non-secretors. On the contrary, B, 0, and AB secretors had lower caries prevalence than their non-secretors counterparts. The differences between secretors and non-secretors in caries prevalence were statistically significant only in B blood group.

REFERENCES

Bell C.E. and Fortwengler H.P. (1971), Salivary Anti-A and Anti-B Activity of Group O males. *Vox Sang* 21: 493-508.

Boettcher B. (1967), ABO Blood Group Agglutinins in Saliva. *Acta Haemat* 38: 351-360.

Bogtish B.J. (1993), The Feeding of A Type Red Blood Cells in Vitro and the Ability of Schistosoma Mansoni Schistosomules to Acquire A Epitopes on their Surface. *J. Parasitol* 79: 946-948.

Caqrmichael A.F. (1965), The Distribution of the ABO Blood Groups in Cases of Periodontal Disease. *Dent Mag* 82:255.

Chattopadhyay P.K. and Ganeson D. (1983), Salivary Agglutinins in an Indian Population. *Anthrop Anz.* 41:221-224.

Clarke C.A. (1961), Blood Groups and Disease. In Steinberg A.G. (ed.): *Progress in Medical Genetics* Vol. 1. New York: Grunne and Stratton.

Denborough M.A., Downing H.J. and McCrea M.G. (1967), The ABO System in Milk and Saliva. *Austr Ann. Med.* 16: 320-325.

Gawrzewska B. (1975), ABO, Rh and MN Blood Group Systems and ABH Group Factors in Saliva Related to Periodontal Diseases. *Czas. Stomatol* 28:1007.

Gibbons R.J. and Van Houte J. (1971), Selective Bacterial Adherence to Oral Epithelial Surfaces and its Role as an Ecological Determinants. *Infect. Immun* 3: 567.

Grizzle J.E. (1967), Continuity Correction in the χ^2 test for 2x2 tables. *Am. Statist* 21: 28-32.

Hummel K. and Schoch J. (1967), Untersuchungen Uber Die Ausscheidung Vov Anti-A und Anti-A Hemagglutininen im Menschlichen Mundspeichel. *Z Immunitaetsforsch* 133:80-100.

Hardman P.K. and Hardman J.T. (1983), Salivary ABO Antibodies and Periodontal Disease. *J. Periodont* 54:351-353.

Jakobowicz R., Graydon J.J. and Simmons R.T. (1966), Observations on Saliva Agglutinins. *Med. J. Austr* 1:399-401.

Kaslick R.S., West T.L. and Chasens A.I. (1980), Association between ABO Blood Groups, HLA Antigens and Periodontal Diseases in Young Adults: A Follow-up Study. *J. Periodontal* 51:339.

Mourant A.E. (1973), Association between Hereditary Blood Factors and Diseases. *Bull WHO* 49: 93-101.

Pradhan A.C., Chawla T.N., Samuel K.C. and Pradhan S. (1971), The Relationship between Periodontal Disease and Blood Groups and Secretor Status. *J. Periodont Res.* 6:294.

Rios M. and Bianco C. (2000), The Role of Blood Group Antigens in Infectious Diseases. *Seminar Haematol* 37:177-185.

Roy S. and Bhalla V. (1977), Variations in the Incidence of Anti-A and Anti-B Agglutinins in Saliva and their Racial Significance. *Acta. Anthropogenetica* 1: 45-49.

Schiff F. (1934), Zur Kenntnis Der Blutantiqine Des Shigabacillus. *Z. Immunitaets forsch* 82:46.

Scott M.L. and Corry J.E. (1980), Effect of Blood Group Active Micro Organisms on the ABO Grouping of Human whole Saliva. *Forensic Sci. Int.* 16:87.

Springer G.F., Williamson P. and Brandes W.C. (1961), Blood Group Activity of Gram Negative Bacteria. *J. Exp. Med.* 113:1077-1033.

Van Houte J., Gibbons R.J. and Banghart S.B. (1970), Adherence is a Determinant of the Presence of Streptococcus Salivarius and Streptococcus Sanguis on the Human Tooth Surface. *Arch. Oral Biol.* 15: 1025.

Williams R.C. and Gibbons R.J. (1972), Inhibition of Bacterial Adherence by Secretary Immunoglobulin A : A Mechanism of Antigen Disposal. *Science* 177:697.

18

FREQUENCY OF ABO(H) ANTIGENS ON RED BLOOD CELLS AND SALIVA OF EPILEPSY PATIENTS

S.K. Pal, K. Sharma, A. Pathak and S. Prabhakar

INTRODUCTION

Soon after the discovery of ABO blood groups by Landsteiner in 1900, their association with the etiology of disease was suggested (Mourant, 1973). The first intensive phase of research on the topic started in 1920' s after the inheritance of ABO blood groups had been worked out and it became aptly clear that frequency of these blood groups differed widely among human populations. Almost every common disease was considered to be associated with blood groups. In these initial years, most of studies were based on inadequate methods and insufficient sample sizes. The results were contradictory in approach and consequently the topic lost its preeminence position till 1950's, when the second phase of such studies started with better understanding of human genetic methods and discovery of many new blood group systems. The literature on the topic is now voluminous. ABO blood groups have been correlated with pathological process like malignancies congenital abnormalities, infectious diseases, autoimmune disorders, blood coagulation disorders, heart and other diseases (Mourant et al, 1978; Mourant 1985; Ndamba et al., 1997).

The undirected research for association between blood groups and diseases has raised considerable controversy (Vogel, 1970; Weiner, 1970). Some of the criticisms made to this approach is undoubtedly true, but basic approach is not a matter of conjecture alone. Cell surface molecules containing blood group epitopes play important roles in modulation of protein function, infection and cancer and hence these may be involved in the disease susceptibility maintenance and progression (Springer, 1970; Lublin, 1995).

Inheritance of ABO blood groups and secretion of ABH substances are independent phenomena involving genes at different loci. The secretors have ABH substances in most body fluids. The non-secretors have been reported to have higher frequency of stomal and duodenal ulcers than secretors (Clarke et al, 1956; Hanley, 1964; Langman et al, 1967; Pratibha et al, 1995). Their association has been investigated with other bacterial infections (Kinane et al, 1982). Adherence of bacteria to carbohydrate receptors on the surface of epithelial cells may play some critical role in susceptibility to epilepsy. On this basis, it has been hypothesized that ABO blood groups and ABH secretion may also be associated with the susceptibility to epilepsy. With this major aim in view, the present study was undertaken. The literature review reveals that Fedrick (1972) had earlier investigated association between epilepsy and ABO blood groups in England. But this investigation did not analyze ABO blood groups separately with reference to idiopathic and symptomatic types of epilepsy and their secretor status was also not studied. Moreover, no such study has been done on Indian populations.

MATERIALS AND METHODS

The data for the present study were collected from Neurology outpatient department (OPD) and epilepsy follow-up clinic at the Postgraduate Institute of Medical Education and Research (PGIMER), Chandigarh. A total of 400 epileptic patients (200 idiopathic and 200 symptomatic) and 100 normal and healthy subjects, serving as controls, were studied. Both, patients and controls belonged to the northwestern region of India (Punjab, Haryana and Himachal Pradesh). The control sample was matched for age, sex and ethnic background with the sample of patients. The patients were subjected to electroencephalography (EEG) and computed tomography (CT). A few doubtful cases were investigated for magnetic resonance imaging (MRI). On the basis of these investigations, the patients were categorized as idiopathic or symptomatic. The idiopathic category included 114 males and 86 females with a mean ±S.D of age as 23.22± 9.92 years, while the symptomatic category included 119 males and 81 females with a mean age of 25.7±11.07 years. Hence, both the samples were comparable for age and sex.

ABO blood group testing was done by the slide method using washed red cells of subjects and standard antisera. Saliva samples were collected in test tubes and kept in boiling water bath for 10 minutes. After centrifugation, the supernatant fluid was typed for ABH salivary secretion by agglutination- inhibition technique using uniformly titred (1:4) anti-A, anti-B, and anti-H sera following the techniques given in Dunsford and Bowley (1967).

Relative incidence (RI) was calculated to study association between blood groups and disease following Woolf (1955). All the possible pairs of the ABO blood group phenotypes were used to calculate relative incidence as suggested by Vogel (1960).

RESULTS

The frequency distribution of ABO blood groups and allele frequency estimates are given in Table 1. A lower frequency of AB is observed in idiopathic epileptics and a higher frequency of A is seen in symptomatic epileptics. However, Chi-square test (Table 2) does not reveal any significant differences in the frequency distribution of ABO blood groups between epileptics and controls and between idiopathic and symptomatic epileptics. The relative incidence (RI) of ABO blood groups for various blood group combinations is given in Table 3. RI is more than two in three instances (O: AB, A: AB; and B: AB) in idiopathic epileptics and in all cases the common factor is AB blood group. The differences are statistically significant. No significant differences are observed in RI in symptomatic epileptics.

Table 1
Frequency Distribution of ABO Blood Groups Among Epileptics and Controls

Type	*Locus*	*Phenotype*	*N*	*%*	*Gene*	*Frequency*
IDIOPATHIC	ABO	A	42	21.0	A	0.168
		B	87	43.5	B	0.312
		AB	14	7.0	-	-
		O	57	28.5	O	0.520
SYMPTOMATIC	ABO	A	52	26.0	A	0.208
		B	71	35.5	B	0.270
		AB	23	11.5	-	-
		O	54	27.0	O	0.522
CONTROLS	ABO	A	19	19.0	A	0.165
		B	41	41.0	B	0.315
		AB	15	15.0	-	-
		O	25	25.0	O	0.518

Table 2
Chi-square Test of Homogeneity between Epileptics and Controls

Locus	*Idiopathic vs Controls*	*$^*\chi^2$ Idiopathic vs Symptomatic*	*Symptomatic vs Controls*	*df*	*p*
ABO	0.050	0.096	0.226	3	>0.05

*Non-significant .

The frequency distribution and allele frequency for ABH secretion are given in Table 4. 30% of the idiopathic epileptics and 37% of the controls are non–secretors. The frequency of non-secretors in symptomatic epileptics is very low (18%). Chi-square test (Table 5) shows significant differences between idiopathic versus symptomatic epileptics and symptomatic versus controls for ABH secretion. RI of secretors versus non-secretors is significantly higher than one in symptomatic epileptics, but not in idiopathic epileptics (Table 6).

Table 3
Relative incidence of ABO Blood Groups with Reference to Type of Epilepsy

Phenotype pairs	*Relative incidence formulae*	*Idiopathic*	χ^2 *Idio. Vs Control*	*Sympto-matic*	χ^2 *Symp. vs Control*	*Total*	χ^2 *Total vs Control*
A : O	$\frac{A_P X O_C}{O_P X A_C}$	0.96	0.01	1.26	0.43	1.06	0.10
O : A	$\frac{O_P X A_C}{A_P X O_C}$	1.03		0.78		0.94	
B : O	$\frac{B_P X O_C}{O_P X B_C}$	0.93	0.06	0.80	0.50	0.87	0.25
O : B	$\frac{O_P X B_C}{B_P X O_C}$	1.07		1.24		1.15	
O : AB	$\frac{O_P X AB_C}{AB_P X O_C}$	2.44	4.19**	1.40	0.70	1.68	2.46
A : B	$\frac{A_P X B_C}{B_P X A_C}$	0.40		0.70		0.29	
B : A	$\frac{B_P X A_C}{A_P X B_C}$	0.95	0.01	0.63	1.91	0.82	0.67
A : AB	$\frac{A_P X AB_C}{AB_P X A_C}$	2.36	3.54	1.78	1.86	1.78	3.15
AB : A	$\frac{AB_P X A_C}{A_P X AB_C}$	0.42		0.56		0.56	
B : AB	$\frac{B_P X AB_C}{AB_P X B_C}$	2.27	4.00**	1.12	0.10	1.46	1.62
AB : B	$\frac{AB_P X B_C}{B_P X AB_C}$	0.43		0.88		0.68	

**Significant at $p < 0.01$ level.

Table 4
Frequency Distribution of ABH Secretions between Epileptics and Controls

Type	*Locus*	*Phenotype*	*N*	*%*	*Gene*	*Frequency*
IDIOPATHIC	Secretor	(a) Secretor	140	70.0	Se	0.45
		(b) Non-secretor	60	30.0	Se	0.55
SYMPTOMATIC	Secretor	(a) Secretor	164	82.0	Se	0.82
		(b) Non-secretor	36	18.0	Se	0.18
CONTROLS	Secretor	(a) Secretor	63	63.0	Se	0.39
		(b) Non-secretor	37	37.0	Se	0.61

Table 5
Chi-square test of homogeneity between epileptics and controls

Locus	χ^2 *Idiopathic vs Controls*	χ^2 *Symptomatic vs Controls*	χ^2 *Idiopathic vs Symptomatic*	*df*
ABH Secretion	3.41	13.07**	7.89**	1

**Significant at $p < 0.01$ level.

Table 6
Relative incidence(RI) of ABH secretions

Locus	*Patients*	*Sec: Non-sec RI*	*Non-sec: Sec RI*
ABH	Idiopathic	1.3703	0.7297
	Symptomatic	2.6754*	0.3738

*p<0.01; Sec: Secretor, Non-Sec: Non-Secretor.

DISCUSSION

The results of the present study indicate the existence of association between ABO blood groups and idiopathic epilepsy secretion. Relative incidence is significant in three instances where it is greater than one in idiopathic epileptics. However, in all these cases, the blood group AB is involved. This observation raises some doubt in the simple interpretation of the data. It may be just co-incidental or due to inadequate data. The confirmation must await more data.

ABH secretor locus reveals strong association between non-secretors and symptomatic epilepsy. Such an association may not be surprising because cell surface molecules containing blood epitopes play important role in modulation of protein function, infection and such factors that may be involved in disease susceptibility, maintenance and progression (Lublin, 1995).

Fedrick (1972) reported ABO blood group data of epileptics from England. He found excess of A blood group among epileptics than controls, and the differences were found to be significant. The present study also shows excess of A blood group in symptomatic epileptics. No other study on epileptics has come to our notice. A large number of studies exist in the literature on frequency of ABO blood groups in various diseases. The studies become incomparable because of geographical and ethnic differences in the frequencies of ABO blood groups in various human populations. However, for the sake of comparison and completeness, frequencies of ABO blood groups with reference to various diseases have been given in Table 7. The studies have been arranged in descending order of A blood group frequency. These biases can be corrected by reporting differences between blood group frequencies observed in patients and the normal controls from the same ethnic population belonging to same geographical area. Table 8 lists differences in ABO phenotypic frequencies between patients and controls and these have been arranged in descending order with reference to blood group A. This would enable to have proper perspective of the association between disease and blood group. A critical analysis of Table 8 reveals that symptomatic epilepsy falls in first 20% of diseases when arranged in descending order of O-E differences for blood A. While idiopathic epilepsy category almost falls in the middle of the Table 8. This indicates differential susceptibility of the two types of epilepsy with reference to A blood group.

Table 7
A Comparative Picture Showing Association between ABO Blood Groups and Susceptibility to Diseases in Different Population

S.N.	Type of disease	A (%)	B(%)	AB (%)	O(%)	Reference
1.	Carcinoma stomach	74.8	10.0	2.6	12.6	Navak, 1971
2.	Cancer of stomach	53.12	7.53	3.13	36.22	Aird et al., 1953
3.	Epileptics	52.47	6.93	3.96	36.63	Fedrick, 1972
4.	Gastric cancer (Macroscopic)	46.47	8.82	2.94	41.77	Beasley, 1960
5.	Gastric cancer (Histological)	46.4	9.18	2.62	41.8	Beasley, 1960
6.	Cancer of pancreas	46.0	7.6	2.6	43.9	Aird et al., 1960
7.	Carcinoma cervix	44.6	27.2	8.6	19.6	Navak, 1971
8.	Cancer of oesophaqus	42.6	9.8	2.6	44.9	Aird et al., 1960
9.	Gastric ulcer	41.05	9.09	5.57	44.28	Merikas et al., 1966
10.	Chromophobe adenoma of pituitary	41.2	9.3	2.2	47.3	Aird et al., 1960
11.	Leukemia	39.3	24.8	2.6	33.3	Navak, 1971
12.	Bleedinq qastric ulcer	37.60	6.40	8.00	48.00	Merikas et al., 1966
13.	Cancer of cervix	37.02	33.19	6.25	23.58	Gupta, 1968
14.	Peotic ulcer	36.68	12.15	5.41	45.74	Merikas et al., 1966
15.	Oropharynx cancer	36.36	36.36	0.00	27.22	Hurkat et al., 1971
16.	Duodenal ulcer	35.88	12.71	5.38	46.01	Merikas et al., 1966
17.	Bleeding duodenal ulcer	34.64	11.68	4.32	50.35	Merikas et al., 1966
18.	Cancer of other Qenital organs	32.76	34.48	10.34	22.41	Mitra et al., 1962
19.	Breast cancer	31.57	27.36	11.57	29.47	Hurkat et al., 1971
20.	Colon cancer	28.57	21.42	14.28	35.71	Hurkat et al., 1971
21.	Vitiligo	28.3	36.4	9.4	25.6	Sonia, 1991
22.	Rheumatic disease	27.23	37.62	9.41	25.74	Sinha et al., 1971
23.	Epilepsy-Symptomatic	26.0	35.5	11.5	27.0	Present study
24.	Lung cancer	25.0	33.33	25.0	16.66	Hurkat et al., 1971
25.	Oesophagus cancer	25.0	37.50	12.50	25.0	Hurkat et al, 1971
26.	Penis cancer	25.0	45.0	10.0	20.0	Hurkat et al., 1971
27.	Peptic ulcer	25.0	28.0	12.0	35.0	Raghvan, 1962
28.	Enlarged prostate	23.34	40.31	7.42	7.42	Hurkat et al., 1971
29.	Diseases of women	22.67	38.28	5.10	33.93	Hurkat et al., 1971
30.	Peptic ulcer	22.22	50.0	2.77	25.0	Chuttani et al., 1964
31.	Anorectal cancer	22.0	40.0	4.00	34.0	Hurkat et al., 1971
32.	Cancer of cervix	21.89	39.15	5.95	33.02	Mitra et al., 1962
33.	Cancer of breast	21.43	35.72	8.33	34.52	Mitra et al., 1962
34.	Tuberculosis	21.24	39.49	7.15	32.10	Hurkat et al., 1971
35.	Epilepsy-Idiopathic	21.0	43.5	7.0	28.5	Present study
36.	Cervix cancer	20.83	48.61	4.16	26.38	Hurkat et al., 1971
37.	Gastrointestinal disorders	20.8	38.8	9.7	30.5	Sonia, 1991
38.	Uterus cancer	20.0	50.0	0.00	30.0	Hurkat et al., 1971
39.	Caecum cancer	20.0	10.0	10.0	60.0	Hurkat et al., 1971
40.	Other collagen disease	20.0	40.0	10.0	30.0	Sinha et al., 1971
41.	Peptic ulcers	19.48	24.67	9.09	46.75	Hurkat et al., 1971
42.	Smallpox	19.6	27.0	5.3	48.1	Downie et al., 1965
43.	Non-ulcer dyspepsia (NUD)	19.3	38.1	10.9	31.6	Sonia, 1991
44.	Periodontitis	19.3	41.9	12.9	25.8	Sonia, 1991
45.	Gastritis	18.2	40.8	11.8	29.0	Sonia, 1991
46.	Calculi	17.37	49.83	9.18	23.60	Hurkat et al., 1971
47.	Dental caries	17.6	44.1	11.7	26.4	Sonia, 1991
48.	Oesophaaitis	16.2	47.2	10.8	25.7	Sonia, 1991
49.	Leukemia cancer	15.15	43.93	1.515	39.39	Hurkat et al., 1971
50.	Pulmonary tuberculosis	15.7	27.0	10.0	47.3	Laha et al., 1963
51.	Stomach cancer	14.70	52.94	5.882	26.47	Hurkat et al., 1971
52.	Duodenal ulcers	13.3	33.3	7.6	45.7	Sonia, 1991
53.	Benian enlarQement of prostrate	8.0	56.0	8.0	28.0	Nayak, 1971
54.	Ovary cancer	11.11	33.33	33.33	22.22	Hurkat et al., 1971
55.	Urinary bladder cancer	7.69	53.84	0.00	20.0	Hurkat et al., 1971
56.	Tuberculosis	6.6	45.0	0.8	47.6	Nayak, 1971
57.	Peptic ulcer	5.2	38.5	0.3	56.0	Nayak, 1971

Table 8
Distribution of Differential Phenotypic Frequencies of Various ABO Blood Groups with Respect to Diseases (0-E)

S. No.	*Type of Disease*	*A*	*B*	*AB*	*0*	*Reference*
1	Cancer of the cervix uteri	14.92	-2.41	-1.30	-11.21	Venkataraman et al., 1968
2	Cancer of pancreas	14.7	-16.5	-0.4	-8.4	Aird et al., 1960
3	Oropharynx cancer	14.54	-2.08	-5.88	-6.55	Hurkat et al., 1971
4	Breast cancer	9.75	-11.08	5.69	-4.36	Hurkat et al., 1971
5	Epilepsy	9.75	-2.3	0.9	-9.55	Fedrick., 1972
6	Symptomatic epilepsy	7.0	-5.5	-3.5	2.0	Present study
7	Colon cancer	6.75	-17.02	8.41	1.89	Hurkat et al., 1971
8	Cancer of other genital organs	6.66	0.28	3.24	-9.19	Mitra et al., 1962
9	Cancer of oesophagus	6.2	8.9	-0.3	-6.3	Aird et al., 1960
10	Rheumatic heart disease	5.8	-3.0	-0.8	-2.1	Maxted (Bristol), 1940
11	Rheumatic disease	5.77	0.5	1.05	-7.32	Sinha et al., 1971
12	Cancer of stomach	5.0	-0.5	-0.3	-4.1	Aird et al., 1953
13	Rheumatic carditis	4.9	4.2	-0.2	-8.9	Clarke et al., 1960
14	Rheumatic heart disease	4.9	4.2	-0.2	-8.9	Addis (Glasgow), 1959
15	Rheumatic heart disease	3.4	0.4	1.0	-4.8	Buckwalter et al., (Iowa), 1962
16	Lung cancer	3.17	-5.12	19.12	-17.17	Hurkat et al., 1971
17	Penis cancer	3.17	6.55	4.12	-13.83	Hurkat et al., 1971
18	Oesophagus cancer	3.17	-0.95	6.62	-8.83	Hurkat et al., 1971
19	Idiopathic epilepsy	2.0	2.5	-8.0	-3.5	Present study
20	Gastric ulcer	1.73	-5.7	0.42	3.54	Merikas et al., 1966
21	Rheumatic fever	0.6	-3.1	-1.1	3.6	Maxted (Bristol), 1940
22	Rheumatic heart disease	0.2	1.2	0.2	-1.4	Addis (Glasgow), 1959
23	Anorectal cancer	0.17	1.54	-1.89	0.16	Hurkatetal., 1971
24	Cancer	-0.32	-3.32	4.11	-0.47	Mitra et al., 1962
25	Adenoma of pituitary	-0.9	0.5	-0.8	1.2	Aird et al., 1960
26	Rheumatic heart disease	-0.5	0.3	0.6	-0.4	Khattab and Ismail (Cairo), 1960
27	Cervix cancer	-0.99	10.17	-1.72	-7.44	Hurkat et al., 1971
28	Small pox	-1.1	-6.4	-0.5	8.0	Downie et al., 1965
29	Other collagen disease	-1.46	2.88	1.64	-3.06	Sinha et al., 1971
30	Caecum cancer	-1.83	-28.45	4.12	26.17	Hurkat et al., 1971
31	Uterus cancer	-1.83	11.55	-5.88	-6.55	Hurkat et al., 1971
32	Peptic ulcer	-2.64	-2.64	0.26	5.0	Merikas et al., 1966
33	Duodenal ulcer	-3.44	-2.08	0.23	5.27	Merikas et al., 1966
34	Cancer of the cervix	-4.21	4.95	-1.15	0.41	Mitra et al., 1962
35	Cancer of the breast	-4.67	1.12	1.23	1.92	Mitra et al., 1962
36	Leukaemia cancer	-6.67	5.49	-4.37	5.58	Hurkat et al., 1971
37	Pulmonary tuberculosis	-7.1	-11.8	3.0	15.9	Laha et al., 1963
38	Stomach cancer	-7.12	14.49	-	-7.37	Hurkat et al., 1971
39	Ovary cancer	-10.72	-5.11	27.46	-11.61	Hurkat et al., 1971
40	Urinary bladder cancer	-14.14	15.39	-5.88	4.63	Hurkat et al., 1971

The frequency of ABH secretors in patients having various diseases in descending magnitude has been given in Table 9. The table clearly shows that the frequency of non-secretors is very low in symptomatic epileptics. The results suggest that there is need to study prevalence of epilepsy with reference to frequency of secretors in various human populations by keeping other controls intact.

Table 9
Prevalence of ASH Secretors/Non-secretors in Certain Diseases

S.N.	Type of disease	Secretors (%)	Non-secretors (%)	Reference
1.	Tonsillectomy	84	16	Havenkorn et al., 1969
2.	Filariasis	82.14	17.6	Ayres et al., 1976
3.	Epilepsy-Symptomatic	82.0	18.0	Present study
4.	Non-ulcer dyspepsia (NUD)	80.3	19.7	Sonia, 1991
5.	Mitral stenosis	79.95	20.5	Havenkorn et al., 1969
6.	Rheumatic heart disease (RHO)	79.46	20.54	Haverkorn et al., 1969
7.	Helicobacter pylori negative	79.8	20.	Sonia, 1991
8.	Acute nephritis	78.3	21.7	Haverkorn et al., 1969
9.	Streptococcal pharyngitis	77.0	23.0	Haverkorn et al., 1969
10.	Rheumatic fever	76.69	23.31	Haverkorn et al., 1969
11.	Vitiligo	75.6	24.3	Sonia, 1991
12.	Rheumatic fever	74.2	25.8	Buckwalter et al., (lowa) 1962
13.	Gastritis	73.1	26.9	Sonia, 1991
14.	Oesophagitis	73.0	27.0	Sonia, 1991
15.	Helicobacter pylori positive	72.7	27.3	Sonia, 1991
16.	Acute rheumatic fever	72.6	27.4	Pham-Hun-Trung et al., (Paris) 1961
17.	Rheumatic carditis	72.2	27.8	Clarke et al., (Liverpool), 1960
18.	Rheumatic fever	71.1	28.9	Glvnn et al., (Taplow), 1959
19.	Rheumatic fever	70.15	29.85	Dublin et al., 1964
20.	Epilepsy-Idiopathic	70.0	30.0	Present study
21.	Gastrointestinal disorders	69.4	30.5	Sonia, 1991
22.	Rheumatic fever	68.62	31.38	Gershowitz and Neel, 1965
23.	Dental caries	68.6	31.3	Sonia, 1991
24.	Rheumatic fever	66.34	33.66	Wan NQO Um et al., 1965
25.	Duodenal ulcers	61.9	38.1	Sonia, 1991
26.	Gall stone disease	60	40	Sonia, 1991
27.	Periodontitis	51.3	48.6	Sonia, 1991
28.	Ulcerative colitis	45	55	Trikha et al., 2000
29.	Coeliac disease	45	55	Trikha et al., 2000

To conclude, there is excess of A blood group frequency and lower AB frequency in epileptics than controls. A very low frequency of ABH non-secretors has been observed in symptomatic epileptics, while no significant difference has been seen between idiopathic epileptics and controls.

SUMMARY

The data for the present study were collected from Neurology outpatient department (OPD) and epilepsy follow-up clinic at the Postgraduate Institute of Medical Education and Research (PGIMER), Chandigarh. A total of 400 epilepsy patients (200 idiopathic and 200 symptomatic) and 100 normal and healthy subjects, serving as controls, were studied. Both, patients and controls, belonged to the northwestern region of India and were matched for sex and ethnicity. Their blood and saliva samples were analyzed for ABO and ABH secretion. The division of idiopathic and symptomatic types of epilepsy was done on the basis of clinical findings (EEG, CT scan and MRI). A lower frequency of AB and excess of A were observed among epilepsy patients. However, chi-square test failed to reveal any significant differences between epilepsy patients and controls for ABO blood groups. The relative incidence (RI) was significantly higher than one in three instances (O: AB, A: AB; and B: AB) in idiopathic epilepsy patients (IEP), but for none in symptomatic epilepsy patients (SEP). A lower frequency of non-secretors was observed in epilepsy patients. 30% of idiopathic and 18% of symptomatic epilepsy patients were non-secretors compared with 37% in controls. The study demonstrated statistically significant differences between symptomatic versus controls and idiopathic versus symptomatic, but insignificant between idiopathic versus controls for ABH secretion. Relative Incidence (RI) of secretors versus non-secretors was significantly higher than one in symptomatic epilepsy patients. The results supported the hypothesis that ABH secretion might be associated with the susceptibility to epilepsy.

REFERENCES

Addis G.J. (1959), Blood Groups in Acute Rheumatism. *Scot Med J.* 4: 547-548.

Aird I., Bentall H.H. and Roberts J.A.F. (1953), A Relationship between Cancer of the Stomach and the ABO Blood Groups. *Brit Med. J.* 1: 799-801.

Aird I, Lee D.R. and Roberts J.A.F. (1960), ABO Blood Groups and Cancer of Oesophagus, Cancer of Pancreas and Pituitary Adenoma. *Brit. Med J.* 1: 1163-1166.

Ayres M., Salzano F.M., Helena M., Franco L.P. and Desouza Barros R.M. (1976), The Association of Blood Groups, ABH Secretion , Haptoglobins and Haemoglobins with Filariasis. *Hum. Hered.* 26: 105-109.

Beasley W.H. (1960), Blood Groups of Gastric Ulcer and Carcinoma. *Brit. Med. J.* 1: 1167-1172.

Buckwalter J.A., Naifeh G.S. and Auer J.E. (1962), Rheumatic Fever and Blood Groups. *Brit. Med. J.* 2: 1023-1028.

Chuttani P.N. (1964), Peptic Ulcer in the Punjab. *J. Ind. Med. Ass.* 42: 422-428.

Clarke C.A., Edwards J.W., Haddock D.R.W. et al. (1956), ABO Blood Groups and Secretor Character in Duodenal Ulcer. Population and Sibship Studies. *Brit. Med. J.* 2: 729-731.

Clarke C.A., McConnell R.B. and Sheppard P.M. (1960), ABO Blood Groups and Secretor Character in Rheumatic Carditis. *Brit. Med.* J. 1: 21-23.

Downie A.W., Meiklejohn G., Vincent St. L., Rao A.A., Babu S.B.V. and Kempe C.H. (1965), Smallpox Frequency and Severity in Relation to A, B and O Blood Groups. *Bull Wld Hlth Org.* 33: 623-625.

Dublin T.D., Bernanke A.D., Pitt E.L., Massell B.F., Allen F.H. and Amezcue F. (1964), Red Blood Cell Groups and ABH Secretor System as Genetic Indicators of Susceptibility to Rheumatic Fever and Rheumatic Heart Disease. *Brit. Med. J.* 2: 775-779.

Dunsford I., Bowley C.C. (1967), *Techniques in Blood Grouping* Vol. II. Edinburgh: Oliver and Boyd.

Fedrick J. (1972), ABO Blood Groups and Epilepsy. The Lancet 1034.

Gersowitz H. and Neel J.V. (1965), The Blood Groups and Secretor Types in Five Potentially Fatal Diseases of Caucasian Children. *Acta Genet Statist Med.* (Basel). 15: 261-308.

Glynn A.A., Glynn L.E., Holborow E.J. (1959), Secretion of Blood Group Substances in Rheumatic Fever-A Genetic Requirement for Susceptibitity. *Brit. Med. J.* 2: 266-270.

Gupta P. (1968), ABO Blood Groups and their Relationship with Cancer of the Cervix Uteri. *J. Ind. Med. Ass.* 51: 69-71.

Hanley W.B. (1964), Hereditary Aspects of Duodenal Ulceration: Serum-Pepsinogen level in Relation to ABO Blood Groups and Salivary ABH Secretor Status. *Brit. Med. J.* 1: 936-940.

Haverkon M.J., Goslings W.R.O. (1969), Streptococci, ABO Blood Groups and Secretor Status. *Am. J. Hum. Genet.* 21: 360-375.

Hurkat P.C., Mittal S.R. and Gupta S.N. (1971), ABO Blood Groups and Susceptibility to Diseases. *J. Ind. Med. Ass.* 57: 455-447.

Khattab T.M. and Ismail A.A. (1960), ABO Blood Groups in Relation to Rheumatic Heart Disease. *J. Egypt Med. Ass.* 43: 431-445.

Kinane D.F., Blackwell C.C., Brettle R.P. et al. (1982), ABO Blood Group Secretors State and Susceptibility to Recurrent Urinary Tract Infection in Women. *Brit. Med. J.* 285: 7-9.

Laha P.N. and Dutta M. (1963), Association between Blood Groups and Pulmonary Tuberculosis. *J. Ass. Phys. Ind.* 2: 287-291.

Langman M.J.S, Doll R., Saracci R. (1967), ABO Blood Group and Secretors Status in Stomal Ulcer. *Gut.* 8: 128-132.

Lubin D.M. (1995), Functional Roles of Blood Group Antigens. In Silberstein L.E. (ed): *Molecular and Functional Aspects of Blood Group Antigens.* American Association of Blood Banks, Bethesda, MD 163-192.

Maxted G.R. (1940), The Incidence of the Four Main Blood Groups in Rheumatic Heart Disease. *Arch. Dis. Child.* 15: 181-183.

Mericas G., Christakopoulos P. and Petropoulos E. (1966), Distribution of ABO Blood Groups in Patients with Ulcer Disease. *Am. J. Digestive Dis.* (New Series) 11: 790-795.

Mitra S., Modal S. and Basu A. (1962), The Study of ABO Blood Groups in Cancer of the Female Genital Organs and Cancer of the Breast. *Cancer.* 15: 39-41.

Mourant A.E. (1973), Association between Hereditary Blood Factors and Diseases. *Bulletin WHO* 49: 93-101.

Mourant A.E, Kopac A.C. and Domanhwaska Sobczak K. (1978), *Blood Groups and Diseases.* Oxford University Press, England, pp. 23-25.

Mourant A.E. (1985), Association between Blood Groups and Disease. *Disease Markers* 3: 1-7.

Mourant A.E. (1988), Recent Advances in the Study of Association between Infection and Genetic Markers. *Disease Markers* 1:

Nadamba J., Gomo E., Nyazema N. et al. (1997), Schistomiasis Infection in Relation to the ABO Blood Groups Among School Children in Zimbabwe. *Acta Trop* (Basel) 65: 181-190.

Nayak S.K. (1971), ABO Blood Group in Different Diseases. *J. Ind. Med. Assoc.* 57: 449-452.

Pham-Huu-Trung, Bessis A. and Mozziconacci P. (1961), Les Groupes Sanguins et Le Rheumatisme Articulaire Aigu. *Ann Pediat* (Paris). 37: 423-426.

Pratibha N., Padma I., Murthy J.S. (1995), ABO Blood Group Antibodies and ABH Secretion in Duodenal Ulcer Ind. *J. Hum. Genet* 1: 71-75.

Raghavan P. (1962), Epidemiology and Clinical behavior of Peptic Ulcer in Bombay, India. *Gastroenterology* 42: 130-143.

Sinha B.N. and Mishra J.N. (1971), ABO Blood Groups and Rheumatic Diseases in the Population of North Bihar. *J. Ind. Med. Ass.* 57: 452-454.

Sonia (1991), *ABH Secretion in Health and Disease.* Ph.D. Thesis (unpublished), Panjab University, Chandigarh.

Springer G.F. (1970), Importance of Blood Group Substances in Interactions between Man and Microbes. *Ann. NY Acad Sci.* 169: 134-152.

Trikha B., Sharma K., Singh V., Nain C.K. and Singh K. (2000), Genetic Epidemiology of Gallstone, Ulcerative Colitis and Celiac Disease. In: *Anthropology at the turn of the Century.* Vashisht R.N., et al. (eds.), Department of Anthropology, Panjab University, Chandigarh.

Vogel F., Pettenkofer H.J., Helmbold W. (1960), Uber Die Populationgenetik der ABO-Blutgruppen 2. Mitteilung, Genhaufigkeit und Epidemieesche Erkrankungen. *Acta Genet. Stat. Med. Gemell.* 10 : 267-294.

Vogel F. (1970), ABO Blood Groups and Disease *Am. J. Hum. Genet.* 22: 464-475.

Wan Ngo Lim, Kellner A., Schweitzer M.D., Smith D. and Wilson M.G. (1965), Association of Secretor Status and Rheumatic Fever in 106 Families. *Am. J. Epidem* 83: 103-111.

Wiener A.S. (1970), Blood Groups and Disease. *Am. J. Hum. Genet.* 22: 476.

Woolf B. (1955), On Estimating the Relation between Blood Group and Disease. *Ann. Hum. Genet.* 19: 251-253.

Part-IV

ETHICS AND OTHER ASPECTS OF HEALTH

19

LEGAL AND ETHICAL IMPERATIVES OF NATIONAL HEALTH IN INDIA

Abhik Ghosh

It is the mark of the cultured man that he is aware of the fact that equality is an ethical and not a biological principle.

—Ashley Montagu

In the hands of the discoverer, medicine becomes a heroic art...wherever life is dear he is a demigod.

—Ralph Waldo Emerson

Not for self, not for the fulfilment of any worldly material, desire or gain, but solely for the good of suffering humanity, I will treat my patient and excel all.

—Charak

INTRODUCTION

Ethics comes from the Greek *ethos* which means "custom or practice, a definitive manner of acting along with somewhat constant mode of behaviour in the deliberate actions of man". In Latin, ethics focuses more on manners, morals and the character of human beings. Ethics deals with the morality of human acts through the medium of natural reasons. Ethics teaches us to judge between the good and the bad.

For the purpose of this work, I shall follow a certain pathway of Ethics, developed from the work of Agnes Heller in *General Ethics* in 1990. According to her, there are three levels of ethics in the world (see figure 1).

At the *first* level, there is individual ethics. This kind of ethics is developed from the personal idiosyncrasies and expediencies of the individual. They include personal viewpoints and ideas. They are formed by the particular worldviews of individuals, especially through personal experiences.

At the *second* level are group or community ethics. In so far as the individual is part of local cultures and communities, and is encultured

INDIVIDUAL ETHICS/MORALS

↕

Personal experiences

Worldviews

Researchers impact personal privacy

Rapport establishment

Keyserlinck; 1993

GROUP/COMMUNITY ETHICS/MORALS

↕

Enculturation/

Socialization

Infiltration through research data

Ethnography as link/facilitator

Hoffmaster; 1993

NATIONAL/GLOBAL/HUMANITARIAN ETHICS/MORALS

Concept of the GOOD man
Valid everywhere
Level of partial paradigms/theories
Beyerstein; 1993
Winkler; 1993

Fig. 1: The Structure of The Ethical System of Humanity (After Heller; 1993)

and socialized by them, a set of ethical and moral values are picked up. These are added on to individual ethics and morals, sometimes in opposition.

At the *third* level, are general ethics. It consists of the concept of the *good* man, a man who is valid as good from the viewpoint of all cultures in space and time. Such a concept seems to exist, even if vaguely, in all cultures.

There are, of course, problems in the linkages of these three levels. They may dovetail but more often they clash. As a result an individual may carry more than one set of ethical maps in his mind.

All ethics and morals are relative. Hence, the problem of determining a universal rule of law or a system of ethics, especially for biomedicine. This has been highlighted by Beyerstein (1993). Such a system may also involve partial theoretical systems or paradigms (Winkler; 1993).

Our collection of data infiltrates into the subspaces of the self and the community. They are very much annoyable and invariably we do intrude into personal and confidential lives. The autonomy of individuals is broken into or hacked by the professional fieldworker by accessing the moral or ethical codes of humanity or the local cultural norms and values, whose subsystems are ethics and morals. We do this by a process we call rapport establishment. This respect (or disrespect) for autonomy may or may not be a multi-cultural principle (Keyserlink; 1993), but it is certainly a contested territory.

To the extent that we believe our fieldwork is benign and helpful to individuals and communities in the long run, we tend to be sincere in our persuasion of individuals to speak to us. In the autonomous territory of the individual and the subsuming and hegemonic spaces of national health policies, perhaps only sincere and detailed ethnography can again link up the spaces between the micro and the macro (Hoffmaster; 1993).

THE BACKGROUND

In the 19th century, the Hippocratic Oath was being widely stated as an essential part of practice. The distinguished radiologist, Sir Robert Hutchison prayed that, "From...too much zeal for the new; and contempt for the old; from putting knowledge before wisdom, science before art: cleverness before common sense: from treating patients as cases, and for making cure of the disease more grievous than the endurance thereof: the good Lord deliver us."

Napoleon Bonaparte is said to have stated that, "I do not want two diseases, one Nature made and one Doctor made." By 1910, it was stated by the Flexner Report that, "One must educate the public that seldom does a patient receive the best treatment."

By the 20th century, it was assumed that the doctor was a trusted person and dominant. The patient often remained uninformed of his disease and the mode of his cure. Being grateful to the doctor was second nature. Believing in fate came first. If something went wrong, very few knew of it and the rest never complained.

By the 21st century, it became clear that there were fewer presumptions. There are more opportunities for errors due to a greater complexity. A perception grew that holding doctors and hospitals as being accountable for treatment will improve the delivery system. Even if doctors do not like to give away information relating to details of a disease, symptoms and treatment, the works are available for consultation either in libraries or on the Internet. By December, 2003, there were 246,000 articles on headache, 112,000 on aneurysms (including 2490 on incidental aneurysms), 93,300 on deep brain stimulation, 47,200 on skull base surgery, 39,600 on radio surgery, 10,100 on cerebral embolisation, and so on. The perception of the health industry has changed. It is now seen as being too big, dangerous and costly for it to be left solely to doctors (Ganapathy; 2003).

The doctor then becomes a health care provider with quality control, audits, protocols, regulations, guidelines and frequent inspections. The patient, the consumer, is a hard negotiator buying a product, calling the shots and capable of changing the system. Systematic measurement of outcome of patient care is the precursor for instituting continuous quality improvement (CQI) techniques used in monitoring industrial processes (Ganapathy; 2003).

At present, the Indian government's tertiary health care infrastructure consists of 117 tertiary medical colleges and hospitals, 1,200 ESI and PSU hospitals, 4,400 district and *taluk* hospitals, and about 2,400 community health centres as part of secondary care with 23,000 primary health care centres, 137,000 sub-centres and 1,500 urban health posts as part of primary healthcare (Trehan; 2004). However, the 4.03 crore slum population of India as of 2001 are unlikely to receive the best part of this infrastructural support. 300 CGHS dispensaries also cater to 44 lakh beneficiaries. However, such services are now in a shambles.

Even while the total amount spent by India annually per capita on health at average exchange rates is $ 24, the total spent being equivalent to 5.1% of GDP (this figure is still being debated), it is very low as compared to the developed countries (USA doing $ 4887 per capita per annum at 13.9% of the GDP) though it does better in comparison with the developing countries. It is spending more on healthcare than Sri Lanka and Malaysia. However, Indians spend the most on medicare from their own pockets as compared to many other countries, amounting to about 82.2% of the total costs. The comparable figures for the US are 15.3% and for UK are 10.6%. According to the figures, 22 lakh people are being pushed below the poverty line due to the high medical costs. By 2005, this figure was estimated to be two crores. It is said also that in India more than 26 crore people cannot afford healthcare (the amount doubled between 1986 and 1995). If the poor pay a premium of Rs. 248 per annum on health insurance, the health insurance scheme would cost the state Rs. 1,200 crore. Further, India has 48 doctors for every 100,000 individuals.

Recent studies have substantiated this. There is a difference in healthcare available in rural areas and that available in urban areas in India. This difference has not become any better in recent years. Even in urban areas, the 22% Indian population residing in slums get poorer treatment as compared to others. Further, those in urban areas in India seem to spend more out of their own pocket on in-patient care than in rural areas. There are also major differences in this spending between public and private healthcare. As a result of government spending on healthcare having decreased, the poor have also been forced to spend on private healthcare to a much larger extent. The case of Mumbai cited by the authors is a case where in spite of there being healthcare needs, adequate infrastructure still does not exist to meet those needs (Dilip and Duggal; 2004).

Poverty being a factor that leads to worse healthcare may also be seen from its indirect effects. Another study shows that a lower economic status of a household may cause infectious diseases to occur in early childhood. In order to achieve a better healthcare rate in such cases the nutrition of children should be enhanced. The 2001 census data also shows only 36% Indians to have access to a toilet facility, 77% to safe drinking water and only 52% households have houses of permanent materials (Ghosh; 2005). The same care is also required to be taken of the aged, especially of the retired, since retirement seems to have an adverse effect on health (Chattopadhyay and Roy; 2005). Differential access to healthcare requirements are also indicated, especially with regard to caste status and this should be looked into (Raj and Raj; 2004). Some help in this regard was given by mobile hospitals, especially in hilly areas (Pant; 2004). However, while the ordinary man sees financial problems in healthcare, Rs. 5 crores were spent on Narasimha Rao's health in the US, Rs. 15 crores on V.P. Singh's healthcare in UK and US and the present Prime Minister has 32 doctors, 27 paramedics and 7 ambulances working round the clock at a cost of Rs. 23 lakh/month (Das and TNN; 2004).

Only 17% of healthcare costs are borne by the government, making it one of the most privatized in the world. In 1996-97, the central government spent Rs. 45.09 crores which has come down to Rs. 7.3 crores in 2001-02. The per capita public health expenditure is Rs. 160 only. The National Health Policy 2002 suggests an increase to 25% of the government's contribution to public health investment with the present rate being 15%. The bulk of the money goes into vaccination programmes like Pulse Polio and TB while basic healthcare is ignored and as a result 6 lakh children die of diarrhoea every year in the country. In 2003-04, health and family welfare spendings amounted to Rs. 6,846 crore out of Rs. 474,255 crore, about 0.0144%. In 2004-05, health, drinking water supply, urban employment and poverty alleviation, elementary education and literacy together were paid Rs. 12,835 crore, marginally lower than CBI, IB and

SPG. In the same period, the police were given Rs. 115,000 crore by the centre and state governments (Singh; 2005).

According to the *World Health Report 2005*, the annual growth rate of India's population is 1.7%, and in 2003 the aged (60 years and above) were 7.8%. The life expectancy in 2003 was 62, and deaths under 5 years of age were 85 for males and 90 for females. The total health expenditure as percentage of GDP in 2002 was 6.1% (a figure seen by many to be too inflated). It was reported in 1991 to be 6.0% of which 21.7% is public spending (Sen Gupta; 1995). The current rates are claimed to be 0.9% which should be increased to 5% claims the World Health Organisation. Some would even be happy if this could be raised to 2-3% of GDP. The crude birth rate was 23.5 and the crude death rate 8.6 (per 1,000). The total fertility rate per woman is 2.9, the age-specific fertility rate for ages 15-19 being 71 per 1,000. Only 43% births were attended by trained health personnel. The life expectancy at birth for males was 62 while for females it was 66 years. The infant mortality rate was 64 while mortality under age 5 years was 92 per 1,000.

At present, 130,000 mothers die during childbirth, while the maternal mortality rate has gone up from 424 to 540 deaths per 100,000 live births. The infant mortality rate is 68 per thousand live births per year. Only 38% of PHCs have all the critical staff, 69% have at least one bed and only 20% have a telephone. The drugs that are under price control were 347 in 1979, at present they are only 74 and even this is proposed to be decreased to 34. No care is taken to ensure essential medicines are kept at a low price and it is not true that market forces keep prices low. This is also true for recent drugs for treatment of HIV/AIDS. Only one organisation, LOCOST, produces generic drugs and sells them at low prices (Narrain; 2004).

Public awareness of unsafe drugs should be increased. For instance, phenyl propanolamine used in cough and cold drugs is banned in the US but is used in India. Doctors should report to the Adverse Drug Reaction monitoring centres who should report to the Drugs Controller General. The Drugs and Cosmetics Act also need modifications to remove loopholes. However, this cannot be done very effectively since many patients resort to self-medication. In alternative medicines, there is even less standardization of procedures and ingredients (Tripathi; 2005). Even unnecessary exposures to X Rays should be avoided and unavoidable ones should be as low as possible (Parthasarathy; 2005).

Another study shows that the number of people falling into poverty due to hospitalization could be as high as 25%. In Bihar and Uttar Pradesh the number is about 35%, it is about 30% in Punjab, 27% in Madhya Pradesh, 25% in the North-East, 23% in Maharashtra, 22% in Orissa, 21% in Karnataka, 20% in Tamil Nadu and 16% in Kerala. Out-of-pocket medical costs may push 2.2% into poverty every year. The data is from the NSSO which were presented to the National Advisory Council last year (Jain; 2004).

In fact about 75% of patient costs go to pay unnecessary tests and costs for paying off middlemen. When tests are conducted about 40% often return back to the doctor. These include the MRI centres, the directors, representatives at the top. At the middle level are Junior residents and peons or ward boys as well as senior residents and consultants. Then come the private practitioners (Khanna; 2004).

In the mid-1990s, the amount of household income spent on healthcare was seven per cent. Now it is 12% and growing, with the poor spending more than the rich. High quality medical treatment is often being claimed by many health service providers as being equated with high-technology gadgets. It may actually be judged by rigorous medical and nursing audits and seen in the function of its routines and practices, the discipline of its staff and the transparency of its management. While money is always required, it is not just money that has to be given to the system. Firstly, there should be a sharply defined health policy. Basic healthcare should always be delivered by the state, since "the mantra of privatizing healthcare and its institutions, including its avatars such as user-fees and cost-recovery, is largely irrelevant to basic health services."

The private health industry should be regulated like any other industry. There is a basic asymmetry of knowledge between the providers and the users for this regulation to occur on its own. Without changes in its composition or procedures the Medical Council of India will not suffice. Secondly, the government health delivery system is flawed, fragmented, without any clear line of command or control. It has become dysfunctional due to the creation of multiple departments, cells, schemes and quasi-autonomous societies, created through the will of donors but who are maintained even after funding dries up. The centrally-sponsored schemes need to be looked into since many have outlived their usefulness. This wastefulness often eats into budgets. Finally, all public services should be based on the user, the user's family and community. Too much of the detail of the health delivery system is decided centrally, leaving little scope for local bodies. One way to do this would be to empower local political bodies like the panchayati raj institutions (David; 2004: 20). The use of panchayats for health services has also been implemented in some areas as in Madhya Pradesh through the help of DANIDA (Diwan and DeCosta; 2004).

LEGAL ASPECTS OF THE NATIONAL HEALTH POLICY

The National Health Policy admits that the total legal aspects related to health and medicine are scattered over a large number of areas and Acts. An integrated, unified comprehensive legislation in the health field enforceable all over the country is proposed (see also Ghosh; 2001). The major articles of the constitution which are related to the health and medical practices are Articles 21, 32 and 226. They include the all-important "right to life."

The doctors in India are guided by the Indian Code of Medical Ethics. Their training is guided by the Medical Degrees Act of 1916. The other major Acts related to the medical profession *per se* are the Indian Medical Council Act of 1933, the Medical Registration Act of 1858, and the Indian Medical Act of 1956 (amended in 1964).

The people of India are protected from fraudulent practices and the use of fraudulent drugs by the Drugs and Magic Remedies (Objectionable Advertisement) Act of 1954. Other drug-related Acts include the Drugs and Cosmetics Act of 1940 and the Drugs Control Act of 1956. Related with this, a Drug Control Policy was enacted in 1986. The use of chemicals and other organic products as insecticides are controlled by the Insecticide Act of 1968.

The sale of unhealthy, diluted or adulterated foods is a criminal offence under the prevention of Food Adulteration Act of 1956 (amended in 1973). The consumers of drugs and foods, among other consumable items, is regulated by the Consumer Protection Act of 1986. On a larger scale, the practice of trading of such articles is regulated by the Monopolies and Restrictive Trade Practices Act of 1984 (amended).

The effect of X-Rays on the human body, among other things, are also a matter of concern in the Atomic Energy Act of 1962. Many other Acts, especially related to the environment, have come up in recent years to control the polluting effects of various kinds of industries, etc. These include the water (Prevention and Control of Pollution) Act of 1974, the Air (Prevention and Control of Pollution) Act of 1981, and the Environment Protection Act of 1986. The Motor Vehicles Act of 1988 also deals with the control of pollution in vehicles driven on roads. A recent bill colloquially known as 'Delhi Quackery Bill' was being attempted to be passed in Parliament in October 1998 in order to control the practice of medicine by uncertified doctors.

Recently, the Ministry of Food Processing Industries proposed an integrated food law called the Food Safety and Standards Bill, 2005. It involves the repealing of the Infant Milk Food Substitutes, Feeding Bottles and Infant Feeds (Regulation of Production, Supply and Distribution) Amendment Act, 2003. The latter Act promotes breast-feeding, the former Bill does not. As a result, a battle was enjoined to protect the earlier Act and save millions of children every year (Rajalakshmi; 2005).

However, it is the affected people who have to make use of such Acts, Articles and Policies. The major drug companies work with large funds at their disposal, and so do a lot of doctors and private practitioners, and hence the poorer population are unable to compete with them or carry out protracted and costly legal wrangles in the courts. In spite of Legal Aid given by the governments, welfare and voluntary organisations, the cost of such practices becomes prohibitive.

Functional foods are an everyday food transformed into a potential lifesaver by the addition of an ingredient. Foods and medicines have different laws. With functional foods, one has the problem of deciding whether it is a food or a medicine (Coghlan; 1996). In the case of the Drug Industry, the All India Drug Action Network has declared a majority of 50,000 drug formulations marketed in India as being irrational. Hence, more stringent controls are required to ensure that the claims made on the item be true.

The Delhi Medical Council Act of 1997 claims that a DMC on its part may initiate an inquiry upon receipt of a complaint of a malpractice of a medical practitioner. However, there are few cases where such cases are taken up. There have been cases in Delhi where patients, especially female, have been criminally assaulted by doctors in hospitals. One minor female was assaulted by a doctor in the Holy Angels Hospital in 2003. There is a rule that male doctors cannot examine a female patient without a nurse or a member of the patient's family being present but this is frequently ignored. Experts feel that this crucial community is least being targeted in the fight against women-related violence (Nayar; 2003).

MEDICAL MALPRACTICE AND THE LAW IN INDIA

The consent of the patient for undergoing any kind of medical treatment is taken for granted, and often no information is given to the patient or the next of kin relating to what the doctor is about to do to the patient. Finally, it is notoriously difficult to elucidate in an Act and bring to book doctors having a lack of dedication or a feeling of humanism for their patients. Further, it is extremely difficult to pinpoint cases of medical malpractice in the case of a doctor (Duggal and Jessani; 1992). We have no reliable statistics of how often medical "misadventures" occur in India. Even in the United States, it has been claimed by one article in *The New England Journal of Medicine* in 1995 that about 5% doctors "ought not to be practicing medicine" (Ganapathy; 2003).

However, some health activists claim that every 11th Indian doctor has a malpractice case against him or her. Further, it is one of the most corrupt professions. According to a study conducted in 2001 by Transparency International, health providers in India were paid 28% of the bribes paid in the country, amounting to Rs. 7,578 crore. Organizations like the Kolkata based People for Better Treatment (PBT) are already fighting this trend (Wadhwa; 2003).

In 1995, there were fewer than 10,000 medical malpractice suits filed in consumer courts. By 1999 the number became 29,944. By 2000, only about 20% of the healthcare of the country was taken care of by government hospitals. At this time there were only 350 registered nursing homes, a ridiculous figure. Many became clinics, which were under the Shops and Establishment Act and could be multi-speciality including MRI and ECG. Many such clinics operated from Delhi Development Authority built homes and other houses (Thapa and Menon; 2000).

Health is a state subject. Technically every state enacts its own legislation. The doctors' lobby prevented it in Andhra Pradesh. The 1,200 private nursing homes were under the Bombay Nursing Act of 1948. As of 2000 AD the records of the Medical Council of India (MCI) show a registered five lakh doctors, a majority in urban areas (Thapa and Menon; 2000).

Dr. C.M. Gulhati, editor of the monthly medical journal *MIMS India*, had once listed the following reasons for the aiding and abetting of medical malpractice (Wadhwa; 2003):

- A doctor's lack of knowledge.
- Lack of continuing education in medicine.
- Absence of a system of re-examining doctors to see if they have kept up with the progress in medicine.
- Unethical practices like taking cuts from each other for cross-referring patients (called cut practice with the general practitioners called gatekeepers because of the referral systems they use). The cut could be as much as 20-30% of the amount paid by the patient.
- Over-treatment of patients to get a heftier fee.
- Drug misuse and overuse.
- Acceptance of bribes from pharmaceutical companies to push their products. This may include foreign junkets, houses, cars for doctors and retail schemes for chemists.
- The near-ineffectiveness of our 19 state medical councils and their umbrella organisation, the Medical Council of India (MCI) – bodies which have the power to deregister doctors guilty of professional misconduct.

The Medical Councils of India was constituted under the Central Statute in 1956. They operate very lackadaisically and make a farce of the medical profession. Few cases of malpractice are returned in favour of the patient and at the most a stern warning may be issued. The Delhi High Court had declared the MCI "a den of corruption" in 2001. It received 118 complaints against doctors between April 2001 and March 2002. As a result 4 doctors were deregistered and none know for how long. 65 complaints were referred to state medical councils. The Tamil Nadu Medical Council (TNMC) was dysfunctional for about 20 years. It started functioning again in December 2002. They were receiving about 4 complaints per week then. Most state Medical Councils are largely inactive and often exist only on paper. Cases of negligent driving and medical negligence are included in the same Section 304A of the Indian Penal Code. It is punishable with up to two years of imprisonment or with fine, or with both. In May 2002, in Alipore Court in Calcutta, a landmark ruling was made in the case of Anuradha Saha where the doctors responsible for her death due to negligible and inappropriate treatment got away with no more than three months' imprisonment and Rs. 3,000 fine. Bail was set at Rs. 5,000 each, keeping both of them out of jail (Wadhwa; 2003). In November 2004, 65 doctors were debarred from practice till 2007 by the MCI, especially with relation to teaching (Jain and TNN; 2004).

As a result people have been reacting in violent ways. The Dhanalakshmi Hospital in Kannur was burnt down by mobs in May 2002 after a patient died after piles surgery. A gynaecologist at the Ernakulum government hospital refused to treat a poor woman for a lower fee. She was mobbed, put on public trial and garlanded with slippers. In return, the Kerala chapter of the Indian Medical Association organized the first ever strike of doctors protesting against unacceptable levels of harassment on 1 October 2002 (Wadhwa; 2003).

In fact Eco (for Economic or those who are for making money) and Thera (for Therapeutic or those who are to be given really needed treatment) describes the two kinds of patients at private medical clinics in India (Wadhwa; 2003).

Many doctors conduct wrong treatments and surgery. Unnecessary appendicitis operations are often coded as chronic remunerative appendicitis. Many low-back pain hospitalizations are being found to have been unnecessary. Constant monitoring of the foetus has probably led to increase in Caesarian sections. Quicker acting antibiotics cause more problems. Many patient deaths are preventable. There are surgeries on the wrong part of the body, or wrong procedures performed or wrong patient surgeries (Ganapathy; 2003).

Cases of patients forced into unnecessary treatments or tests for the lucrative vested interest of the doctors has become so commonplace that it is ordinary. Physicians in India have certain "duties" towards their patients, laid down by the Indian Medical Council (Professional Conduct, Etiquette and Ethics) Regulations 2002. Patients, however, have no "rights" as such. A physician is free to choose to serve but cannot ignore emergencies. Unnecessary consultations are to be avoided and whenever it is given the benefit of the patient should be of foremost importance. Any variation in treatment should be discussed/explained to the patient. These issues are mandatory in the US including a patient's access to medical records (Ghosh; 2004(b)).

Further, goons who get themselves treated as VIPs after giving the names of prominent politicians, those who need to be treated for longer periods to show that their injuries are more serious than reality, declarations for trumping up false criminal cases and doctors beaten up whenever VIP patients or VIPs die has become the norm in some areas (Ghosh; 2004(a)).

A recent spate of articles show that the number of quacks practicing in India could be far higher than had been supposed earlier. They stay in the heart of major cities like Delhi and practice within view of major hospitals without having the requisite degrees or being otherwise recognized (Ghosh; 2004(d)). Delhi has an estimated 40,000 quacks while there are about 25,000 registered MBBS doctors. To open a clinic one has only to show proof of registration with either the Delhi Medical Council, Bharatiya Chikitsa Parishad or Homoeopathy Board. So far 30,000 have been so registered. No commercial licences are required to open clinics in residences but water and electricity have to be paid at commercial rates. Unless complaints are made the State Health department does not check them (Ghosh; 2004(c), Times News Network; 2004). About 2,000 illegal nursing homes thrive in Delhi. Any nursing home should comply with the municipal laws, and have more than 30 beds. Below this it can only be a health centre. The rooms need to be well-ventilated, clean, and arrangements for heating and cooling. Any operating theatre should have 280 sq feet of floor space. A high pressure sterilizer, an instrument sterilizer, apparatus for transfusions, intravenous apparatus, oxygen cylinder are essential. There should be one nurse for every three beds and for 10 beds should have at least 2 nurses (Ghosh; 2004(e)).

In West Bengal an estimated one lakh quacks as a conservative estimate were seen to exist (Ganguly; 2004). Further, faced with a lack of doctors, West Bengal government decided to give charge to homoeopaths and ayurveds of at least 322 primary health centres. The MBBS doctors would only be in the Block health centres from where they would visit once a week (Majumdar; 2004). In Karnataka, the number of quacks are 400 as estimated by the health department, while the IMA which gets about three complaints per day from here claim the number is about 75,000. The health department invokes the Drugs and Magic Remedies Act of 1954 to attend to this crime. However, the state government is reportedly sitting on the Karnataka Quackery Prohibition Bill Act, 2001 which imposes a fine of Rs. 35,000 and three-year imprisonment (S.; 2004). In Haryana, especially Panchkula, doctors certified under the State Council of Ayurvedic and Unani Medicines, Bihar are operating. The number of them enrolled is about 110 in 2003. However, Rule Two of the Drugs and Cosmetics Rules, 1945, forbid them to practice in another state. Haryana has 11,000 quacks and there are only 15-16 drug inspectors. It seems that some, if not many, enjoy political patronage (Sharma; 2005). In Punjab, under the Drugs and Magic Remedies (objectionable advertisements) Act, 1954, those putting out such advertisements may be caught but in reality such advertisements are rarely taken action upon. 54 diseases are covered under the Act like obesity, diabetes, disorder of the brain, epilepsy, blood pressure, rheumatics, sexual impotence, asthma, etc. (Ashk; 2005). In Mumbai there are 30,000 registered practitioners and an equal number of quacks. In 1998, the General Practitioners' Association did a survey and turned up 10,000 quacks. One boy who swept the floor of a doctor's clinic later set up his own clinic. To set up a dispensary one only needs to set up shop under the Shops and Establishments Act, seeing that they open and close on time and do not employ children (Iyer; 2004).

Doctors are also not trained enough for cross-practices. For instance a non-allopathic medical practitioner may not practice allopathy. From 22 April 1992, after a landmark judgment by the Supreme Court, this became a legal issue. In response to an appeal by Dr. A.K. Subhapathy, the Kerala Government's permission to allow persons not qualified in modern medicine to practice allopathy was struck down (Phadke; 1997:1). Further, in "the Pramod vs. Dr. Ashwin Patel case, the Supreme Court ruled that the homeopathic doctor was guilty of negligence *per se* because section 15(3) of the Indian Medical Council Act prohibited any person without the requisite qualification in the allopathic system of medicine to practice that system" (Phadke; 1997: 1).

How then is one to incorporate the ISMs in this kind of a system? It is proposed that a minimum list of 50 essential drugs can be drawn with their treatment profiles and usage. This can be used to train non-allopathic doctors in the system for quick cures in case they are required. Beyond this, they have to refer to an allopathic specialist (Phadke; 1997: 2-3).

According to doctors, the medical service is not a commodity. They prefer to judge competence and timeliness, but not results. They claim that judges cannot grasp the technical nature of medical cases. The lack of court fees and stamp duty means that frivolous cases will be tried out. 'Defensive' medicine will lead to greater costs and many would withhold service in critical cases. There is fear that an USA-like situation of huge awards will be created.

On the other hand, consumer activists claim that medicine is like any other professional service, and doctors are needed to do only what is professionally possible. Civil and criminal courts have been judging with the help of expert testimony. The CPA should be amended to avoid frivolous cases. All civil court procedures are followed. Medical costs are already high to recover costs of equipment. Doctors also withhold services to avoid medico-legal complications in critical cases. India's limited insurance market will ensure that large claims are not made.

A Supreme Court ruling in 1992 has also dictated that medical practitioners also fall in the purview of the Consumer Protection Act, 1986, Section 2(1)(o). Under this Act it was found that only 0.1 to 2% of the total cases pertain to medical malpractice. The cases where such victims have found redressal include:

1. K. Gracykutty versus Dr. Annamma Ommen and another reported in 1992(1) CPR 256, with the Kerala State Consumer Disputes Redressal Commission.
2. The supply of contaminated blood in Harish Kumar versus Sunil Blood Bank reported in 1991 (1) CPJ 645.
3. For not providing post-operative care in Shekar Hegde versus Dr. Sudhanshu Bhattacharya reported in 1992(2) CPJ 449.

Consumer Protection is only one of the routes that are available to the victim. There are other routes possible also. For instance, it may be negligence as Tort, a case where tortuous liability arises from the breach of a duty primarily fixed by law. It may also be a negligence under Contract where contractual liability depends upon the express or implied terms agreed upon by the patient and the doctor. Negligence as Crime involves criminal liability, depending on the amount and degree of the negligence. When a First Information Report (FIR) is filed against a doctor for the death of a patient under his treatment, it is under Section 304-A of the Indian Penal Code. Such a doctor may be arrested and be provided bail. If proved guilty the doctor may be jailed for a maximum of two years or fined or both. If the patient is alive the complaints are filed under IPC sections 337 and 338 (Lawz Bureau; 2004).

Some protection may be gained by the doctors by going in for insurance schemes against professional liability. At present about 15% of Indian Medical Association's (IMA's) one lakh members are estimated to be insured. Doctors would also now advise the patients to take more and more tests in order to avoid making mistakes. It would make health care costlier. Further, doctors frequently do not standardize their fees, they give away physician's samples after inadequate knowledge and offer radically different treatment regimes for the same illness. The results of the CPA will tend to standardize these practices (Subramaniam; 1995).

Under the CPA the following people would be liable:

1. Doctors with independent practices, unless rendering only free service.
2. Private hospitals charging all.
3. All hospitals having free as well as paying patients. They are liable to both.
4. Doctors/hospitals paid by an insurance firm for treatment of a client, or an employer for that of an employee.

Doctors in hospitals which do not charge any of their patients and hospitals offering free service to all patients are not liable.

Either way, the issue of ethics remains unnoticed. In recent years, the issue of malpractice among health practitioners has swung both towards the patients as also towards the doctors.

It has been stated that about 6 million Indian women undergo abortion every year, according to a study by the Abortion Assessment Project India. Further, 69% of the syringes used in India are unsafe, according to the Union health minister A. Ramadoss. This was a quote from a draft report of a study funded by the World Bank. 34% were found to be unsafe due to improper sterilization and another 34% were found to be unsafe due to the poor skills of those who administered the injection. To prevent this there was a move to introduce Auto Disable Syringes which could not be used again (Times of India; 2004). These were invented by Marc Koska of UK who was in Delhi in July 2005 to set up the SafePoint Centres for promoting public awareness on syringes (Koska; 2005).

In 2005, a report of an All India study conducted by India Clen, funded by the Ministry of Health and the World Bank also found that 63% of the total injections given are unsafe. 6 out of every 10 injections carry pathogens like HIV, hepatitis B or C. 74% immunizations carry the risk of blood-borne infections. Annually, 4.2 billion injections are given in India. 83% of these are in therapeutic care and 17% are used for immunizations. Of every 100 prescriptions, 48 are for injections. 46% of these are for fever, cough and diarrhoea. Every year 30,000 new HIV infections are diagnosed. There are also 20 lakh cases of hepatitis B and 4 lakh cases of hepatitis C every year. PATH with Niloufer Hospital in Hyderabad opened the first ever Model Injection Centre of India in the last week of January 2005. They advocate the use of injections solely by qualified personnel only when it is found to be necessary (Vasudev; 2005).

Following a Punjab and Haryana High Court directive, the state government has undertaken the exercise of identifying unqualified doctors in the state of Punjab. By August 1999, 30,000 fake medical practitioners running illegal health care centres, mostly in the rural areas, were identified. Though lacking qualifying degrees, they have big nursing homes. Others are running their business in the guise of the names of either non-existent or missing people. This system worked well due to a lack of government infrastructure in rural areas. The health department forwarded some cases for action to the police. Many such doctors have temporarily closed down their business centres. The police have filed challans in 1,500 cases. However, action slows down during the Lok Sabha elections, with health department officials being pressurized not to forward all the cases to the police for action. Such quacks also act as nodal recruiters for pulling in patients to health practitioners in nearby urban areas. In 1998, the government drive to detect fake registered medical practitioners (RMPs) was resisted by RMPs (Bharadwaj; 1999).

P.R. Kumaramangalam, the Union power minister, was admitted at Delhi's Indraprastha Apollo Hospital for treatment of his blood cancer on 14 April. His subsequent death was caused by mis-diagnosis. They should have conducted a bone-marrow examination, a mandatory for long-term fever. Four months later, he was admitted to AIIMS where he later died (Menon; 2000).

A few senior medical officers (SMOs) have become known of accepting kickbacks from private doctors for remaining absent from their jobs. A son of an SMO was also found collecting money from doctors and also sanctioning them leaves. The complaints were received from the public as well as from staff members. Surprise raids at some centres have found the entire staff being absent. Further, though none were present at one dispensary, with an average of three to five patients per day visiting it, there were two doctors on the rolls who were supposed to have been present, a very high doctor-patient ratio (Rana; 2003).

On 8 October 2003, the Primary Health Centre at Morni was instructed to pay a woman Rs. 70,000 on account of deficiency of services to Sheela Devi by the District consumer grievances and redressal forum. Having five children already, she had agreed to a tubectomy. The PHC had conducted the operation. Inspite the operation, she had conceived again in 2001 and then again in 2002 (TNN; 2003(a)).

In September 2004, the vigilance department caught Dr. Ramesh Maheshwari, at the civil hospital in Bathinda, Punjab, taking a Rs. 4,000 bribe from a representative of a reputed pharmaceutical company. It was alleged by the representative that the doctor forced him to pay. As a result of this practice, commonly known but rarely caught, doctors take bribes from medical representatives and prescribe costlier medicines to patients. In other words, even in other areas, the patient is rarely given a choice between less costly alternatives of the same medicine. It was also commented by a doctor in Guru Gobind Singh Medical College, Faridkot, that pharmaceutical companies had given gifts of airconditioners, refrigerators to doctors, even organizing trips for them to hill stations during summer. An orthopaedist and ENT specialist in Faridkot has accepted a Zen vehicle and a scooter from a Ferozepur company for prescribing their drugs to patients (Garg; 2004(c)). In other areas in West Bengal, such large gifts are common to those taking large orders of such medicines, also including the gift of bungalows and vehicles.

Publications regarding a new drug are published through the drug companies without adequate peer review in less ethical journals. Then they are displayed to doctors as examples of the drug's efficacy and lack of side effects. The articles are often ghost written by others. Even editorials of such journals may be ghost written by the drug manufacturer. Further, a reprint of an article that praises a drug may have several hundred thousand copies bought off by the drug manufacturer (costing upto half a million pounds). Such sales usually tempt many journals to publish such articles. Peer reviews may also be pushed into less critical directions. Some of the journals which have maintained a high standard of ethics include the *Lancet* and the *British Medical Journal* (Prasad; 2005).

In many cases, biases are built into the experiment right from the beginning of a drug trial. Multicentric drug trials involve a series of tests in different areas. Such tests generate multiple sets of data. Originally conceived as a safe method for checking out new drugs, the drug companies only publish the favorable result data sets while ignoring others. Researchers involved in trials funded by companies have no say in what is published in a journal. Often such researchers just add in their name to an already-written paper after being paid huge sums of money (Prasad; 2005(a)).

Drug trials were carried out illegally in India on patients with aplastic anaemia through the Institute of Immunohaematology, Mumbai (IIH), by TriStem Corporation (TSC) from Britain. TSC approached ICMR in 2003 for these tests. The medical consultancy firm GG Haemhealth Technologies Private Limited (GGHTPL) in Chandigarh was asked to conduct trials in India. It perhaps became a go-between in the collaboration. It was carried out in gross violation of ethical guidelines for biomedical research. The studies were not subjected to peer-review before the trials. The trials began in August 2004 with Dipika Mohanty, IIH director and Farha Jijina, haematology professor at King Edward Medical Hospital (KEMH). The patients showed some improvement initially. Abuljadayel was chief scientific officer at TSC. He did some work and then gave patients false hope without knowledge or consent of other team members. The TSC website had given 'before' and 'after' photos of patients which had been fudged by lighting techniques. Further, *New Scientist* on 9 October, 2004 carried articles showing a miracle cure and explaining the study when the study was only a month old. Abuljadayel had also wiped cytometric or experimental data from the laboratory, though it still has clinical data. One patient died on 19 December, 2004 (Jayan and Vijayalakshmi; 2005).

It is often no matter of surprise that doctors behave in this manner. In the current scenario, a payment of Rs. 16 to Rs. 20 lakhs ensures that a child may clear the CBSE (Medical) or Pre Medical Entrance Test (Punjab) in North India. In such cases either dummies write the exams or papers are leaked and filled the night before the exams. Results depend on the amounts paid (Ahluwalia; 2005).

In Bathinda, wrong blood given to a woman in transfusion cost a pregnant woman her life (Garg; 2004(a)). Three doctors have been accused by the Amritsar civil surgeon Dr. H.S. Gill of being in the service of quacks, conducting pre-natal diagnostic tests and medical termination of pregnancy at Mehrok Nursing Home (Tur; 2004(a)). Ajay, a 25-year old matriculate *halwai* from Hamirpur in Himachal Pradesh was abducted from opposite the Golden Temple in Amritsar and kept incarcerated, tortured, till he agreed to give up his kidney which was extracted forcibly from him at Kakkar Hospital, in addition to being robbed of Rs. 13,000 (Tur; 2004(b)).

Munni Devi Barthwal, aged 43, was a teacher at a Kendriya Vidyalaya in Landsdowne. She suffered a partial paralysis on 30th November, 2004 and lost sensation in both feet. She was brought to Delhi and admitted at the emergency in the Vidyasagar Institute of Mental Health and Neurosciences (VIMHANS). On the night of 4th December they gave her some steroids intravenously causing her hand to swell. The nursing staff and junior doctors, on being informed, claimed there was nothing to worry about. The hand became so swollen that it had to be amputated on 20th December, 2004. The doctors then claimed that they would not charge money for the mishap and would fit her with an artificial hand worth Rs. 2 lakh. By the time she was to be discharged on 7th February, 2005, the authorities asked them to pay the Rs. 4 lakh bill. When they did not pay it, they were prevented from leaving the hospital. The police registered a case of causing grievous hurt and a case of medical negligence has been registered. The doctors refuse to admit there was any negligence. She had spinal cord disease, and was also suffering from hypothyroidism and hypertension and possibly acute dorsal myelitis. This caused the necrotising disability of her right hand which had to be amputated. Without it she might have died (TNN; 2005). Perhaps, time will tell who was right in this case.

From 1 July, 2004, the US health regulators promulgated new rules, demanding doctors and hospitals to take specific steps to implement a protocol to prevent wrong person, wrong procedure and wrong site surgery. The Universal Protocol mandated by the Joint Commission on Accreditation of Healthcare Organisations may be implemented with little cost. It involves identifying the patient positively before the operation, the surgeon marking and signing the operation site while the patient is awake and the mark not being washable in the operating room. A 'time out' immediately before starting the procedure to double-check everything would be the culmination. This was done since from 1995 to the end of January 2004, there had been 300 cases of such surgical errors. This is an underestimation. Of this number 59% involved the wrong side of the body, 10% the wrong procedure and 12% the wrong patient. 19% had surgery on the wrong site. In a classic case, Indian film actress Sridevi's mother Rajeswari Ayyappan was operated by Dr. Ehud Arbit at Sloan-Kettering Cancer Center, New York on the right side of her brain on 26 May, 1995, when her cancer was on the left side. Dr. Arbit had believed that 59-year Gupta from Delhi was on the table. He was suspended on 8 June, 1995, receiving a censure and reprimand, one-year probation including practice monitoring and a $ 10,000 fine after signing a consent order agreeing not to contest the charges. He later became the Director of neuro-surgical oncology at Staten Island University Hospital. On 5 January, 2001, he was found by the New York State Health Department to have conducted gross professional misconduct by operating on the wrong part of a patient's spine. It has been suggested that India also follow this Universal Protocol to avoid such mistakes (Parthasarathy; 2004).

In a Supreme Court verdict on 5 August, 2004, it was stated that an error of judgement on the part of a doctor does not make him criminally liable. A doctor is only criminally liable if it was proved that a patient died due to their gross negligence or recklessness. This was after a case where a plastic surgeon faced a charge under Section 304-A for causing the death of a person during surgery for removing his nasal deformity in April 1994. It was decided by a Bench of Justices Y.K. Sabharwal and D.M. Dharmadhikari. The former Attorney General and senior advocate Ashok Desai defended the plastic surgeon. Further, the doctor is not bound to provide treatment-related information to a patient or his/her family. Such rights are from the Indian Medical Council (Professional Conduct, Etiquette and Ethics) Regulations, 2002. Doctors, of course, feel that it is a just judgement and that it is now up to the doctors to create their own standards of practice. Based on this, the patient may then choose doctors (Ghosh; 2004(f)). However, cases show that patients are far from being satisfied with such a decision (Sen; 2004).

The Medical Council of India also suggests that in the future non-medical members would also be included in various states to act as an ombudsman in cases of medical negligence. At present only Delhi has three such members. Human rights activists, however, are beginning to feel that such a decision may not help the poor since they could not afford the courts and would embolden doctors to continue such malpractices, especially in government hospitals (Venkatesan; 2004, TNN; 2004). A multitude of cases now show that it is near impossible to advance cases of medical malpractice, even though many such cases exist, as in Bhatinda and Amritsar. Some hospitals are also becoming zones where such cases abound, like the Breach Candy hospital in Mumbai. Books like *In the Pink of Wealth* by Sumit Ghoshal and *My God is Dead–Chinny's Story as Told by His Mother* by Neeru Khattar of Panchkula, Haryana detail many such cases. Some NGOs like Health Watch in Uttar Pradesh, Association for Consumers Action on Safety and Health in Mumbai and a website (www.antidoctor.crimsonzone.com) are involved in recording, contesting and preventing such medical malpractice cases (Mukerji et al; 2004, Garg; 2004(b), HT Correspondent; 2004).

On 1 August, 2003, the Punjab government decided to abolish non-practising allowance (NPA) for the doctors. The government has given the go-ahead to Punjab Civil Medical Services to "undertake private practice". Since the lack of NPA would mean a loss of Rs. 3,000 to Rs. 7,000 per month to a doctor, they now claim that their priority would be private practice. Hence, patients in government medical centres are likely to suffer since doctors are unlikely to stay longer in government hospitals. Further, patients will be encouraged to admit themselves to the private clinics by the doctors themselves. Since, diagnostic tests would also be referred to private clinics, the Punjab government is likely to lose revenue due to this also. As a result, the national level disease control, intervention and immunization programmes are likely to suffer. Thus, 'under deputation' doctors from Chandigarh and Punjab working in the Chandigarh Administration would have lesser take home pay than the doctors from Haryana. The 30-40% of the present shortage of teachers in non-clinical departments is likely to increase also (Sanyal; 2003(a)).

Even at the prestigious PGI in Chandigarh, such mistakes and blatant misuse keeps happening. In 2001, a patient named Saroj was to be operated in the neck but was wrongly operated upon by ENT doctors. The cause was the presence of another patient called Saroj who was to be operated on that day by them. A patient who was diagnosed with terminal ovarian cancer found herself to have only a slight infection later. It turned out that her medical records had gotten exchanged with someone else's. Errors like this occur in Gynaecology, Surgery and Medicine at the rate of 3-5 times in a fortnight. Further, many laboratories have now sprung up around PGI which now conduct a battery of tests for patients coming to PGI. Each of these laboratories, however, may conduct the same test for variable rates, in other words, a stressed out poor patient might have to do some market survey first if he/she wishes to get her tests done cheaply. The rates vary by as much as Rs. 150 (Yadav; 2004, Siwach; 2004). Such tests at private centres were banned by an order in November, especially when these tests were available at the General Hospital and all dispensaries (Siwach; 2004(a)). In another five years, while patient intake would exceed 15 lakhs per year and resources would never be able to keep up the load, Union health minister Dr. A. Ramadoss' suggestion that PGI doctors should also take up private practice in order to generate funds for the institute seems to be an unusual suggestion (Yadav; 2005). As a result, a 60:40 ratio split was to be made of the proceeds. At Rs. 250 per patient and 5 patients per day, it would amount to Rs. 3.37 crore per year (Yadav; 2005(a)).

It became apparent that even recipients of free services were being exploited by unscrupulous hospitals. Rajindra Hospital in Patiala is the only hospital giving service to thalassaemics. However, it forced people to get tests conducted by private clinics at high rates, were asked to pay Rs. 100 per unit of blood and were asked to purchase Cannula IV and BT sets from the market though these were given free by the Thalassaemic Society (Ashk; 2004).

The issue of NPA was taken up by the Punjab Civil Medical Services Association (PCMSA). They decided to contact the central Congress leadership for redressal on the issue. They claimed that it was a move powered by an underhand deal of top bureaucrats and a powerful lobby of corrupt government doctors, who had built huge nursing homes through their illegal practice which they have been doing unchecked under the politico-bureaucratic umbrella (Sanyal; 2003(a)). The Chandigarh Administration decided to wait and watch since it usually follows Punjab Government rules (TNN; 2003).

The fourth Punjab Pay Commission had recommended the payment of NPA (amounting to 25%) of basic pay (provided that the pay plus NPA not exceed Rs. 25,500) in the case of PCMS Class I doctors. It also recommended strong action against medical malpractice. The Himachal Pradesh government, which also usually follows Punjab government in its rules refused to make a cut in the NPA. In the meantime, the doctors have asked that instead of cutting NPA, giving the government only 23 crores of savings, a cut would be acceptable in all similar class officers of the Punjab government in their fringe benefits thus giving greater savings to the government. The PCMS cadre had about 4100 individuals, only 45 being promotional posts. As a result 99% doctors join and retire from the same posts (Sanyal; 2003(b)).

Many private medical care centres operate without regulation. Medical Councils can help in stopping government appointments and taking in full-time members. They need to update their registers and make their proceedings public. They also need to make continuous education compulsory and arrange for imposing fines on erring doctors.

The Government may set clear standards for health institutions, standardise fees and invest in the health sector. Confusion also exists regarding the fees paid and the sequence of examinations of various medical colleges in the country (Garg and Betab; 2004).

Many private medical colleges have insufficient faculty and patients. Most do not fulfill the Medical Council of India norms. Such medical training colleges turn this noble profession into shady and cynical commerce. For instance the size of the faculty as well as the area of the college is enhanced at inspections and later used for other courses. Fake staff and patients are shown. A nexus between politicians and promoters exists in some states as a result of which No Objection Certificates are issued. In 2001, the Darbhanga Dental College was de-affiliated from the Mithila University because it did not have an NOC from the Bihar government. As a result students suffer in getting their degrees for up to 12 years and some have even attempted mass suicide. Some do not even have their own hospitals (Vasudev, et al.; 2004).

What we, perhaps, really need are doctors with the ability to learn patiently and train themselves well. While the complexity of the tools lead to a load of information, the ultimate action has to be taken by the doctors. A 'clinical judgment' is now being transformed into the ability of the doctor to standardize his care with a view to consistency and predictability. Doctors may not be aware of one recent study, may ignore a second and follow a third (Ganapathy; 2003).

The patient then actively becomes a major impact on the system which demands and tries to get better care in a continuous process. In distinct contravention of the above practices, doctors in various government hospitals in West Bengal resigned out of the desperation caused due to faults in the healthcare system. It led to the government reviewing its own methods (Mukherjee; 2004).

DEATH, EUTHANASIA AND THE INDIAN CONTEXT

What happens when a patient prefers death to a long term suffering which drains the person of meaning as well as finances? Some recent cases have brought this interesting ethical issue to the fore.

Euthanasia is a case where one person takes the life of another on account of mercy. MTL or 'Medical Termination of Life' involves a person's wish to die. Venkatesh, the chess champion, died trying to die by non-violent means. The law would claim that taking one's life or another's is a crime. One may not even commit suicide. Death is defined now by the cessation of brain activity. It was earlier considered to be a cessation in the working of the heart ('cardio-respiratory arrest'). Some, like Raghavan (2004: 12), would claim that it should be granted to those where disease and debilitation as well as old age cause the person to live a life without quality. It then becomes a moot point whether those without immediate reasons to live, suffering from immense debts and long-term criminals in jails as well as the poor would also be allowed to die under the same conditions?

The case of Terri Schiavo in the US who was living for years in a state of irreversible brain damage is also a case in point. She was finally removed from life support and allowed to die. However, Gupta (2005: 8) would object to such a procedure. Since, 1997, an organization called CanSupport has cared for more than a thousand people with terminal cancer in Delhi and the surrounding region, trying to give meaning and support to a dying person. In such a context Gupta claims that a revival of the human relationship is crucial rather than a more technologically oriented decision that considers a mere 'switching off' decision that may be taken in the public sphere through orders of state.

This issue came up again in a new case where Abdul Rauf from Mulukgram Dakhin Para, Birbhum district, in West Bengal, aged 70 years, asked the Chief Minister's permission to kill two of their daughters Fatima (40) and Regina (36) who were 95% disabled with polio, since they found no means of taking care of them or feeding them. He used to feed them while he had a job as a bus driver, now, having lost his job, he is forced to beg. While considering the petition as illegal, it is now seen that the authorities are in a quandary for doing nothing could condemn the family (Datta; 2005).

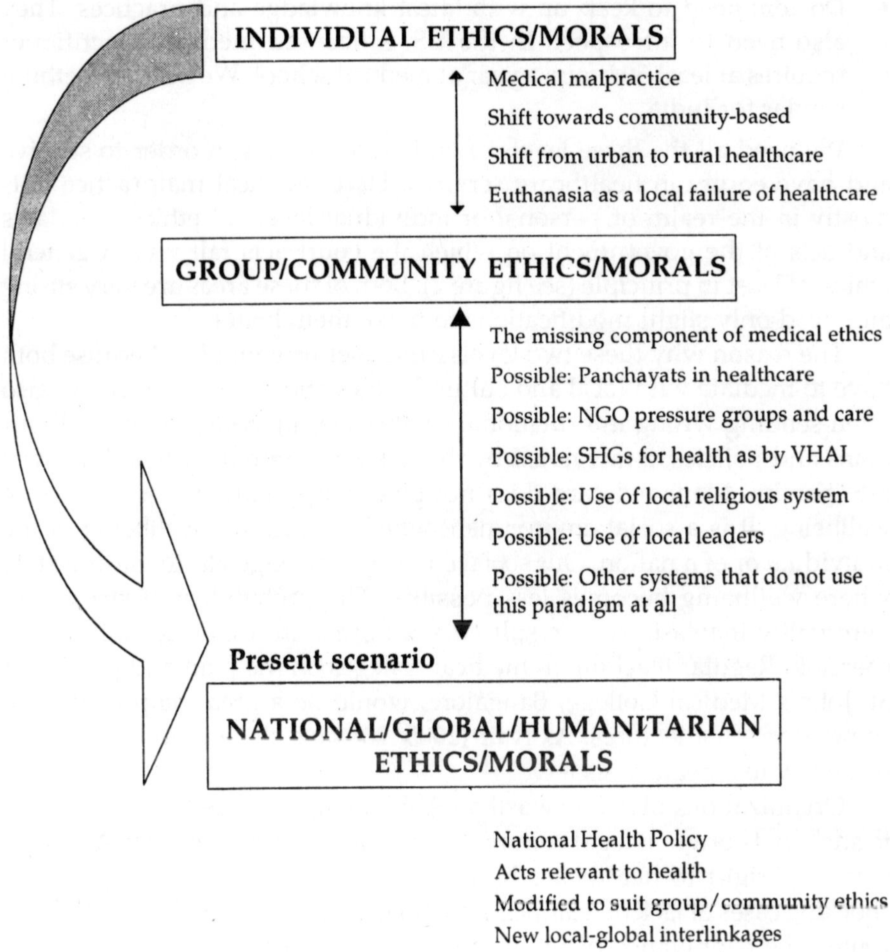

Fig. 2: The Structure of The Ethical System of Health In India

CONCLUSIONS

Some of the possible solutions to the problem of medical malpractice and accountability are given as follows:

- An active Union Health Ministry is required. A new health policy that looks into these aspects of the regulation of private hospitals is a necessity. Even the fee structure needs to be made more uniform.
- Transparency is a must and hospitals must take urgent notice of patient complaints.
- Accountability of those doctors who give others a bad name needs to be tackled on an urgent basis. A broad-based medical audit committee in each state which looks into cases of malpractice is required.

- Doctors need to keep up with latest knowledge and practices. They also need to introspect. In the US, a licensed medical practitioner requires at least 50 hours a year at medical school. We need something similar for India.

We need all the three levels of ethics and morals in order to survive and have equity in healthcare services. Here, medical malpractice falls mostly in the realm of personal or individual levels of ethics. The laws and acts of the government on which the court acts fall within general ethics, at least in principle (see figure 2). Both of these areas are very strong and need only slight modifications to make them better.

The reason why these two levels can never be enough is because both have to mediate with local and cultural ethics and morals, which are also often sending wrong information. It is the missing component of all our plans and policies, a fact noted by the famous community health activist K.S. Sanjivi. Managed care does not give happy patients or a sense of wellbeing. It is a social environment which defines the wellbeing of the individual or of a nation. Our social environment edges us towards a state where wellbeing becomes less possible. The probability of stress and immorality increase. As a result ethical norms are followed only under coercion. Regular teaching in medical colleges on the plan and pattern of St. John's Medical College, Bangalore, would be a great help instead of some occasional lectures. As Nair (2005: 23) says, "community medicine is the key to a healthy society."

Organizations like Jan Swasthya Abhiyan try to force the government to stick to its original legal commitment to delivering Health for All. They want the right to healthcare be made a legal right. They have found shocking cases of lack of healthcare and neglect and recorded them (Shukla; 2005). The connivance of politicians was also an issue in Punjab when whistle-blower Dr. Ashwani Ahuja asked the CBI to probe the health department's working. He claimed that the Punjab Health Minister R.C. Dogra's son Micky Dogra had tried to force him to issue a no dues certificate to the chief pharmacist even after the latter owed the department upward of Rs. 17 lakh. He was then transferred after which he approached the Punjab and Haryana High Court after which his transfer was stayed (Garg; 2005). Many medical colleges are also owned by politicians and run by them (Vasudev et al.; 2005).

Our cultures used coercion also. They used them in the guise of community feeling or of the sense of humanity at large (two levels of ethics used to influence and align a third). Cultures use coercion in the guise of community feeling as sanctions. Instead of using general ethical sanctions (the police, the courts, often seen as hegemonic and absolutist), we must use the second level of ethics also. Whether this is used in the guise of Habermas' public sphere, or the local panchayat, we must bring a range of local and community organizations that are empowered to work at these levels. There is a need for NGOs and others to act as regular pressure groups on a regular scale and for them to participate in healthcare more than they have done so far. Self-Help Groups or SHGs would also become a necessity, especially in the field of health. This has already been begun by the Voluntary Health Association of India. The use of local religious, political systems as well as local leaders would also be required. Finally, there is a need to think out of this box and to create other systems that use other methods for delivering healthcare and caring for those who are ill. For those vested interest bodies at the level of the general ethical national model, I believe this emancipatory mode of action strikes at the very root of their legitimacy and power. In other words, one must expect resistance from those whose interest it is to maintain this power and hegemony.

REFERENCES

Ahluwalia, Khushwant (2005), Want Medical Seat? Just Tell the Mafia... in *Times of Chandigarh*, Friday, 11 March, p. 10.

Ashk, Gur Kirpal Singh (2004), Hospital Bleeds Thalassaemics' Parents...Forces Them to Spend on Free Facilities in *Times of Chandigarh*, Thursday, 25 November, p. 9.

Ashk, Gur Kirpal Singh (2005), Who Says Quackery is Dead? in *Times of Chandigarh*, Tuesday, 25 January, p. 10.

Beyerstein, Dale (1993), The Functions and Limitations of Professional Codes of Ethics In Earl R. Winkler and Jerrold R. Coombs (eds.) *Applied Ethics: A Reader*. Oxford (UK) and Cambridge (USA): Blackwell, pp. 416-425.

Bharadwaj, Ajay (1999), More Than 30,000 Quacks in Punjab in *Times of India*, Tuesday, 17 August, p. 1.

Chattopadhyay, Aparajita and T.K. Roy (2005), Does Retirement Affect Healthy Ageing? A Study of Two Groups of Pensioners in Mumbai, India in *Asia-Pacific Population Journal*, vol. 20, No. 1, April, pp. 89-115.

Coghlan, Andy (1996), A Plateful of Medicine in *New Scientist*, 2 November, pp. 12-13.

Das, Arun Kumar and T.N.N. (2004), PM's Health Bill: Rs 23 lakh/mth in *Times of India*, Sunday, 18 July, p. 1.

Datta, Saikat (2005), The Death Wish in *Outlook*, 11 July, p. 62.

David, L.H. (2004), Medical Miasma: A Blueprint for Healthcare Reforms in *Times of India*, Wednesday, June 30, p. 20.

Dilip, T.R. and Ravi Duggal (2004), Unmet Need for Public Health-Care Services in Mumbai, India in *Asia-Pacific Population Journal*, Vol. 19, No. 2, pp. 27-40.

Diwan, Vinod K. and Ayesha De Costa (2004), *Challenges and Opportunities: 25 Years of Danida Support to the Health Sector in Madhya Pradesh, India*. Bhopal: Madhya Pradesh Basic Health Services.

Duggal, Ravi and Amar Jessani (1992), Medical Ethics: Awaiting a Patient's Movement in Alok Mukhopadhyay (ed.) *State of India's Health*. New Delhi: Voluntary Health Association of India, pp. 365-375.

Ganapathy, K. (2003), Patient Power in *The Hindu*, Sunday, December 14, Magazine, p. 4.

Ganguly, Arnab (2004), 1 Lakh and Still Quacking in *Times of India*, Thursday, 10 June, p. 3.

Garg, Balwant (2004a), Woman's Death Due to Wrong Blood Sparks Stir in *Times of India*, Sunday, 18 July, p. 5.

Garg, Balwant (2004b), Youth's Death May Create Medical Crisis in *Times of India*, Monday, 9 August, p. 6.

Garg, Balwant (2004c), Doc in the Dock for Graft in *Times of India*, Monday, 6 September, p. 5.

Garg, Balwant (2005), Whistle-Blower Wants CBI to Probe Health Department's Working in *Times of Chandigarh*, 8 February, Tuesday, p. 10.

Garg, Balwant and Parshotam Betab (2004), Official Indecision May Hit 10,000 Students' Career in *Times of India*, Sunday, 18 July, p. 6.

Ghosh, Abhik (2001), The Rise and Fall of the National Health Policy in *Indian Anthropologist*, Vol. 31, No. 2, pp. 27-48.

Ghosh, Abantika (2004a), Vaghela's 'PA' Runs Amok in Hospital in *Times of India*, Monday, 7 June, p. 3.

Ghosh, Abantika (2004b), Watch Your Wallet, Dr. Greed Is On The Prowl in *Times of India*, Monday, 7 June, p. 4.

Ghosh, Abantika (2004c), Medi-Shame: Quacks Duck Authorities in *Times of India*, Wednesday, 9 June, p. 3.

Ghosh, Abantika (2004d), No Checks: Quacking Away to Glory's Name in *Times of India*, Thursday, 10 June, p. 3.

Ghosh, Abantika (2004e), City's Medical Network Needs Healing Touch in *Times of India*, Sunday, 13 June, p. 3.

Ghosh, Abantika (2004f), Whose Life Is It, Anyway? In *Times of India*, Sunday, 12 September, p. 7.

Ghosh, Saswata (2005), Does Economic Inequality Matter in Cases of Infectious Childhood Diseases? An Analysis for India in *Asia-Pacific Population Journal*, Vol. 20, No. 1, April, pp. 37-62.

Gupta, Harmala (2005), Gentle Into the Night: Terri Schiavo and the Issue of Dying With Dignity in *Times of India*, Friday, 1 April, p. 8.

Heller, Agnes (1990), *General Ethics*. Oxford: Basil Blackwell.

Hoffmaster, Barry (1993), Can Ethnography save the Life of Medical Ethics? In Earl R. Winkler and Jerrold R. Coombs (eds.) *Applied Ethics: A Reader*. Oxford (UK) and Cambridge (USA): Blackwell, pp. 366-389.

HT Correspondent (2004), Doctors Booked for Negligence in *Hindustan Times*, Sunday, 2 May, p. 10.

Iyer, Malathy (2004), As Easy As Setting Up a Grocery Store in *Times of India*, Tuesday, 8 June, p. 3.

Jain, Indu (2004), Bliss to Boom: Market India's Wellness Wisdom in *Times of India*, Tuesday, June 29, p. 16.

Jain, Kalpana and T.N.N. (2004), Shock Treatment: MCI Debars 65 Docs in *Times of India*, Saturday, 6 November, p. 7.

Jayan, T.V. and E. Vijayalakshmi (2005), What Ethics? In *Down to Earth*, 28 February, p. 15.

Keyserlinck, Edward W. (1993), Ethics Codes and Guidelines for Health Care and Research: Can Respect for Autonomy Be A Multi-cultural Principle? In Earl R. Winkler and Jerrold R. Coombs (eds.) *Applied Ethics: A Reader*. Oxford (UK) and Cambridge (USA): Blackwell, pp. 390-415.

Khanna, Aman (2004), Diabolical Diagnosis in *Tehelka*, Saturday, 28 August, pp. 16-21.

Koska, Marc (2005), When the Syringe Threatens to Kill in *Times of India*, Thursday, 21 July, p. 10.

Lawz Bureau (2004), Consumer Redressal in the Health Sector in *Lawz*, Vol. 4, No. 8, Issue 36, August, pp. 14-17.

Majumdar, Bappa. 2004. Quack Quack Goes Bengal in *The Telegraph*, Monday, 7 June, p. 1.

Menon, Subhadra (2000), The Final Diagnosis in *India Today*, 25 September, pp. 48-50.

Mukherjee, Shankar (2004), Doctor Quit Jolt to Health Reform in *The Telegraph*, 12 December, Sunday, p. 1.

Mukerji, Debasish, et al. (2004), Let Off The Hook in *The Week*, 22 August, pp. 32-39.

Nair, V.K.G. (2005), Gender and Community Medicine in *Yojana*, July, pp. 22-23.

Narrain, Siddharth (2004), In a Critical Condition in *Frontline*, 18 June, pp. 19-21.

Nayak, A.N. and B.V. Babu (2004), Recording and Reporting Process of Health Information by the Health System: A Study from Khurda District of Orissa, India in *Journal of Human Ecology*, vol. 15, No. 4, pp. 295-297.

Nayar, Mandira (2003), Medical Bodies' Silence Draws Flak in *The Hindu*, Sunday, 28 September, p. 3.

Pant, C.S. (2004), Hospital on Wheels in *Times of India*, Thursday, 18 November, p. 10.

Parthasarathy, K.S. (2004), Prevention of Medical Errors During Surgery in *The Hindu*, Thursday, 26 August, p. 14.

Parthasarathy, K.S. (2005), Health Risks to Patients and Radiation Workers in *The Hindu*, Thursday, 14 July, p. 16.

Phadke, Anant (1997), The (Il) Legality of Cross-Practice in *FRCH Newsletter*, Vol. XI, No. 1, Jan.-Feb. pp. 1-3, 8.

Prasad, R. (2005), Publish or Perish in *The Hindu*, Thursday, 6 January, p. 14.

Prasad, R. (2005a), Doctoring Trials is the Name of the Game in *The Hindu*, Thursday, 7 July, p. 16.

Raghavan, T.S. Sreenivasa (2004), Freedom To Die: Law Should Respect Right to End One's Own Life in *Times of India*, Wednesday, 29 December, p. 12.

Rajalakshmi, T.K. (2005), A Bill and Its Import in *Frontline*, 11 March, pp. 128-130.

Raj, Papia and Aditya Raj (2004), Caste Variations in Reproductive Health Status of Women: A Study of an 'Epistemic Community' in *Sociological Bulletin*, Vol. 53, No. 3, September-December, pp. 326-346.

Rana, Yudhvir (2003), How 'Money-Smart' Absent Doctors Make System Sick...in *Times of India*, Monday, 10 November, p. 6.

Seethalakshmi S., (2004), Undaunted, They Rule the Roost Here in *Times of India*, Thursday, 10 June, p. 3.

Sanyal, Sourav (2003a), Private Practice First, Patients Last? in *Times of India*, Thursday, 31 July, p. 1. Also PCMSA: Roll Back NPA or Else...'We Will Go To Congress High Command, Launch Agitation', p. 3.

Sanyal, Sourav (2003b), We're Ready If There is Uniform Policy: Doctors in *Times of India*, Friday, 1 August, p. 5. Also And Doctors Make Private Calculations..., p. 5.

Sen Gupta, Amit (1995), Retreat of the Indian State in Health Care in *People's Democracy*, 18 June, pp. 10-11.

Sen, Rachna Subir (2004), SC Decision Opens Old Wounds in *Times of India*, Saturday, 7 August, p. 3.

Sharma, Seema (2005), No Medicine for Swelling Tribe of Quacks in *Times of Chandigarh*, 6 May, Friday, p. 7.

Shukla, Abhay (2005), Medical Nemesis in *Times of India*, 25 January, Tuesday, p. 8.

Singh, Jasvir (2005), Skewed Priorities: Budget Exercise Overlooks Needs of the Majority in *Times of India*, Tuesday, 22 February, p. 8.

Siwach, Sukhbir (2004), Test Laboratories Mushroom Near PGI in *Times of Chandigarh*, Thursday, 25 November, p. 3.

Siwach, Sukhbir (2004a), General Hospital Bills to Be Free From Private Ills in *Times of Chandigarh*, Saturday, 27 November, p. 1.

Subramaniam, Arun (1995), Enforcing Accountability in *India Today*, Dec. 15, pp. 143-155.

Thapa, Vijay Jung and Menon (2000), Growing Distrust in *India Today*, 25 September, pp. 38-50.

Times of India (2004), Minister: 69% Injections in Govt. Hospitals Unsafe in *Times of India*, 18 December, Saturday, p. 9.

Times News Network (2004), For Every Doc in City There's A Killer Quack in *Times of India*, Tuesday, 8 June, p. 3.

T.N.N. (2003), UT Plays Wait & Watch Game in *Times of India*, Thursday, 31 July, p. 3.

T.N.N. (2003a), Health Dept Told To Pay Up Woman Who Conceived...despite Tubectomy Done At Primary Health Centre in *Times of India*, Thursday, 9 October, p. 3.

T.N.N. (2004), SC Lets Doctors Off The Hook in *Times of India*, Friday, 6 August, p. 1.

T.N.N. (2005), Woman Loses Hand As VIMHANS Goofs in *Times of India*, Wednesday, 9 February, p. 2.

Trehan, Naresh (2004), The Health of Rural India in *The Hindustan Times*, Sunday, 5 September, p. 16.

Tripathi, C.D. (2005), Healing With Care in *Times of India*, 3 February, Thursday, p. 10.

Tur, Jatinder Kaur (2004a), Man Robbed of Kidney Looks for Justice in *Times of India*, Sunday, 18 July, p. 6.

Tur, Jatinder Kaur (2004b), Three Doctors in Service of Quacks in *Times of India*, Tuesday, 20 July, p. 1.

Vasudev, Shefalee, Amarnath K. Menon, M.G. Radhakrishnan, Stephen David, Sanjay Kumar Jha and Sheela Raval (2004), Oath of Hypocrites in *India Today*, 23 February, pp. 64-70.

Vasudev, Shefalee (2005), Prickly Discovery in *India Today*, 7 February, p. 61.

Venkatesan, J. (2004), Patients Aggrieved Over Supreme Court Judgement in *The Hindu*, Sunday, 8 August, p. 10.

Wadhwa, Soma (2003), Hypocratic Practice in *Outlook*, 3 February, pp. 50-58.

Winkler, Earl R. (1993), From Kantianism to Contextualism: The Rise and Fall of the Paradigm Theory in Bioethics In Earl R. Winkler and Jerrold R. Coombs (eds.) *Applied Ethics: A Reader*. Oxford (UK) and Cambridge (USA): Blackwell, pp. 343-365.

Yadav, Priya (2004), Errors Do Not Make A Comedy At PGI in *Times of Chandigarh*, Thursday, November 25, p. 1.

Yadav, Priya (2005), Allow Private Practice By PGI Doctors in *Times of Chandigarh*, Friday, 25 February, p. 3.

Yadav, Priya (2005a), A Win-win Situation for PGI Doctors and Patients in *Times of Chandigarh*, Saturday, 26 February, p. 3.

20

SOCIO-PERSONAL AND PSYCHOLOGICAL PROBLEMS OF INMATES OF SENIOR CITIZEN HOMES OF LUDHIANA (PUNJAB)—AN ANALYSIS

Archana Handa, A.K. Gupta & Balbir Kumar

INTRODUCTION

The number of 'Senior Citizens' and their ratio to the total population has been increasing rapidly in both the developed as well as developing countries. Advances in medical science, better nourishment and improved standards of public health have contributed to increased longevity. The developing countries have so far failed to take sufficient notice of this problem. Plans to support the elderly are generally inadequate. Thousands of them continue to be a neglected lot.

According to the United Nation's Projections by the year 2050, every third person on the earth will be aged 60 years and above. By the year 2020, India will be among the top ten countries globally with the largest population of the aged. The population of the aged above sixty is increasing rapidly in our country from 56 million in 1991 to 70 million in 1998 and expected to be 177 million by 2025.

As a part of the Welfare Policy, Indian Government is trying to promote Old Age Homes and Day Care Centres for the destitute elderly. In 1998, India had 728 Old Age Homes catering to the needs of the poor, destitutes, widows and for the sick and handicapped elderly. One in the seven old age homes is meant for the elderly who can afford to pay for their boarding and lodging. According to Helpage India, one-third of them are receiving financial and material support, while two–third of them are managed by Non-Governmental Christian Organisations for meeting infrastructural expenses only. The highest number of old age homes are situated in Kerala (124), followed by Tamil Nadu (121), Andhra Pradesh (78) and Karnataka (66). More than half of the old age homes (51.43 per cent) are located in South Indian States (Helpage India).

The 'Senior Citizens' have certain needs which may be grouped under four heads: (i) financial security (ii) medical care (iii) physical support; and (iv) emotional support. Each one of these needs is so vital, that non-availability of any one of them will make their life miserable (Nayar 1987).

According to National Sample Survey Organisation, reported by Narula (1998), 36.7 per cent of 70 million elderly people wanted to shift to old age homes. Another study (Wig 1999) quoted at a seminar organised by the Institute of Human Behaviour and Allied Sciences in New Delhi, that 40 per cent of the elderly in the capital have no care-takers.

The problems of the old age are rapidly increasing in magnitude. Low income, inadequate accommodation, loneliness, ill health and non participation in community life are the main problems faced by the elderly population of the country. They often feel themselves unwanted and dejected as their retirement and subsequent joblessness epitomizes absolute rejection and removal of the individual from the main stream of the society. This significantly effects their personal well-being and family relations. This also results in serious socio-psychological problems for the aged, where rapid social changes have wiped off many traditional sources of strength without evolving new ones to fill up this gap. In most countries of the world the older persons do not enjoy a decent status in society (Ramamurthy 2003). The situation is even worse in the developing countries like India.

The Senior Citizens are thus in need of urgent attention. It is our duty to see that they do not spend the twilight years of their life in isolation, penury and misery. The 'Old Age Homes' can provide the elderly with a sense of security and self respect. Such 'homes' are need of the hour. Older people are, therefore, in need of viable support for improving their overall quality of life. The present study was therefore conducted in Ludhiana with specific objectives as follows:

(i) To know reasons which forced the aged to shift to 'Senior Citizen Homes'.

(ii) To study the socio-personal and psychological problems of inmates of 'Senior Citizen Homes'.

(iii) To list the facilities available and suggest improvements in the functioning of the 'Senior Citizen Homes'

MATERIALS AND METHODS

The study was conducted in Ludhiana district of Punjab State during 2003-2004. A list of all the Senior Citizen Homes (SCHs) in the district was prepared. In all, there were five such 'homes' in the city dwelling 90 inmates. All of them were taken as the 'respondents' for the present study. The respondents were personally interviewed to collect the information on a pre-tested interview schedule. Part I of the interview schedule dealt with various reasons which forced the aged to go to Senior Citizen Homes (SCHs). Part II contained questions on various socio-personal and psychological problems of the inmates of these SCHs. Part III of the interview schedule dealt with the facilities available in 'SCH' and the suggestions to make improvements in the functioning of the 'Senior Citizen Homes'. Data were collected from the respondents personally on the interview schedule consisting of both structured as well as open -ended questions. Data were analysed by using simple tabular analysis with the help of percentage, mean score etc.

RESULTS AND DISCUSSION

Reasons for staying at Senior Citizen Home

Table 1 reflects the fact that a majority of the respondents (52.22 per cent) were compelled to stay in 'SCHs' due to non-cooperation of their family members. While 37.78 per cent of them were staying there after the death of their spouse. On the other hand, 24.44 per cent of the respondents lived in SCH because they wanted to lead calm and quiet life while for 22.22 per cent respondents, nobody was there i.e. they did not have any male child in the family to look after them.

Table 1
Distribution of the Respondents According to the Reasons for Staying in Senior Citizens Homes, Ludhiana, 2003-04

(Multiple Response)

Reasons	*Male* (N = 56)	*Female* (N = 34)	*Total* (N = 90)
Non-cooperation of family members	29 (51.79)	18 (52.94)	47 (52.22)
Death of the spouse	21 (37.50)	13 (38.24)	34 (37.78)
Nobody to look after/no male child	11 (19.64)	9 (26.48)	20 (22.22)
Own choice	21 (37.50)	12 (35.29)	33 (36.67)
Wanted to lead quiet life	16 (28.57)	6 (17.65)	22 (24.44)
Non-availability of proper housing	19 (33.93)	11 (32.35)	30 (33.33)

Figures in parentheses indicate percentages.

Physical and Health Problems

Table 2 shows that majority of the respondents i.e. 64.44 per cent suffered from eye problem. Whereas 45.56 per cent of the inmates suffered from joint pains. The percentage of such females (i.e. 55.88 per cent) was more than that of males (i.e. 39.29 per cent). On the other hand 41.11 per cent of inmates had heart ailment. The incidence was more among males than females. Another 38.89 per cent of the respondents had blood pressure, gastroenteritis and diabetes, 17.78 per cent were suffering from Asthma (percentage of females was more i.e. 20.59 in relation to males i.e. 16.07 per cent).

Table 2
Distribution of Respondents According to their Physical and Health Problems, Ludhiana, 2003-04

(Multiple Response)

Problems	*Male (N = 56)*	*Female (N = 34)*	*Total (N = 90)*
Heart problem	28 (50.00)	9 (26.47)	37 (41.11)
Blood pressure	21 (37.50)	14 (41.18)	35 (38.89)
Eye-sight	37 (66.07)	21 (61.76)	58 (64.44)
Asthma	9 (16.07)	7 (20.59)	16 (17.78)
Diabetes	19 (33.93)	16 (47.06)	35 (38.89)
Gastroenteritis	23 (41.07)	12 (35.29)	35 (38.89)
Joint pains	22 (39.29)	19 (55.88)	41 (45.56)
Common infection (chronic cold, cough)	18 (32.14)	8 (23.53)	26 (28.89)

Figures in parentheses indicate percentages.

Personal Care

A majority of the respondents (i.e. 70 per cent) received good personal care and attention at the SCHs. Whereas about 21.11 per cent of the inmates contradicted the above perception and rued that they received less than desired level of personal care and attention Table 3. There were, however, 8.88 per cent of the inmates who felt unconcerned.

Table 3
Distribution of the Respondents According to Personal Care Received by them at Senior Citizen Homes, Ludhiana, 2003-04

Personal Care	*Male (N = 56)*	*Female (N = 34)*	*Total (N = 90)*
Very Much	39 (69.64)	24 (70.59)	63 (70.00)
Less	12 (21.42)	7 (20.59)	19 (21.11)
Unconcerned	5 (8.92)	3 (8.82)	8 (8.88)

Figures in parentheses indicate percentages.

Psychological Problems

Most of the respondents (55.56 per cent) felt that they were loose tempered and had become easily irritable. About fifty per cent of the respondents felt that they remained depressed. Whereas another psychological problem faced by the inmates was of loneliness (36.67 per cent). It was however heartening to note that 31.11 per cent of the inmates perceived themselves psychologically fit and did not face any such problem.

Social Problems

Table 5 reflects the social problems of the respondents. A majority i.e. 61.11 per cent responded that they found it difficult to maintain social relations with other people. While 57.78 per cent inmates said that there was a downward trend in their social status. More than one–half (53.33

per cent) inmates confessed that there was an increase in frustration level, the women being more affected than men.

Table 4
Distribution of Respondents According to their Psychological Problems, Ludhiana, 2003-2004

(Multiple Response)

Psychological Problems	*Male (N = 56)*	*Female (N = 34)*	*Total (N = 90)*
Loneliness	19 (33.93)	14 (41.18)	33 (36.67)
Irritation	31 (55.36)	19 (55.88)	50 (55.56)
Tension	24 (42.86)	12 (35.29)	36 (40.00)
Frustration	13 (23.21)	7 (20.50)	20 (22.22)
Depression	28 (50.00)	16 (47.06)	44 (48.89)
No Problem	17 (30.36)	11 (32.35)	29 (31.11)

Figures in parentheses indicate percentages.

Table 5
Distribution of Respondents According to their Social Problems, Ludhiana, 2003-04

(Multiple Response)

Social Problems	*Male (N=56)*	*Female (N=34)*	*Total (N=90)*
Downward trend in social status	34 (60.71)	18 (52.94)	52 (57.78)
Decreasing economic independence	28 (50.00)	16 (47.07)	44 (48.89)
Difficulty in maintaining social relations	31 (55.36)	24 (70.59)	55 (61.11)
Increase in frustration level	26 (46.43)	22 (64.70)	48 (53.33)

Figures in parentheses indicate percentages.

Table 6
Respondent's Opinions Regarding Medical Care at Senior Citizen Homes, Ludhiana, 2003-04

Availability of medical care	*Male (N=56)*	*Female (N=34)*	*Total (N=90)*
Very much (2)	6 (10.71)	4 (11.76)	10 (11.11)
Less (1)	21 (37.50)	10 (29.41)	31 (34.44)
No (0)	29 (51.79)	20 (58.83)	49 (54.45)

Figures in parentheses indicate percentages

Facilities Available at Senior Citizen Homes

A majority of both male (51.79 per cent) as well as female respondents (58.83 per cent) had complained of non-availability of proper medical care at Senior Citizen Homes Table 6. Whereas 34.44 per cent of the inmates had alleged that although medical facilities did exist but these were inadequate. There were however, 11.11 per cent respondents who expressed satisfaction with the medical facilities available at Senior Citizen Homes. The mean satisfaction level was 0.57 whereas mean per cent satisfaction was 28.50.

Table 7 shows that majority of the respondents i.e. 63.33 per cent were satisfied with the food facilities available at their respective SCHs. While satisfaction level for clothing for both male and female was 70 per cent, it was surprising to note that 88.88 per cent of the respondents were dissatisfied with the medical and telephone facilities at the Senior Citizen Homes.

Table 7
Distribution of Respondents According to their Satisfaction or Dissatisfaction with the Facilities Available at Senior Citizen Homes, Ludhiana, 2003-04

(Multiple Response)

Facilities available	*Male (N=56)*	*Female (N=34)*	*Total (N=90)*
Food			
Satisfied	34 (60.71)	23 (67.65)	57 (63.33)
Not satisfied	22 (39.28)	11 (32.35)	33 (36.66)
Clothing			
Satisfied	39 (69.64)	24 (70.59)	63 (70.00)
Not satisfied	17 (30.35)	10 (29.41)	27 (30.00)
Medical facilities			
Satisfied	6 (10.71)	4 (11.76)	10 (11.11)
Not satisfied	50 (89.28)	30 (88.23)	80 (88.88)
Transport facilities			
Satisfied	24 (42.86)	21 (61.76)	45 (50.00)
Not satisfied	32 (57.14)	13 (38.23)	45 (50.00)
Provision of literature/library			
Satisfied	19 (33.92)	22 (68.75)	41 (45.55)
Not satisfied	37 (66.07)	12 (35.29)	49 (54.44)
Religious facilities			
Satisfied	32 (57.14)	22 (64.70)	54 (60.00)
Not satisfied	24 (42.85)	12 (35.29)	36 (40.00)
Sanitation facilities/hygiene			
Satisfied	20 (35.71)	8 (23.52)	28 (31.11)
Not satisfied	36 (64.28)	26 (76.47)	62 (68.88)
Telephone facility (STD/ICD etc.)			
Satisfied	8 (14.28)	2 (5.88)	10 (11.11)
Not satisfied	48 (85.71)	32 (94.11)	80 (88.88)

Figures in parentheses indicate percentages

Suggestions

Table 8 reflects the response of those respondents who were not satisfied with the facilities available at the SCHs. They were asked to give suggestions for bringing about improvements in the functioning of SCHs. Majority suggested availability of proper bathroom facilities could lead to improvement. Whereas 67.57 per cent opined that tasty and variety food could increase their level of personal care and attention. Room cleanliness and provision of literature can improve the personal care and attention level of 59.46 per cent of inmates, whereas providence of clothing and proper washing facilities could satisfy 48.65 per cent of the inmates.

The aged are not a spent force, they are a treasure house of knowledge.
They are not to be sidelined, they are to be mainstreamed.
These flowers may be faded but they still smell sweet"

Table 8
Suggestions for Brining about Improvements in the Functioning of Senior Citizen Homes, Ludhiana, 2003-2004

(Multiple Response)

Suggestions	*Male (N=27)*	*Female (N=10)*	*Total (N=37)*
Proper bathroom facilities	18 (66.67)	8 (80.00)	26 (70.27)
Proper Washing facilities	11 (40.74)	7 (70.00)	18 (48.65)
Room cleanliness/disinfectants	14 (51.85)	8 (80.00)	22 (59.46)
Provision of literature/newspapers	13 (48.15)	9 (90.00)	22 (59.46)
Medical Care	16 (59.26)	7 (70.00)	23 (62.16)
More varietal and tastier food	19 (70.37)	6 (60.00)	25 (67.57)
Proper personal care	12 (44.44)	6 (60.00)	18 (48.65)
Phone facility	16 (28.57)	7 (20.59)	23 (25.56)
Easily digestible food	23 (41.07)	12 (35.29)	35 (38.89)

Figures in parentheses indicate percentages.

SUMMARY

The present study was undertaken to investigate the socio-personal and psychological problems of the inmates of Senior Citizen Homes of Ludhiana city of Punjab. A systematic procedure was designed for conducting the investigation. A list of all the Senior Citizen Homes (SCHs) in this district was prepared from where all the ninety inmates were taken as respondents for the present investigation. The data were collected through interview method. The reasons which forced the aged to go to Senior Citizen Homes and their problems were analysed. Then, the suggestions for reducing such problems and making improvements were also solicited from the respondents. The statistical tests employed for analysing the data included simple percentages, rank order and mean score. Majority of the respondents were in the age group of 60-70 yrs. A majority belonged to the Hindu religion having urban residence. Most of the respondents had stayed for more than two years in these SCHs. Some of the them were staying there for the last 20 years. Mainly they belonged to service class. Most of the respondents were literate but lowly educated i.e. upto primary or middle level. A substantial majority was of married respondents, however 5.56 per cent were either widow or divorced. Most of the respondents had monthly income of upto Rs. 5000. The inmates were brought to SCH by some non-family members/friends/relatives. A paradoxical situation was witnessed in the sense that although a majority did come to these SCHs unwillingly but they did like their stay at the SCH thereafter. Viewing TV was their main recreational activity. Majority complained of inadequate or non-availability of medical care in these SCHs. They mainly suffered from eye and heart ailments, besides joint pains and blood pressure. The majority was frequently seeking medical advice on their own expenses and made fortnightly visits to medical doctors. A few, however, could not afford this and were looked after by their relatives or friends. The respondents expressed satisfaction with the meals served, the personal care and attention being bestowed on them at the SCHs. The respondents mainly suffered from psychological problems of isolation, loneliness and the consequent emotional vacuum in their personal lives. They stay in SCHs due to non-cooperation of their family members and suggested that better medical facilities could improve the functioning of SCHs. Moreover better room and food facilities could make the SCHs a better place where one could feel more homely than otherwise.

REFERENCES

Helpage India, C-14, Qutab Institutional Area, New Delhi-16.

Nayar P. (1987), Aging And Society. *J. Social Welfare* 34: 28-36.

Ramamurthy (2003), Decay In The Family Dynamics of Interaction, Relation and Communication as Determinants of Growing Vulnerability Amongst Elderly. *Indian J. Gerontology* 18:173-86.

Narula R. (1998), The No Where People. *The Tribune* Sept. 98: 1.

Wig N.N. (1999), Why Be Afraid of Ageing. *The Tribune* Sept 99: 13.

21

DIALOGUES ON MORALITY AND ETHICS IN PERCEPTIONS ON MASCULINITY AND SEXUALITY: CROSS-CULTURAL CONVERSATIONS IN ANTHROPOLOGY

Shalina Mehta & Nongmeikapam Inoaba Singh

The tradition of generating dialogues is intrinsic to anthropological research. Its efficacy in interpreting social dilemmas is rooted in the belief that people want to share and exchange views. Dialogues are critical to paradigmatic concerns. Construction of notion of morality and ethics has explored texts beyond religion and philosophy. It is constructed and reconstructed by individuals in their experiences. It transcends psychological and social boundaries created by processes of enculturation. It evolves beyond encrusted worldviews generated through primary and secondary socialization processes.

Ethics and *Morality* are invariably used as intertwined or interchangeable 'codes of conduct'. The concepts are generated in the domain of individual perceptions but are extended to be complied with in contexts and situations that are socially defined. It is also expected that in its extension individual choices are secondary to social expectations. It also insists that emotions be not allowed to overrule socially appropriate rules which are imposed as *morals* but are expected to be internalized as *Ethics.* It is this fine distinction that is often ignored in common discussions on *ethics* and *Morality.* Morality is a tool used by various sections of leadership and opinion makers in the society to control people's conduct. It has an over arching arm asking and expecting people to conform and if need be sacrifice felt physical and psychological desires and needs. In addition to the fact that every society prescribes codes that qualify as ethics and are accompanied by moral servitudes, these social sanctions are integral to people's dialogues. They question before conforming, or on occasions deciding to differ, even under the fear of being labeled as bohemian, thereby opening a space that is critical for building a social science edifice.

LOGIC OF GENERATING DIALOGUE

There is a growing shift in anthropological methodologies used for generating data and ascertaining its representative-ness. Notions of neutrality and objectivity in pursuance for more than hundred years in anthropological texts are also under reconsiderations. Anthropologists in the past have adapted various methods to invoke information that generally remains confined to the domain of research "requires disclosure of behaviour or attitudes which would normally be kept private and personal, which might result in offence or lead to social censure or disapproval, and/or which might cause the respondent discomfort to express" (Kaye Wellings, Branigan and Krisiti Mitchell, 2000:2560).

This paper attempts to evolve a methodological shift in which a researcher pursues a dialogue on issues relating to ethics and morality in understanding perceptions on masculinity and sexuality, regarded as 'sensitive issues'. The data for the paper is generated by the second author of the paper from two sub-sets of populations. The first sub-set comprised of Manipuri students studying in Chandigarh. The research investigator is an insider to this sub-set. He came from Manipur to Chandigarh to study along with number of his respondents in this sub-set. They have experienced social transitions from one cultural milieu to another, often collectively. Typical of small immigrant student populations, they interact at two distinct levels. First and foremost to them is the desire to share common bonding, common food habits, common cultural activities and resolution of any adjustment problems that any one of them may be confronting. Within this profile articulation of their social mores become a crucial concern to them. And it is here that exchange with their cultural peers on questions of morality and ethics becomes a significant component of their regular conversations.

Locating 'self' in a research situation is never easy for any first time researcher wanting to gain some experience and expertise in anthropological research methodologies. There are two very interesting articles that were of considerable influence in moderating the way, methodology in this paper finally defined itself. First was Karen Larson's (1987) unpublished paper* 'Ethno politics and Research Ethics for the Non-Native Researcher' and second was Stella Mascarenhas-keyes (1987) publication 'The Native Anthropologist: Constraints and strategies in Research'. Larson's understanding of the kind of role relationship in field work situations involving native and non-native researcher is summed as:

> *Intercultural discourse becomes that non-oppositional "other", which native and non-native researchers can pursue jointly in paradigmatic harmony, and in the context of a social relationship in which both are equally the knower and the known (Chance 1986:10). Our resulting theoretical and methodological discourse should make reference not only to observations of both cultures..............but also to the intellectually and emotionally based cultural foundations of the discourse itself.*

Taking a clue and wanting to experiment with a field situation in which the researcher has the responsibility of collecting and interpreting data from two different situations, one in which he is the insider and in many ways a native researcher, even when the cultural space he was exploring was located far away from his native home state. I really do not know whether 'Ethnography is an arrogant enterprise' as proclaimed by Agar (1980:41) but it certainly is an exciting and forever challenging 'enterprise'. Field work is decidedly 'the balanced reciprocity of relationships and information' as suggested by Mayer (1975: 28), though as Stella (1987:428)* rightly comments 'the demands for reciprocity *are* different with respect to different social categories'. I substituted Stella's 'were' for 'are' and extend meaning of 'social categories' to encompass 'sociological populations' that any anthropologist or sociologist decides to study.

One of the interesting highlights of studies involving native studies is admission of the fact that the information that we are seeking from the 'other', in many instances we are not willing to divulge it ourselves. Following admission from Stella's paper makes interesting reading, though it calls for detailed anthropological discussion and introspection:

> *Like the natives, I had little hesitation in divulging impersonal information but was wary of disclosing personal details. Furthermore, since it was obvious that through 'gallivanting around the village', as my behavior was referred to, I had undoubtedly gathered 'salacious information' and there were many attempts to prise it out of me. Hence, with most Catholics, reciprocity led to heightened vulnerability of Self, and I generally circumvented questions by resorting to evasive answers, lightening and subtle changes of conversation, partial answers, half truths and so forth-the very strategies I tried to steer 'my people' from. While everyday native social interaction, particularly for women, was articulated in the exchange of ' personalized' information, I could only engage partially and cautiously in this activity because had I acceded to their excessive demands, not only would I have epitomized the 'bad native' but also breached professional ethics. (428 cf. Srivastava, 2004).*

Stella's very honest confessions open vistas for defining boundaries within which a native researcher is expected to commit to conversations-the cultural spaces that he/she invade and subsequent cultural space that they recreate. If he is not willing to accept half truths for information then he has to be integral to the conversations that he is supposedly recording as data. Researcher has to be as much involved as the 'other' from his own community, in particular when he is discussing or generating information on intimate subjects like sexuality or adolescent behavioural practices. The researcher in this instance has decidedly gone beyond being a 'self-effacing creature without any reaction other than being a recording machine' (Nash and Wintrop 1972:527). Stella would like social anthropologists to 'incorporate the creative use of emotional reactions of self and other as methodological tools in field work' (429, ibid). I encouraged my co-author and field worker in this context to make comprehensive use of impromptu reactions, and emotional responses that emerged in conversations. I may not be in a position to narrate dialogues that I had with him on numerous occasions after he returned from the field but there were moments that I felt he was 'emotionally stressed' though it would be difficult for me to suggest whether he converted 'anxiety to method' as Stella reportedly did during her own fieldwork. What was of immense interest to me during my co-author's training was his virgin enthusiasm which was so different from years of my own controlled experimentation with my own field work training and learning.

The conflicts and emotional reactions that the researcher experienced, do surface in the dialogues and sometimes in the analysis. I must admit here as the first author of this paper, that this research work was, largely inspired, by my experiences of having researched in the field of HIV/AIDS for more than a decade now. The limitations experienced by research investigators in the course of data collection for various research programmes and 'communication needs assessment studies on HIV/AIDS', that I was involved with for various AIDS control societies, prompted me to experiment with a method in which researcher first becomes familiar with his inhibitions and articulation conformities. I also subscribe to the view that 'the exportation of a *research* model in which the rational, the logical, and the empirical is systematically separated from, and more highly valued than the emotional and the subjective has clearly been a form of 20th century mental colonialism' (Larson, 1987 italics mine) and in the 21st century given the kind of research questions that we are faced with, we must reexamine techniques of data collection and analysis.

With this premise after three months of preliminary data collection in Chandigarh, we moved on to research the 'other', the 'unknown' the 'exotic'. The primary researcher was trained and equipped with dialogues from his own community on issues of *ethics and Morality* with regard to *Perceptions on Masculinity and Sexuality.* He was now ready to test his exploratory skills in a cross-cultural milieu. I was hoping that by now he had mastered the art of keeping 'sensitive' data in the realm of resources defined as 'private' and 'confidential'. In the context of other culture, it was also important that he learnt to command his own attitudes and develop a research language that is rooted in 'non-condemnatory attitudes' (Lee and Renzetti, 1990; cf. Wellings et.al. 2000). It was at this stage that he accompanied his post-graduate class for a short term training field work to a small town in Himachal Pradesh[1]. I also happened to be the class field supervisor and accompanied post graduate students to the field. I must admit that I was little apprehensive. My first impressions were that he was not fluent in the language and may have problems discussing a very complex question in an alien setting. In the beginning, I tried to be present in the vicinity, if not involved in the conversations myself, but soon realized that he had established excellent rapport and was quite comfortable talking to peers from an undergraduate college in Himachal Pradesh. My presence was infact distracting free flow of conversations.

However, it must be authenticated that I was never present for any of the dialogues that researcher had with his friends or selected respondents from his own community in Chandigarh. I must also acknowledge that the data generated in this paper may not be adequate for suggesting any pervasive changes in methodology on studies on sexuality but it certainly charts an alternative route to exploring a very complex and intimate process of recording conversations and seeking meanings and methodologies for intervention in applied research.

CONCEPTUALIZING ETHICS AND MORALITY

Theoretical issues

We said in the beginning of this paper that as social scientist we need to distinguish between 'ethics' and 'Morality'. One is reminded of differing positions that leading intellectuals of the world have taken on the issue. Ernest Hemingway in his characteristic literary style says:

> *So far, about morals, I know only that what is moral is what you feel good after and what is immoral is what you feel bad after.*

But to Voltaire:

> *All sects are different, because they come from men; morality is everywhere the same, because it comes from God.*

It is often argued that values imparted as ethics are to give guidance to our lives. It provides a kind of code book that promotes 'optimal living' for the self and society. Morality is devised as an external control mechanism. It is brought in to the domain of social by religious and social leaders. It is then by social consent extended to the realm of legal as we notice in the case of various legal codes being practiced in various societies to prevent moral turpitude. Man assumes that he is making the right choices. But many would argue that man is not always in awareness as to what will benefit him. He is also not always right in making decisions as to with whom should he interact with, and there is visible need to tell him what is right and wrong, an extension of what Ernest Hemmingway says feeling good or bad about. Emotions and feelings are determined by social rules that one is taught to behave by, since early socialization. Values taught as ethics are repeatedly delivered as messages endorsed in dialectics of good or bad. If one fails to conform to these ethical practices, then one suffers guilt. In many spiritual texts guilt or remorse is an internalized correction mechanism by which individual resolves internal tensions to conform to the social expectations.

Ethics and Morality operate in the realm of social interactions. It is stated by both sociologists and psychologists that 'personal morality can, and must form the foundation to social morality, political and legal systems. Judging the morality of social norms, public policy and laws can only be done with reference to what is good for individual' (*www.optimal.org/peter/rational_ethics.htm*).

When we portray external resorting for conducting our day to day to interactions, another argument generally mooted is that our cognitive and reasoning skills in complex situations are rather restricted. If we have access to external control mechanisms that are learnt and facilitate control over impetuous responses, then there are greater possibilities of sustaining social order in societies. One may be prompted to endorse the statement that 'subconscious assimilation leads to automatic emotional responses that are in harmony with our explicit conscious values' (ibid).

Social science literature has documented four separate but interrelated sources that constitute popular systems of morality:

- Social rules or customs that are either agreed on by the majority or enforced by some kind of law.
- Some authority, usually claimed to be 'divinely inspired', that establishes an absolute dogma.
- Intuitive, emotional 'knowledge' of what is right and wrong- a personal moral compass.
- Rational or common sense rules and principles aimed at achieving a given objective. (ibid)

From the domain of individual to that of universal, the journey that construction of morality makes has a huge impact in the domain of empirical and intervention research. To transmit HIV virus to your partner in construction of universal empiricism should be immoral and in the domain of individual it should fall in the category of 'feeling bad after'. Similarly rape, physical violence, abuse of your partner should all fall in the domain of 'immoral'. Transference of values considered 'moral' or 'immoral' are parts of systems of knowledge dispensation. The process of internalization of the value system in the format of being ethical or not is something that is exclusive to the individual. This rather difficult pathway requires tremendous meandering. Self is not willing to internalize social and visualizes threat perception as being distant and remote. The moral doctor who in the context of this paper often happens to be either a doctor of medicine or behavioral research finds it extremely difficult to construct his messages, fearing that he is transgressing zones that were not taught to him as part of his training.

CONSTRUCTING NOTIONS OF SEXUALITY AND MASCULINITY

Empirical issues

There is near consensus among scholars from different disciplines exploring notions of masculinity that masculinity is a multi-cultural construction, (Morerell, 2001, Sorrell & Raffaelli, 2005) endowed with plural perceptions both within cultures and across cultures. In a minimalist sense it can be defined as 'a set of role behaviours that most men are encouraged to perform' (Sorrell & Raffaelli, 2005). In a cross-cultural context, Gilmore (1990) attributed it with the distinction of what Linton called 'an achieved status'. Gilmore also endorsed most commonly perceived conceptions of 'toughness', 'aggressiveness', 'stoicism' and 'sexuality' as general constructions in popular worldviews of masculinity. The last listed characteristic 'sexuality' is interrupted in many cultures as 'virility' or license that men have, to many sexual partners both before and after marriage. The cultures that we are discussing in this paper have had numerous folktales in which sexual exploits of men are often narrated with lot of aplomb. 'Semen anxiety' is regarded by many scholars across disciplines as an important theme in discussions on 'Indian Sexuality' (Srivastva, 2004; Alter 1992; Carstairs, 1958). Discourse on 'semen anxiety' in India, in a peculiar way entwined with legends rooted in Hindu Scriptures. Polarities symbolizing focus on Shiva, lingam and related conception of procreation at one end and veneration of Hanuman symbolizing valor, and conservation of energy following Brahmacharya that is celibacy at the other end; constitutes the paradox that defines cultural construction of masculine sexuality speaking in a hegemonic sense 'the Indian masculinity'. In a strange way this notion transcended boundaries of religion, language and ethnic identification and has only occasionally challenged by forces of westernization, modernization, popular culture and relatively recently by cyber revolutions and globalization.

This debate is often caught in a myriad of suppositions and oppositions. Kakkar the Indian Guru of Psycho-sexual social analysis reasons that the 'Hindu version' of the 'mother-whore dichotomy........is crucial for understanding the culture's public and official attitudes towards women and wives' (Kakar, 1990:17). Kakars' supposition is challenged by Srivastva's (2004) argument that 'it is not clear, ... that analytical recourse to *The laws of Manu'*.......... is adequate to an understanding of the sexual present' (ibid, 14). It is not our attention in this paper to debate or to establish any hegemonic notions of masculine sexuality. We are on an ethnographic journey. We are in agreement with Srivastva (2004) that 'we need to distinguish between normative rules of sexuality and those practices and beliefs that are contingent: a flux dictated by the overwhelming circumstances of social and cultural processes' (ibid: 15).

It is location of these social and cultural processes[2] that is critical to anthropological explorations in this qualitative methodological exercise.

The attempt in this paper is to record conversations made in the present, as it is called in the ethnographic present. But in any analytical pursuit, importance of tradition and history can not be denied. It is through the folklore that ideal notions of masculinity are constructed and even in the local context cultural hegemony established. It is against this ideal construction of what is to be defined as 'masculine' that most other men in that cultural group measure themselves against and are measured by others (Connell, 1987, Morell, 2001, Sorrell & Raffaelli, 2005).

CONVERSATIONS DECONSTRUCTED

Conversations on masculinity in empirical data generation have often been victim of what is described in scholarly and social circles as 'conspiracy of silence' (John and Nair, 1998). John and Nair other than making significant contributions to the understanding of sexuality are relatively critical to anthropological understanding and explorations of sexuality in empirical ethnographic texts. Their criticism hovers around the question 'that the caste/community/gender nexus framed by anthropology, so critical for any approach conceptualizing sexuality in rural and urban India, has largely turned into a lost opportunity?' One may not concur with the spirit of this argument given the liberal spirit in which the discipline has generated a huge body of empirical data. There is no denying that this valuable data is left often enough with half or little explanations-a praxis that any evolving discipline, struggling to master the art of theory and practice is not going to be comfortable with.

It is pertinent to emphasize that all disciplines evolve within the existing socio-political climate. Issues relating to sexuality as pointed out in the beginning of this section of the essay have been victims of silence, hypocrisy and moral policing by the law enforcing agencies[3]. It is only in the face of rising challenges posed by virtually unstoppable rising numbers of HIV infections that there are debates in the public domain. However, these debates are being pulled in opposite directions because of immediacy of health concerns and political compulsions of various political parties that thrive on public ignorance and take respite in judicial system. The paper is being revised at a time when debates on section 377 that regulates homosexuality is hanging balance in judicial wisdom, political correctness and demands by the stakeholders. Before we dwell on the arguments put forward by various contenders, we want to sum up what our respondents from Himachal and Manipur had to say on the issue of *Trans-sexuality, Homosexuality* and *Bisexuality*:

> *Gays and Lesbians are talk of the town. Person like Bobby darling is part of the celebrity circle. Characters like that are becoming too popular. But if somebody*

in my neighbourhood dressed like that I will be far too embarrassed (Santos-graduate student from Himachal Pradesh)*

An engineering student from Himachal says:

We sometimes find a person wearing clothes of the opposite sex .... I personally have no problems ....'but something happens in the mind though one accepts later as every one has the freedom'. But the same respondent had firm ideas on article 377-he said homosexuality is against nature, humanism and ethics.

A twenty two year old, studying in BA first year and coming from a remote rural area in Himachal reacted sharply to the question responding:

If any of my neighbour ever came close to me wearing a woman's clothes 'Joote Mareunga sale ko' (I will beat him with my shoes).

Rajinder another twenty year old coming from a far flung rural area gave a cultural explanation and said,

Culture decides how a person must dress up and behave.

The opinion that subset of our respondents belonging to the state of Manipur, currently studying in Chandigarh to which the second author and primary field investigator also belonged had this to say:

Santon a post graduate student at Panjab University, Chandigarh said:

Though homosexuality is legalized in Britain, I do not think it should be legalized in India. But, punitive action should not be taken against them.

Lalminthang-a Naga student from Manipur, studying in a college in Chandigarh was convinced that homosexuality was a eugenic disorder:

I do not accept that sexual identity is learnt in the childhood. It has been scientifically proved that Gays and Lesbians have genetic problems. .... We cannot legalize homosexuality. It is abnormal and should be eliminated from the society.

Tondon from Kakaching in Manipur gave a vivid description of transsexual practices:

In Manipur there are persons who are sexually male but their nature, behaviour and looks are almost like a woman. In many street plays they act as leading female actor and also participate in local beauty pageant. Some people in my native village would even organize dance parties for them. But others hate all this. I personally have nothing against it but Homosexuality should not be legalized as it is against nature.

With these qualitative imprints from the field, we can attempt to map how boys/men in the age group of 19-32 envision homosexuality. If quantitative evidence in such studies is to be regarded as any kind of marker*, then we may summarize that 65% of the respondents (n = 35) from Himachal and 47.5% (n = 35) from Manipur were in favour of banning the practice of Homosexuality, if it occurred in their state. Quantitative markers in a research area that requires discussing sensitive issues is not really a very effective tool. It was often found in the course of data generation that respondents were evasive in their replies, when they were being interviewed with the help of a pre-designed semi-structured schedule. They opened up with the field researcher over a cup of tea in a canteen, while going for a walk in the evening or sharing a meal in the hostel. Written responses from college students from Himachal were often sketchy but the students from Manipur with distinct advantage of having access to better quality education were more cogent and argumentative. What is striking to us in this data is that not even a single respondent stated either in discussions or in-depth interviews that legal sanctions against homosexuality should be removed.

Students of HIV/AIDS research programmes, and we happen to be among them are in a dilemma. The ambiguities in the response of the state and respondent's upfront rejection or refusal to comprehend alternative sexualities as integral to social systems is further confounding. On 1st December 2005, the World AIDS day–there were two conflicting messages delivered by the state. While addressing what has come to be described as Youth parliament, Prime Minister Dr. Manmohan Singh said:

> *You should fully comprehend the need to educate our young people about the modes of transmission of this deadly disease. Leading a healthy and safe sexual life is one of the commitments we must all make. This is particularly important given our traditional inhibitions about discussing such matters within our families and among our colleagues, quite apart from doing so in public.*
>
> *This quite obviously, has to change, if we are to succeed in this war against HIV/AIDS, if we are to succeed in creating awareness of the hazards of unsafe sexual practices. .... One reason why I am focusing on the need for us to take up challenge of AIDS in right earnest is the simple logic of demography. India is today at the threshold of major demographic transition with the age profile of our population favouring the youth. .... But what if we begin to lose our youth to this disease?*

This will have serious consequences for our society, our economy, and indeed our entire Indian polity. Like all epidemics, AIDS does not discriminate among its victims, but the youth are the highest risk segments. Consequently we must focus on this threat to our survival, threat to our future.

The crux of his address was a strong message to the youth and other opinion makers of India:

> *Youth leaders, members of the media and social activists can contribute a great deal to shaping public opinion, attitudes and behaviour through their work and their own life styles. .... We are committed to, we are determined to prevail and to overcome. I am certain that you will unleash the vast latent energy of your youth to overcome and to triumph over the constraints that have inhibited us so far in the past.* (AIDS-INDIA@yahoogroups.com)

If one is to interpret these messages as precursors to the direction that social policy is likely to take in the future, in particular in fighting 'silence over sexualities' and a more liberal attitude towards accepting 'alternative sexualities', then the Union Home Ministry's affidavit submitted to the Supreme Court of India is in marked contrast. In response to a petition submitted by the Naz foundation challenging the validity of section 377 of the Indian Penal Code, the affidavit of the Ministry states:

Public opinion and the current societal context in India do not favour the deletion of the said offence from the statue book. On a more positive note it also said that it was "examining" recommendations of the Law Commission of India which favoured delection of the clause from the IPC. However, the content of the affidavit submitted by Deputy secretary (Judicial) Y. Baweja, states "even if it is assumed that the rights of sexual minorities emanates from a perceived right to privacy cannot be extended to defeat public morality which must prevail over the exercise of any private right".

The affidavit further submits:

The question of homosexuality is not mere question of personal preferences but may involve behavioural sanctions of legislative authority of the state as it tends to affect the social environment .... In fact, homosexuality/sodomy is still an offence in large number of countries all over the world"(The Indian Express, December 1st 2005).

The affidavit submitted by the ministry invited angry response from the stakeholders. In an article dated December 4th 2005, Ashok Row Kavi, chairperson of Hamsafar Trust, a well reputed organization that fights for the rights of the *Gays* wrote:

Obviously, the left hand of the government does not know what the right hand is doing. .... If the most important health programme of the government accepts Homosexuals (reference is being made to NACO's intervention programmes) as a vulnerable group, how on earth does the very important Home Ministry, ... go about policing something as private as sexuality? What was interesting in Kavi's angry response was reiteration of the fact that section 377 of the IPC introduced by British was brought into common law from Ecclesiastical Law, more specifically the st.James Bible where Leviticus rants and raves against the same sex relations. Britain threw out its anti-Sodomy statues in 1968. But obviously, it is all right to defend a law that Christian evangelists keep on selectively quoting as the main flood gate against morality.

Kavi's critique acquires tremendous significance as discourse on morality, ethics and sexuality is invariably drawn from Hindu mythology and its source is traced to be historically rooted in Hindu scriptures. Political right or those parties that claim to be located somewhere in the middle between the left and the right, find it difficult to take categorical and relevant stance. The data that we cited in the earlier part of this section of the paper suggests that public mood is not perceptive to accepting legalizing of Homosexuality. It is this political compulsion that encourages translation of personal hypocritical stands into public representations.

As a student of social processes we are familiar with the content of contradictions and discontinuities in public discourse. We are also accustomed to reading the meaning that these contradictions invoke and familiar with the limitations of these representations. It brings to the fore conflict between political wisdom and scientific thinking and rationale that political survival is impinged upon maintaining an oscillating balance between them. Kavi seeking representation for a sexual minority and also the larger agenda of meeting the challenge of confronting HIV/AIDS voices his conflict:

> *It is trifle puzzling that it should come from as liberal a party as the Congress that has always stood for reformation and welcomed change through progressive movements. Maybe homosexuals do not form a constituency who can vote and insist on their rights being defended on consensual relations in private between two adults. This profoundly disturbing repetition of an old argument has to be brought to a logical end.*

The concern of HIV/AIDS researcher goes beyond the question of violation of human rights of a sexual minority or limitations of a political middle path. It explores limitations of restrictive mind-sets and world views. Social experience suggests that legislations and political movements take a long time to become popular public conversations. The epidemic is growing at a pace that, it may not wait for the social process to gain momentum. The two cultural locales from where data for this paper is generated are located at different end of AIDS axis. Manipur is a high prevalence state and Himachal is still a low prevalence state. But there is remarkable sharing of attitudes on the issue of Homosexuality though responses in other domains of sexuality, in particular openness in heterosexual relations are strikingly different.

'Eve Teasing' was another domain that we tried to examine through cross questioning. In the north and in this case in the rural areas of Himachal Pradesh, eve teasing is admitted as a criminal act in community perceptions. Some of the responses from the field study in Himachal are cited as affirmations of public articulation:

> *Light teasing not involving physical overtures may be fine but overt sexual pestering is a public nuisance (response by a 24 year old undergraduate student).*
>
> *Eve teasing is symbolic of defective mentality and psychological deformity (28year old postgraduate student)*

Focusing on right family values as instrumental in determining your attitude towards women and eve teasing, a 20 year undergraduate student had this to say: *Eve teasing is simply foolish. Man's behaviour should be gentle; he must show concern for his family and serve people rather than waste time on these foolish things. Himachali society teaches us to care for our family and society.*

At the other extreme was response of a 20 year rural youth, who had just moved from his village to the city saying *'Ladki Bahar Jaygi to Samaj kee Nazar me Giryaegi'* suggesting that if girls decide to move out of the house they are likely to be objects of public scrutiny and susceptible to eve teasing.

Public perceptions towards what is viewed as 'eve teasing' in the northern part of India are relatively viewed differently in Manipur. This was aptly stated by a young M.Phil student hailing from Manipur, currently studying in Chandigarh:

> *To biologist, eve teasing and passing remarks to the opposite sex are signs of sexual attraction and a move towards the opposite sex for intimacy. This mode of behaviour is more prominent among the males. If not for al men, at least for some it is symbolic of being masculine. And also girls in Manipur are happy, when they are being pursued by several boys. They are treated like queens as they are in demand for becoming prospective bides.*

Another respondent from Manipur aired similar views- *Eve teasing is part and parcel of male personality.*

A student from Nagaland belonging to Meitei community thought- *eve teasing is nothing, it is just a way of demonstrating that one is acting little naughty.*

Another student from Manipur summed up his perceptions- *Eve teasing is the culture. It depends on the society, even girls tease men.*

A first year student from Manipur perceived eve teasing as a romantic allure and said *eve teasing is not at all a nuisance, it is rather a way to reach a woman's heart and it should be taken as a blessing rather than being seen as a crush.* .

These arguments, perceptions, responses and dialogues that we had with our respondents from Himachal Pradesh and Manipur emphasize the role that culture plays in moderating voices. What is important is 'how the other is culturally constructed'. In both the societies women are regarded by men as being both biologically and sociologically different. There is also a resolve, often stated at times hesitant among this young group of our respondents that women are objects that need discerning treatment. In one subset if they move out, dress up in a particular fashion then they become objects of eve teasing, in the other it is natural for them to seek male attention for future bonding. These translations are problematic, as they represent two contrasting arguments but with similar implications. In the first case, women must not objectify themselves as men get provoked, in the second women must objectify their bodies to draw attention of the opposite sex. Eve teasing is perceived as ridicule in the conversations coming from Himachal Pradesh and is projected as a compliment in discussions drawn from Manipur.

When we examine, these dialogues and conversations within the existing scope of feminist theories that gender is largely socially constructed, and all that focus on sex roles being determined by biology, is rather misplaced or is an essentialists argument to sustain male hegemony. Judith Lorber, the founding editor of *Gender and Society* argued that *the long term goal of feminism must be no less than the eradication of gender as an organizing principle of post industrial society* (1986,568). Coltrane in the same context argues:

> *For men to concur that gender should be unimportant in everyday life, however, opens them to criticism because men have often blithely assumed that gender could be ignored, or at least argued that competence rather than biology, provided them with special privileges. Historically, men's experiences have been universalized, allowing them to overlook discrimination against women and legitimate male dominance (Kimmel, 1990). Many profeminist men avoid this regressive potential by highlighting gender and paying attention to men's overt and subtle exercise of power. .... By linking the ways that men create and sustain gendered selves with the ways that gender influences power relations and perpetuates inequality, feminist men's studies support and compliment the critical perspectives of women's studies. Despite research and theories to the contrary , most people continue to conceive of gender differences as innately given reflecting some underlying dichotomy between men and women (p. 44-45)*.*

We cite these excerpts from Scott Coltrane's excellent review of studies on masculinity to assert our view that perception of gender differences is not an exclusive attribute of people located in specific cultures but is a near universal presumption in sociological narratives and analysis as well. Men and women think differently, behave differently and are conditioned by expectations that societies through active and alert processes of socialization impinge upon them. It is this perception that made Robert Bly talk about exclusive male retreats to restore what he described "Zeus energy" in his book *Iron John*. It is also the gendered argument that has made classical evolutionary theorist talk about hunting being the exclusive prerogative of men. It is the same sentiment that has conjured innumerable fables and folklores in which women the temptress uses her body to attract men, and men the virile hunter uses his masculine energy and physical ability to attract women.

Ethnographic evidence is often cited to augment the case that men and women are different. The areas that are chartered include physical difference (Mead 1949, LaBarre, 1954), the division of labour (Durkheim, Murdock 1937, 1949, M.E. Spiro, 1956, Washburn & Devore, 1961), Sex distinctions in social structure (Aberle, 1961), Sexual behaviour (Ford & Beach 1951) and authority, aggression, conflict and responsibility. Roy G. D'andrade from Stanford University summarized these studies in a paper titled *Sex differences and Cultural Institutions.* Most anthropological explanations focus on the complex equation that biological differences have with environmental, social and technological factors. What is perturbing to a student of sexuality research confronting issues of sexual violence and subsequent pattern of spread of HIV/AIDS is the conclusion that these ethnographic explorations portray. It is important to pay attention to the concluding paragraph of D'Andrade's assertions in his thesis:

> *The cross-cultural mode is that males are more sexually active, more dominant, more deferred to, more aggressive, less responsible, less nurturant, and less emotionally expressive than females. The extent of these differences varies by culture. And in some cultures some of these differences do not exist (and occasionally the trend is actually reversed). These differences are related to and presumably influenced by which sex controls economic capital, the extent and kind of division of labour by sex, the degree of political "authoritarianism", and family composition.*
>
> *Maleness and femaleness are institutionalized as statuses in all cultures. Such statuses become psychological identities for most individuals. Usually individuals learn to want to occupy sex status they are assigned: however, special cultural conditions can affect the degree to which one sex envies the status of the other (p. 201).*

D'Andrade's assertions and references that we draw from the narratives in the field bring us in proximity of a near universal model of how sexuality is generally perceived in hugely diverse societies. What makes these translations complex is the second part of the assertion, when individuals try to accommodate their idiosyncrasies to specific cultural constructs. Take for instance the assertion that men have the right to dominate because he is the primary provider of economic sustenance. Idioms in sorne contexts have changed. Women are substantial providers. Men find it hard to accept this change and are strapped in the traditional format wanting to persist with ideologies of dominance and control, subsequently increasing extent of oppression and prosecution of the opposite sex. Tradition is re-crafted to insist that traditional role models and accompanying status positions are for ever to stay. Interpret it in the context that we are addressing- HIV positive male believes it is legitimate for him to persist with unsafe sex and his wife has no right to deny him sexual favours even if she knows that she is exposed to grave danger.

Through out this paper, we are trying to address the question of our ability or inability to restructure institutionalized practices of looking at the other sex. Our conviction is that unless we generate a movement to address this question, all our efforts at generating awareness about the HIV/AIDS epidemic will have little impact.

RESOURCING DIALOGUE

It is important for any discipline to generate a dialogue within the discipline itself to evolve an understanding of complexities that confront native and non native researcher dealing with any sensitive issue of the kind discussed in this paper. The arguments are persuasive on both counts of familiarity and non-familiarity.

'The deeper familiarity of the native researcher with the culture (Colson 1982: 260) is offset by the difficulties of viewing the culture through a reflective prism of its own values. The non-native researcher lacks depth of familiarity, but is naturally endowed with the ability to see the culture from another perspective, a perspective albeit potentially influenced by the values of his or her home culture. The difficulties faced by each researcher in establishing rapport with informants as a relatively unknown outsider and as a previously socially identified insider are distinct .... The root of this conflict lies in western culture, specifically in the 17th century rationalism which informs western science, and in the social separation that is philosophically inherent in the Cartesian-based conceptual dualism of mind and body .... The resultant positivism in social science creates a philosophically based social schism between researcher, identified with more highly valued objectivity and rationality, and informant or subject, identified with the unreflective and pristine state of nature. It is this Cartesian based model which is currently endangered in anthropology (and a good deal of anthropology is endangered along with it) (Larson, 1987).

The dualism that confronted us throughout this paper is appropriately summarized by Larson in the above paragraph. The paradox is our ability or inability to come to terms with locating self in construction of these conversations. Our dilemma summed up by Stella Mascarenhas-Keyes:

> *'A desire to locate an autobiography within a cultural biography'.*

She concludes saying that 'by using self as Informant the culturally induced sources or stress can be subjected to systematic analysis and used a s a methodological tool in field work' and finally adds that 'because the dialogue with natives does not terminate with fieldwork for the native anthropologist, as it does for most outsiders, their demands, as well as those of the profession, influence the production of anthropological texts' (432, 434, ibid).

The kind of issues contemporary anthropology is grappling with, it is becoming imperative upon many of us to address these questions in a transparent manner to facilitate our own search for data.

CONCLUDING DIALOGUES/CONVERSATIONS

Dialogues, Conversations and discussions in this paper, have gone beyond the confessed limitations of having a discourse only on inbuilt notions of morality and ethics in construction of notions of masculinity. We have come to conclude that masculinity is a plural construction. It also has to be perceived beyond the dichotomous constructions of opposites that of being masculine or feminine or gay as opposed to being normal. Both men and women are products of social dialectics. We have also in this paper focused on the cultural construction of notion of Masculinity, while admitting that somewhere 'deep there', masculinity lies behind 'mere culture' (Bly, 1990). The concept of masculinity as a plural construction is also not without problems. Social construction of masculinity may craft it as a hegemonic notion or fashion it as impression of subordination often implying that 'men are in command but they have their women's permission to be in control'-seemingly contradictory but culturally relevant constructions. What is important is to remember that 'masculinities are no longer individual possessions, but are institutional practices located in structures of power' (Hearn, 1987).

SUMMARY

Dialogues are critical to empirical methodology of reproducing ethnographies. They have come to acquire pivotal role in understanding ambiguities that govern human relations and exercise control on emotions and desires. Dialogues also bring to the fore cross-cultural variations that anthropologists often confront in generating data from different cultural contexts. This paper examines questions of methodology and interprets narratives to address complex questions of sexuality and ethics. Evolving sensitivities to differing discourse on cross-cultural conversations on sexuality is the urgent need of the hour to evolve effective intervention strategies to meet the challenge of HIV/AIDS.

NOTES

1. To protect confidentiality of respondents' exact location from where dialogues from college students form Himachal Pradesh were generated is kept confidential.
2. It is important as asserted by Srivastva (2004) repeatedly in his work that 'sexual landscape-or rather, a landscape where sexuality is an unspoken spectre-is only one of many social topographies, and a fuller picture must include other 'little' traditions that are too frequently regarded as aberrations and not representative of the underlying truth'-this paper is an attempt to acknowledge not only the presence of these 'little' traditions but also the role that these traditions play to neutralize or balance the hegemonic influence of larger 'Indian sexuality'.
3. Moral policing by the Meerut Police (Indian Express, Times of India, Media reports .... dated 21st, 22nd December 2005) in which young couples sitting in a public park were brutally beaten by the police constables (both men and women) to prevent 'eve teasing'. Controversy surrounding south India's popular film star's comments that men should not expect their newly married brides to be 'virgin all the time' and political hue and cry, that was generated on various political forums is a classic example of hypocrisy that is integral to our social system.

REFERENCES

Aberle D.F. (1961), 'Navaho: Matrilineal Descent in Cross Cultural Perspective.' In D.M. Schneider and K. Gough (eds.), *Matrilineal Kinship*. Berkeley: University of California Press.

Alter J.S. (1992), *The Wrestler's Body: Identity and Ideology in North India*. Chicago: Chicago University Press.

Bly R. (1990), *Iron John: A Book about Men*. New York: Addison –Wesley.

Carstairs M.G. (1958), The Twice Born. London: Hogarth Press.

Coltrane S. (1994), 'Theorizing Masculinities in Contemporary Social Science'. In B. Harry and M. Kaufman(eds). *Theorizing Masculinities: Research on Man and Masculinities*. Thousand Oaks: Sage.

Connell R.W. (1987), *Gender and Power: Society, the Person and Sexual Politics*. Stanford, CA: Stanford University Press.

D'Andrade R.G. (1962), *Paternal Absence and Cross Sex Identification*. Unpublished Doctoral Dissertation, Harvard University.

Ford C.S. and Beach F. (1951), *Patterns of Sexual Behaviour*. New York: Harper & Sons.

Gilmore D. (1990), *Manhood in the Making: Cultural Concepts of Masculinity*. New Haven, CT: Yale University Press.

Hearn J. (1987), *The Gender of Oppression: Men, Masculinity and the Critique of Marxism*. Brighton: Harvester Wheat Sheaf.

John M.E. and Nair J. (1998), *A Question of Silence? The Sexual Economies of Modern India*. Delhi: Kali for Women.

Kakar S. (1990), *Intimate Relations: Exploring Indian Sexuality*. Chicago: University of Chicago Press.

La Barre W. (1954), *The Human Animal*. Chicago: University of Chicago Press.

Larson K. (1987), Ethno Politics and Research Ethics for the Non-Native Researcher (unpublished paper).

Lorber J. (1986), Gender and Society, Editorial Comments.

Mascarenhas-Keyes S. (1987), 'The Native Anthropologist: Constraints and Strategies in Research' in Anthony Jackson (ed), *Anthropology at Home*. London: Tavistock Publications.

Morrell R. (2001), The Times of Change: Men and Masculinity in South Africa in R. Morell (ed) *Changing Men s Southern Africa* Pietermartizburg: University of Natal Press.

Nash D. and Wintrop R. (1972), 'The Emergence of Self-Consciousness in Ethnography', *Current Anthropology*, 13:527-42.

Sorrell J., Brown J. and Raffaelli M. (2005), 'An Exploratory Study of Constructions of Masculinity, Sexuality and HIV / AIDS in Namibia, Southern Africa' *Culture, Health & Sexuality*, November-December, 2005, 7 (6), pp. 585-598.

Srivastava S. (2004), Sexual *Sites, Seminal Attitudes: Sexualities, Masculinities and Culture in South Asia* (ed.) New Delhi: Sage Publications.

Srivastava VK. 2004. *Methodology and Fieldwork*(ed). New Delhi: Oxford University Press.

Wellings K., Branigan P. and Mitchell K.(2005), "Discomfort, Discord and Discontinuity as Data: Using Focus Group to Research Sensitive Topics', *Culture, Health & Sexuality* 2: 255-267.

NEWSPAPER REPORTS/ARTICLES

Kaví A.R. (2005), 'Old Wine in Very old Bottles' in *Hindustan Times* 4th December 2005 p. 8.

Ananthakrishnan G. (2005), 'India not Ready for Gays, Public Morality Supreme: Centre to SC' *The Indian Express* 1st December 2005 p. 1.

WEBSITES

AIDS-INDIA@yahoogroups.com
www.optismal.org/peter/rational_ethics.htm
www.fwbo.org/articles/sexual evolution.html
www.teachingssexualethics.org/writing/history.htm
www.relgion-online.org

22

APPROACHES TOWARDS SEX BIASED HEALTH CARE PRACTICES: A STUDY ON RAJBANSIS OF DARJEELING DISTRICT, WEST BENGAL

Subir Biswas & Ganesh Chandra Mallick

INTRODUCTION

The Rajbansis is a numerically predominant scheduled caste community of West Bengal, mainly concentrated on northern part of West Bengal. According to 1971 census, they occupy near about 14% among total population of North Bengal. The Rajbansis is a patriarchal community and that's why in their society males get more preference than females. Like many other communities of India, the Rajbansis have their own traditional system of health care and disease treatment pattern; and in the past they show more conservativeness in acceptance of another system of health care and disease treatment pattern like immunization of the children (launched by the Government of India) and various welfare programmes of various non-Governmental organizations. But in recent time this conservativeness gradually relaxed and now a large portion of this population accept modern facility of health care practice; but this advantage goes mostly in favour of males. The same is reflected on sex ratio pattern of the population. The Sex ratio depends not only on the biological factors but also on several socio-cultural factors influences it. If the sex biased health care practices, disease treatment patterns are continued, then higher mortality rate may be observed in favour of a particular gender, either male or female; which result on imbalance of sex ratio pattern of the population.

A series of study was conducted by social scientist to highlight the sex biased health care practices among Indian as well as third world population and consequences because of that. Visaria and Visaria examined male biased sex-ratio composition of Indian population, and factors responsible for it (Visaria and Visaria, 1981). Dasgupta examined the risk and vulnerability of women's health in India as well as violence against women (Dasgupta, 1998). Krishnaji examined the correlation between poverty and male biased sex ratio, which may be treated as an effect of sex biased health care practices (Kishnaji, 1987). Arokiasamy and Pradhan examined gender bias against female children in India with regional differences, after analyzing national Family Health Survey-2 data set; and find out the gender bias in schooling, nutrition, immunization, illness, treatment etc. (Arokiasamy and Pradhan, 2004). The study of Jatrana also suggests gender disparities for children in child health, disease incidence, use of preventive and curative health care services (Jatrana, 2003). In above two cases the use of National Family Health Survey–2 data suggests a sex biased health care in favour of males (NFHS, 1995). Later study on India (NFHS, 2001) as well as West Bengal by NFHS also indicates the prevalence of gender biased health care systems (NFHS: WB, 2001). Again estimation of maternal mortality in rural West Bengal and identify the underlying the causes was done by Pal et al. (2002).

Not only India but almost all of the developing country may have similar type of environment. Li et al.(2004) examined gender differences in child survival because of disparities between sexes in the form of food, nutrition, health care, as well as socio-economic and cultural factors The disparities in the form of duration of Breastfeeding (Quinlan et al., 2005) as well as negligence in Reproductive Health (Raghavan-Gilbert, 1999) also examined by scholars of different regions.

We select the village Rangia, which possess the lowest sex ratio (770.92 according to 2001 census) in the Matigara block; the Matigara block also occupy the lowest position in case of sex ratio pattern (902 according to 2001 census) in Darjeeling District [which possess slightly higher sex ratio (943) than state level (934) and even than national level (933 according to 2001 census)]. The aim of this paper is to highlight how the disparities in the form of sex bias plays its role in case of health care practices and disease treatment pattern among the Rajbansi population of Rangia village of district Darjeeling in West Bengal, India.

MATERIALS AND METHODS

Data were collected from the village of Rangia; district Darjeeling of West Bengal, India, during 11th January 2004 to 25th June 2004 as part of an ongoing study of demographic study of Rajbansis of this region. The village Rangia was chosen because of its sex ratio pattern as indicated earlier. The Rajbansi was chosen because of its numerical strength; as they shares more than 90% of total village population. Altogether 976 people of 200 families were covered during the fieldwork, among them 525 are male and 451 are female.

Several surveys was designed and conducted during field time including household survey questionnaire, interviews and observations.

The survey includes both qualitative and quantitative data, which was designed by the manner so that it can examine the disparities in the form of sex bias on health care practices.

The household survey was conducted with a format and questionnaire consisted of four sections. The first section includes duration of breastfeeding, the second section includes vaccinations of children, the third section was about their nutritional status and the fourth to highlight disease treatment pattern.

We have used a multiple indicator approach to study of the level of gender bias of each section. For statistical inference, we calculated simple percentage and averages of all stages to identify sex bias of various stages. The sex ratio was calculated as number of females per 1000 males, to identify the gender differences among them (Srinivasan, 1998). Chi-square (X^2) analysis and Z-test were conducted to test the differences between various proportions (Rosner, 2000). The Z-test was used to test the sex differences between boys and girls on Breastfeeding duration. The Chi-square (X^2) test was conducted to test the differences on immunization, malnutrition as well as disparities in the form of disease treatment pattern. Statistical calculation of the data was also conducted by using PAST, version 1.34 (Hammer et.al, 2001). Values of $p< 0.05$ were considered to be statistically significant.

RESULTS

Sex Bias in Breastfeeding Duration

Breastfeeding duration may be defined as child's age at weaning i.e., complete cessation of breastfeeding. It is always attributed to resource allocation inequality: the girl child was breastfeed for a smaller time span than boys (Agnihotri, 2000). The weaning decisions may not be entirely conscious, there may be some sort of sex-biased psychological mechanisms, which plays its role for weaning (Quinlan et al. 2005). The same situation is evident from our field experiences. Table 1 indicates a sex-biased 'Breastfeeding duration (BFD)' of the population. 42.6% female baby breastfeed for less than one year, whereas in case of boys only 29.46% fall under this BFD group. Next consecutive groups show a tendency to have fewer girls in all stages. Statistical tests for difference among boys and girls by Breastfeeding duration was found to be significant at $p<0.0005$ level. The figure 1 indicates a tendency towards less BFD in case of female than their male counterpart.

Sex Bias in Immunization

Here the immunization mean the Universal Immunization Programme (UIP) launched by the Government of India, aim to vaccinate all the children against 6 preventable childhood diseases viz. tuberculosis,

Figure 1: Duration of Breastfeeding.

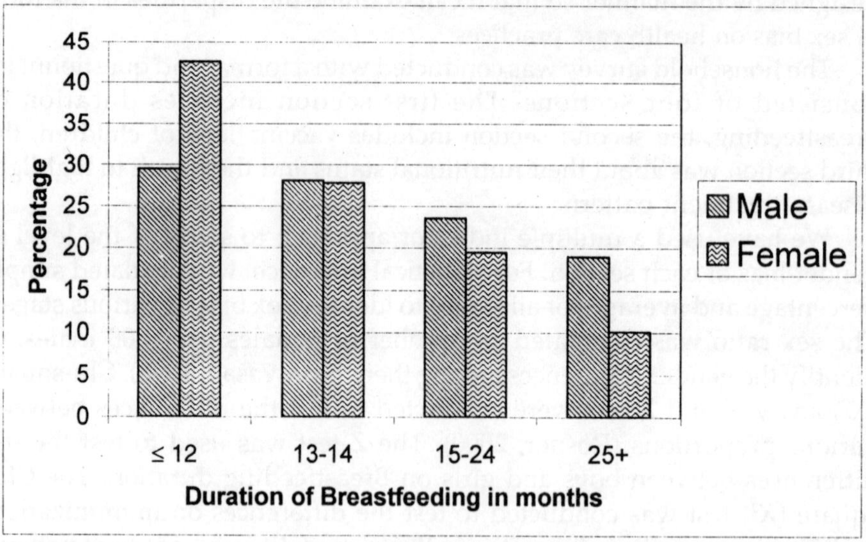

diphtheria, whooping cough (pertusis), tetanus, poliomyelitis and measles. Besides these, the pulse polio vaccination also counted for the study. The classification was made on the view to identify level of acceptance of the programme, sex wise. The first stage includes those who have completed all the above said vaccination while the last stage comprising of child with no vaccination. A second stage has to constitute as many of them receives immunization vaccines but not completed property.

Table 1
Duration of Breastfeeding

Duration of Breastfeeding in Months	Boys (%)	Girls (%)	Total (%)	Sex Ratio
≤ 12	104 (29.46)	118 (42.60)	222 (35.24)	1134.6
13-14	99 (28.05)	77 (27.80)	176 (27.94)	777.77
15-24	83 (23.51)	54 (19.49)	137 (21.74)	650.6
25+	67 (18.98)	28 (10.11)	95 (15.08)	417.9
Total	353	277	.630	784.7

*Significant at $p < 0.0005$ level ($Z = 4.1138$).

The boys have a greater access over vaccination, though the differences between properly vaccinated boys (27.75%) and girls (25.40%) are not so gigantic. However, the disparity lies in second and last stages. The girls of never vaccinated group (42.22%) are numerically much more than boys (33.25%). Again, more number of boys started their vaccination (39%) than girls (32.38%) but have to leave because of socio-economic reasons. The differences are statistically significant at $p < 0.05$ level. The figure. 2 may be act as a glimpse of sex biased immunization of the population.

Figure 2: Immunization of Children

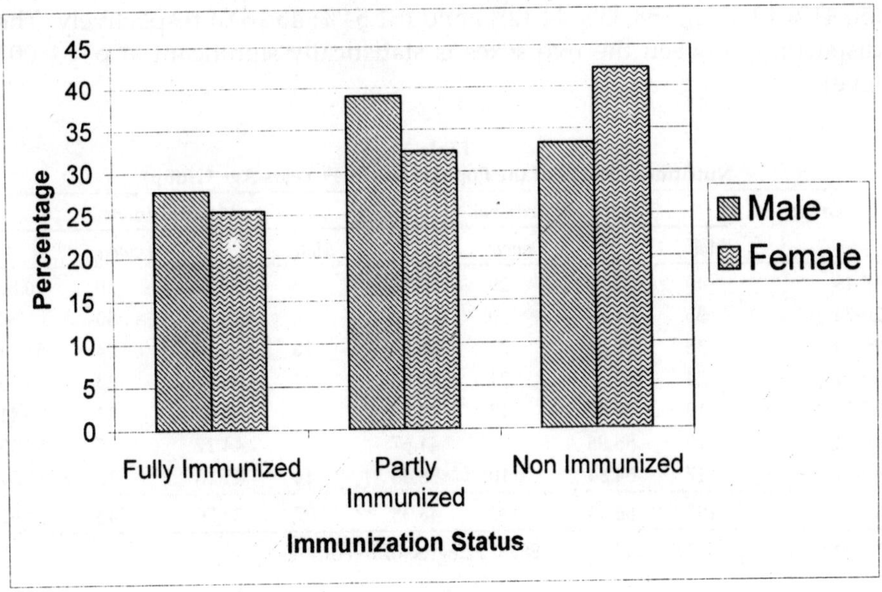

Table 2
Immunization of Children

Immunization Status	*Total No. of Children*			
	Boys (%)	*Girls (%)*	*Total (%)*	*Sex Ratio*
Completed	106 (27.75)	80 (25.40)	186 (26.70)	754.71
Partly Completed	149 (39)	102 (32.38)	251 (36)	684.56
Not Taken	127 (33.25)	133 (42.22)	260 (37.30)	1047.24
Total	382 (100)	315 (100)	697 (100)	824.61

*Significant at $p< 0.05$ level (X^2=6.1899, 2 degree of freedom).

Sex Bias in Nutrition

A framework may be constructed by which we can understand how health and nutritional status produce the mortality differentials among the population. The major forms of illness among the people of developing countries are protein-calorie mal-nutrition and some common infections like diarrhea, measles and respiratory diseases. Protein-calorie malnutrition is determined by two major indicators: food intake and infections (Chen, 1982). Food intake is fundamental necessities for nutritional well being; but infections too are important to determine by two indicators-high susceptibility and exposure to disease transmission.

The table 3 categorized the female and males (15-49 years) based on nutritional status. In all age groups, females are more malnourished than their male counterpart. The corresponding figure of malnourished females and males of age groups 15-19, 20-24, 25-29, 30-34, 35-39, 40-44 and 45-49 are (40.82%:27.27%), (50.00%:18.61%), (51.11%:32.14%), (54.35%:36.84%), (56.41%:40.63%), (58.33%:44.12%) and (61.54%: 45.16%) respectively. The disparities between the two sexes is statistically significant at $p < 0.001$ level.

Table 3
Nutritional Status of the Population (15-49 Years Age Group)

Age Group	*Properly Nutritional*				*Mal-Nutritional*			
	Male	*%*	*Female*	*%*	*Male*	*%*	*Female*	*%*
15-19	40	72.73	29	59.18	15	27.27	20	40.82
20-24	35	81.39	30	50	8	18.61	30	50
25-29	38	67.86	22	48.89	18	32.14	23	51.11
30-34	24	63.16	21	45.65	14	36.84	25	54.35
35-39	19	59.37	17	43.59	13	40.63	22	56.41
40-44	19	55.88	5	41.67	15	44.12	7	58.33
45-49	17	54.84	10	38.46	14	45.16	16	61.54
Total	192	66.44	134	48.38	97	33.56	143	51.62

*Significant at $p< 0.001$ level (X^2=18.8898, 1 degree of freedom).

Again, nutritional status of the group is of age biased i.e., peoples are more malnourished with their ages. However, there is an exception in case of 20-24 age groups of males (See Figure 3).

Sex Bias in Disease Treatment Pattern

A common way in which gender bias manifests is that girls tends not to be taken for health care as often or as early in their illness as boys; as well as girls may receive less attention from parents (Arokiasamy et al., 2004). The situation is very much similar in our reference area.

Figure 3: Nutritional Status (Mal-nutrition) of the Population

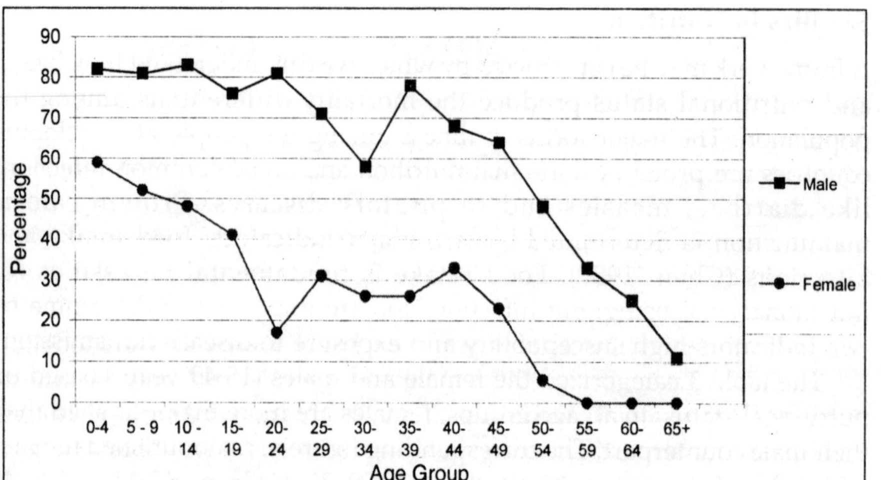

Beside less attention to any illness, the females have less access over modern medical facilities. Sex differentials in the source of treatment may explain the sex differentials in mortality. The women are to be taken to doctor/health centre only after deterioration of their condition. It is observed from table 4 that males in all age groups have a greater access over doctor/health centre than females. About 71.43% males have an access over modern medical facilities whereas only 34.15% of females enjoy the same. The differences between male and female is statistically significant at $p < 0.001$ level. Because of less access over modern medical facilities, they (female) have to go to Ojha's house or depend upon home remedy (See Figure 4).

Table 4
Gender Bias Disease and Treatment Pattern

Age Group	*Doctor/Health Centre*				*Ojha/Local Practitioner*				*Home Remedy*			
	Male		*Female*		*Male*		*Female*		*Male*		*Female*	
	No.	*%*	*No.*	*%*	*No.*	*%*	*No.*	*%*	*No.*	*%*	*No.*	*%*
0-4	46	8.76	29	6.43	8	1.52	13	2.88	2	0.38	7	1.55
5-9	46	8.76	26	5.76	8	1.52	12	2.66	3	0.57	12	2.66
10-14	57	10.86	22	4.88	10	1.90	13	2.88	2	0.38	11	2.44
15-19	42	8.00	20	4.43	12	2.28	20	4.33	1	0.19	9	1.99
20-24	35	6.66	10	2.22	7	1.33	42	9.31	1	0.19	8	1.77
25-29	40	7.62	14	3.1	12	2.28	15	3.33	4	0.76	16	3.54
30-34	22	4.2	12	2.66	13	2.47	14	3.1	3	0.57	20	4.43
35-39	25	4.76	10	2.22	5	0.95	12	2.66	2	0.38	17	3.77
40-44	23	4.38	4	0.89	7	1.33	3	0.66	4	0.76	5	1.11
45-49	20	3.80	6	1.33	7	1.33	10	2.22	4	0.76	10	2.22
50-54	12	2.28	1	0.22	6	1.14	8	1.77	7	1.33	9	1.99
55-59	4	0.76	.	.	5	0.95	2	0.44	3	0.57	2	0.44
60-64	2	0.38	.	.	4	0.76	2	0.44	2	0.38	1	0.22
65+	1	0.19	.	.	5	0.95	3	0.66	3	0.57	1	0.22
Total	375	71.43	154	34.15	109	20.76	169	37.47	41	7.81	128	28.38

*Significant at $p < 0.001$ level (X^2=145.2870, 2 degree of freedom).

DISCUSSION

After analyzing the data, the results provide a concrete base to conclude the presence of sex biased health care practices among the Rajbansis of village Rangia. The four indicators viz., breast-feeding duration (BFD), immunization, nutrition and disease treatment pattern of the group suggests a sharp disparities between two sexes.

The finding indicates the sex biased health care starts immediately after birth. The causes are not always conscious but may be due to psychological or social mechanism of the parents and the society. The girl child breastfeed for a short duration compared to boys. Then the girls have a less access over vaccination of preventable diseases. They (women)

Figure 4: Disease and Treatment Pattern (Access over Doctor/Health Center)

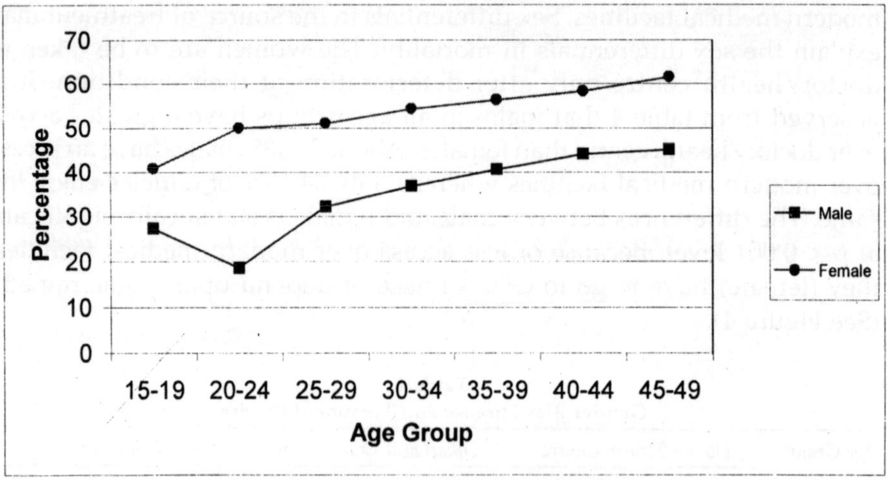

have to take less quantity of food as well as quality of food may differ in favour of males. Another serious concern is disparity in disease treatment pattern. The male have a greater access over modern medical facilities like doctor or health centers in all age groups. Whereas, the females have to go for Ojha's or local practioner or sometimes to home remedy only. Few of them have an access over modern medical facilities.

However, the gender disparity affects more brutally in terms of malnutrition and access over doctor/health centre than others. The situation is so serious that it affects the sex ratio of the village by eliminating more females than males of all age groups. That is why the sex-ratio of the village stands last on the block, the block, in turn, again stands on last within the district.

This sort of sex bias is of negative implication for achieving development goals of India as well as West Bengal. The sex biased health care might have negative impact on women survival. If the entitlement failure against women would reduce by the help of governmental and Non-governmental efforts as well as after proper consciousness of the population, then a part of developmental goals may achieved in near future and we are waiting for it.

SUMMARY

Rajbansi is a numerically predominant Scheduled Caste community of West Bengal. Like many other communities of India, the Rajbansi also have their own health care system, which reflects sex bias practices. Due to differential health care practices, they have a more number of female death. Not only their health care system but also their disease treatment pattern shows a sex-biased pattern favouring males, having a greater access to modern medicine than their female counterpart. This type of sex-biased treatment also accelerates female death, as they have to go for local medicine or house remedy instead of modern ones. This sex biased health care system and disease treatment pattern may be one of the major causes behind low sex ratio of this community of that region. The present paper is an attempt to identify such health care bias and their consequences on Rajbansi community of Rangia village of Darjeeling district, West Bengal.

ACKNOWLEDGEMENT

The authors wish to acknowledge Miss. D. Bagchi, Mr. B. Gan and Miss. S. Roy for their co-operation during field survey.

REFERENCES

Agnihotri S.B. (2000), *Sex Ratio Pattern in Indian Population: A Fresh Exploration.* New Delhi: Sage Publication India Private Ltd.

Arokiasamy P. and Pradhan J. (2004), Gender Bias Against Female Children in India: Regional Differences and Their Implications for MDGs. In Seminar Proceedings of Promoting Human Rights and Social Policies for Children and Women: Monitoring and Achieving the Millennium Development Goals. New York: New School. 28-30, April, 2004.

Census of India (2001), *Provisional Population Totals.* New Delhi: Govt. of India.

Chen L.C. (1982), Where Have The Woman Gone? Insight from Bangladesh on Low Sex Ratio of Indian Population. Economic and Political Weekly. March 6: 364-72.

Dasgupta M. (1998), *Women's Health in India Risk and Vulnerability.* New Delhi: Oxford University Press.

Hammer O., Harper D.A.T. and Ryan P.D. (2001), PAST: Palaeontological Statistics Software Package for Education and Data Analysis. Palaeontologia Electronica 4(1): 9 pp. http://folk.uio.no/ohammer/past.

International Institute for Population Science (1995), *National Family Health Survey (MCH and Planning) India.1992-93.* Bombay: International Institute for Population Science.

International Institute for Population Science (2001), *National Family Health Survey: India, 1998-99.* Bombay, International Institute for Population Science: 131-149.

International Institute for Population Science (2001), *National Family Health Survey: West Bengal. 1998-99.* Bombay : International Institute for Population Science.

Jatrana S. (2003), Explaining Gender Disparity in Child Health in Haryana State of India. Asian Meta Centre Research Paper Series. No. 16.

Krishnaji N. (1987), Poverty and Sex Ratio: Some Data and Speculation. Economic and Political Weekly. June 6: 892-897.

Li S. Zhu C. and Feldman M.W. (2004), Gender Differences in Child Survival on Contemporary Rural China: A Country Study. *J Biosoc Sci.* 36:83-109.

Pal M., Bharati P., Vasulu T.S., Chaudhuri A., Bhattacharya B.N., Das R.N. and Ghosh R. (2002), Maternal Mortality in Rural West Bengal : Estimation of Its Rate and Identification of Underlying Causes. *Demography in India.* 34 (2) 253-58.

Quinlan R.J., Quinlan M.B. and Flinn M.V. (2005), Local Resource Enhancement and Sex-biased Breastfeeding in a Caribbean Community. *Current Anthropology.* Vol. 46. No. 3: 471-480.

Raghavan-Gilbert P. (1999), Gender Issues in Reproductive Health: Let's Get Serious. Reflections. No. 1: 1-4.

Ravindran T.K.S. (2000), Engendering Health .Seminar 489.

Rosner B. (2000), *Fundamentals of Bio-statistics (5th ed.).* Pacific Grove: Duxbury Thomson Learning.

Srinivasan K. (1998), *Basic Demographic Techniques and Application.* New Delhi: Sage Publication.

Visaria P. and Visaria L. (1981), Indian Population Science After 1981 Census. *Economic and Political Weekly.* (Special Issue): 727-30.

INDEX

I-40051